BLACKPENTECOSTAL BREATH

FORDHAM UNIVERSITY PRESS   NEW YORK 2017

COMMONALITIES

Timothy C. Campbell, series editor

BLACKPENTECOSTAL BREATH

BREATH

The Aesthetics of Possibility

ASHON T. CRAWLEY

Visit us online at www.fordhampress.com.

Library of Congress Cataloging-in-Publication Data
Names: Crawley, Ashon T., author.
Title: Blackpentecostal breath : the aesthetics of possibility / Ashon T. Crawley.
Description: First edition. | New York : Fordham University Press, 2017. | Series: Commonalities | Includes bibliographical references and index.
Identifiers: LCCN 2016027587 | ISBN 9780823274543 (cloth : alk. paper) | ISBN 9780823274550 (pbk. : alk. paper)
Subjects: LCSH: Aesthetics. | Performing arts—Philosophy. | Pentecostals, Black. | Experience. | Symbolism. | Ritual.
Classification: LCC BH39 .C734 2017 | DDC 306—dc23
LC record available at https://lccn.loc.gov/2016027587

Printed in the United States of America

19 18   5 4

First edition

A book in the American Literatures Initiative (ALI), a collaborative publishing project of NYU Press, Fordham University Press, Rutgers University Press, Temple University Press, and the University of Virginia Press. The Initiative is supported by The Andrew W. Mellon Foundation. For more information, please visit www.americanliteratures.org.

CONTENTS

INTRODUCTION

"I can't breathe." July 17, 2014, sharpened it. Eric Garner repeated it eleven times while camera phones captured his murder, while the excesses of police violence—the excesses that are central to and the grounds of policing itself—accosted him, grounded him, choked him. "I can't breathe," the announcement of his intensely singular experience, *his* experience of the ongoing act of racial animus, antiblack racism, violent policing, policing as segregation and the implementation of dispossession and displacement as policy that structures life in the United States. Yet and also, "I can't breathe," the announcement—through ventriloquizing, some voice enunciating modernity's violence—of what had been set into motion before him, a modality of thinking and conceiving black flesh as discardable, as inherently violent and antagonistic, as necessarily in need of removal, remediation, a modality of thinking and conceiving that is not just American but western, global in its reach. "I can't breathe" as both the announcement of a particular moment and rupture in the life world of the Garners, and "I can't breathe" as a rupture, a disruption, an ethical plea regarding the ethical crisis that has been the grounds for producing his moment, our time, this modern world.

The announcement, "I can't breathe," is not merely raw material for theorizing, for producing a theological and philosophical analysis. "I can't breathe" charges us to do something, to perform, to produce otherwise than what we have. We are charged to end, to produce abolition against, the episteme that produced for us current iterations of categorical designations of racial hierarchies, class stratifications, gender binaries, mind-body splits. "I can't breathe," Garner's disbelief, his black disbelief, in the configuration of the world that could so violently attack and assault him for, at the very worst, selling loosies on the street. "I can't breathe," also, the enactment of the force of black disbelief, a desire for otherwise air than what is and has been given, the enunciation, the breathing out the strange utterance of otherwise possibility. If he could not breathe it was because of the violence of white supremacist capitalist heteropatriarchy, a violence that cannot conceive of black flesh feeling pain, a violence that cannot think "I can't breathe" anything other than ploy, trick, toward fugitive flight. Garner's plea, his "I can't breathe," an ethical charge for those of us who are alive and remain to be caught up in the cause of justice against the violence, the episteme, that produced his moment of intensity, the moment of his assault and murder.

I

There is a vibration, a sonic event, a sound I want to talk about, but its ongoing movement makes its apprehension both illusory and provisional. Illusory because the thing itself is both given and withheld from view, from earshot. Provisional because it—the vibration, the sonic event, the sound—is not and cannot ever be stilled absolutely. It keeps going, it keeps moving, it is open-ended. It can be felt and detected but remains almost obscure, almost unnoticed. And this for its protection. And this, its gift. Giving something of itself while remaining a resource from which such force can eternally return and emerge. It is a resource that is plenteous, that exists in plentitude, always available and split from itself, split from while transforming into itself. It is the gift, the concept, the inhabitation of and living into *otherwise possibilities.* Otherwise, as word—otherwise possibilities, as phrase—announces the fact of infinite alternatives to what *is.* And what *is* is about being, about existence, about ontology. But if infinite alternatives exist, if otherwise possibility is a resource that is never exhausted, what *is,* what exists, is but one of many. Otherwise possibilities exist alongside that which we can detect with our finite sensual capacities. Or, otherwise possibilities exist and the register of imagination, the epistemology through which sensual detection occurs—that is, the way we think the world—has to be altered in order to get at what's there. Moving in and through us like the trillions of neutrinos that pass through each square inch of Earth every second, there but undetected until we create and utilize certain technologies in the service of harnessing that which is unseen to naked eyes. How to detect such sensuality, such possibility otherwise, such alternative to what *is* as a means to disrupt the current configurations of power and inequity? How to detect, how to produce and inhabit otherwise epistemological fields, is the question of Black Study.

I believe in Black Study and *Blackpentecostal Breath: The Aesthetics of Possibility* is about the movement toward and emergence of collective intellectual projects.[1] Black Study is the force of belief that blackness is but one critical and urgently necessary disruption to the epistemology, the theology-philosophy, that produces a world, a set of protocols, wherein black flesh cannot easily breathe. *Blackpentecostal Breath* argues that blackness is released into the world to disrupt the institutionalization and abstraction of thought that produces the categorical distinctions of disciplinary knowledge. To make a claim for *belief*—in and of Black Study—is to trouble and unsettle epistemological projects founded upon pure reason, pure rationality, in the service of thinking with and against how that which we call knowledge is produced and dispersed. Black Study is a wholly unbounded, holy, collective intellectual project that is fundamentally otherwise than an (inter)discipline. This refusal of disciplinary boundaries is important because disciplinary knowledges attempt resolution, attempt to "resolve" knowledge "into objectivity . . . that ha[s] characterized modern knowledge . . . with certainty."[2] *Blackpentecostal Breath* is not about resolve but about openness to worlds, to experiences, to ideas. *Blackpentecostal Breath* does not so much arrive at conclusions as it tarries with concepts. In this book, I attempt to think about and with otherwise possibilities with regard to the production of knowledge, a production predicated on the performance of resistance, a resistance that precedes what exists before any encounter.

Imagination is necessary for thinking and breathing into the capacities of infinite alternatives. Blackpentecostal aesthetics, this work will argue, are but one enactment of alternative modes, alternative strategies, for organizing, performing and producing thought. In a very real and material way, *Blackpentecostal Breath: The Aesthetics of Possibility* is a meditation on the violence that infused and produced the occasion for Eric Garner's announcement. *Blackpentecostal Breath* attends to the fact that racial categorization and distinction is but one way to think the world, one way to consider organizing, and racial categorization and distinction is, in many and fundamental ways, about the disruption and interruption of the capacity to breathe in the flesh.

Blackpentecostal Breath contributes to interdisciplinary scholarship by existing in the nexus of performance theory, queer theory, sound studies, literary theory, theological studies, and continental philosophy. This to explore how social life emerges—in thought, sound, and sexuality—for those considered occupying "the position of the unthought."[3] The immediate objects of study I engage are the aesthetic practices found in Blackpentecostalism, a multiracial, multiclass, multinational Christian sect that finds one strand of its genesis in 1906 Los Angeles, California. I argue throughout that the aesthetics of Blackpentecostalism constitute a performative critique of normative theology and philosophy. Indeed, the tradition of these performances is an *a*theological-*a*philosophical project, produced against the grain of liberal logics of subjectivity. Theology and Philosophy both, I argue, have at the core a subject, a subjectivity, enacting the categorical distinction of thought. Blackness is an abolitionist, decolonial project that resists the role of the subject and, thus, has no capacity to produce the thought of the would-be theologian, the would-be philosopher. In contradistinction to the desire for subjectivity, *Blackpentecostal Breath* elaborates upon the extra-subjective mode of being together that is the condition of occasion for envisioning, and living into such envisioning, a critique of the known—the violent, oppressive, normative—world. The performative practices of Blackpentecostalism constitute a disruptive force, generative for imagining otherwise modes of social organization and mobilization.

Blackpentecostalism is an intellectual practice grounded in the fact of the flesh, flesh unbounded and liberative, flesh as vibrational and always on the move. Such practice constitutes a way of life. The practices I analyze are a range of sensual, affective, material experiences: "shouting" as dance; "tarrying" as stilled intensity and waiting, as well as raucous praise noise; "whooping" (ecstatic, eclipsed breath) during praying and preaching; as well as, finally, speaking in tongues. These practices of Blackpentecostalism not only trouble the assumptive logics of gender but also unmoor the matters of sex and sexuality. I ultimately argue that these choreographic, sonic, and visual aesthetic practices and sensual experiences are not only important objects of study for those interested in alternative modes of social organization, but they also yield a general hermeneutics, a methodology for reading culture. What I am arguing throughout is that the disruptive capacities found in the otherwise world of Blackpentecostalism is but one example of how to produce a break with the known, the normative, the violent world of western thought and material condition. Black aesthetics are Blackpentecostal; they are unbounded and found in the celebration of the flesh.

Blackpentecostalism does not belong to those Saints called Blackpentecostal, those Saints that attend traditionally considered Pentecostal church spaces. Rather, Blackpentecostalism belongs to all who would so live into the fact of the flesh, live into this fact as a critique of the violence of modernity, the violence of the Middle Passage and enslavement, the violence of enslavement and its ongoing afterlife, live into the flesh as a critique of the ongoing attempt to interdict the capacity to breathe. The aesthetic practices cannot be owned but only collectively produced, cannot be property but must be given away in order to constitute community. Blackpentecostalism—and those that would come to describe themselves as such—is *sent* into the world; it is an aesthetic practice that was sent and is about being sent: "to be sent, to be transported out of yourself, it's an ecstatic experience, it's not an experience of interiority, it's an experience of *exteriority*, it's an *exteriorization*. And so we're sent. We're sent to one another. We are sent by one another to one another . . . we're sent by one another to one another until one and another don't signify anymore."[4] Being beside oneself, beside oneself in the service of the other, in the service of constituting and being part of an unbroken circle, a critical sociality of intense feeling: this is Blackpentecostalism. Focusing on this particular religious group brings into view, brings into hearing, the way such performances produce otherwise possibilities for thought, for action, for being and becoming.

How to go about this, to go about producing a critical analysis and a way forward, a way otherwise, is the work in this book. In *Blackpentecostal Breath,* I consider categorical distinction and how the possibility for producing pure distinction is the grounds for racism, sexism, homo- and transphobia, classism and the like. I do this by considering the categories of theology and philosophy to ask: What counts, and who decides what counts, as a theological and/or philosophical thought? Analyses of aesthetic practices found in Blackpentecostalism—of, for example, speaking in tongues and whooping during preached moments—urge against these categorical distinctions. The theologian and philosopher ground their identity in the capacity to produce categorically distinct modes of thought *as* theological, *as* philosophical. And what then obtains as theological thought, as philosophical thought, is decided by the would-be theologian, the would-be philosopher. Circular logic, indeed. Blackpentecostal aesthetics, I argue, are against such distinctions grounded in the identity of the one making such a claim for thought.

Whiteness is a way to think the world; it has its theological and philosophical resonances and employments; it has its theological and philosophical emplotments. It is a violent encounter, an encounter and way of life that is fundamentally about the interdiction, the desired theft, of the capacity to breathe. Eric Garner is but one example of this. As a way to think the world and one's relation to it, whiteness is about the acceptance of violence and violation as a way of life, as quotidian, as axiomatic. Black social life has been the constant emergence of abolition as the grounding of its existence, the refusal of violence and violation as a way of life, as quotidian. Black social life, to be precise, is an abolitionist politic, it is the ongoing "no," a black disbelief in the conditions under which we are told we must endure. Cheryl Harris in her influential "Whiteness as Property" demonstrated the ways whiteness in this particular epistemological moment, this long moment, is grounded in the capacity for ownership, for acquiring objects.[5] Whiteness is a capacity for possession as the grounds for identity, and we learn from indigenous and settler colonial studies that the settler state stakes its claim on the acceptance of violence, the claim of property that produces a displacement from land, a violent encounter with peoples. Those of us accepting the fact of our living in, our inhabitation of the flesh seek abolition from this way of life, from this way of thinking relation. Life in the flesh is seeking otherwise possibilities not just for our "own" but for the world to live, to be, truly liberated. And insofar as being sent, Blackpentecostalism is the performance of otherwise possibilities in the service of enfleshing an abolitionist politic. I take the idea of enfleshing and enfleshment from M. Shawn Copeland's work.[6] I think of enfleshment as distinct from embodiment and will argue throughout the text that enfleshment is the movement to, the vibration of, liberation and this over and against embodiment that presumes a subject of theology, a subject of philosophy, a subject of history.

Blackpentecostalism is a social, musical, intellectual form of otherwise life, predicated upon the necessity of ongoing otherwise possibilities. I do not say new. I say otherwise. Using otherwise, I seek to underscore the ways alternative modes, alternative strategies, alternative ways of life *already* exist, indeed are violently acted upon in order to produce the coherence of the state. I look particularly at the *tradition*—I do not say history intentionally—of the religious twentieth-century Pentecostal movement's roots in blackness, blackness the testament to the fact of object's resistance.[7] I consider dancing, singing, noise making, whooping, and tongue talking as ways to resist normative modes of theological and philosophical reflection, the same sorts of thought that produce categorical differentiation-as-deficiency such as race, class, gender, slave, and so on. I argue that the aesthetic practices of Blackpentecostalism constitute a performative critique of normative theology and philosophy that precede the twentieth-century moment. The practices existed, in other words, before they were called Blackpentecostal, before a group cohered on Bonnie Brae Street for prayer in April 1906.

During the antebellum era, both clergy and scholars alike levied incessant injunctions against loud singing and frenzied dancing in religion and popular culture. Calling for the relinquishment of these sensual spiritual experiences, I argue that these injunctions led to a condition where Blackpentecostal aesthetics were and are considered to be excessive performances, unnecessary because of their purported lack of refinement, discardable because of their seeming lack of intellectual rationality and rigor. And this because the flesh performing such aesthetic practices, the intellectual capacity, the capacity for thought and imagination, came to be racialized and gendered, and such racializing and gendering meant the denigration of black flesh. *Blackpentecostal Breath* investigates how discourses that emerged within the cauldron of spatiotemporal triangular trades in coffee, tea, sugar, and human flesh of new world slavery necessitated a theology and philosophy of race and, consequently, the racializing of aesthetic practices. Theology and philosophy would come to work together to target the object of blackness, thus theology-philosophy. Before and against this discursive theology-philosophy were the performance practices of Blackpentecostalism, an *a*theology-*a*philosophy. These sensual experiences were not merely performed through duress but were the instantiation and sign of life and love. As life and love, these performative dances, songs, noises, and tongues illustrate how enjoyment, desire, and joy are important for the tradition that antiphonally speaks back against aversion, embarrassment, and abandonment, against the debasement and denigration of blackness. Fundamentally, *Blackpentecostal Breath* is about the possibility for Black Study, about the capacity for aesthetics typically deemed excessive to be constitutive, can provide new models for collective intellectual practice. Black Study is a methodological mode of intense, spiritual, communal intellectual practice and meditative performance. I write about the forms life takes that rise to the occasion of particular moments—a mode of thinking of performance *as* a critical intervention into the very concept of the historical, of historical being. This may prove troubling for religious historians, but I want to pressure the assumption about the narrativity of historical events to think through other lineages, to move toward, after Foucault, genealogy rather than archeology.[8] This is no history of the modern global Pentecostal movement. I am not looking so much for missing documents as much as I am looking for the "broken claim to connection"[9] between anything that has receded into the *ago* and that which bears down on the *now* moment through its categorical *soon*-ness. I am not primarily concerned with creating an historicist project with names, dates, and primary, spectacular events that took place on Azusa Street, and things that both preceded and came after that particular flashpoint.[10] As a critique of the concept of *the historical*, to be elaborated in Chapter 3 particularly, *Blackpentecostal Breath* may prove troubling for those seeking a historical review of dates, times, and events. *Blackpentecostal Breath* presses against the assumption about the narrativity of historical events to think through other lineages, other inheritances, for performance practice. That is, performance constitutes a tradition, tradition against History.

Blackpentecostal Breath: The Aesthetics of Possibility is about, and is an attempt to produce, Black Study. Black Study is similar to what Denise Ferreira da Silva describes as "knowing (at) the limits of justice," that is "at once a kind of knowing and doing; it is a praxis, one that unsettles what has come before but offers no guidance for what has yet to become."[11] And Black Study is a particular strategy of mixture, "self-life-writing" of both "cultural and political critique."[12] For this reason, *Blackpentecostal Breath* moves in and out of the autobiographical, the fictional, the performative, the theological, and the philosophical in order to enact a politicocultural criticism, one that is unflinching in its belief in blackness as a social, traditioned, anoriginal force of change, resistance, pleasure, and love in the world. *Blackpentecostal Breath* is an exercise of the otherwise possibility, thinking and desiring more than what we have, knowing we already have enough to produce flourishing in the world.

Though not producing a history of Pentecostalism, it still seems consequential to place the tradition I explicate to guide you, the reader, through the work. So briefly: Blackpentecostalism has one strand of its genesis in April 1906 in Los Angeles, California. I choose the April 1906 moment for what is known colloquially among believers as the "outpouring of the Spirit" for ethical and political reasons, because of the characters that were there in that moment. William Seymour is a character of prominence. Born and raised in Centerville, Louisiana on May 2, 1870, to parents that were emancipated just years previous to his birth, Seymour was baptized in the Catholic tradition at the Roman Catholic Church of the Assumption, and his family attended the New Providence Baptist Church near their home. From an early age, he was used to various confessions and traditions, such that a certain openness to seeking spiritual fulfillment would be a structuring logic for his life. This openness meant a refusal to denigrate various traditions; indeed, Seymour was against the various denominational factions that would spar over doctrinal truths years later. Seymour was not interested in beginning a denomination or a sect; he believed the outpouring of Spirit was available for all regardless of confession.

Seymour left his hometown of Centerville in the 1890s and traveled north, itinerating mostly as a restaurant server. "A critical turning point came when he moved to Indianapolis in 1895, where although he continued to visit other states for brief periods, he stayed until 1900."[13] It was in Indianapolis where he attended Simpson Chapel Methodist Episcopal Church, a black congregation. There, he accepted the call to ministry and began to preach. He was a seeker of experience, profound experience and encounter, with his notion of the divine. And it was his encounter with a group called the Evening Light Saints that Seymour saw the first evidence of the possibility for interracial reconciliation and fellowship grounded in faith. "This socially progressive, radical Holiness group preached racial equality and reconciliation around the beginning of Jim Crow segregation and actively reached out to blacks."[14] Whatever would come to animate Seymour's idea about faith and conviction would have to include an openness to those that have been marginalized and such openness would have to be lived out as a way to disrupt the normative world. "The [Evening Light] Saints provided him with one of his first visions of a racially egalitarian church—a vision he remained true to the rest of his life."[15] Ordained by the Evening Light Saints, he eventually left the north to find lost family members in Texas. And it was in Texas that he first heard the message of tongues.

Seymour joined a Holiness church pastored by Lucy Farrow in Houston. "In Houston Seymour met Pastor Lucy Farrow, the woman who would introduce him to the doctrine and experience of Pentecostal Spirit baptism and began attending her Holiness church."[16] In addition to leading a church, Farrow worked for Charles Parham, a prominent figure in Pentecostal history. He founded a school that taught Spirit baptism including speaking in tongues as evidence of this work of grace. Because of her relationship with Parham, Farrow was able to arrange for Seymour to attend the school, though because of segregation, he was not allowed to sit in the same classroom or pray in the same space with the white students. After learning as much as he felt possible from sitting under Parham, and after having preached several times under Parham's tutelage, in 1906, Seymour told Parham that the Lord told him to go to California. Parham was not happy about this and tried to get Seymour to relent, but he would not.

Seymour left Texas and arrived to Los Angeles in February 1906. He began a prayer meeting at 216 North Bonnie Brae Street with Ruth and Richard Asberry, a prayer meeting wherein they would tarry—wait with fervent prayer and song—intensely for the experience of Spirit baptism. April 9, 1906, was the first day someone of the group experienced Spirit baptism, Edward S. Lee. And a couple of days later, April 12, was the first time Seymour himself experienced Spirit baptism. People heard about the prayer meeting and began to gather at the house of the Asberrys so Seymour had the group move from North Bonnie Brae to 312 Azusa Street, a converted horse stable. It was the Azusa Street building where news spread globally of the "outpouring of the Spirit" in ways unlike any of the other revival similar revival meetings that occurred previous to this April 1906 flashpoint.

Named the Apostolic Faith Mission, people came from across the country to experience what they heard was occurring. And because of Seymour's experiences with the Evening Light Saints and others, he was committed to intentional egalitarianism in the meeting space. White men and women prayed for and with black women and men, Latinx persons were there at the very beginning, Korean and Jewish too. It was noted, even in the first news story about this new group, how the interraciality was a flout to the normative ideals of racial categorization and distinction.[17] Seymour harnessed the power of Spirit baptism, he—in other words—marshaled the power of aesthetic practice in the service of imagining, and living into such imagining, otherwise possibilities. He wanted to create an alternative mode of existence that would disrupt the here and now of his inhabitation. Unlike Parham (about which more in Chapter 4), Seymour was not content to allow the organization and hierarchies of race, gender, and class to remain intact after an encounter with Spirit baptism. Rather, Seymour and those in his tradition, utilized the various aesthetic practices discovered on the wooden floors of 312 Azusa Street to become a disruptive force. And it is for this reason that I write April 1906 as the beginning of this movement, the beginning of the movement of otherwise possibilities already set into motion and being enacted before Seymour's moment. Such that the "beginning" is misnomer, is impure, is—to return to the beginning— illusory and provisional. Seymour and the ones that would move with him simply lived into the black aesthetic, the black radical tradition, the already moving tradition of Blackpentecostal performance.

II

What does it mean—to riff on, and thus off, Immanuel Kant—to orient oneself in thinking ... *theologically* and *philosophically*? What does it mean to place oneself into a conceptual zone and category of distinction and to think from such a "place"? How does thought emerge from that which has been deemed, a priori, a categorically distinct modality of thought? And just what desires for purity undergird such a drive toward thinking from the categorically distinct zone? Air, the impure admixture, had to be let out of thought, had to be evacuated. Thought's flourishing, its leaps and bounds, must be strangled. Thought, through desired categorical distinction, is made to not breathe. The possibility for distinction that is categorical, that is in the end pure, is the *problem* of Enlightenment thought. Pure difference. This is what theological and philosophical thought attempt to achieve. Thought from within its own delimitation, purely different from—through excluding—*other* thought. Racialization is but one modality of creating a purely distinct category as a means to confront and contend with difference. The difference that is racialization must be made to be pure, and must be made to be maintained by the very possibility of pure difference.

The nominational moment convoking color as a means to think distinction—from within theology, philosophy—distinction that is race, to think blackness and whiteness, did not simply mean that skin was targeted. An entire range of sensual experiences—sound, smell, touch—were selected for such a racializing thought project. Thought had to be, in effect, made to be pure. Such thought was to be categorically distinct while *creating* the means through which categorically pure zones of thought could emerge. In a word, provocative though it may be: to think theologically, to think philosophically, is to think racially. It is to produce thought through the epistemology of western constructions. To attend to the necessary antiblackness of raciality is to summon us to be attentive likewise to the necessary antiblackness of theological-philosophical thought. They both emerge from the desire for pure thought, thought that is purely different from other modalities of cognition. Blackness was, is, and is still to come, as a destabilizing force against the project of racial purity, of aesthetic distinction. This remains to be elaborated through *Blackpentecostal Breath*.

I turn to two specific examples—not as a means to dismiss thought that emerges from within—but to illustrate the very delimitation with which we are confronted. So to turn to black womanist and queer theology is, for me, to demonstrate both the force of thought and the perniciousness of the epistemology of western civilization. As an example, concerns about blackness and the logic of western civilization inform my reading of Kelly Brown Douglas's offering, *Black Bodies and the Black Church: A Blues Slant*.[18] Douglas's main thesis is that the black church has a problem with bodies, with what she calls a *blues* body: "The black woman's body is a blues body. The highs and especially the lows of blues culture are associated with their bodies. It is the black woman's body that has been at the center of the contestations about blues in the black community."[19] Central to Douglas's text is the experience of black womanhood, as she believes the testimonies and songs of black blues women is most emphatically, intentionally, and explicitly illustrative of what it means to be rendered both central to and marginalized within the black church. The blues body, the black woman body, is a disruption to notions of civility and decorum; the more this body performs its wildness—the more one accepts one's condition of fleshliness—the more disruptive and in need of coercive control.

What Douglas demonstrates is the capacity for the blues to be an irruptive force for social life, how blues bodies manifest a mode of being in but not of worlds of normative function and form. Not only disruptive of racialist, classist, elitist ideologies of which whiteness serves as foundational, the blues has the capacity to interrupt black church aspirations toward respectability. The black church will be at its best when it leaves behind aspirations for respectability because such aspirations are, at base, antiblack. It is the antiblackness of white theological thought that renders black bodies lascivious, that renders our sexualities and gender expressions—a priori—in need of conversion.

> This body-denying/body-phobic culture in large measure points to the impact of a 'white gaze' upon the black church community. As black people tried to gain acceptance within white society by changing the black image in the white mind, they adopted white cultural standards of 'respectability.' In the main, these standards reflected Western dualistic perspectives that did not respect the body.[20]

Douglas successfully points readers to the antiblackness of aspirational modalities of black Christianity, the antiblackness that undergirds respectability politics even when that politics is deployed in the name of, in the service of, people who have been—historically and contemporarily—marginalized because they are, because we are, through the ideation of racial purity and categorical difference, rendered "black." But how do western dualistic perspectives affect how we think the capacity to produce thought as theological? How is western dualistic thinking grounded in the desire for pure difference such that the dualism can be obtained? How, in other words, is theology, as categorically pure and distinct from other modalities of thought, also a construction of western dualistic perspectives? How is theology antiblack and, thus, antiblues?

Intriguingly, for this reader at least, is how the concern over purity that sets off the very concept of theology as a modality of thought—a mode of thought that disavows materiality—runs against the very elaboration of the blues that Douglas is so very attentive. That to ask: Does not the blues in all its varied enfleshed manifestations Douglas describes—blues bodies, blues hope, blues bonds, blues song, as examples—act as an antagonism not merely to the black church's resistance to blues, to secularity, but to the very conceptual domain, zone, field of categorical distinction called theology? Theology produces the notion of heterosexual life that needs to be contained and controlled:

[Marcella] Althaus-Reid argues that the theological tradition is sexually saturated by male heterosexual fantasies. As a result, nonnormative persons—heterosexual and lesbian women, gay men, bisexuals, transgender[] persons—and their desires are placeless, shadow realities amid the small reiteration of supposed truths about God, which are always also stories about proper sexual conduct in service of heterosexist spiritual governance. Theology is effectively much more about the control of women's bodies than about God, or rather discourse about God is a way of keeping nonnormative experiences and desires marginal. Theology's official heteronormativity is tightly interwoven with colonialism and the silencing of non-Euro, non-modern, noncapitalist 'others.' Systematic theology is a way that church intellectuals keep sexuality from the ambiguous, polymorphic expressions—that 'others' press and sublimate—that would otherwise open new vistas on divinity. [(Systematic) Theology is a] pornographic system that holds women in place by inventing and policing the difference between 'decent' and 'indecent' talk about experience . . .[21]

Tom Beaudoin argues that theology, theological tradition, is about the control of flesh, about the fantasies of heterosexual desire and the muting of nonnormativity. Blues are nonnormative, and Douglas's blues bodies would be likewise. Such that if the blues does anything—and Douglas's attentiveness to the refusal of distinction between sacred and secular in the songs and lives of blues folks is instructive—it compels us to rethink the efficaciousness of the categorical distinction. That is, Douglas ends up reproducing the logic of exclusion by forcing the blues into to the hermeneutic work of theology, by asking it to do the work that perhaps ends up participating in the fantasy of heterosexuality and male control. And this would not only be true of Douglas. We can perhaps ask how theologies *black*, theologies *womanist*, theologies *mujerista*, theologies *liberation* do the work of reifying the seeming import of theology as categorical. How is it the production of theology ends up being a mode of respectability, constricting the bluesiness of blues to the strictures of an abstracted, delimited zone and field of inquiry?

What the blues are, what the blues do—if we trust Douglas's elaboration of them, which we should—is to break altogether with the imperative of the categorical distinctive. It must be interrogated: What counts, and who decides what counts, as a theological thought? Douglas submits the wildness and irruptive force of the blues to a *Christological* theological rendering, a doubled submission that abstracts and mutes—as so many trumpets in Harlem nightclubs—without the aesthetic adornment, excesses, or flourishes. The theologian's very identity is produced through the capacity to "think theologically" as a pure category, as a purely distinct mode of thought. And this is not only true for theology but philosophy as well. "Establishing identity, the identity of the philosophical through the work of differentiation, takes place, for example, in Hegel's argument that while philosophy may involve thought it needs to be distinguished from what he describes as 'thought in general'. The force of this distinction lies first in the possibility, once it is formulated, of presenting philosophy as escaping any reduction to common sense."[22] It is the thought in *general*, the social, the common, that is target of remediation in Hegel's thought, in philosophy generally. Though speaking specifically about Hegel, what Andrew Benjamin offers about the establishment of identity through the capacity to think a discipline, to think a field of categorical distinction, can and should be generalized. And I want to generalize against the ways generality is thought to be an obstacle, a problem, for proper thought and intellectual reflection. The blues antagonize such distinctions grounded in the identity of the one making such a claim for thought. The aesthetic practices of the blues moves us beyond simply interrogating who gets to make such a declaration about certain modalities of thought being theological in order to argue that the declaration itself—that some thought is theological over and against other kinds of thought—is a problem. It does not matter if the adjectival appendage is black, womanist, liberation, or queer. The capacity to make the distinction seems grounded in the necessity for exclusionary practice. What the blues demonstrate is not the working of theological thought but a critique of the capacity to make something theological, which is to say the capacity to make the pure distinction, the purely different.

In EL Kornegay's *A Queering of Black Theology: James Baldwin's Blues Project and Gospel Prose*, I find another iteration of the way theology, as method, constrains the radical potentiality of the object of study, the object of observation. James Baldwin is an important figure to consider because of the lingering presence Blackpentecostalism was in his life, the way it interrupted and infused his social, political, ethical projects—from the fictive to the poetic, from the theater to the essay critical. There is no James Baldwin without the radical force of Blackpentecostalism, the sound and feel, the feel and verve, the verve and movement of the religious social practice. In Kornegay's work, it becomes clearer to me why the focus on blues in black and womanist theology reproduces the delimitation of categorically distinct and pure modalities of thought. It is because of a dematerialization of the blues, the way the blues becomes rendered as disconnected from the sound, from the vibration, from the note. Kornegay, in his work, describes the ways he believes Baldwin is guided by what he calls a "blues poetics," yet this poetics is dematerialized, abstracted, not the result of the blues as material fact, as texture and weight, not the result of the blues as sound, as note. Writing about Baldwin's metaphorization of the Blues, Kornegay says:

> The term music does not refer here to a rhythm accompaniment of horns, symbols [sic], drumbeats, but what Baldwin calls the experience of black life. . . . [He] write[s] about how James Baldwin's use of the blues as the language/linguistics/semiotics of sexualized discourse signifies on the limitations of depravity placed on racialized and sexualized blues bodies [and that] the blues is a sexual and sensuous language enabling racialized, sexualized, and othered blues bodies to resist theological violence.[23]

Yet what of its sound, what of the blue note, the flatted fifth? That is, what of the materiality of sound, the vibratory frequency with which such a project of sound and song cuts and augments, is made manifest in the world? The reduction of blues to linguistics is a dematerialization, it seems to me, that is of necessity in the project of theology itself. It is a dematerialization not unlike the problem posed by the smell and funk that emanates from Argentinian women while selling lemons on the street without underwear that cuts against producing theology.

> Should a woman keep her pants on in the streets or not? Shall she remove them, say, at the moment of going to church, for a more intimate reminder of her sexuality in relation to God? What difference does it make if that woman is a lemon vendor and sells you lemons in the streets without using underwear? Moreover, what difference would it make if she sits down to write theology without underwear? The Argentinian woman theologian and the lemon vendors may have some things in common and others not.

In common, they have centuries of patriarchal oppression, in the Latin American mixture of clericalism, militarism and the authoritarianism of decency, that is, the sexual organisation of the public and private spaces of society. However, there may be differences too. The lemon vendor sitting in the street may be able to feel her sex; her musky smell may be confused with that of her basket of lemons, in a metaphor that brings together sexuality and economics. But the Argentinian theologian may be different. She may keep her underwear on at the moment of prayer, or whilst reflecting on salvation; and maybe the smell of her sex doesn't get mixed with issues of theology and economy. Writing theology without underwear may be punishable by law, who knows . . . Yet, an Argentinian feminist theologian may want to do, precisely, that. Her task may be to deconstruct a moral order which is based on a heterosexual construction of reality, which organises not only categories of approved social and divine interactions but of economic ones too. The Argentinian theologian would like then to remove her underwear to write theology with feminist honesty, not forgetting what it is to be a woman when dealing with theological and political categories.[24]

Marcella Althaus-Reid offers a way to think about the way nonnormative flesh undoes the project of theology and perhaps that might be the point. Perhaps we should remove those layers of material and intellectual cloth that have us bound within projects of normativity. Althaus-Reid offers a way to read and think and produce otherwise than theology by attending to the flesh, by considering the *primacy* of flesh for intellectual projects collective. Althaus-Reid, in the name of theology, writes against the project of theology. This writing against is what I attempt. What is dematerialized in theology is the materiality of funk, the materiality of unworn cloth. This dematerialization shares with the dematerialization of the blues. Perhaps we need become indecent and queer *against* theology. So to return to Kornegay, queering theology is forcing the radical potentiality of otherwise possibility that is queerness, its enactment, its otherwise modality and way of life, to inhere, to be subject to, to submit to the forces of a predetermined and given line of thought.

What can we make of the material trace that lingers within and makes itself felt, known, in Baldwin's writing, the material trace of Blackpentecostal aesthetic practice, the breath and tongues, the choreography and sonicity, that remains in his work, even when he writes against religion? I quote Baldwin at length:

Well, that winter in Switzerland, I was working on my first novel—I thought I would never be able to finish it—and I finally realized that one of the reasons that I couldn't finish this novel was that I was ashamed of where I came from and where I had been. I was ashamed of the life in the Negro church, ashamed of my father, ashamed of the Blues, ashamed of Jazz, and, of course, ashamed of watermelon: all of these stereotypes that the country inflicts on Negroes, that we all eat watermelon or we all do nothing but sing the Blues. Well, I was afraid of all that; and I ran from it.

When I say I was trying to *dig back* to the way I myself must have spoken when I was little, I realized that I had acquired so many affectations, had told myself so many lies, that I really had buried myself beneath a whole fantastic image of myself which wasn't mine, but white people's image of me.

I realized that I had not always talked—obviously I hadn't always talked—the way I had forced myself to learn how to talk. I had to find out what I had been like in the beginning, in order, just technically as a writer, to re-create Negro speech. I realized it was a cadence; it was not a question of dropping s's or n's or g's, but a question of the *beat*. Bessie had the beat. In that icy wilderness, as far removed from Harlem as anything you can imagine, with Bessie and me. . . .

Those Swiss people really thought I had been sent by the devil; it was a very strange . . . they had never seen a Negro before. In this isolation I managed to finish the book. And I played Bessie every day. A lot of the book is in dialogue, you know, and I corrected things according to what I was able to hear when Bessie sang, and when James P. Johnson plays. It's that *tone*, that sound, which is in me.[25]

What is needed is an *a*theological-*a*philosophical accounting, a *digging back*, a movement within, listening to and feeling the vibration of the tone, black tone. Theology, as a project, seeks to remediate the verve and flow of tone, black tone, it seeks to move forward, eschatologically toward some future end when instead, perhaps we should have a preferential option for the *digging back*. Baldwin's attention to the sound, to the tonality by which speech happens and his desire to recover it for his poetics, means that the work needs to be materialized through the sound, through the tone, to mark its true achievement. His writing is not antithetical to the material force of the form that speech, song, takes but must be materialized *through* the materiality, the texture and weight, the thickness and intensity, of vibration, of sound, of sonic force.

The blues were never only ever about language, were never only about lyricism. Many churches were wary of Georgia Tom's music even after he converted, became Thomas Dorsey, and began writing for the church. And this because the sound of the song, not simply the lyrical content. Listen to, for example, "Deep Moaning Blues" with Ma Rainey on lead and Georgia Tom on piano:[26]

> *My bell rang this morning, didn't know which way to go*
> *My bell rang this morning, didn't know which way to go*
> *I had the blues so bad, I sit right down on my floor*

It is not just the lyrics that resolve after the two repetitions in the lines beginning "My bell rang . . ." It is also the melodic line that resolves, that ends on the dominant, that ends on the tonic. The resolve, in the blues form, is a cause for joy, it is a displacement that is about the abandonment of strife that gives way to, that produces, feeling of the possibility of anxiety and solace. Nathaniel Mackey assists: "The orphan is such an archetypal figure, recurrent not only in my work but in world culture, because it tugs at the roots of our sense of belonging and the mix of anxiety and solace that goes with that sense."[27] Such production of the feeling of the possibility of anxiety and solace is enfleshed in a poetics that is about the practice of orphanage, of seeking, of journeying. And this orphanage, seeking, journey is heard not just in the lyrics but in the sound, in the resolve, in the movement away from and to the tonic. The blues ain't just the lyric. The blues is enfleshment; the blues is material. "The word is our rescue, whether spoken, written, sung, or nonverbally intoned, in part because the language of music and the music of language accent a tending-toward— 'pointing-beyond-itself' in Victor Zuckerkandl's analysis of tonal motion, Ezra Pound's 'tone leading of vowels,' etc.—that might well be the beginning of kinship, or a therapeutic or cathartic analogue to it, at least . . . The song sung in a strange land asks how can it be sung in a strange land, lamenting lost connection and reaching toward would-be connection, tenuous connection perhaps."[28]

Baldwin's writing is not dematerialized but a gathering of the vibration, the ongoing movement of matter, in the cause of plays, poetry, prose.

Like Baldwin's poetics, the blues is but one iteration of a way of life whose "underlying drive is a longing that outlives its ostensible fulfillments, reaching beyond its ostensible objects."[29] The blues is a gathering of the materiality of vibration and announced as enunciation, announced as the displacement of air, announced—that is—as sound. What does this mean for an analytics, a theory, that thinks blackness, black flesh, the blueness of blackness as a drive that is never meant to be contained, never meant to reach some there? We can then ask what Douglas's and Kornegay's moves to the blues prepare us for but that of which they each, in their own ways, stop short: What makes thought theological in the first place, particularly when one resists western dualistic thought? These various black womanist theological focuses on the blues were to trouble the ease with which dualistic thought flourishes, created by the very strictures of whiteness and the aspirational qualities undergirding respectability politics. Yet, if the sacred/profane split is a result of enlightened thought, that split is also always racialized, gendered, classed, sexed. But if dualism is actually *not*, if categorical distinction of sacred from profane is unsettled through otherwise epistemologies, then what is thought that can be considered categorically as "theological" over and against other modalities of thought? If theology is "god talk," as is often colloquially offered, but talk in blackness is never categorically distinct or pure, what does it mean to do, think or be theology or theological? This is not to say that thought does not occur from within the zone called theology. *Blackpentecostal Breath* could not be offered into a conversation without the clearing work of those theologians *black* and *womanist* and *mujerista* and *liberationist* and *queer*, their work cleared ground through which I now move. The work I present is indebted to the various thinkers of these concepts, thinkers from within these zones and disciplines whose thinking, it seems to me, pushes up against the limits of those zones and disciplines. I am simply unsure about the efficaciousness of the delimitation placed on thought from the outside, then calling thought—delimited through forced violent encounter, a violence at least as old as the Middle Passage, though without a doubt older—"theological," "philosophical."

III

Charles Mingus knew. Composer and musician, Mingus recognized the importance and impact of the midweek gathering of black folks at the Holiness-Pentecostal Church at 79th and Watts in Los Angeles that he'd attend with his stepmother or his friend Britt Woodman. Mingus tells the story of how his stepmother traveled weekly to the lively church services: "My father didn't dig my mother going there. . . . People went into trances and the congregation's response was wilder and more uninhibited. . . . The blues was in the Holiness churches—moaning and riffs and that sort of thing between the audience and the preacher."[30] These visits were the impetus for "Wednesday Night Prayer Meeting," a song that used 6/4 rhythmic propulsion in order to convey its message, in order to approach the aesthetic-intellectual force of what he'd feel on any given Wednesday night prayer service. Scott Saul described Mingus's 6/4 rhythm as taking "the traditional gospel rhythm and, by accelerating the overall tempo, [the rhythm] brought out the swinging cross-rhythms that had been hidden in the loping advance" of other recordings. Brought out in the song is that which was hidden from view, the excess—the gospel rhythmning—that prompts gathering, an excess that at the same time constitutes and is the grounds for gathering. The sounds of love, the smells of food, the praising flesh. This is captured in the extended 11'54" performance of the song recorded in 1960 at Juan-les-Pins during the Antibes Jazz Festival for the album *Mingus at Antibes* released in 1976.

It opens with Mingus on bass, the announcement of pitch low, vibration slow. Feel the pulse-pulse of the movement, divine call and encounter, in and of openness to spirit. Like open doors to a church, like a prayer meeting for study, gathering together the dispersed parts of severed sociality. Refusing enclosure, refusing seclusion. Throughout this particular performance, the song increases in speed moment by moment. The saxophone solo at 7'40", the sax breaking off into what sounds like speaking in tongues. At 6'19", a clap interlude. The handclaps function to both keep and break with rhythm. The drums, the bass, the piano. Each instance of the solo enfleshed the airy space with the black symphonic. You hear the density of the space when there is abandonment and reanimation of sound, when there is the leaving and arrival, the breaking away from and coming back to of instruments.

And there is the ethical demand of the prayer meeting felt, experienced, that Mingus's song attempts to capture. This ethics, this demand, is for openness and hospitality, improvisation and refusing to be done with seeking otherwise. To hear the saints testify, sing before the Lord, shout, get happy and do their dance. "Wednesday Night Prayer Meeting" was Mingus's memorial, homage, to black sociality. Mingus figured out that those gatherings were the constant repetition of an ongoing, deep, intense mode of study, a kind of study wherein the aesthetic forms created could not be severed from the intellectual practice because they were one and also, but not, the same. To transform such force of testimony, song, shout, happiness, dance into otherwise modality, otherwise feel. It was the black symphonic, the sounding out together of the ecology of gathering black being, blackness as becoming, as a force of critique and ethical demand upon the world. What one hears in the density of the space made through these prayer meetings is the sound of love, the sound of radical welcome beckoning the margin to join in. The sound of radical hospitality.

Yet radical hospitality did not stop murder. Dylan Roof's massacre of the nine parishioners at Emanuel African Methodist Episcopal Church in Charleston, South Carolina illustrates the ongoing ecological, ethical crisis. He said both: "everyone was so nice" and, "I had to go through with the mission." The parishioners were not nice but *so* nice; excess was the grounds of their engaging him, excess was the solicitation that made a space for him to leave the margins of the meeting and join with the others. Yet, he still performed the heinous act.   What those saints in study offered him, through prayer and song and inviting him to be part of an unbroken circle, was nothing short of radical possibility of otherwise. What Roof experienced, however, he transformed into a merely aesthetic encounter, not one that had intellectual content, not one that could move him and let him, with reckless abandon, join the handclaps of hard-loved flesh. Beautiful, hard-loved flesh opened and became vulnerable for him, invited him into not the sanctuary but the basement, where the love is felt.

White terrorizing, white supremacist ideology, is produced by the suppression, the gathering and destroying, of such an openness, such a vitality, such a propulsive 6/4 rhythmning. White supremacy, its rapacious and incessant antiblackness, is the constant emergence of fear, the fear of being engulfed, and changed, by this radical abundance. Dylan Roof murdering the members of Emmanuel African Methodist Episcopal Church in Charleston, SC illustrates the ways his was not the violence of someone who believed that social death—the state of total powerless—was achievable but was the violence of one terrified by its impossibility. The people he murdered were not the totally powerless but those who extended life, an otherwise mode of relationality, to him. He began shooting during the benediction when the eyes of the twelve gathered were closed. He began his violence when they were most open and vulnerable, when they were at the height of availability. Such vulnerability was evinced most in their closed eyes, their prayer for sociality of protection: "May the Lord watch between me and thee while we're absent one from . . ." Interrupted. He had to, against the openness of love and hospitality felt and the prayer offered, enclose himself, shut down his sensual capacities, not be moved. He had to repress the desire to join in and with what was extended to him.

This is neither an exercise in "redeeming" Roof nor making less horrific the brutality and horror of his violent acts, his acts of violation. Rather, we hone in on the truly pernicious nature of the horror of white supremacist antiblack violence if we consider Roof as *responding* to the irrepressible life offered, if we consider violence of the state against racialized communities that has been intensifying *as a response* to protest, life as protest, life in general. Because that is the key. Such that we must answer: What to do, how to move, in such a world wherein your resistance against violent conditions—resistance as prayer meetings or protests, resistance as simply wishing to breathe—produces the occasion for violence? This is the ethical crisis to which we must be attuned, the ethical crisis to which *Blackpentecostal Breath: The Aesthetics of Possibility* attempts to engage and offer reply.

IV

To produce a choreosonic encounter wherein not one—the choreographic nor the sonic—is privileged is the purpose of the work in *Blackpentecostal Breath: The Aesthetics of Possibility*. What I attempt to do in the pages to come is elaborate what I have come to think of as *otherwise possibilities* for organizing, for thinking projects that neither make the flesh diminutive nor discardable. Rather, I want to give careful and thoughtful attention to the flesh, life in the flesh as the liberative position, as the liberative modality, life in the flesh—following Hortense Spillers—as the way of empathy.[31] How to discover in a religious practice normatively deemed excessive, excessive because of the performance of the flesh, the performance of the flesh grounding the critique of such a world as unthoughtful—and as such, not philosophical nor theological—is what I set out to do in *Blackpentecostal Breath*. Thinkers I engage throughout the work include Hortense Spillers, Nahum Chandler, Fred Moten, Nathaniel Mackey, Michel Foucault, Saidiya Hartman, and Denise Ferreira da Silva. They inform the way I have come to think the keywords of the text: flesh, sociality, blackness, otherwise. And the text attempts to approach something of the aesthetic force of Blackpentecostal worship, though this certainly is no argument in favor of conversion. One does not enter into a church, for example, with explanations of all that will occur but often one will experience, one will hear, smell, see, touch before one is given explication of what has happened or the meaning thereof. The text desires something of this force of suggestion while also remaining clear that it is a theoretical intervention, a performance of the sociality elaborated.

I am not, it should also be said, making an argument that Blackpentecostalism is utopic, that it is free of the problems of marginalizing. Having grown up in the Blackpentecostal movement, as a member of the Church of God in Christ (COGIC), as a former choir director, musician, preacher, as the son of preachers, as one that was well on his way to ordination within the social world, I am all too familiar with the world's proclivities for classism, sexism, homophobia, and transphobia. I am not making an argument that the world exists without participating in practices that marginalize. But something is *there*, in the aesthetic practices, aesthetic practices that *are* collective intellectual performances, that serve as antagonistic to the very doctrines of sin and flesh that so proliferate within the world. What I mean is that the resource for critiquing the ways sexism, homophobia, transphobia, and classism inform the world exist within the world itself, the breakdown and critical analysis is an otherwise possibility full in its plurality and plentitude already within the world. It is a world of Black Study even against its sometimes vulgar and vile declarations of sin. Otherwise is a word that names plurality as its core operation, otherwise bespeaks the ongoingness of possibility, of things existing other than what is given, what is known, what is grasped. Otherwise possibility is what I think Blackpentecostal aesthetics produce for thinking blackness and flesh, for thinking blackness and performance, as gathering and extending that which otherwise is discarded and discardable, those two modalities as modes of being and existence. Otherwise names the subjectivity in the commons, an *a*subjectivity that is not about the enclosed self but the open, vulnerable, available, enfleshed organism.

Black Study is the affirmation of and belief in blackness, though belief is radically under assault, coded through and attacked as "the religious." One need only read contemporary philosophical work of the "New Atheist" movement—Sam Harris and Christopher Hitchens as two examples—for the ways belief becomes racialized, and how that racialization is part of, not distinct from, a general antiblackness sentiment.[32] Characterized by Harris as the most virulent and dangerous strain of belief, one wonders at his inter-articulation of Islam and otherness that seems to animate Harris's thought. It is not simply that belief is a problem, but belief that is accompanied with overt, explicit aesthetic practices—wearing *hijab*, praying five times a day eastward—that makes of such belief a general antagonism, a general threat. I opine that the general antagonism and threat of belief is because belief, when borne out through certain aesthetic behaviors, is considered to be blackness itself. Whiteness is considered the absence of such purportedly primitivist behaviors, and thus, a lack of belief that moves the flesh.[33] As such, *Blackpentecostal Breath* considers the aesthetics of belief, the performative behaviors and gestures that accompany collective modes of intellection and knowledge of divine, otherworldly worlds. I invoke Harris and Hitchens not just to serve as straw men but to consider the ways belief *as* practice of sociality comes under assault for certain groups. I am intrigued by the ways Islam is cast in the New Atheist movement as a modality of thought and practice that is most violent, and it seemed to me, this is asserted because of the public prac-tice of belief, the way belief is worn on the flesh (in the case of the khimar, niqab, burka, and hijab, as examples). Such belief is worn—like the racial-ization of the flesh—and such wearing produces a crisis in the meaning of belief as practice. We might call this wearing of *belief in the flesh*—"in" here indexing both *internal* to and *the state or condition of* the flesh. This belief is not unlike the aesthetic practices of Blackpentecostalism I elaborate. What remains to be done in future work, work I hope this writing will prompt, are ways to think the relation between Islam and Christianity grounded in the flesh, black flesh, a certain move and movement, a certain vibration toward liberation. The distinction between belief and practice is one interrogation *Blackpentecostal Breath* stages.

In "On the Jewish Question," Karl Marx interrogates Bruno Bau-er's idea that integration into German society for Jews depended upon forced relinquishment of their relationship to Jewishness—the cultural and historical performative practices of religiosity.[34] Usually figured as antireligious, Marx indeed otherwise and famously claimed that religion and opiates were co-constitutive for masses. However, in "On the Jewish Question," which queries the possibilities for Jewishness, Marx demonstrates how relinquishment to gain freedom and citizenship—what he calls "political emancipation"—is a ruse. Giving up cultural and historical performative practices does not produce abolition but another set of strictures and bondage. In another register and key, we can say that one gains political emancipation through aversion, embarrassment, and abandonment over practice, over *belief in the flesh*, and this political emancipation is the condition that occasions the theological-philosophical production of "the body." The body, here then, is a coherence, a stable entity that can be entered into something like civil society. But perhaps what is needed is an excess to, an exorbitance of, political emancipation. *Belief in the flesh* will get us there. In *Blackpentecostal Breath*, I try to think about not only the generalizability of Marx's analysis to consider the ways in which black flesh are denigrated, but how Blackpentecostal aesthetics rise to the occasion of, and overcome, the denigration of and aversion for blackness.

I utilize the portmanteau Blackpentecostalism because I consider both blackness and Pentecostalness to be forces in the world that do not belong to any group, that *are* only insofar as they are given away. Both are transformational energies that are carried in the flesh, and I think the two concepts together, each as constitutive of the other. If blackness is the tradition of resistance that inheres objects,[35] and if Pentecostalness is the capacity for otherwise beginnings ongoingly,[36] Blackpentecostalism is the capaciousness of otherwise resistance that rises to, while emerging from, the occasion of its genesis. I use the term theological-philosophical throughout the text and do so because I think the two *together* constitute a worldview, a way to think about blackness and attendant fleshly practices and performances. I hone in on and interrogate the ways theology and philosophy are sometimes thought as distinct from the other rather than are co-constituted. I hope for it to become clear that the ways blackness is conceived in western theology and philosophy is through averting blackness, black flesh, through an ongoing antagonistic relation to it. I also use the couplet *a*theological-*a*philosophical to name the intimate relationship of the collective intellectual project that is Blackpentecostalism for thinking about "god talk" as well as concepts of being, morality, knowledge, and law. But like the resolve that is the aspiration of knowledge in theology and philosophy, as da Silva noted above, I am interested in the otherwise than theology and philosophy that is no less intensely concerned with these various ideas. And the object of Blackpentecostalism, of Black Study, what Black Study tries to produce and analyze, is a collective possibility for belief in otherwise worlds, one that is a creative critique of the one(s) in which we exist. That otherwise can be constituted in our now moment does not mean that otherwise worlds are utopic. It means that otherwise is possible and after such an analytics, after such an interrogation into the ways otherwise performs itself into being, we are charged with producing otherwise in the cause of justice. But we cannot rest with having been the otherwise but must be capacious and unfolding, open and committed to equity.

In Chapter 1, "Breath," I construct the theory of tradition embedded in the performance and transference of breath as the necessary physiological and spiritual force that is the constitutive element of Blackpentecostal performative production. As breath is the vivifying force enlivening and quickening flesh, this chapter sets the theoretical groundwork and structure for thinking the *a*theological-*a*philosophical concept. Breath is a reminder of the connection with divinity and Jean-Christophe Bailly writes about how the "slightest breath" is the sign of irrepressible life.[37] To consider the aesthetics of breathing, I first analyze "whooping" practices of three Blackpentecostal women preachers to illustrate the performance of intentional breathing practices. Then, I turn to Pneumatology—the study of *pneuma*, the Greek word for "breath"—as pneumatology is about the relation of spirit to flesh. However, most pneumatological writings repress the concept of breath itself in ways similar, I argue, to how black flesh *as* Blackpentecostalism is repressed in pneumatological writings. Chapter 1 extrapolates a "blackness pneumatology," an *a*theology-*a*philosophy of breathing that informs Blackpentecostal aesthetic cultural production, as a poetics and a form of life. Analyzing lynching practices between 1880 and 1930, I argue that Blackpentecostal whooping during preaching and praying responds to the eclipsing of black breath through aesthetic breathing. Ida B. Wells-Barnett and her antilynching campaign shows up in this chapter. I want to demonstrate the ways the Blackpentecostal intellectual practice of critique finds its way in, infuses, and produces the critique that Wells-Barnett staged throughout her career.

"Shouting," the second chapter, is primarily an analysis of Immanuel Kant's Enlightenment anthropological thought as well as a staging to consider the relation between Enlightenment and the Calvinist doctrine of predestination. Chapter 2 defines what I term the "choreographic itinerary and protocol," a series of placements and arrangements for how blackness was cognized, creating the concept of racial-religious difference. This choreographic is different from what I call the choreosonic, a portmanteau underscoring the fact that choreography and sonicity—movement and sound—are inextricably linked and have to be thought together. "Shouting" as a Blackpentecostal practice undoes the distinction between movement and sound. In this chapter, I analyze the "choreo" of the choreosonic, illuminating how both predestination theology animating the Great Awakening revivals, as well as Enlightenment philosophy were the theological-philosophical conditions of emergence for thinking time and space without blackness that not only instantiates subjectivity but marks the dividing line between white bodies and the complex modes of fleshly disembodiment that are called blackness. A case study in aversion as a concept, this chapter argues that there is movement-sound, a vibration, a choreosonics of *a*theological-*a*philosophical thought that exceeds normative theological-philosophical figurations, found in performance of moving flesh—that which exists before the abstraction of spatial and temporal coherence. Moving flesh speaks back and against problematic conceptions of blackness. I thus analyze the tradition of Blackpentecostal dancing flesh through interrelations among Afro-Arabic Islamic *saut*, nineteenth-century Ring Shout, and twentieth-century Blackpentecostal "shouting."

In Chapter 3, "Noise," I analyze the *sonic* in choreosonic performances of the *a*theology-*a*philosophy of blackness aestheticized by a specific kind of singing and praise noise heard during two particular moments of the Blackpentecostal church service—that is, Testimony and Tarrying. These songs and sounds offer sharp criticism of the given world, a political economy that is foundationally built on exploitation and abstraction, exploitation and alienation. An attention to the songs and sounds, as ephemera, is urgent for thinking about the ways Blackpentecostalism manifests before the 1906 Azusa Street revival in Los Angeles, how the sonic resources of resistance in Blackpentecostalism are found in varied contexts, some seemingly secular and others purportedly only sacred. Offered in the chapter is a critique of *historical being*, of the concept of history. Three Jennys—an enslaved woman,

Jenny von Westphalen (Marx), and Jenny Evans Moore (Seymour)—ground the chapter, using the "sonic" aspect of the choreosonic as a critique of racial capitalism and its abuses. Listening to the sound of singing during Testimony Service and praise noise during Tarrying makes the *a*theological-*a*philosophical antiphonal resistance to aversion and embarrassment audible. Embarrassment—an affective response produced through a submission to respectability politics—is the concept untangled in this chapter that the three Jennys refuse. Rather than embarrassment, they each utilize the politics of avoidance, an *a*theological-*a*philosophical intellectual performative practice. Such refusal of embarrassment is against historical being.

In the fourth chapter, "Tongues," I write about how, at the turn of the twentieth-century, a crucial debate emerged amongst the nascent Blackpentecostal movement: Was speaking in tongues *glossolalia*, "heavenly language," or *xenolalia*, speaking a language that the individual has not learned? What was the breath doing in the flesh and how was that aestheticized breath registered in this community? More, how is the distinction between *glosso* and *xeno* grounded in abandonment? Rather than leaving behind the aesthetic spiritual practice, Blackpentecostals employed speaking in tongues with reckless abandon. I argue that these are two minuscule but inassimilable concepts are each grounded in particular conceptions of personhood. The debate about *glosso* and *xeno* elucidates concerns about capacities to speak for oneself or for another, and to speak to another. Moreover, the debate was also about the possibility of converting an Other—someone in India, for example—without the need to cognize in the language, thought, and mental aptitude of the Other. This debate about performative distinction is the grounds for a Blackpentecostal critique of the liberal subject. And this distinction between *glosso* and *xeno*, it turns out, buttresses different approaches to the study of black life as well as divergent approaches to approaching objects of study in institutions like the university. In the chapter, we also listen in on the Fisk Jubilee Singers to consider the ways the distinction between *glosso* and *xeno* indexes a way to think the social life of blackness, its vibration, its sounding, its translation, its interpretation. Such interpretations have often happened in the university. All this to consider how knowledge is produced and transformed in the setting of the university, how these institutional settings often require a reduction of black sound, of blackness, of Blackpentecostal aesthetic practice.

V

In *Blackpentecostal Breath*, I demonstrate how categorical distinction is a problem of modern thought. Elaborated, alongside the untangling of categorical distinction, are the ways the invention of racialization is a fundamental, foundational aspect of the maintenance of that project. Categorical distinction as a means to organize knowledge is a certain epistemological constraint that bears down on us from the outside since such organizing presumes the possibility of the finding and continuance of pure difference. Thought theological, thought philosophical, is, then, racial thought, racialist thought. Categorically distinct modalities of thinking the world cannot help but be subsumed under the thinking of racialization. Categorically distinct modalities of thinking the world produces the serrations of racialization, this thinking cuts thought, divides it. Such operations happen through aversive logics. But the gift of aversive logic—insofar as there might be one—is that what remains intact is the thing so averted, even if the thing so averted is averted through violence, brutality, horror. There is something that remains, exceeds, is uncapturable and that because of the refusal of sustained engagement. *Blackpentecostal Breath* considers aesthetic practices of Blackpentecostalism—whooping, shouting, noise-making, and tongues speech—to interrogate the ways distinction is produced. And that because each aesthetic practice was only distinguished in order to highlight the ways such distinctions were predicated upon the literal evacuation of breath, *black pneuma*, the slightest breath of living. Such distinctions, in other words, are illusory because each practice is grounded in the flesh, in the breath flesh takes in and expels, is grounded in otherwise modes of existence. The varied aesthetic practices cannot be considered as a stand-alone but part of a social world, an ecology of intense mood and feeling, the practice of otherwise epistemologies against the constraints of western modernity. Looking toward the horizon after setting categorical distinction in relief, we will be able to ask: What does it mean to be black, to exist in blackness, when the categorical distinction as an imperative modality of thought itself has been interrogated? What does blackness have to do, to say, to be if the primary organizing logic of flesh has been disrupted, if racialization is no longer operable as a strategy of containment? The task of this book is to get us to the horizon.

So I HAD to think about it, and it hit me. Before encountering Hortense Spillers's "vestibularity," before Fred Moten's "in the break," before Nahum Chandler's "otherwise," before Denise Ferreira da Silva's "ethical crisis," it was the radically inclusive Pentecostal ministerial work that my friend Kendal Brown was doing that prompted me to really think about the concept of otherwise possibilities. I asked him years ago—because I was frustrated that queer folks wouldn't just attend queer affirming churches rather than those spaces that deemed them sinful—what was the point of having queer affirming churches if people won't leave. And he said to me the point wasn't to have everyone leave their spaces through brute force, to cause them to leave spaces where they are in order to be in affirming spaces against their will. Rather, the point of the work was to create the space of possibility, to create the affirming spaces, and to let folks know that an alternative exists if they so choose to join with it. And that idea has remained with me so many years later. Alternatives exist—*already*—against the normative modes under which we endure. If we so choose to join up with the alternative, all the better. The work is to make apparent the fact of the resonance of alternatives, to let folks know that we are here engaging in otherwise work. And that is a beautiful thing.

1

BREATH

Stories of escape and flight from circum-Atlantic enslavement are numerous. Too numerous, in fact, to recount here. Yet in each instance, in each retelling, is movement emerging from plurality, from the irreducibility of otherwise possibilities. One such movement is the excitement, frustration, exacerbation internal to the narrative that the actor recounts for readers. How one felt. What one thought on the varied routes to flight, the many highways and byways, the hidings and showing forths. The final arrival, relief. All this in these narratives, fugitive stories, about the capacity for producing justice and liberation by stealing oneself away. But there is otherwise movement irreducibly in such narratives, movement of—for example—the incitement to excitement, frustration, exacerbation the narrator wants to produce *for* readers. Does the reader hear the rustling of grass underfoot, the sounds of ship whistles, of whipped flesh? Does the reader see the muddy passageways, the swamps? Does the reader smell the sweaty flesh absconding? All this as an excess of the writing, an excess written into the writing, an excess about desiring for the reader to understand something about the peculiar—the peculiarly violent—institution. Such doubled movement written into and as the text announces the excessive possibility of otherwise, that such otherwise possibility is marked by its plurality. This writing is an exercise in theorizing otherwise possibilities by elaborating upon the various remains, the various excesses yet to be elaborated.

Breathing. There is something that occurs in these texts that typically goes unremarked, or if remarked, is only done insofar as there is a spectacular instance of such. What goes unremarked, though certainly produced in the occasions of recounting movement, is the necessity of the breath, of breathing itself, as performative act, as performative gesture. What goes unremarked is how breathing air is constitutive for flight, for movement, for performance. We do hear about air, breath, and breathing in an indirect way when we read of the varied forms of punishment that were utilized to inhibit or obstruct air from getting into and out of the flesh. We hear, for example—through so many varied examples—of "heart-rending shrieks," so much so that it would seem to be a narrative strategy and rhetorical device. Almost. The various stories, however, are not neatly contained to predetermined strategies. These narratives depend upon the repetition of the idea of how insidious and unvirtuous, how violative and violent, this peculiar institution was.

Writing of heart-rending shrieks during various productions of brutal violence hint at the necessity of air, and its obstruction, for the further-ance of the peculiar institution. Heart-rending shrieks issue forth from the spectacular performances of violation and violence, and following Saidiya Hartman,[1] we must think about the necessity of breathing, of breath, of air, in otherwise than these spectacularized instances. What do air, breath, and breathing have to do with black performance, with Blackpentecostal aesthetics?

Breathing, like the picking up of sticks in woods, is not new.[2] But to keep breathing, like picking up sticks—because of the imposition of theological-philosophical reasoning and understanding; because of the imposition of a juridical-ecclesial mode of thinking the human, the individual—such per-formances of breathing and gathering of sticks became fugitive acts. Pick-ing up sticks was not always illegal; forests were not always enclosed land. This was a form of life, social form, that privileged holding land in com-mon. What befell this already existent social form, this form of life, was law stating that practices that had already been performed—commoning— were now, because of the random declaration, acts of criminality.[3] This criminality did not *create* the social form but attempted to control and repress it, to harness and exploit this already existing social form for use in new modalities of juridical repression and control.

Yet, for Nimi Wariboko, the ongoing emergence of the new is what con-stitutes, for him, what he calls the "pentecostal principle."[4] He describes it as "the capacity to begin," that it is a "demand of new beginning."[5] But what this demand is grounded in a presumption of linear time, of western time, as the movement from past, to present, to future in a smooth transition and progression. "If it is a matter of time, then it is all about the future," is the manifestation, the coming into being of the new.[6] But Blackpentecostal aesthetics resist the conceptualization of the purely new, of western time's forward propulsion. Blackpentecostal aesthetics, rather than a turn to the new, is the production of otherwise, shows the sending forth of otherwise possibilities already enacted, already here. So we turn, again, to the picking up of sticks.

Groups, such as the Levellers and Diggers, formed after such newly defined criminality, gathering in order to enact modes of sociality—to keep the land common and available to all.[7] And this newly formed grouping, this mode of being together, was grounded in their coming together in the service of old, already existing, social form. These groups were new only insofar as they emerged to rise to the occasion of contending against the idea that what they'd already been was in need of eradication. If criminal, if a problem for thought, this concept would be true only insofar as preexisting social forms made it difficult for new juridical-ecclesial repression and control to be imposed without resistance. And it is only *thus* that violence befalls.

This brief beginning excursus informs how I consider Blackpentecostalism and the blackness that is foundational for such a concept. The very idea that juridical violence of western civilization has the capacity to create blackness—and all its attendant deformational, creative potentialities and polarities—is undone by attending to Blackpentecostal performance. Western theology-philosophy has been an unrelenting and incessant drive to repress creative potentia and kinesthesia of blackness because such potentia and kinesthesia are the necessary interruption and disruption of such possibility. To breathe, within this western theological-philosophical epistemology, from within the zone of blackness, from within the zone of Blackpentecostalism, is to offer a critical performative intervention into the western juridical apparatus of violent control, repression, and yes, premature death. Thus the importance of attending to the ways air, breath, and breathing are aestheticized, are intentionally elaborated for one that would so notice.

When narratives of escape were produced as incitement to affect—to intense emotion and feeling—for the reader, air, breath, and breathing were produced as aesthetic performance, announcing one's existence in the world, enunciating one's ongoing displacement and movement in worlds, producing critical disruption into the world of our normative inhabitation.

One can only imagine, for example, the compression in chest Harriet Jacobs endured in the "loophole of retreat,"[8] in the crawlspace above her grandmother's dwelling. Dimensions of only nine feet long, seven feet wide, and three feet high at the tall end, the capacities for breathing deeply, fully, satisfyingly were likely to have been compromised by such compressed space, sharing air with rats and mice. Such compression of space likewise produced an otherwise temporality wherein hearing, wherein listening, became heightened. Jacobs could faintly see her children playing outside the dwelling through cracks in the structure. But as seeing was most obstructed, Jacobs relied on hearing them just beyond the crawlspace outside playing, speaking. All she had to do was keep on breathing.

Or one could imagine, as another example, the varied breathing patterns of the many people that escaped enslavement with the guidance of Harriet Tubman.[9] We know, for example, that she sang to her fellow travelers in the woods in order to announce to them that the paths were clear.[10] Tubman's travelers listened to the enunciative displacement of air, displacement as her voice, in order to know it was indeed her vocalizing, her timbre, her tone. They listened to air's displacement, in other words, to know that her flesh was present. The aestheticization of the entry into and out of the flesh of air, of breath, as necessary for fugitive flight.

Or one could even imagine the changes in breathing for Olaudah Equiano just moments before receiving manumission papers that would, in law, free him from enslavement.[11] Did his breathing become perhaps labored, shallow, faint, nervous, flights of butterflies in in his stomach, tightness in chest anticipatory? All this because of his wanting to seize hope for a future but considering that anything was, yet and still, possible? Did the breathing, in other words, come to match the intensity of emotion and feeling that was no doubt occurring during those moments? The reader of his narrative, no doubt, breathed heavy and deep and sighed and felt exasperated throughout the duration of the text.

In each instance, what goes unremarked—what we might almost (but not) consider marginal to the retelling—is the way one had to keep on breathing, panting, for such a narrative occurrence. Narratives of escape, collectively, are simply one figuration of the ways in which air, breath, and breathing are important considerations for black performance. There are certainly other instances, other stagings, other spaces and "texts" from which emerge the possibility for such analysis. Breathing, I mean to say, was integral though not generally the matter, the materiality, of narrative performance. Yet it is there, was there, in all its enunciative force. And enunciation is the precise word for what I attempt to consider in this chapter.

From the Latin *ex-* meaning out and *nuntius* meaning messenger, enunciation at base is about an irreducible showing forth and making apparent of one that would perform, act, in the world. What happens when we bring enunciation close, make the concept rub up against, fugitivity, two terms moving, seemingly, in antithetical directions? The fugitivity of escape as the showing forth of the "out messenger," the one that carries a word, a phrase, a plea, a praise, a prayer, a psalm. This messenger, this fugitive messenger in blackness, this messenger carrying the word of blackness, releases oneself out into the world, in plainclothes, hidden view. And such releasing becomes the grounds from which to be enfleshed anew, to announce an otherwise desire than what is normative. The fugitive enacts by enunciative force, by desire, by air, by breath, by breathing. Breath and breathing of air, in other words, not only make possible but sustain such movement.

So. Pause. Deeply breathe, in. Now slowly, out.

Air. It is an object that is shared, that is common, that is necessary for each movement, each act, each scene—whether of subjection or celebration. Air is an irreducible admixture of nitrogen, oxygen, other minute atmospheric gases and particulate matter that enters the flesh through the process of breathing. This process of breathing can be, certainly has been, is and will be, aestheticized, performed. Children play breathing games, seeing who can hold one's breath longest; singers breathe to hit high and low notes, to climb and descend scales; people dance and run, sleep and snore. All necessitate the performance, the process, of breathing.

Air is an object held in common, an object that we come to know through a collective participation within it as it enters and exits flesh. The process by which we participate in this common object, with this common admixture, not only must be thought about but must be consumed and expelled through repetition in order to think. The always more than double gesture of inhalation and exhalation is a matter of grave concern given the overwhelming presence of air as shared object, the overwhelming presence of breathing as shared, common performance. In each movement of dilation is a displacement of one kind of matter into the space and plane of another. To fill lungs with air is to displace the carbonite matter that was previously within. To write narratives of flight is to displace the common conceptions of the human, the subject, the object. Blackpentecostalism, I argue, is grounded in this process of movement and displacement, movement as displacement. Of material, of flesh, of concepts. So we turn to instances of breathing as an intentionally aesthetic production, a mode of life, a politics of avoidance.

If there was a movement that "began" in Los Angeles on Bonnie Brae Street in 1906, which would eventually be called Pentecostalism, this movement would always and everywhere be claimed by what Laura Harris calls the "aesthetic sociality of blackness": "The aesthetic sociality of blackness is an improvised political assemblage that resides in the heart of the polity but operates under its ground and on its edge. It is not a re-membering of something that was broken, but an ever-expanding invention. It develops by way of exclusion but it is not exclusionary, particularly since it is continuously subject to legitimated, but always incomplete, exploitation."[12] Blackpentecostalism is an enactment of this aesthetic sociality. Blackpentecostalism is the performance of plural possibilities for otherwise, is the enactment of irreducible openness, the experience of displacement as common, the performance of displacement as a critique of the violent modernity that produced violent possession, colonialism, enslavement. Blackpentecostalism is the ongoing emergence of otherwise than "spatial and temporal coherence,"[13] is not about human possibility but the possibilities that exist in plurality for those that have been rejected from the zone of the human. This ongoing emergence of otherwise is not, in the first instance, out of duress and violence, but out of and grounded in love. Prompted by sounds, such as of rushing mighty winds, Blackpentecostalism compels the analysis of the ongoing necessity for escape as one condition of emergence for the perpetual reconfiguration—and, with hope, the dismantling of and building something otherwise—of normative, violative modes of repressive and regulatory apparatuses.

Blackpentecostalism is ever expansive, emerging through having certain aesthetic religious practices excluded from categories of the "mainline," excluded because these practices were considered excessive and discardable, practices that were obstructions for achieving pure theological-philosophical *thought*, pure theological-philosophical *reflection*. Yet these practices, these aesthetic sacred performances were always critical analyses of and performed positions against the categorical distinctions of theology and philosophy that would come to define normative religious practice. Blackpentecostalism, though excluded from the mainstream, was ever inclusive of those that would be excluded. It is an egalitarian mode of Spirit indwelling, wherein that which those filled with the Spirit have is immediately given away to others through aesthetic proclamation, through linguistic rupture that announces and enunciates expanded sociality. The sound of violent wind is matched with, but also exceeded by, an intensive, intentional, and pullulating capacity for otherwise sociality. And what is held and given away, what is involved in reciprocity of gift and exchange, is air through the performance of breathing, that which animates the flesh and makes it move. The energy of Pentecost found in the biblical Luke-Acts 2 narrative was carried into, and given away within, the early twentieth century by an intergenerational, interreligious, multigender people, an enactment of a spiritual "motley crew."[14]

The aesthetic production of breath in Blackpentecostalism is what I will index as *black pneuma*, the capacity for the plural movement and displacement of inhalation and exhalation to enunciate life, life that is exorbitant, capacious, and fundamentally, social, though it is also life that is structured through and engulfed by brutal violence. This life, life in blackness, otherwise black life, exceeds the very capacities of seemingly gratuitous violence to be totalizing. What I will expand upon in this chapter are the ways that breath is not only important but also holy, and this holiness is not reducible to confessions of faith or anything that could simply be called "religious." Analyzing the Blackpentecostal tendency for praying and preaching to be inclusive of, and often end with, "whooping"—the speaking of phrases melodically, with excitement, usually breaking into loud exclamations and declarations repetitiously; the disruption of air through intentional, intense breathing—will yield robust analyses of liberal concepts of subjectivity and of the body. It's all about breathing.

Pneumatology—as a field of inquiry within Christian theology—is a relatively new series of studies, emerging approximately fifty years after the Azusa Street revival in Los Angeles 1906. Though theologians and philosophers have spoken about spirit generally, and the Holy Spirit since the days of—if certainly before—Pentecost, the "third person of the Trinity" was often cast as the forgotten member, with God the Father and God the Son taking precedent in treatises, tomes, and testimonies. Jürgen Moltmann, perhaps the most renown theologian of pneumatology, says that as late as the 1970s, "it was usual to introduce studies on the Holy Spirit with a complaint about 'forgetfulness of the Spirit' at the present day generally, and in the Protestant theology in particular."[15] Veli-Matti Kärkkäinen discusses the recent interest in the Spirit under the rubric of a "renaissance": "In recent years, one of the most exciting developments in theology has been an unprecedented interest in the Holy Spirit."[16] This renaissance is response to—not the forgetfulness of the Spirit—but its subordination, its repression: "Rather than speaking of a *Geistvergessenheit* (oblivion of the Spirit), we should speak of a pneumatological deficit."[17] Though the Spirit has a prominent place in various biblical narratives, the "birth" of the church in the Luke-Acts narrative of flames and speaking in various tongues as an emphatic example, discourse about the role of the Holy Spirit, the power and force of this entity, remained largely peripheral until the mid-twentieth century. Moltmann credits a nonspecific, general Christian ecumenical movement as part and parcel of this sweeping interest in the Spirit: "[it] is without a doubt the most important Christian event of the twentieth century. For the first time, there is a revolution of feeling."[18]

The Pentecostal movement that began in Los Angeles 1906 was intergenerational, interreligious, interracial, and internationalist in its composition. Women and men preached and prayed together, white men glorifying the fact that black women and men prayed for them—laid hands on them even—and they worshipped together. Children spoke in tongues, prophesied, and interpreted the meaning of such words with boldness, conviction, and clarity. Los Angeles in 1906 was a meeting place for a many-headed hydra of internationalism and interraciality, from Chinese to Mexican, from Irish and German to American descendants of the enslaved. Prior to 1906, in 1900, members of the Evening Light Saints would testify that they were "saved, sanctified, and prejudice removed," intriguing because in later Blackpentecostal Testimony Services, people often say that they are "saved, sanctified, and filled with the precious gift of the Holy Spirit."[19] To have prejudice in the heart seems to be at odds with having the Holy Spirit—the breath of divinity—working in the flesh.[20]

Pneumatology is the study of *pneuma*—the Greek word for "breath." The Holy Spirit's labor in biblical narratives is connected, particularly, to the invisible world of intangible, but also material, animation:

In the Septuagint (LXX), the Greek term *pneuma* is almost always equivalent of the Hebrew *ruach*. . . . The idea behind *ruach* is the extraordinary fact that air should move; the basic meaning of *ruach* is, therefore, "blowing." Both terms in the Bible, the Old Testament *ruach* and the New Testament *pneuma*, carry the same ambiguity of multiple meanings: "breath," "air," "wind," or "soul."[21]

This plentitude of meaning, this exorbitance of terminology, for what the Spirit does, is an instance of black pneuma, the otherwise-than-coherent and static, the otherwise-than-determinant. This plentitude of meaning, this exorbitance is originary displacement, anoriginal difference of black performance, the otherwise possibilities of respiratory function and form. Theologians speak about the radical sociality—as hospitality—of Spirit: "The Spirit who gives life is evident in hospitality shown toward strangers."[22] Such that we might say that Spirit—*pneuma*, breath, that which animates the body—is grounded in the necessity for sociality. Not only does Spirit give life, but that life is evident in how one leans toward others, how one engages with others in the world. We do not merely share in sociality; we share in the materiality of that which quickens flesh; we share air, breath, breathing through the process of inhalation and exhalation.

This radical sociality, this sharing of breathing, of breath, of air, occurred previous to an ecumenical movement, so named intentionally as such. This ecumenism was enacted in brush harbors and praise houses. This ecumenism was certainly a primary feature of the Azusa Street congregants. So it is odd, indeed very curious, for Moltmann to assert, "The successful growth of pentecostal churches outside the ecumenical movement is also a serious challenge to all the old, mainstream churches."[23] A challenge to mainstream, to normativity? Certainly. But how is it that Pentecostalism—Blackpentecostalism—is removed from the figuration, how is it that Blackpentecostalism is "outside" ecumenism? This "outside"—Blackpentecostalism, black performance—materially enacted while also the constitutive force for thinking ecumenism as a modality for thought.

What I am tracking, in other words, is the way theology—in the name of theological studies called pneumatology—represses blackness internal to its elaboration by glossing over, if ever even mentioning, the fact, the lived experience, the case of breathing on Azusa Street. The April 18, 1906,

Los Angeles Times begins, "Breathing strange utterances and mouthing a creed which it would seem no sane mortal could understand, the newest religious sect has started in Los Angeles."[24] *Breathing.* That such a term, such a concept, would be what was immediately noticed as producing a rupture, a disruption, with normative conceptions of religiosity, that such a word and concept were noticed because of the blackness of the Azusa Street revival is integral to the argument here. The breathing that the journalist described by attempting to lampoon the worshippers was considered strange, nonnormative, black.

If the Spirit has been subject to being forgotten, what drops out of the study of *pneuma* is air, breath, breathing itself, and how breath moves and changes and performs in the world, the world that is made at the moment of the emergence of being together with others. William Seymour and Azusa serve the role of intellectual practitioners of an *a*theology-*a*philosophy. The wooden floors of the Azusa Street Mission are the grounds upon which incoherence and indeterminacy were played out to create something like a radical sociality of intense feeling. The theological study of pneumatology created the condition to repress the enunciative force *of* black pneuma, of Blackpentecostal aesthetics, of black performance, that was internal to the very capacity for emergence of the object studied.

Plentitude, otherwise possibility, unfortunately for Moltmann, are problems for pure theological reflection: "Talk about Eastern or African spirituality unfortunately blurs this precise sense of the word and reduces it again to 'religiousness.'"[25] This is not to assert that pneumatological theologians do not ever consider the concepts of gender, sexuality, ecology, and race, but that such thinking constitutes itself through the presumption of the existence of modern man, what Sylvia Wynter describes as the coloniality of being/power/truth/freedom.[26] This presumption, however, does not operate on the wooden floors of the Azusa Street Mission. In the world but not of it; of some other world but not in it. Nahum Chandler's critique cuts along the bias of the problematics for thought, holding up for analysis and critique the concept of purity that grounds many philosophical and theological projects.[27] Pneumatology—as a mode of theological-philosophical positioning—is structured by the nonconvergence of blackness and thought. The materiality of blackness, the animating breath that is gathered and dispersed in Los Angeles 1906, is given scant attention. The particularity of the margin—the African, the Eastern, blackness—produces a blurring effect, a blurring of boundedness. But what Moltmann would desire to maintain is the categorical distinction that blackness comes to disrupt. The margin, here and yet again, is a problematic for thought. Coherent thought, coherence itself, emerges from the dislodging of difference as originary in the service of the search for purity: pure thought, pure space, pure practice. The very social form and field that yields an emphatic and intense elaboration of Spirit—the fact, the lived experience, the performance of breathing—is not only repressed but discarded after presumed nonconvergence has been theologically-philosophically established. The Spirit—*pneuma*, breath, air—is evacuated from flesh, productive of a thought body, a corpus, of work. Pneumatology is the "body" of which Azusa is flesh. So I want to consider specific performances of breathing in black, breathing in Blackpentecostal performance practices, to think about more fully how breathing is not just a sign of life but is an irreducibly irruptive critique of the normative world. I turn to specific modalities of breathing in black so as not to continue the theological forgetting of blackness, of black flesh, the continued forgetting and discarding of sociality. Thus, whooping. This is not to save theology but to illustrate the ways theology is insufficient for the task of thinking blackness.

THE "WHOOPING" IN praying and preaching invites congregants to intense performances of deep antiphony as celebration. Homiletician Evans E. Crawford describes this climactic process:

> Sermon delivery is a creative and inclusive moment where the preacher embodies for the whole congregation or group of hearers their celebrative gifts. It is a time when all that has been generative in the pulpit, pew, or elsewhere is seen as organic to life. What results is not far from chant. . . . In some circles this is called "whooping," where meter and message not only meet but celebrate. . . . The sound of the sermon is not simply something added to the substance but rather is inseparable from the experience of participant proclamation, which is a communal event in the life of the congregation.[28]

Whooping is the moment of celebration, the moment when the sermon is unleashed. Whooping allows for the deep and intense modes of improvisation, often breaking off to what almost sounds like song but stops short of singing. Whooping is the intentioned apportioning of breathing, the making of breathing stylistic, the making audible the flow of air into and out of lungs. The whooping moment incites the congregation to ecstasy, heightens the intensity of emotion, is the solicitation to which congregants respond with energy and conviction. That this would be celebratory, that this would announce joy and pleasure, is what I wish to attend to.

While Crawford concentrates on the role of the preacher and preaching, the enactment of Blackpentecostal force in congregations demonstrates that this mode of meter-meeting-message through celebratory proclamation occurs when people testify during "Testimony Service" as well as when people pray to open or close services, before or after the sermons, or even during the offering. Blackpentecostal services privilege the "move of the Spirit" and often punctuate printed programs with declarations such as, "The Order of Service is Subject to the Move of the Holy Spirit." The aesthetics of Blackpentecostalism operate, in other words, through irreducible openness, never adhering to containment, to producing specific performative behaviors during specific, predetermined moments of church services. Blackpentecostalism privileges interruption, eruption, of air, of breath and breathing as being contingent, on edge, waiting for the perculatory movement of the otherwise breaking into and surprising the service. Though speaking specifically about the sermon, what Crawford says about "the pause"—that it "is much more than a break in delivery" but also "an opening in the preacher's consciousness through which the musicality of the Spirit breathes so that the musicality of the sermon resonates with the living truth"—is instructive for theorizing otherwise possibilities for breathing, the process of breathing as aesthetic production.[29] That is, as an otherwise possibility, breathing is more than merely aesthetic and the whooping from within the space of Blackpentecostalism makes explicit a fact that is and everywhere achievable.

The pause or the break when one prays or preaches is an atemporal eclipse of speech, allowing a collective deep breath—audibly and often with intensity wherein the materiality of the flesh is confirmed by the forceful vibrations of nasal passages, the tongue smacking the roof of the mouth, the constricting of the pharynx, the augmentation by admixture of linguistic vocable appendages to words—to gather more resource from which to continue performance is invitational in its enactment, it creates a gap wherein the voices of congregants can "fill" the otherwise than "empty" silence.

With whooping comes the expiration, the giving out of the excess, the constitutive that exists on the outside, the other side of breathing. Dorinda

Clark-Cole and Juandolyn Stokes, Blackpentecostal preachers both, illustrate this point. I turn to two examples to demonstrate how "musicality is a sonic manifestation of various social and cultural forces alive" in the preacher-as-performer.[30] And when we consider the whooping as antiphonal—as the congregation speaking back to the preacher and vice versa—evident is how antiphony allows for the internally differentiated group of the congregation to breathe aesthetically, productive of fundamentally social centripetal and centrifugal force of giving and withholding air, collectively performing and enacting *black pneuma*. Crawford states, "We often ignore the climatic factor that is most obvious yet essential to all preaching: that our speaking is surrounded by silence and that it is in the 'pause' of delivery that 'sound' or 'pitch' resounds or reverberates."[31] How the words, how the sounds, how the whooping is received, then, is determined fundamentally by the break and pause, its discontinuity, its openness and vulnerability on all "sides." And such a break, pause, discontinuity would be ongoing, would be foundation for praise.

Blackpentecostal aesthetics, when we attend to whooping as one enactment of this practice, produces a critique of western theological and philosophical traditions. The production of the falling away of "sides" through irreducible openness, for example, offer a critical analytic resistant to Enlightenment thought. Enlightenment thought constructed its conception of the subject through a desire for reducing openness and vulnerability, Enlightenment's subject was one created by the shoring up against movement, created a subject through containment and enclosure. Enlightenment's subject is one that can withdraw into an absolute silence, unbothered and unconcerned by the ongoing verve and noise of worlds. But the Blackpentecostal pause illustrates how silence that surrounds is illusory at best, it demonstrates how there is no such thing as absolute silence. What silence indexes, rather, is a certain quality of seeming noiselessness, but this quality is effectuated by context.

In a sermon titled "Why Do I Come Back for More," preacher Dorinda Clark-Cole, member of the famed Clark Sisters singing group and a prominent figure in the Blackpentecostal organization Church of God in Christ, I find an explicit example of whooping.[32] In the particular performative interval of interest, Clark-Cole is engaged in an exchange between her words, the congregation and the musicked response. At 3'26", we notice her sitting on the steps that lead to the pulpit, seated while proclaiming with voiced force, with voiced texture, the wonders of the gospel. She speaks a phrase and a chorus of "yes!" and "amen!" and the sounds of the Hammond organ and drum all punctuate the statements. She is preaching "hard," preaching with conviction and clarity, preaching with excitement and exuberance. Such hard preaching utilizes the breath, the texture of sound created through inhalation and exhalation of interaction of air with the flesh. At 3'26", she says

I wonder if I got some women'hah /
That'll open up your mouth'hah /
And say lawwwd'hah!
Oh lawwwd'hah!
Oh-oh law-aw-awd'hah!
OOOOH-Aaaaaaye-eah-eah!

then retreated into a silence, of sorts, but immediately her whooping produced the sonic space as discontinuous and open, open to the other voices that both proceeded her moment of being overcome with Spirit—such that other women gathered around, held and hugged her—and extended the preacherly moment by sociality, through opening up and diffusing the very grounds for the concept of preaching, for listening, for breathing. They all in that space breathed the same air, the same irreducibly impure admixture: Clark-Cole gave it, they received it, they gave it, she received it. The fundamental quality of such aesthetic sociality is not that it can be shared, but that it must be common and used by all, for vitality, for life. This sharing in and as commons enacts violence against any form of marginalization or oppression.

What is merely hinted at in the attempt to transcribe Clark-Cole is more explicit in Juandolyn Stokes. In a sermon titled "This Closed Door Will Be Your Best Opportunity,"[33] Stokes is soliciting, is convoking a response from the congregation through the grain in her voice, the grain made audible through the inhalation and exhalation of air, through the interaction of air with and in her flesh. Throughout the video, one hears and sees how Stokes utilizes increases and decreases in volume, how she at times rushes phrases and at others draws out and appends syllables onto words for emphasis. Like Clark-Cole, Stokes's preached moment needs antiphony; it needs a speaking back from the congregation and music in order for the moment to constitute itself. The point of it all is to excite the congregation into a moment of intense reflection and raucous praise, to excite the congregation to shout, to move their flesh in the space in order to think otherwise possibilities for their inhabitation in the world. One moment in Stokes's sermon I hone in on is found at 4'15" when she says:

Tell'em neighbah'tuh /
God's gonna deliva you tonight, hah /
Thank you, Jesus, hah /
So the Bible said'tuh /
So Amnon laid down, hah /
And he made himself sick, hah /

There is an excessive otherwise of breath, which enunciates itself with vocables such as "hah" and "tuh." These are "impure" appendages to words that are no less important for, no less generative of, meaning. With Stokes's preacherly performance, one finds that not even the word "neighbor" could be contained, enclosed, by grammar, by logic of boundaries and borders. The preached moment of the word, at the level of grammar, refused "silence" and enclosure. The word "neighbor," at once vernacularized through the replacement of "or" with "ah" but also extended through "tuh." This "tuh" has no inherent value; its content lacks reproductive meaning. Yet, it is there, it elucidates the air that not only leaves the flesh, but escapes, absconds through its excess, is enunciated emphatically and with joy. Escapes like so many narratives of fugitive flight. The appendages to words are extensional, outward leaning, open. Or, simply, fleshly.

Whooping aestheticizes breath, which is also and likewise to assert that whooping makes vividly apparent the fullness and plentitude of life, even when such life the project of white supremacist antiblack violence seeks to destroy through the surround of totalizing force. Such life, such breathed critique, speaks back and against this totality, makes evident the incompleteness, the incompletion, of the project of white supremacy. And this because of the open-endedness to movement, to change. Even when the "scientific" community takes up the concern over respiration, the relationship of breathing to emotion is theorized as one wherein physiological response of the flesh is in accordance with emotional posture: "Specific respiratory symptoms are frequently reported in association with emotionally stressful states, a sudden scare takes the breath out of each of us, we can easily observe the connection in ourselves or among others between certain states of consciousness and changes in breathing (e.g. sleep-wake differences or acute fear), and we know that the particulars of speaking and other behavioral activities must be coordinated with our breathing."[34] Moreover, "Breathing leads the list of vital needs in terms of the limits of time of deprivation; without an adequate supply of oxygen (O_2) cells die within minutes and life ends."[35] Finally, "The activities of breathing in and breathing out are a curious mechanism because this activity comes from the unconscious regulation of a metabolic requirement, and simultaneously expresses emotion involuntarily."[36] Consensus is the idea that physiology shares with emotionality, that what the flesh does and emotive disposition are not easily disentangled. We might say that they entangle with and produce each other. They work together, refusing the border, categorical coherence and difference of flesh from mind, of mind from emotion. If such a difference exists, it would not be categorically irreducible, it could not be maintained as absolute.

Whooping is an aesthetic practice, utilizing the breath physiologically to effect affective mood of the one preaching, the one praying and the congregation. What is notable in the two examples above is the effort necessary to sustain the performative moment, which is not only the sound and melodic phrasing but the fleshliness of such an enterprise. The flesh is forcefully foregrounded by the intentioned respiratory process. We might ask, simply, what is the purpose of praying, of preaching, *like that*? The *like that* is a concern fundamentally about, and the intellectual work that is done through, form.

Jean-Christophe Bailly claims that living is porous, intimating its capacity to be an antidote against enclosure, seizure, capture, enslavement.

> We are used to the range of breath—from a prolonged, even dilation to gasping and panting, and from joy to suffocation. It is the animal form of being in life, the space of our most proper emotion, and the fundamental rhythm through which we identify life and the living. . . . [W]hat persists does so with the thinness of a thread, since the thread of existence only holds as long as there is an accord with the immense outside, whose air, passing through the nostrils, is the final messenger. . . . [L]iving is immediately constituted and produced, until the end, as a porosity.[37]

It is not a certain kind of living, but the fact of living itself, the fact, that is, of the breath, of the performative process of respiration undergirding the facts of life—from Mrs. Garrett's, Tootie Ramsey's, and Blair Warner's to whomever reads this present writing. Whooping is the intellectual practice of aestheticizing the gap between the fact of breath and the lived experience of breathing. Fred Moten in "The Case of Blackness" explicated the concern about the space between "fact" and "lived experience" and for him, the cut between fact and lived experience is the occasion to consider the case of blackness.[38] As case, we might simply call it the performance. Here, I am interested in the generativity of the case, the performance, of breathing, of respiration, for intellectual practice. This bridge, whooping, is necessary because there is a long tradition of "studies" of blackness that are grounded in the purportedly pathological behaviors, conditions, and constraints of the curious black figures, from antebellum worries over Drapetomania to post-Reconstruction concerns about the problematic patricidal tendencies of negro families.

The "fact" of breathing, so some theories could attempt to claim, would not be evidence of life, social or otherwise. The fact of breathing in figurations of blackness-as-death would submit this double-gesture to the *merely* biological, and those relegated to the zone of breathing's "fact" would be said to have no lived experience because we are likewise, and as an a priori principle, said to lack the capacity for experience. But the performance of breathing, the otherwise possibilities in respiratory processes as black pneuma rises to, while it emerges from, its specific occasion. Breathing is a resource from which to perform the resistance that is prior to power and whooping is but one audible example of such performance. And the occasion—whether with Harriet Jacobs's insurrectional inhabitation or being violently forced to abide in the hold of The Lord—the case of breathing is an ongoing openness to life that is always and exorbitantly social: from W.E.B. Du Bois's predeath, posthumously read note, "As you live, believe in life!"[39]; to Sethe's pondering the handholding and play of shadows, "A life. Could be."[40]; to, finally, Gilles Deleuze's inhabitation of the break of immediate liminality, "pure immanence," "A LIFE . . . [that] is everywhere,"[41] and even so, ever so abundantly. The zone of the purportedly merely breathing, those whom are "socially dead,"[42] must be rethought and this mode of thought must be an other-than-theological, other-than-philosophical project. The intellectual practice of the *a*theology-*a*philosophy of black pneuma, the breathing exercises of Clark-Cole and Stokes above, the birthing of refusal, is my concern.

Whooping, as an intentioned aesthetic of breath, elucidates concerns about gender and performativity. It is neither haphazard nor random that I selected women as the "sound" of Blackpentecostal breathing exercises. Homiletic writing about preaching and style tend to focus on theology and, when writers do consider "style," cisgender male-identified preachers become the anchoring point of aesthetic analysis.[43] However, Jerma Jackson's writing offers a fresh perspective regarding gender and the sound of Blackpentecostalism:

> Barred from the pulpit, women used musical forms that became the rudiments of gospel to testify to their religious convictions, sustain fellowship, and pursue missionary work. In the process they helped shape the contours of gospel's solo tradition. Their influence was not confined to the church. The proscriptions against female preaching that initially inspired women to pursue gospel also gave them an incentive to push the music beyond church doors, as they ventured first onto city streets and then into the commercial arena.[44]

Gender befalls—like a border, like a juridical announcement of newly construed criminal social form—on the flesh, creating through such bordering, the concept of the body itself, and the notion of "gender" and "sex" as originary markers of deficiency for those who do not have "it." But it is the sound of women—on street corners evangelizing; in churches testifying—that set the sonic environment from which all Blackpentecostal sound participated and from which sound was drawn. Being barred from the pulpit, being rejected and ejected from *the* place where the divine is supposed to be encountered and elaborated for congregants, gender distinction was created through such a spatial logic. But because categorical distinction is undone by the aesthetics of Blackpentecostal practice, these same gendered distinctions would produce a space otherwise, and in such production illustrate the ways *any* space can be sacralized, whether pulpit, pew, or platform on the street-corner. Gender befalls, bordering on the flesh creating a body, but the spatial logics of gender are critically interrogated by the street-corner-preaching women that Jackson discussed. It is urgent, then, to consider the ways the sounds of whooping, as signs of life, are a critique of violence and violation that produce the terms of gendered order, of sexuality and difference as deficiency.

Why did Clark-Cole and Stokes preach *like that*? Why did they intention breath in such a way as to be gratingly audible in the ears of the congregation? What does the like that, the form in performance, elucidate about the performative force of breathing? They could have easily preached without the flourishes and embellishments, without pushing the lungs to capacity. There are far too many examples of sermonizing that do not include such accents, and there are much too many critiques of the excessiveness of *this* mode of sermonizing to recount. What is this sort of performance of breathing sent into the world to do, do illustrate, to make audible, visible, felt, known? The performative force of breathing invites consideration of choice and will that is not circumscribed through violence and violation, but choice and will that emerges within the context of its utterance, choice and will that is produced by antiphonal collectivity. Through meter-meeting-message in the celebratory enunciations of whooping—the speaking of a phrase with a momentary eclipse of speech with a pause—foregrounds the intensity of the pause, felt instantaneously, as absolute potentiality, absolute capacity, in the split second that builds, that constructs, that forms what architects call a *parti*, through sonic accrual.

A *parti*, according to Julio Bermudez, is "the most basic organizational principle that expresses [the] architectural design. It is the scheme, main concept, or idea that explains better than anything else the character and appearance of your design."[45] Moreover, a *parti* "provides a horizontal thrust that connects program, site, experience, form, and tectonics together in such a way that, if very well done, it also points to a vertical dimension."[46] I want to pause to specifically consider how the *parti* offers explanation for "character and appearance" as well as how it is the anoriginal locus for "horizontal thrust" and "vertical dimension[ality]" of design. Character, appearance, horizontal thrust, and vertical dimension are, I argue, otherwise examples of black pneuma, whooping, that materialize before any "end"—before any presumed final destination or point of nadir—and these four categories are, when together, nothing but originarily celebratory.

To consider the "character and appearance" of Blackpentecostal aesthetics takes us back to where we began with narratives of fugitive flight and their being grounded in the enunciative force of blackness.

As a very young child when I thought I was a budding artist, the method I was taught for drawing was to create a border first then "color within the lines" so ascribed. The border, the line, would precede and be the guiding principle for coloring, for shape making, for art. Whatever would

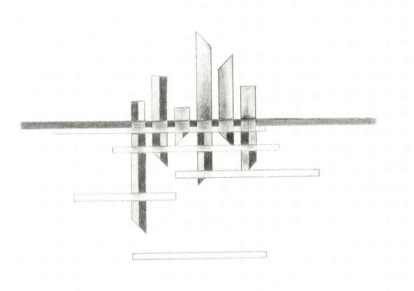

Figure 1. Author's personal collection (2002)

emerge from the artistic practice—a shape, a head, a three-dimensional box—would not be from the sociality of color internally differentiating the object through gradation, but through being contained, as N. would say, "previous to situation."[47] However, much later in life, I had the occasion to take two architecture courses while an undergraduate student at University of Pennsylvania. In those courses, we were taught the skills for coloring and shading, for drawing straight lines, making shapes and coloring in within borders. In my initial drawing exercises in architecture, I brought with me the knowledge of my grade-school teachers; I would first draw the bold outline—darkly—then color the shape after. The two images above (Figures 1 and 2)—*parti* drawings for what would eventually be a built design—are evidence of this method. In the *parti* above, one is immediately struck by the ways the borders are very thick and defined. The thin rectangles underneath the assemblages in both *parti* are most pronounced.

However, what I needed to do was unlearn the preceding ideology regarding borders and shade. The architecture professor encouraged students to think otherwise than preceding boundaries and constraints, and encouraged us to think design methodology without necessitating the

Figure 2. Author's personal collection (2002)

creation of initiatory, originary borders. Rather, shading itself could create the contours of the "space," not a border that encloses as an *a priori* principle. In the following two images (Figures 3 and 4), notice how though there are blocks of color, none of them are "defined"—set, formed—by a border but each block is shaded *to its limit.*

This is not to say that there were no guiding principles or desires for design previous to when the shading began. What Figures 3 and 4 illustrate is that those guiding principles and desires do not take precedence over the presencing of the design itself. The difference between Figures 1 and 2 from Figures 3 and 4 offers critical insight into the distinction between the wholly bound subject and the one that is discontinuous; these figures are, in effect, theological-philosophical propositions. Susan Buck-Morss has the following to say about discontinuity:

> The nervous system is not contained within the body's limits. The circuit from sense-perception to motor response begins and ends in the

Figure 3. Author's personal collection (2002)

world. The brain is thus not an isolable anatomical body, but part of a system that passes through the person and her or his (culturally specific, historically transient) environment. As the source of stimuli and the arena for motor response, the external world must be included to complete the sensory circuit.[48]

We are back at the fact of the flesh, the flesh as liberative, the flesh as unbounded, open, available, vulnerable. The flesh is that which senses worlds, the possibility for sensate experience is through discontinuity. Brian Massumi would simply call this open system of nervousness "the charge of indeterminacy carried by a body [that] is inseparable from it" because that which is called the body "is a passage or in process . . ."[49] The first two *parti* drawings are figurations of classical continental western philosophy of the subject that is wholly bound, enclosed, encased. This is something like John Locke's possessive individualism, wherein one is enclosed through grasping and containing rights. And this as an a priori

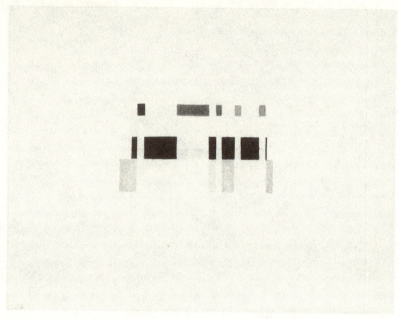

Figure 4. Author's personal collection (2002)

principle. This boundary would be defined previous to any material filling, any spirit indwelling, compelling a normative comportment in order
to "fit." The final two *parti* drawings, however, are critical performative
interventions into the concepts of boundedness, such desire for enclosure.
The blocks of color in the final two *parti* are not easily isolable from the
environment in which they are a part, the capacity for making a distinction
between background and shape withers away because of the unspecified,
the refusal for, bordering.

As Buck-Morss states, the external world is not excluded but included in
making a system; the external world likewise passes *through* the seemingly
internal one. There is an intense and intimate relay between external and
internal, they are—even at the level of artistic objects in *parti* drawings—
figurations of otherwise modalities for existence, modalities that do not

presume distinction as maintainable. In the final two *parti*, the shapes appear, as a city, standing forth and out, presencing: "The city appears to you as a whole where no desire is lost and of which you are a part, and since it enjoys everything you do not enjoy, you can do nothing but inhabit this desire and be content."[50] What is important is not the "whole" of desire wherein one walking through the city should be fully content with its contents. What is important is that the city, as a collection of reciprocal relations, stands and furnishes forth.

This collection of discontinuous breaths, figurations of whooping, may at first appear unfamiliar, but there is, yet, an occasion for celebration: "The more one was lost in unfamiliar quarters of distant cities, the more one understood the other cities he had crossed to arrive there; and he retraced the stages of his journeys, and he came to know the port from which he had set sail, and the familiar places of his youth, and the surroundings of home, and a little square of Venice where he gamboled as a child."[51] That which is at present unfamiliar is the accrual and distance of that which has been traversed; the ago, then, acts as alluvial, sedimentary. The unfamiliar is compression, as in held breath, forced exhalation. The unfamiliar heightens the awareness of that which is now receded from view, sharpens memory. Out of the unfamiliar, then, is an outreaching of knowledge of the withdrawn. The unfamiliar is only an otherwise possibility for knowledge, not the lack but the sharp relief of knowledge, of pastness.

> from: a
> to: a
> Wednesday, April 21, 2010, 4:13 PM
> subject: Re: mp
> mp,
> It happened again and i don't know what to make of it. Not staring but the sorta moment you feel someone looking at you from across the room and you look up from the convo you'd been engaging and, sure enough, there he is, looking. You make brief eye contact, he takes a deep breath and looks away, almost as if his looking—the very fact of his doing it—stunned him, so he also was not immediately able to look away. You're the trainwreck. The fire to which the moth is attracted. Beautifully so [or, at least, you convince yourself]. But also: he's cute. Very cute. So the hesitant averted gaze, the stalled look away, the wary worry which announces, before any "hello," the emergence of problems.

It was at Calvin's art opening a few weeks ago, his first gallery showing in fact, so things were abuzz and he was rather excited. Wine was
flowing and there was genuine giddiness in the air. I was pleased to
support and met all sorts of folks: people I'd never seen or heard of
before—who knew so many cool, artsy folks lived here?—and finally
met folks that I've known online but never in person from twitter
and facebook, for example. Anyway. The artwork was nothing short
of amazing. Called it his "music and movement" installation where
he'd taken all sorts of media and used oil paint to create these abstract
swirls and strokes, all based on the music to which he'd be listening
at the time. The painting was to approach a kind of sonic referential-
ity, was a type of metaphorization of the sounds, of the music. I was
moved by the colors he used, mostly darker gradations :: deep purples
and blues, dense, full-bodied reds, and lots of black. He used a variety of surfaces, "to bespeak the everydayness of our encounters with
music. This is a piece about the sublime's relation to the ordinary."
Sure, I laughed a bit at his description, but more because I never pay
attention to what artists say about their own shit . . . it's always on the
edge of self-congratulatory "look at this cool shit I did and now please
pay me" message implicit in their self-referential descriptions, and so
they always misread their own motives. But aside from his description, it truly was amazing. Couldn't deny it.

The problem, of course, was that there was this hella cute dude there
with his girlfriendofthreeyears [he said it, rushed just like that, while
she was in the restroom]. Calvin wanted me to meet this guy because
he's a likewise nerd and sometimey musician, so he thought we'd hit
off. Dude had been glancing at me even before the official introduction,
when I stood across the gallery space talking with some other folks. And
then we were introduced and of course I was surprised to learn that
the young woman was not just a friend but was, in fact, the girlfriendofthreeyears. But anyway, nice guy and his girlfriendofthreeyears were,
in fact, cool as hell. The three of us talked for at least an hour, conversation moving through all sorts of terrain, from theology to the presi-
dency. Needless to say, I got along with them very well, so Calvin wasn't
wrong at all. The problem? Well . . . you know how I tend to get a bit on
the edge of loud, and insistent, when I've had one too many glasses of
wine. Not the sorta belligerent volume but speaking my mind, no filter,

so also full of conviction. I was on some, "I voted green party! Not even gonna vote the next time around if things keep going the way they're going" shit. And though true, it's always weird to sorta feel that settled with folks you'd just met. Anyway, girlfriendofthreeyears went to the restroom but saw an old colleague and stopped to talk to her for a while. So dude and I kept talking and it was nice. It goes without saying that I noticed how handsome he was and how, had there been no girlfriendofthreeyears present, I would've overtly flirted. But I'm not desperate. Nor that needy. Nor grimy. But things *did* cross my mind. His smile, his eyes, his lips? So good. Anyway.

After this hour or so convo and girlfriendofthreeyears returned, I bid them adieu so that I could meet/talk to other friends I hadn't seen in a while. We facebooked each other and I scurried away. Whispered to Calvin "oh my god . . . he's cute! ugh!" He laughed. I settled on a new group of old friends with whom I could catch up. But while drinking this newest glass of wine and having convo where I laughed a lot and made several points, I looked up and saw him. Not quite staring but definitely looking with an almost insatiable desire. I felt it. Felt it in me. Knew someone was looking, just had to find the directional field from which the energy emanated. And each time [it happened about four times throughout the duration of the evening *after* we'd met to say nothing of the before] when he realized I realized he was looking at me, he'd sorta almost—faintly—smile but not really, because there was also a slight hint of embarrassment on his face, in his heart I presume as well, that he was looking at me *like that* in the first place. Made me question what it was that prompted his search that landed in my face, in my eyes, each time, causing him to further still: search.

[Are metaphors a displacement of thought? Do they get us closer to the heart of the matter? Or are they some other kind of complication?]

I think he saw something familiar in me that he'd not ever named. It almost sounds egotistical to think it the way I'm thinking it but that's not what I mean. I wish things were much less complex but this has happened with so many dudes that it's pretty common now. Declarations of heterosexuality are cool but then they long for something otherwise and see me, and act as if whatever that otherwise might be is somewhere hidden in me, is something familiar. And I had this weird experience when I was a kid that was all about familiarity.

We took a bus trip when I was in the fifth grade to Baltimore or some other city and the trip included everyone in the fifth grade so all the teachers, most of whom I did not know, went along. There was one teacher on the bus who, upon catching my eye in the rear view mirror the first time [she was staring at me], continued to look at me. I would turn around to someone behind me and begin to talk and she'd walk up to me, grab my arm, tell me "didn't I tell you to turn around?! Stop talking! And look forward!," forcing me to turn around on the bus so she could continue to look at me in the rear view mirror. She would not let me talk to others, made me to face forward. She stared into my reflection in the mirror. Needless to say, I was more than a little bit uncomfortable.

Upon my return home, I told my parents about the entire affair and when I told them who it was, they said "the next time you see her, ask her if she knows Elder so-n-so." So the next time I saw her I asked her if she knew my mother and when I did, she exclaimed loudly, hugging me hard, "I knew it!" Turns out, she saw my parents—daddy's mouth and lips, mother's voice [even though I was too young, fifth grade . . . but I suppose I had pre-pubescent hints of the voice to come, it's otherwise possibility already with me and if I learned anything from my mother, it was the insistence in voice, the conviction]—in me, on me. The point is that familiarity shows up in all sorts of weird ways. Something about— literally external—to me bespoke something in me. But that something was noise at best, incoherence, or at least, incomprehensible, ineffable audiovisuality [sorta like how cell phones used to produce all of this static whenever you'd go out of range]. Nevertheless, it was a certain sort of knowledge, a knowledge of having known, a knowledge of know- ing, a knowledge of desire to know. That knowledge—the who that I was—was there, while withdrawing with each pondered "but how do I know him? But where do I know him from?" furrow of her brow. I felt abused by her force on the bus, felt ashamed and felt that she was misunderstanding my simple wish to talk to other kids. And I'm not the least bit disabused of the erotics that sorta underpinned the staring into a mirror to figure me out. She was trying to remember something without knowing what it was.

And so dude with the girlfriendofthreeyears, I think, also was cathected by some sorta erotic-libidinal excess, provoked by the insistence of my voice, an insistence that produced in him some desire to know more. To "get" what was so familiar. Maybe he thought he could, if he stared enough, figure out what it was for which he was longing. Of course, a few days after the event, it all became a bit clearer with a message on facebook that would feign the flirting that was certainly implied, so vague that a claim of ignorance and misunderstanding—another sort of noise and static—could be made, though the apparentness of the interactions is no less there.[52]

The unfamiliar is often a cause for anxiety and anxiety—as emotional response—has a physiological affect on the process of breathing. It happened when "A" looked across a room and noticed someone staring at him, and upon such a stare being noticed, the one staring breathed deeply with a slight sigh. To return to the final two *parti* images refracted through the fictional story "A" recounts, the images can now be considered instantiations of aestheticized flesh—what Hortense Spillers describes as such: "But I would make a distinction in this case between 'body' and 'flesh' and impose that distinction as the central one between captive and liberated subject-positions. In that sense, before the 'body' there is 'flesh,' that zero degree of social conceptualization that does not escape concealment under the brush of discourse or the reflexes of iconography."[53]—and the borderless *parti* drawings are illustrative of whooping, of the irreducible plural nature of respiratory functions. Flesh is that which stands forth, unbounded, discontinuous, open, vulnerable. Flesh is anoriginal. Flesh designates a borderless, discontinuous object, previous to its being sexed, previous to its being raced. As Spillers would have it, the "body" that comes after flesh is produced through rhetoric, through discourse, through—what Judith Butler would say—discursive practice. For Butler, the "body" is constituted by the discursivity of "sex": "Sex is . . . not simply what one has, or a static description of what one is: it will be one of the norms by which the 'one' becomes viable at all, that which qualifies a body for life within the domain of cultural intelligibility."[54] The "body"—through sex, through rhetoric—is a categorical coherence, it is a theological-philosophical concept of enclosure, a grammar and logic producing something like bodily integrity. But breathing flesh makes apparent the importance of openness, of otherwise grammars, against borders.

Zero degree flesh, the shapes in the *parti* image, the irreducibly plural process of breathing, whooping, *black pneuma* is thrust upon its environment, it literally enfleshes itself and stands forth. Let "thrust" designate the force of that which has been, to follow Martin Heidegger, "thrown" (*Geworfenheit*). According to Heidegger's thrownness, Being—Dasein—is "thrown into its There (*Da*)" and thrownness is likewise "a constant accompaniment of Dasein's existence."[55] Dasein's thrownness also has the capacity for infinite possibility: "Dasein confronts every concrete situation in which it finds itself (into which it has been thrown) as a range of possibilities for acting (onto which it may project itself). Insofar as some of these possibilities are actualized, others will not be, meaning that there is a sense in which not-Being (a set of unactualized possibilities of Being) is a structural component of Dasein's Being."[56] Bermudez intimates that the force of the horizon, its thrust, also has within it the capacity for verticality; thrust is the locus, that which holds the gathering of exorbitant potentiality. This is because, as Brian Massumi asserts, "a path is not composed of positions. It is nondecomposable: a dynamic unity."[57] He uses the example of an arrow thrust from its bow with force and it is only after it hits its target, after it stops, that "the arrow is in position. It is only after the arrow hits its mark that its real trajectory may be plotted."[58] But the horizon is never exhausted; it always recedes even as an arrow approaches it as target. Thus, thrownness is constant and thrust eternal.

Clark-Cole and Stokes, in this particular instance—because the compression of song into the singer's body is animated by breath, by the capacity to aestheticize and stylistically render respiration otherwise than the merely biological, and thus the merely biogenetic—are engaged in intellectual practice by their "vivid thereness," targeting and presencing, enfleshing through performance.

> The Burkean pentad of fiction—agent, agency, act, scene, and purpose as the principal elements involved in the human drama—is compressed in the singer into a living body, insinuating itself through a material scene, and in that dance of motives, in which the motor behavior, the changes of countenance, the vocal dynamics, the calibration of gesture and nuance in relationship to a formal object—the song itself—is a precise demonstration of the subject turning in fully conscious knowledge of her own resources toward her object. In this instance of being-for-self, it does not matter that the vocalist is 'entertaining' under American

skies because the woman, in her particular and vivid thereness, is an unalterable and discrete moment of self-knowledge.[59]

These preachers breathe stylistically toward a horizon that recedes as they approach, but their movement, their inhalation and exhalation push respective congregations to ecstasy. And this because they not only preached, but preached *like that*, they performed a form of intentional sustained breathing as an intellectual practice over and against the range of other possibilities for preaching the same text with the same congregation. Out of infinite possibility, even in constraint, never exhausted. Creativity rises to the occasion of constraint, and in such rising, exceeds. Blackpentecostal aesthetics, in other words, operate out of—and produce—a different epistemology altogether.

Calvino's invisible cities are epistemic. If one does not experience the depth, even when confronted with it as a *parti* that stands forth, presences, eventuates, one has refused the thrusting gesture, the extensional movement that reaches out for sociality. This sociality occurs through what Michel de Certeau describes as "walking through the city" where the built environment participates in the acoustemological possibility.[60] Acoustemology also means that the presencing, the standing forth of the city, is not reducible to ocularcentrism, but happens for varied enfleshed abilities.

Though his eyes were removed at the age of three, Ben Underwood was able to utilize sound to "see" depth of the environment, that which stood forth.[61] At the age of two, Underwood developed a malignant tumor affecting the retinas of his eyes, *retinoblastoma*, and had his eyes removed in order to stem the spread of the cancer. Ben Underwood learned how to use sound to hear into the shape of his environment. As he walked, he'd create a clicking sound with his tongue, listening in on the depth of his surround, a perceptual seeing that was not distinguishable from hearing. His clicking into the environment, his utilization of breath in order to perceive depth and shape, allowed him to play basketball, to find objects in the house at his mother's call, to sense the world otherwise. His "seeing" was made possible through vibration, through the way sound moves in and around objects. Utilizing an otherwise-than-whooping aesthetics of breathing, creating a clicking sound by sucking in air and forcing it toward the surfaces in the mouth, the sound—once released—would bounce off the surrounding environment through echo. "An echo . . . cannot occur without a distance between surfaces for the sounds to bounce from. But the resonation is not on the walls. It is in the emptiness between them. It fills the emptiness with its complex patterning."[62] Underwood's ability to experience different worlds was predicated upon a sociality of sound, but importantly, through the discontinuity of what is called "the body" and what is called "the world." It was the space *between*, in the pause and eclipse, that experience manifested. This is true for the entire range of sensual experience. Nearness and distance, proximity and approach, the capacity for encounter. This brokenness is an occasion for celebration such that it is in the break, pause and broken discontinuity that assembling, that gathering together, happens and this broken break, this pause, is anoriginal. Underwood's creative engagement with environments compel the queries: What is the sound of the city? What depth of perception is possible through listening, through the air that moves both in the city and in flesh? What is the sound of the *parti* drawings?

The *parti* drawings (Figures 3 and 4) are figurations of fleshly experience, of what it means to be thrown into the world and stand forth, and in such standing—creating one such surface among many other surfaces—are the conditions of emergence for experiencing worlds. Prior to sexing, racing, prior to being theologically-philosophically conceived as a body: flesh. "The field of emergence is not presocial. It is open-endedly social. It is social in a manner 'prior to' the separating out of individuals and the identifiable groupings that they end up boxing themselves into (positions in gridlock). A sociality without determinate borders: 'pure' sociality."[63] As sociality, what is necessitated is an aninstitutional, anoriginal practice, what Michel Foucault calls "friendship" that is nothing other than "a way of life."[64] Life, breathing flesh as irreducibly social, must "invent, from A to Z, a relationship that is still formless, which is friendship: that is to say, the sum of, everything through which [one can have] pleasure."[65] I am attempting to call attention to various enactments of the aestheticization of breathing that, rather than the institutionalization of function and form—bordering—that exists *in the service of coherence with the state*, is the refusal of figurations.

In Calvino's theorizing, unfamiliar territory is generative for thinking the past, thinking previous crossings, with nuance; the unfamiliar "now" produces knowledge of the "ago." The unfamiliar is that which posits, that which extends, knowledge of the past. But the unfamiliar, at its realization of its unstable ground and incoherence, is also the point of departure: the crossings of the path were not mere gestural, but were choreosonic, were otherwise epistemologies. When one crossed by way of paths created in order to arrive at some unfamiliar territory, though one may not have been conscious of the knowledge project of crossings, the very movement toward some unfamiliar was also the movement of the production of knowledge.

LYNCHING VIOLENCE, AND its varied antithetical campaigns, were all about the breath. Both Billie Holiday[66] and Nina Simone[67] sang about the terror of southern trees bearing strange fruit, a song that neither of them wrote.[68] The difference with which they sang, the way in which they participated in the performance and dispersal of affect, was through the breath, through the aestheticizing of the reciprocal always more than doubled process respiration. For example, in Billie Holiday's rendering, there is but a slight pause between "trees" and "bear" in the first ten seconds of the performance. Yet with Simone, when she sings, the pause—the break and space—between "trees" and "bear" is much more pronounced, much more elongated than Holiday's version. Such difference—in timing, in increases and decreases of volume, in key signature—endures throughout both performances, they are announced through their difference from one another. The fugitive inhalation of oxygen plus more and fugitive exhalation of carbon dioxide plus more was the method through which the terrible and terrifying was *a*theologically and *a*philosophically critiqued through the enunciative force of breathing's performance. And the nuance, the "slightest breath" each used, gathered up and dispersed the air that was eclipsed in victims' bodies.[69] Their performances illustrate the always available otherwise possibility, the irreducible otherwise of flesh.

They participated in a sonic "public zone," a zone that is fugitive and insurrectionary, where borrowing from a common store is a way of life, not as theft, but as a means to producing a social world where sound and song are both gift and object of exchange. The performance of song and sound from the public zone is a social experiment such that singing and sounding out are tentative, improvisational processes, open-against-enclosure. The social experiment of utilizing the same song and sound produces inflection, accent, and most importantly, critical distance from other performances. But not only do they set into relief the distance between the two performances, what such distance emphatically illustrates is that even the "original" version is one produced by critical distancing. The originary is irreducibly, but not categorically, different. The distance is not categorical because the distance is shared, shared in difference, is an impurity of difference, the difference of otherwise than categorical enclosure. The object—whether song, sound, image or text—has within the capacity to be a multiplicity, the performative force of diaspora, what Édouard Glissant described as "the passage from unity to multiplicity."[70] What the passage, as performance, enfleshes, what it lets stand forth and burst free, is that the multiple is a fact of the unit, that within any object are multitudes. This multiplicity is integral to ascertaining the force of an otherwise theoria-aesthesia, a mode to redeploy that which is at once denigrated and improper, a means to critical distancing as an intellectual performative practice, a way of life.

The performative force of diaspora—the critical distance between Holiday and Simone—is heard, is rehearsed, as a matter of air, of breath, of breathing. Perhaps authenticity is not a grasping for a foundational claim of origin/ality, but is a reaching—with depth and breadth—inward and outward, an extensional mobility, a centrifugitive movement and dilation that seeks escape and refuge, creating sonic spaces in which one can inhabit that are, at the same time, the public zones in and through which contact occurs. Yet it is not only pleasurable intimacies that occur in public zones of contact. The behaviors of lynching—"an offense has been committed to which the group responds in community spirit with burning, mutilation, gathering trophies, and initiating children," what Trudier Harris calls "ritual violence"—likewise took place in public zones of contact.[71] From trains and automobiles into and out of city centers, to the photographing, selling, buying, and mailing images of killed, swollen, burned, mottled flesh—not always black, not always male—lynching practices were the instantiation of what Joseph Roach calls the "It-Effect": not only was black flesh made into bodies through discourse and material violence, but those bodies were radically, unalterably—after Spillers, "vividly there"—available to the public, what Roach calls "public intimacy" that is "the illusion of availability."[72] But not illusion but the forcing, the nonconsensual violence demanding availability.

Unlike Roach's description of Uma Thurman on the cover of a magazine,[73] however, the It-Effect of blackness is not the ruse of public availability but a violent performance that attempts to make It available, that attempts to furnish forth It itself. In the case of racial mob and lynching violence, making It available meant closing off objects, silencing and shutting them up, it was to force enclosure, to create a boundary, to produce, that is, a liberal subject, the possessive individual, through violence. Roach's chapters include "Accessories," "Clothes," "Hair," "Skin," "Flesh," and "Bone," and each of these categories were integral to mob violence against conceptions of blackness with the theft shoes and rings, with the stripping bare by removal of sartorial stylings, with the cutting of hair to serve memorial, with the severing and cutting of skin, with the lacerating of flesh and breaking bones—Roach's primarily eighteenth-century history of It leaves open to be elaborated the question about racialization of the modern world that produces the It-Effect. That celebrities said to have It often cause so many affectations of the breath, so much breathlessness, the It-effect also has something to do with the case of breathing.

Holiday and Simone, because theirs are performances that illustrate the efficacy of intentioned voice, of intentional patterned breathing exercises, perform Blackpentecostal aesthetics, perform multiplicity even through rehearsing scenes of violence and violation. Though participating in the commons of aural worlds, airy zones, Holiday and Simone made this one song's lyrics their own by giving it away, through the exhalation of the always attendant plus more of carbon dioxide. That is, Holiday and Simone breathed in such a way as to melodically break down the theological-philosophical conception of enclosure; theirs were performances of multiplicity. Just breathe because the capacity for undoing any scene of subjection exists within the scene itself. Singing, praying, preaching—through breathing exercise—are intellectual practices. Turning to Ida B. Wells-Barnett's and the National Association for the Advancement of Colored People's (NAACP) antilynching campaigns show them as likewise breathing exercises, and as such, Wells-Barnett's and the NAACP's campaigns participated in—through anticipating and extending—the Blackpentecostal practice of whooping.

In 1892, the then thirty-year-old Ida B. Wells(-Barnett) published the antilynching pamphlet, "Southern Horrors: Lynch Law in All Its Phases," which proclaimed to "give the world a true, unvarnished account of the causes of lynch law in the South."[74] The pamphlet was a "contribution to truth [and] an array of facts," with Wells hoping that it would allow the "demand [for] justice [to] be done though the heavens fall."[75] In this work, Wells contended that rape was a rhetorical device used to veil the fact of antiblackness as the root of lynching violence. When reporting how J.C. Duke questioned the erotic and racial atmosphere in postemancipation Alabama, Wells concluded with the following: "Mr. Duke, like the Free Speech proprietors, was forced to leave the city for reflecting on the 'honah' of white women and his paper suppressed . . ."[76] From h-o-n-*o-r* to h-o-n-*a-h*, the difference between *or* and *ah* was not a little bit about the inter-rogation of southern sentiment, the linguistic, accented, sounded con-struction of whiteness, through linguistic rupture. Wells engaged a literary whooping of sorts, similar to the preaching moments of Juandolyn Stokes above. Wells not only wrote, but she wrote *like that*. I contend the whole of her antilynching oeuvre was quickened by a similar figural gesture, sonic replacement, reintentioning violence and violation of white mobs and journalism against itself. The intellectual practice of breathing as the critique lynching—which is nothing other than the eclipsing of the possi-bility for breathing—is what she wrote into her campaign. Her campaign was animated by the desire for others to breathe deeply, fully, satisfyingly.

In "Southern Horrors," Wells keyed in on the fact that economics was a reason integral to the practice of violence black folks endured: "The leading citizens met in the Cotton Exchange Building the same evening, and threats of lynching were freely indulged, not by the lawless element which the dev-iltry of the South is usually saddled—but by the leading business men, in their leading business centre."[77] Sociologist Susan Olzak corroborates Wells's connecting of violence to economy and politics: "Economic slumps, partic-ularly those that affected the least-skilled workers, increased rates of both lynching and urban racial violence, as did rising competition from immigra-tion."[78] A series of concerns emerge: if the narrativity of lynching was rooted in the protection of white female "honah," what is implicit is white male desire to enforce patriarchal hegemony over the public and domestic spheres, which included economic control of white women. Virtue and honor, thus, had political-economic resonances and consequences. Of course and also, virtue and honor, thus, had theological-philosophical resonances and con-sequences. Anxiety emerged from the threat over control, their not being able to figuratively perform the function, the task, of white masculinity. Virtue and honor should thus be considered—along with the theological-philosophical resonances—primarily economic categories, categories of dis-tinction that are about structuring the antisocial world of whiteness and to enact that hegemony throughout.

Both lynching and urban violence rose during periods of economic turmoil. Following the end of Reconstruction in 1877, the supply of low-wage labor . . . increased competition for jobs and other scarce resources in the United States. Rising competition seriously threatened job monopolies and other advantages enjoyed by native whites in both regions.[79]

And

Professional and entrepreneurial blacks were frequent targets of mob violence in the South, especially when their commercial activities weakened the grip of white business owners who systematically exploited blacks. For Wells, the tragedy and personal loss were extremely difficult to accept, especially when the local white press applauded the violence. That she had long borne witness to white journalists' usual justifications for lynching as the only way to handle black criminals and "Negro rapists" left her no option but to speak truth to power.[80]

Economic forces caused collective anxiety—a racial emphysema—and mass racial violence and lynching appears to respond to very material, physiological responses to black pneuma as a conceptual fugitive breathing, breathing in black flesh. Blackness, let's say, took their breath away and lynching—with its homoerotic sensuality[81]—sought to restore patterned, "normal" breathing. When one has emphysema, "the inner walls of the air sacs weaken and eventually rupture."[82] The shape and function of lungs, of the capacity to breathe, is obstructed. Such that the southern horrors Wells rehearsed were fundamentally a concern about breathing. Whiteness, while being "self-fashioned" at the scenes of subjecting blackness, cohered around this collective political-economic anxiety. And that anxiety was all about air, breath, breathing.

Of anxiety and breathing, Yuri Masaoka et al. state that "emotional experiences are not only productions within the brain accompanied by physiological activity such as sweating, increasing heart rate and respiration; these activities result from an unconscious process."[83] What we discover with racialist mob and lynching violence is an American studies, a masculinity studies, a gender and sexuality studies, grounded in the physiological responses of the body to the political economy. And these studies are in the service of normativity. What we discover in racialist mob and lynching violence, in other words, is the aspiration for picket fences and dreams of stability, a movement toward purity against the impurities of black breath. White anxiety was produced by trying to, metaphorically, breathe pure oxygen, to breathe in air without it fundamentally being an admixture, trying to breathe in (both resonances are necessary here: in as ingestion; in as within) an undiluted, unadulterated, unobstructed "America." The racial emphysema was, it seems, a response to the ongoing question posed about color lines, about feeling like a problem, about "a complex idea formed inside the (historical-transcendental) movement of the constitution of the African American as material idea."[84]

But lynching was more than a metaphor. What's more, lynching was not simply a response to after-the-fact material competition. It was also produced through anticipation. "*Potential competition* [could] spark such antagonism before much direct (head-to-head) competition has occurred. . . . [E]vidence suggests that racial violence in response to potential competition was sometimes not directed against its competitors."[85] Shortness of breath from thinking the very capacity of Others breathing the same air, it seems, was a vivifying force of racial mob and lynching violence. "Charges of improper sexual conduct were often tacked on as a secondary justification for lynching when the primary reason for the lynching was economic or political."[86] Air, breath, breathing share a relation with any political economy. Lynching, as a peculiar performance of moral uplift for whiteness and moral degradation of blackness, was grounded in concerns over economy.

In *A Red Record*, Wells stated, "The purpose of the pages which follow shall be to give the record which has been made, not by colored men, but that which is the result of compilations made by white men, of reports sent over the civilized world by white men in the South. Out of their own mouths shall the murderers be condemned."[87] Perhaps *A Red Record* is something like "unceasing variations around a theme," using the violent tendencies for the destruction of violence itself.[88] Because black journalists could not be trusted, so the narrative went, Wells used the writing of violence and violation—quoting directly from the journals and even including images from those "trusted" news sources—in order to critically address and analyze the racist and sexist posturing. "Out of their own mouths," Wells recognized the expiration, the exhalation, of their performances. But, as with air, there was an admixture even at the level of racist "journalistic" rhetoric, there was an unruly excess, a fugitive excess, written into the recountings.

Wells utilized that which was publicly available, that which was deposited in a public zone, the same air as a means to dissolute the narrativity of white female innocence, white patriarchal protection and black male bestiality. Wells inhaled from the resource that was available, that was public, that was common, breathed it in in order to expire it *like that*, with difference. Something like the intentioned performative to *create* the infelicitous occasion, the creation of the infelicitous in the cause of justice.[89] The undoing of the dominant narrative of lynching practice was internal to its own being reported. Thus text and images are redeployed. Those texts and images that were supposed to incite celebration of the achievement of whiteness over purported black incivility, because of the breath interdicted and held in each image, in each story recounted, in each quantifiable but unidentified deceased victim, Wells was able to call attention to an otherwise aesthetic, an otherwise theory, for black social life.

Wells's antilynching writing in both "Southern Horrors" and the later improvisational and extensional *A Red Record* illustrate the creative radicality and force of Blackpentecostal performance. And this because her work demonstrated the always excessive capacity for otherwise possibilities. That she could redeploy the texts and images meant to shame is cause for celebration. That she was able to produce lament, lament that sought clarification and justice, demonstrates the incapacity of the so-thought totalizing force of antiblack violence. She shared in the fleshing out and of black social life by attending to the brutality of lynching, by enunciating the varied ways breath was eclipsed in defense of white gentility and "honah." The writing itself, in other words, was a scream, heart-rending shriek. In the writing, what informed the writing, what gave the writing its form was breath, was the air in which all participated, was the desire for life against eclipsed breath. The life force was held and contained within the movement to write against violent death itself. Unexhaled, but given, scream. Inhaled and held, air.

Wells-Barnett's antilynching campaign breathed—through attending to shared breath as common resource, even against the rhetoric and appeal to the state—*against* the extrajuridical process of violence. Wells-Barnett's antilynching campaign was, like what would be said of the Blackpentecostals on Azusa Street in 1906, an exercise in "breathing strange utterances." In her writings, what evinces is how the juridical system is predicated upon the granting to itself the powers to produce violence and violation, and that ongoingly. The juridical system coheres around material, physiological anxiety the very possibility of infraction and seeks to account for and amend the capacity, the potentiality, for wrongdoing. Given the fact that lynchers and those who produced mob violence against black people asserted that certain types of crimes placed blacks "outside the pale of humanity," it is our project to elaborate upon social life that emerges "outside" this juridical political system. Lynching, of course, is extrajudicial, but to be extrajudicial is to consider the judicial as the grounding principle, the foundational theological-philosophical claim such that to be "extra" or in excess of the judicial is to still make claims about the rightness of the judicial system itself. But what of other modes of life that do not assent to this judicial system, such that breathing is not the apposite response to extrajudicial killing, but is the otherwise?

Orlando Patterson argues in *Slavery and Social Death* that in contradistinction to conceptions of citizenship and family, slavery denied enslaved people kinship through natal alienation: "Alienated from all 'rights' or claims of birth, he ceased to belong in his own right to any legitimate social order. ... Not only was the slave denied all claims on, and obligations to, his parents and living blood relations but, by extension, all such claims and obligations on his more remote ancestors and on his descendants," and that "slaves differed from other human beings in that they were not allowed freely to integrate the experience of their ancestors into their lives, to inform their understanding of social reality with inherited meanings of their natural forebears, or to anchor the living present in any conscious community of memory."[90] To not belong "in his own right" is about being denied entry into the zone of the human, of modern man, of John Locke's possessive individual. To belong in one's own right is to have belonging predicated upon the capacity to be enclosed, not flesh. Similar to the figuration of the coherent and stable rightness of the law in extrajudicial murders of black folks, Patterson's understanding of violence and alienation presumes the rightness of *this* western theological-philosophical conception of the self, the subject, the citizen. And this because his work presumes that blood relations established by *this* law—the law that includes through exclusion, the law that creates the concept of population as a means to state formation, state coherence—are necessarily the only, or the most important, forms of relationality. Not only does Patterson's "natal alienation" establish itself through aspirational heteronormativity, but also it mines the very rationalist science discourse about the effectiveness of blood as a means to measure—which is also and likewise to say, border—affective modes of relationality.

The problem, of course, is that the idea of kinship here is grounded in a general, nonspecific affectable thing called "the law," that is, if "kinship is denied entirely by the force of law," its very denial obtains through the belief, the confessional posture, that kinship is something the law has the ability to give or withhold. Maybe this is why the Saints are important with the use of sister/brother/mother—means to name congregants. Maybe this is why kith bonds—play cousins, play aunties, mom-moms, and great uncles—are likewise. Not because legal kinship is denied but because legal kinship is the ongoing, repetitive denial of other modes of relationality. Legal kinship, it could be then said, is a figuration of the extrajudicial.

What lynching photographs capture, what they hold, is an instance of paused and held anxiety, desired enclosed purity over and against open breakdowns. They would so obscure this possibility, but the fact of life—of the refusal of borders that befall creating subjects and objects, creating distinctions that are not tenable—is also the performative force of breathing. An image of William Stanley, for example, collected in the *Without Sanctuary: Lynching Photography in America* shows a white crowd at what they described as a "barbecue," an instance of racialist violence.[91] I argue that brutally violent moments like this, and the capturing of these moments in images, occurred with regularity in order to alleviate the pressure in their collective political-economic, physiological chest, a desire to relieve the stressed breathing that blackness purportedly instantiated for them.

Various visual studies have closely "read" the image of Stanley.[92] In the image is the burnt corpse, a sacrificial propitiation for a whiteness inability to breathe easy. Like a Messianic figure with salvific potentiality, Stanley—and many others, both named and unnamed—stood in and was sacrificed for the collective racial emphysema of whiteness. And whiteness, Americanness, cohere—gathers—around that which is sacrificed within its midst. As sacrificial, the words of theologian James Cone are instructive: "The crucifixion of Jesus by the Romans in Jerusalem and the lynching of blacks by whites in the United States are so amazingly similar that one wonders what blocks the American Christian imagination from seeing the connection."[93] Using Cone's analysis, both the cross and lynching tree were about the capacity of mobs—that create something along the order of a nation-state through anonymizing fungibility, what in another register we call citizenship—to inflict harm as a means to control.

Lynching, like the Middle Passage, was the demonstration of the forcing of flesh into a "body," both rhetorical and physical, forced entry into western modes of theological-philosophical cognizing. But this forcing into a body would always be on edge, would always be abject relationally. Though Cone is most concerned with a Christological understanding of lynching violence—and, to be sure, the coherence of white Americanness around a lynching tree or pole, around a burning or bullet-ridden body, is also an articulation of American Christianity and theologies of refusing to see and regard the pain of others—what I am interested in is how there is an *a*theological-*a*philosophical impulse at work in the recasting, repurposing at the heart of antilynching critique. A critique, that is, of the very categorical distinctions theology and philosophy that *produce* modes of thought that cause white bodies anxiety, anxiety that then becomes the grounds of violence against air, breath, breathing while black and within blackness.

The transformation of flesh into bodies could not reduce the irrepressible life that those on the receiving end of violence carried within and dispersed. The breath, literally of life, was in them and the brutality was fundamentally because of this irrepressibility. We need an ethics project that recognizes that the violence of white supremacist capitalist patriarchy as a response to the ongoing refusal of black life, of otherwise possibility. We need an ethics project that understands the violence of white supremacist capitalist patriarchy as set loose to *control* the breathing of blackness from its flourishing. Because with such a recognition, how will we who are called black live? This is the "ethical crisis" to which we must heed, with which we must contend.[94] This was the charge Wells's work rose to the occasion to answer. Performance of air, breath, breathing is the enunciation of excess, of Blackpentecostal aesthetics, grounded in otherwise possibilities. Creative spirit was not destroyed but was continually enacted by reconfiguration of otherwise modes of sociality. Racial mob and lynching violence are confessions of faith, declarations given about the desired interdiction of the capacity to move, to be on the run, to have pleasure in blackness. Simply, the anxiety of whiteness, the racialist emphysema, enacted on black flesh is a theological-philosophical claim that one must believe, that one must confess, about blackness, bestiality, and the capacity to be civil. Racial mob and lynching violence attempted a theological-philosophical production of the human, of desired coherence against indeterminacy. Immanuel Kant conceives of the Transcendental Aesthetic as the production of space and time, and it is on this terrain, this mode of contemplative thought, that those whom "have" a "body" are produced.[95]

Of lynching photography, generally, Leigh Raiford says:

> We can understand these images to be sites of struggle over the meaning and possession of the black body between white and black Americans, about the ability to make and unmake racial identity. In the hands of whites, photographs of lynchings, circulated as postcards in this period, served to extend and redefine the boundaries of white community beyond localities in which lynchings occurred to a larger "imagined community." In the hands of blacks during the same time period, these photographs were recast as a call to arms against a seeming never-ending tide of violent coercion, and transformed into tools for the making of a new African American national identity.[96]

Though wary about the making of a national identity given the fact that nation building, national identity, functions by way of the nation's capacity for exclusion, I think Raiford's untangling of the differences with which whites and blacks handled and passed on images of violence and violation is productive for thinking about the possible grounds of such a distinction. With such a distinction, the question emerges: what created the capacity for any one image to do various things? And isn't the work being in *Blackpentecostal Breath* itself against categorical distinction, isn't it about the interrogation of the possibility of achieving pure difference? Certainly.

And we are back, it seems, to Glissant and the concept of diaspora, that there is multiplicity in any unity, that the idea of unity veils the originary plentitude, the otherwise possibilities, inherent in any object. Recasting the same material for another purpose is to take the common object, breathed air and aestheticize it. The irreducible impurity called air—breathed in and out, inhaled and exhaled, through the respiratory process—is both archive and anarchival.[97] Air and its vibration—the sounds of cracking fire and singed flesh; the screams and pleas of lament and pain; of crowds laughing and children crying—are arrested in each image, a capturing of infinitesimal collective anxiety. The image of the crowd standing around Stanley's black flesh indexes its own undoing through refused relationality.

Even when sent to family members and friends, what is created through lynching photography in the hands of whiteness is the dispersal of anxiety, of racial emphysema, and its desired removal. This anxiety is generative for wholly bound subjects, for fully contained and continuous bodies. This anxiety, in other words, is antisocial and against sociality. Such that sending to family members and friends is not a calling out to others to be together, but one instance among many of the way alienation appears, the way alienation antisocializes through binding and shoring up against porosity.

Like the critique of Blackpentecostal aesthetic practices emerging from the "mainline" that denigrated multiplicity and fleshliness of worship, and the Blackpentecostal gathering up and deepening the practice within such so-called denigrated practices, the "difference" that emerges from the handling of lynching photographs is not because this difference exists through purity; it is a difference that exists because of a previous renunciation of the multiplicity inherent to the photographs, a renunciation of the fleshliness of the photograph, a renunciation of the fleshliness of blackness, a renunciation of air, breath, breathing in black. If there is an antilynching capacity, it is within the image itself, it is within the shared air, as shared breath, of blackness. The various images of lynching produced by white anxiety—through the physiological eclipsing of breath, through the muting of sound-as-breath—illustrate the relation of whiteness, of Americanness, to silence.

Looking at various images of lynching violence, one is struck by the seeming silence that pulsates in and around them. But silence, of course, is never absolute; the most one can achieve is relative silence. How, then, might there be a noise in the image, a captured sonic environment presencing and breaking the enclosure of frame? It is, again, all about the breath. Nimi Wariboko's pentecostal principle elaborates sound as "an opening toward others in a movement that does not have a final object or destiny," building off Victor Zuckerkandl's philosophy of music.[98] For Wariboko, sound "represents excess that cannot be fully incorporated, institutionalized, or controlled by a system or used as a basis for sovereignty or governance."[99] Sound even of silence, then, is never complete or totalizing. Such that the work of Wells-Barnett and the NAACP not only shows the object's capacity for multiplicity, but—nevertheless and in spite of—the object's multiplicity to act as a quickening force of critique against the very conceptual frame that produced the object, and that such force is originary to its having been made. There was something there before the desire for death—premature, physical, social—and that which was there is elaborated through Blackpentecostal aesthetic practice.

There is even a silence, therefore, that can be heard in any image—a silence that makes its sonic force known—felt in any cut cloth or severed finger. A silence—as a sonic event—that escapes, centrifugitive, like life.[100] If air was there at the scene of subjection, and breath was the desired object to be stolen, this slightest breath at any moment of enframing, of eclipsing, evinces the life that escaped, through screams, through moans, through pleas. Whiteness would have itself be totalizing, pure, gratuitous violence. Totalizing, pure, gratuitous violence is the desire of whiteness but has not been achieved.

The air, the breath, allows in admixture, produces the violent force of violence's own dissolution. Can breathing, then, be a collective memory and rememory? Memory is about the proximity, the balance, between remembering and forgetting:

> Then, perhaps, life only offers the choice of remembering the garden or forgetting it. Either, or: it takes strength to remember, it takes another kind of strength to forget it, it takes a hero to do both. People who remember court madness through pain, the pain of the perpetually recurring death of their innocence; people who forget court another kind of madness, the madness of the denial of pain and hatred of innocence.[101]

Rememory would be the remembering of the balance of the necessity of forced recall and compelled forgetting. The rememory of breath as the intentioned performance of breathing—whooping, for example— produces an otherwise-than-history, one not dependent upon Newtonian physics of smooth, linear, contained time and space, but a performance of breathing and its eclipse as the hallucination of life and love in the face of the project of the plentitude of gratuitous violence and violation. But the breath, every breath, even stolen, breaks down the project through rememory. Remembered is the balance between the individual and the social. Generated are variations around the theme of discontinuity and openness as a way, as a form, as a politics against violent silences and enclosures, mutilations and deaths.

REMEMBERING THAT BREATH, and thus life, is in any enactment of violence and violation—against the very desires of whiteness to produce silence; against the very physiological anxieties that produce whiteness itself—allows for the following image to "make sense." This image (Figure 5) of Bishop Charles Harrison Mason, founder of the Blackpentecostal organization the Church of God in Christ, performatively breathes as critique. He stands there in the image repurposing and recasting possibility to demonstrate—even at the same temporal moment and spatial locations that lynchings and mass mob racial violence were prevalent—what it meant to live in enacting otherwise possibilities already existing, criminal, fugitive socialities, as a radical critique of the world from which we escape, to dwell in the present now while disrupting normative, western epistemologies and temporalities. Mason among the crowd, rather than violence, they breathe in the same air as he, likely, prayed for and exhorted the crowd. Not a sacrificial messianic figure but a communal act of love, of caring for flesh that stands out and bursts forth, against the grain of surveillance and possible disruption. Mason stands, his hand atop the head of a man in the crowd, Mason surrounded by believers. He appears to be deeply engaged with them, deeply embedded with them, loving them as they love him. What is seen in this image is the fleshliness of black love, of reciprocity. These images are both "ordinary" and, as Gwendolyn Brooks admonished in *Maud Martha*, can be cherished moments.[102]

COGIC settled, not just in Tennessee, but in the placed from which Ida B. Wells escaped: Memphis. Between 1880 and 1930, "Tennessee had 214 confirmed lynch victims during this period; 37 victims were white, 177 were African American. An additional 34 remain as unreconciled listings. Tennessee ranks sixth in the nation in the number of lynchings behind Mississippi, Georgia, Texas, Louisiana, and Alabama."[103] So though Wells encouraged black people to leave the city, in less than twenty years, COGIC was repopulating it: exhaled, inhaled. COGIC was also the target of racial terrorism and violence well after its inaugural years. Mason, as well, was the target of racial mob and lynching violence because of his pacifistic stance:

Following President Woodrow Wilson's entry of America into World War I in April 1917, Congress approved a massive national conscription campaign. Charles Mason encouraged men in the COGIC to avoid

Figure 5. Bishop Charles Harrison Mason with crowd (*The Commercial Appeal*, Memphis, TN: December 7, 1952).

war-making by registering as "conscientious objectors." Because of this, the FBI began an investigation of Mason and began proceedings accusing him of draft obstruction. When the word got out among whites in Lexington, Mississippi, a lynch mob formed and Sheriff Palmer had to arrest Mason in order to prevent him from being lynched.[104]

Mason was released on bail when it could not be determined if he were of the dangerous sort, and he immediately went to Memphis to deliver the sermon "The Kaiser in the Light of the Scriptures,"[105] which, Craig Scandrett-Leatherman argues, "indicates that Mason understood baptism as an immersion into the way of Jesus' nonviolence. Those baptized into Christ would not seek justice through violence but by speaking the truth and accepting suffering."[106] Mason's conceptualization of personhood was not grounded in the capacity to produce mob and lynching violence, but was an ethical stance of how to be together with others in an unjust world. And given Mason's belief in the aesthetics of Blackpentecostal movement of the spirit, we must attend to the social form that this Blackpentecostal group took as an enactment of an ethics of black pneuma, an intellectual practice of being together with others to perpetually critique the exorbitant violence of normative theology-philosophy. This critique is given in the performance of the fugitive otherwise sociality of blackness.

Craig Scandrett-Leatherman says of COGIC that it is "in part . . . a black ritual system of liberation in response to the white system of lynching" and that "Afro-Pentecostal dance and conscientious objection were affirmations of life, which resisted the expected norms for black men: lifeless acquiescence comportment or life-taking participation in military violence."[107] And as Cheryl Townsend Gilkes argues, "Black women and men have perceived racial oppression to be the most pervasive source of their individual and group suffering, but it has not been the sole catalyst for their collective action," such that the gatherings together are shown to be in the name of, in the cause for, breathing.[108] COGIC organized *like that*, with attention to function and form. Breathing, then, is the cultivation and care of flesh.

The flesh is animated and breathes. This breath is sacred in its antiphonal and social nature, shared in and as common. The flesh steps outside, moves, cares and sustains, rectifies and reproduces. And Baby Suggs, holy, knew about the flesh and the intense necessity for its care against the outside boundary.

> "Here," she said, "in this here place, we flesh; flesh that weeps, laughs; flesh that dances on bare feet in grass. Love it. Love it hard. Yonder they do not love your flesh. They despise it . . . This is flesh I'm talking about here. Flesh that needs to be loved . . . Saying no more, she stood up then and danced with her twisted hip the rest of what her heart had to say while others opened their mouths and gave her the music. Long notes held until the four-part harmony was perfect enough for their deeply loved flesh.[109]

Baby Suggs's sermon at first blush seems to support the claim that blackness is life contained within the totalizing force of social death, with her figuration of *here, in this place* and *yonder*. Though the clearing is where they would come together for sustenance, they would return to society civil, violent. But a return is not what they desired; they would have the logics— the spatial and temporal theological-philosophical thought that produced such illusory distinction—undone. But how are they able to gather, and gather quickly, in the midst of that which bears upon them? And we might ask this question of the nimbleness and quickness of gathering for residents of Ferguson, MO, responding to the murder of Michael Brown contemporarily. It means that even in civil society—even under surveillance of cameras, under lash and whip, hanging from trees and poles, stripped naked and bullet-ridden—they are always in the clearing, they carry the clearing in them, enact the clearing. This mode of gathering in clearing existed before the Middle Passage, but they, indeed, gathered *like that* against the violence of flesh trade. COGIC gathered in public zones *like that* around black flesh against racial mob and lynching violence, instances—captured and held in frame—of black pneuma. Their gathering quickly, *here, in this place*, was an enunciation—a showing out of the messenger, of the ones that carried the word of blackness in their beating hearts, their breathing lungs.

Here I want to elaborate upon Italo Calvino's discussion of invisible cities. Those invisible cities, for me, are enactments of black pneuma, intentionally aestheticized breath. Analyzing invisible cities through what Nahum Chandler calls a general "problematic," will take us toward the horizon. Chandler is critical of a theological-philosophical comportment that animates African American and Africana studies—the possibility of making a distinction, a distinction grounded in the notion of purity even while proclaiming its antithesis, that essentialism is fundamentally flawed. For example, Chandler asserts, "Although it is rather typically assumed, too simplistically, that the grounds of historical and social existence and identification were placed in question for 'Africans,' or 'Negroes,' or 'Blacks,' configured in this vortex, what is not so typically remarked is the way in which a fundamental questioning of the roots of identification and forms of historical existence for 'Europeans' or 'Whites' was also set loose at the core of this historical problematization."[110] Chandler goes deeper and higher still, rigorously arguing about the notion of a pure discourse:

> It naively implies that a nonessentialist discourse or position can be produced. As such, it presupposes an oppositional theoretical architecture at its core, in the supposed and self-serving distinction between a discourse or position that does not operate on the basis of an essence and those that do. It thus all the more emphatically presupposes a simple essence as the ground of its discourse, in both conceptual and practical, that is, political, terms.[111]

The architecture internal to racial mob and lynching violence—as an enactment of theological-philosophical thought—is of the purely oppositional character of desired civil society, of desired whiteness, to blackness. The structuring coherence at the heart of such violence is the conception of full and complete citizen/civil/human/subject's nonconvergence with blackness and that black pneuma—air, breath, breathing in blackness—is a violation, a disruption, an undoing of this nonconvergence. The simple essence at the heart of the matter is distinction, distinction that emerges through the project of producing gratuitous violence and violation. The purity of civil society would be the lack of being target of the project of gratuitous violence. Violence, in this figuration, takes on an aesthetic and quantifiable quality.

The exorbitant violence of whiteness is an aesthetic practice, it is a performance form. Achille Mbembe's influential article "Necropolitics" points in that direction, is ground from which such an argument can be made. He says, "Slave life, in many ways, is a form of death-in-life" and that "Because the slave's life is like a 'thing,' possessed by another person, the slave existence appears as a perfect figure of a shadow."[112] Perfection. Purity. Same thing, differently. Yet, as mentioned above, even the sociality of shadows is generative for intellectual reflection: "A life. Could be," grounded in a celebratory Blackpentecostal *nevertheless* and *in spite of* (about which more below).[113] Mbembe contends that there is, within the cauldron of enslavement practices, a "triple loss" of the notion of "home," "rights over his or her body" and, finally, "loss of political status," such that this triple loss "is identical with absolute domination, natal alienation, and social death (expulsion from humanity altogether)" thus and therefore, the plantation creates the condition in which the slave does not have anything like "community" because community "implied the exercise of the power of speech and thought."[114] But was domination, indeed, absolute? Is there a giving and withholding that could ever be intentional? Is there the capacity for withholding consent: that though one might not give consent to conditions, one can withhold—as in breath—such sentiment.[115] And is the triple loss a loss at all? So we attend to those that dwelt together in presumed nonconvergence, in presumed pure, absolute, perfect space made by those that would so expunge them from zones of thought, of thinking. What did they make in absence of being included, by way of—but not as a result of—being excluded?

THAT WHICH PRODUCES the western concept of the human, the individual, the man was producing itself—through theology and philosophy—at the moment that the African was being stolen. This is important because to speak of "loss" would presuppose an oppositional coherence at the core, an operational architecture that would have home, rights over bodily integrity and political status mean and function universally before the point Cristóbal Colón ever made a journey, before the *San Juan Bautista* ever landed at Jamestown. This is simply repeating what Sylvia Wynter has called "unsettling the coloniality of Being/Power/Truth/Freedom."[116] To unsettle the coloniality of the conceptual ground and frame by which we come to understand the very terms of order, the very things that Africans would have "lost."

For Mbembe, "Colonial occupation itself was a matter of seizing, delimiting, and asserting control over a physical geographical area—of writing on the ground a new set of social and spatial relations."[117] Under colonial relations, that which he calls the "conditions of vertical sovereignty and splintering colonial occupation," Mbembe says, "communities are separated across a y-axis. This leads to a proliferation of the sites of violence."[118] The dispersing of violent locales is the means through which it improvises at specific points of spatial and temporal organization. So we are talking, here, about aesthetic practices of violence, the tension violence creates through spatializing its logic, the form it takes, violence as performance. Blackpentecostal aesthetics, Blackpentecostal performance practices, illustrate how "resistance is prior to power."[119] *Breathing strange utterances* in Blackpentecostal spaces, during various moments in the church service—during what is called Testimony Service, for example—I have many a time experienced a song leader or preacher sometimes scream on the microphone the word "Nevertheless!" And sometimes, Blackpentecostals would be encouraged to "give God an 'in spite of' praise!'" That word, and that phrase, point to the primacy of particularity, that though one may feel encased, enclosed, contained, that—nevertheless, and in spite of—there is an excessive force that sustains, that exists before any situation, violent or otherwise. "Nevertheless" and "in spite of," within this world, link back to an excess that precedes any moment, modality, any encounter or engulfment.[120]

The structural core—the operating assumption—of any thought is the nevertheless and in spite of condition. Something like arguing that though whites were indeed targets of mob and lynching violence historically—nevertheless and in spite of these historical conditions—the so-thought gratuitous violence of which blackness is the target makes of those historical truths but a marginal, untenable example. This structural coherence of the nonconvergence of the marginal, of the otherwise example, allows for the emergence of categorical purity and distinction, of violence against blacks on the one hand and other modes of violence on the other. To hopefully be more precise: those marginal examples might be targeted by violence but it is not *gratuitous*, they might experience alienation but it is not *natal*. The grounds for these form differences are the juridical process that assumes its rightness and universality, that assumes it has been assented to. Thus, nevertheless and in spite of these marginal examples of violence and alienation, a theoretical coherence about the blackness as living death, blackness as slavery, is rendered. "Nevertheless" and "in spite of" mark the always available and plural otherwise possibility, that we can be otherwise than this.

Coherence and categorical distinction are but one possibility among a plentitude, and infinite range, of otherwise possibilities. It is not that knowledge cannot be produced or organized around the concepts of coherence and categorical distinction. Indeed, the long history of western epistemology has demonstrated such a project and aspiration. Yet what has also been demonstrated is the violence and violation necessary for such a project. Otherwise possibilities, other breathing, black breath, breathing in black flesh, places pressure on the range of other modalities for ways of life. Albert Einstein's rejection of pure distinction is instructive: "What Einstein rejects most forcefully of Newton's conception of space and time is its commitment to understanding space and time as separate and physically independent, autonomous entities" and "In Einstein's reconceptualization, space, time and matter are interconnected and interdefined, relative terms."[121] In the first instance, in Newton's instance, there has been much discovered, much elaborated, knowledge produced, through the assumption that separation, categorical distinction between space and time were possible. But in the second instance, otherwise thought opened up to otherwise imaginative worlds that have been equally generative for conceiving math and physics.

The refusal of pure distinction became the grounds for an otherwise epistemological project. And thus, we are thrown back into the horizontal thrust of *parti* drawings, the thrownness of whooping that presences the black flesh of women preachers insofar as the distinction between background and foreground, between that which is thrown and the environment into which Dasein finds itself, withers away. Black being must be thought otherwise than racial distinction that was the gift, that was the problem, of modern thought. The confessional posture of the instrumentality of racial violence breaks down through a general hermeneutics given by black breath, black pneuma, a mode of intellectual practice and performance of the breathing in and the breathing out, the reciprocity of exhalation and inhalation, the giving and sharing in the commons of air.

And if the repression of the breath of blackness is an animating feature of theological pneumatology, studies in humanities and the social sciences predicated on Newtonian physics are not merely reflections of philosophical thought but modalities of violent theologies. Whooping, then, is the anoriginal convergence—against presumed nonconvergence—of blackness and the world, blackness in the world against social death, blackness in the worlds of its own making as a critique of worlds produced through exclusion. While Achille Mbembe asserts, after Patterson, that slavery creates the condition of total, absolute control, "Control, especially 'absolute' control, over someone else's intention requires recognition of that intention: There is no need to control that intention which has no force. This force, the force of an intention other than that of the slave owner's, is signified practically by the risk of flight or escape: The slave can always choose to escape or attempt to escape, including by way of death or suicide."[122] Michelle Koerner offers another way to think about this mode of recognition, as a line of flight: "not [as] a concept of negativity or of destruction; it rather seeks to give consistency to social compositions that are not accounted for by state theory."[123] The intensity of whooping, the double-gesture of respiration, the aestheticized breathing of flesh, is "invented" by the one who is, by the ones who are, performing. The intensity and intentionality of such performance makes the scene "absolute," as it is not determined by the "relative speed" of civil society, of whiteness, of what it means to be human.[124]

The sermons of Dorinda Clark-Cole and Juandolyn Stokes are important for considering the spontaneity of black flesh becoming, of black flesh emergence. Such becoming, such emergence, is the performance of the zero degree of social conceptualization, the performance of the social occasion of blackness. Such becoming, such emergence, is the illustration of the refusal of categorical distinction, that blackness is sent into the world to demonstrate. Those sermons with whooping, with the intensity of breath, show the ways that breathing intentionally are the accretional peaks and points of departure for spontaneous, improvisatory praise. One does not get the sense that they "planned" to perform the sounds and movements they produced. One does not get the sense that Clark-Cole "decided" to preach until overwhelmed and overcome, had to be encircled by other women, had to be carried up and off and to the podium. One does not get the sense that Stokes "planned" to append words with "tuh." Rather, the animated breath made apparent the enfleshment of these women at the moment of performance—vividly there, in the unalterable "now" of unfamiliarity. These moves, these sounds, were not planned but absolutely happened; they was not produced through surveillance and lack of will but the most emphatic enactment of absolute—I do not say pure—capacity.

In the poem "Speech to the Young : Speech to the Progress-Toward (Among Them Nora and Henry III)," Gwendolyn Brooks closes with the following: "Live not for battles won. / Live not for the-end-of-the-song. / Live in the along."[125] A pneumatology of blackness is generative for reading the entire poem, the breaks in lines as solicitations for an intellectual sociality of breathing, of breath, of air. But more, a Blackpentecostal aesthetic compels me to read such breakage as hallucinatory of whooping, a doubled-gesture of respiration, an accretional build of intensity with the barest of phrases. "Live in the along." This is how Brooks chose to end the poem. To "live in the along" is to live as flesh, to refuse the enclosure of language that produces grammar, the enclosures of land that produce private property, the enclosures of flesh that produce the conceptual body. To "live in the along" is to intimate that path and passage are given and prior to Newtonian physics, space, and time. To "live in the along" is to "journey through" worlds, it is to, of priority, steal away. "Live in the along" is the prime meridian of Brooks's poetics, setting the velocity of everything that came before it. *Along* is defined as movement in a direction, as extending in a horizontal line and as in company with others. The word registers these three ideas such that to live in the along is to have a way of life as movement, as *horizontal* and in the presence, in the cause, of others. To "live in the along," as a command, as a solicitation, is to live in and to not desire assumption from out of the flesh, to live at the meridian point is the *parti* that stands and furnishes forth.

So Clark-Cole and Stokes not only preach but they preach *like that*, with absolute intensity, with absolute intentionality. Absolute but never pure. And when they pause—invitational eclipse of speech for congregational antiphony—through their will, through their capacity for intellectual practice, the congregation swells to the point of rupture. And everyone, because of praise, is out of and held within air, breath, everyone is held within breathing as process. To "live in the along" allows for air, breath, breathing to escape, and in such escape, make enfleshment appear and "place" oneself in movement, as movement, altering the normative worlds of juridical violence and violation.

2

SHOUTING

To become an object for theological, for philosophical, reflection. To be an instrument that produces thought as categorically distinct, pure. What does it mean to be such an instrument? But before that question can be answered—the question, the concern over being such an object (what Frantz Fanon might say is an object in the midst of other objects . . . for thinking)—another demands attention. Having attended to air, breath, breathing as the grounds for Blackpentecostal aesthetics, for black sociality, another concern: Just what does it mean to think theologically, to think philosophically? And how does one come to think in such a way *as opposed to* thinking not-theologically, not-philosophically? Having first attended to air, breath, breathing as the grounds for considering Blackpentecostal aesthetics before elaborating the meaning of theological-philosophical thought was intentional. It was to illustrate the ways the concerns about breath, about *black pnuema,* could be cognized without founding it upon the terrain of pure theological, pure philosophical, reflection. It was also elaborated first such that Blackpentecostalism was not forced to cohere with, adhere to, a set of predetermined (Predestined, as in Calvinism? about which, more soon) formulae, a systematics, a series of explaining why Blackpentecostalism should matter to theological-philosophical thought. Like a first visit to a Blackpentecostal church, the explanation for aesthetic practice emerges through experience. One's gotta feel it, have a feeling for it, a desire to be there, an openness to such movement.

Blackpentecostals believe one fundament of experience is to be in the world, *for* the world, as an agent of radical alterity. It is an openness to others while also establishing oneself through a claim for moving through the world differently. Yet this difference obtains by way of its being excluded. Is this difference categorically distinct? Can it be maintained? Is it pure? And what are the grounds for such thinking? This line of questioning is informed by the way Nahum Chandler discusses ontological possibility and difference as such:

> It is widely believed that a real thing called 'America' exists. It is precisely this idea of an America in itself that we should not accept without examination. Is 'America' really the anchorage point that supports the social-cultural practices of African Americans, or is it rather a complex idea formed inside the (historical-transcendental) movement of the constitution of the African American as material idea.[1]

The thing called America is structured by an assumptive logic wherein that which is so named bears the weight of producing ontological difference for the thing that would obtain for the negro—for the black—in time and across space, as African-hyphen-American. The assumptive logic renders America a neutral zone and inhabitation for that which is never in need of, nor in search for, that which comes before the hyphen such that the very designation African-hyphen-America/n would bear a similar ontological necessity for defining itself constantly in relation to this America, and designating what it means to be rendered irreducibly different from, and thus fundamentally disorienting for, this America. Think, then, of America—and its existence through assumptive logics—as a theological-philosophical project, a problem. Nahum Chandler helps us detect the ways belief in an America indexes not just the concept of difference but that that difference is categorical, that it is locatable on maps, for example, that difference emerges on and as smooth space, progressive time.

But to the point, what of exclusion? Cheryl Sanders's influential *Saints in Exile* is a sociological study about Holiness-Pentecostal believers, and she utilizes the category of "exile" as a figuration for the mode of relation that the Saints—what Holiness-Pentecostal believers call themselves, a democratizing of the idea of the veneration—have with the mainline religious sects from which they emerged such as Baptist, Methodist, and the African Methodist Episcopal traditions.[2] Exile is about the forced movement into the exterior, from the interior, of something like having been templed, having something like a geospatial location in which one could worship, a coherent time and space for divine encounter. Exilic communities are those that had a place, and a time, to go, to dwell but that having was violently interdicted. Cheryl Sanders theorizes that the "Saints" can be understood by way of the motif of a violent and violative expulsion. Thus, the Saints are the perpetual seekers of the would-be home after having been pushed out, those who—by way of force—have been separated from the thing with which they desire most: grounding.

The utility of exile as a motif for considering the relationship of Holiness-Pentecostal religious life to mainline African American religious organizations such as the National Baptist Convention and the African Methodist Episcopal Church is understandable: during the "birth" of the modern Pentecostal movement at the turn of the twentieth century, individuals were banished from families for joining the "holy rollers," shunned by friends and lambasted in the media for speaking in tongues, those strange utterances that are not given to coherent rational thought. But those that were pushed out, forced into exile, made a world, a large, strange, and dense world of inhabitation, a world of radical sociality with intense feeling. And it is the aesthetic practices of *cipriéré* communities—maroons of Africans and American Indigenes who escaped conditions of enslavement, existing in the cypress swamps—that offer a fresh figuration for thinking about the intellectual practice of picking up your stuff and leaving where you are not wanted, and making something with a radical potentiality and critical edge.

It is the *cipriéré* communities that give me another means for thinking the Saints, and for thinking the possibility for interrogating categorical difference itself. The *cipriéré* communities compel me to think about the necessary presumptions that obtain in the assertion of exile, that pure difference exists, and we would know it from that which exists in metaphorical hyphenation, on the move with the historic force of violent encounter. That is, to be a Saint in exile locates ontological, categorical difference in the fact of banishment and makes of the relationality stable, coherent and precise, it makes of that performance of rhetorical—and yes, at times, physical—violation and violence the grounding for difference. But not just rhetorical and physical violence but the very *capacity* to be violated, to be acted upon violently, becomes the grounds for grouping. Curious circular logic, tautological force, that does not work itself out. If exile is the figuration, the Saints are different because of something that befell them. And this rather than the Saints being in relation to one another grounded in an intense and intentional seeking *together with others* for the Holy Spirit, for a mode of divine communion, divine encounter, that went further and deeper than they had, at that moment heretofore experienced. The violence of expulsion came after the fact of their having experience—or even desire for such experience—experience that caused them to be in communion with others, experience that caused them to be open to the freshness *of* experience. The violence of expulsion, in other words, did not create the Saints, but was a critique of the already in motion, already on the move, sociality created. And it is the New Orleans *cipriere* marronage community that I think has something important to teach us about agential movement and *a*theological-*a*philosophical critique.

Of New Orleans and the *cipriere*, Bryan Wagner writes that "much of the social life of the city's slaves became concentrated in the swamps where they could talk, dance, drink, trade, hunt, fish, and garden without supervision. The settlements were hidden away, but they were also integrated with the life of the city. Unlike in some places in the United States, these maroon communes had many women and children."[3] In marronage, then, was an always existing aesthetic practice of joy and enjoyment, pleasure and the pleasurable, even with knowledge that the world could befall and produce terror because of the fugitive nature of their world-making. Monique Allewaert writes about the concept of citizenship and marronage, stating, "at precisely the moment citizen-subjects were emerging in metropolitan centers, the plantation zone gave rise to an ecological practice closely linked to marronage, a process through which human agents found ways to interact with nonhuman forces and in so doing resisted the order of the plantation."[4] The practice of marronage was an extensive one, one that produced otherwise ecologies, otherwise interactions, otherwise modes of inhabitation. And this from the force of exclusion. And, finally: "The city fascinates—as all who come to expect it. Do certain country markets necessarily secrete cities about themselves."[5] Samuel Delany's speculative fiction—with the word secrete—is how I will think the relationship between the maroons and the market on the one hand, and the saints and the sanctuaries from which they were uprooted on the other. Secretion is that which has been discharged or released, something that has been, in Heideggerian terms, "let" out, something that lets itself appear, something that presences.

Secretions are things internal to, and thus internal differentiation for, systems, orders, figurations, but it is through a puncture, hole, or other process that a journey is enacted. Timothy James Lockley says, "The Spanish first had to find the maroon communities, and since *palenques* were usually secreted away in remote and inaccessible areas this was not easy. The Native Americans present among the maroons provided vital local knowledge as to the best locations for settlements that were both defensible and had ready supplies of fresh water."[6] Like the city that fascinates in Delany's fiction, Lockley's rhetorical flourish about the maroons *secreting away into* allows me to consider the force, the agential capacity, for the object that journeys, the thing that is seemingly exilic, the thing that is secreted. Following critic Michelle Koerner's analysis of "lines of flight" and fugitivity, we can think of the force of secreting away into as a line of flight, "not [as] a concept of negativity or of destruction; it rather seeks to give consistency to social compositions that are not accounted for by state theory."[7] The intensity of making presence of marronage felt, as an aesthetic force, is "invented" by the one who is, by the ones who are, secreting. The intensity and intentionality of such performance makes the scenes of fugitivity, the scenes of escape and flight, "absolute," as it is not determined by the "relative speed" of civil society, of whiteness, of what it means to be human.

Allewaert keys us in to the fact that maroons were not interested in reproducing logics of citizenship and exclusion but were—at the moment when citizen-subjects were being organized and thought theologically and philosophically in something called America—resisting not only plantation modes of inhabitation and exclusion, but the very world that made plantations possible. Maroons secreted into the interior of the swamp and, therein, created modes of vitality, they established and lived into possibilities otherwise. They were released and let out *into*, interrogating notions of directionality. This interrogation of, this critical intervention into, directionality is just another enactment of Blackpentecostal aesthetics, enacted before such a "group" existed in 1906 Los Angeles. This interrogation of and critical intervention into directionality will be the grounds for critiquing theology-philosophy that misunderstands blackness through aversive logic.

Maroons were known for "Running their own political and judicial affairs [and] they were known for such exotic practices as polygyny, oracular divination, spirit possession, body sacrifice, and plastic arts, and countless other aspects of daily life that served as reminders of their uncompromised heritage of independence."[8] And "Maroons had established and protected their settlements with great ingenuity and had become expert at all aspects of guerrilla warfare."[9] The *cipriré* communities secreted from local plantations, maintaining a relationship to those spaces from which they escaped, but established new patterns of behavior and aesthetic interventions for protection and peace. Setting traps, navigating the waters, having sex, singing, raising children, eating—all these were aesthetic practices that always and likewise had to be practices of preparation. Maroons needed be ready at a moment's notice for encounter, not with the divine, but with the political world of the exterior that would bear down on them and produce violence against them. Each practice, therefore, was a likewise preparation for the possibility of the threat of violation; each practice, thus, highlights the ways in which interventions always likewise have an aesthetic quality and theoretical underpinning. Like the "clearing" carried in the flesh, as belief in the flesh, Baby Suggs preached about, the aesthetics of marronage had to be belief in the flesh, worn in and on the flesh, as modes of preparation. These practices were the ongoing dispersal of intellect-as-spirit, performed in the flesh of maroons.

The Saints are a likewise secretion, of necessity, from "mainstream" and "mainline" religious denominations. Do the Saints and the *cipriré* communities share in an aesthetic, cultural relationship, which is to say, a mode of sociality? Preparation, readiness, practice for encounter, was necessarily an aesthetic, spiritual practice. This is likewise true of the Saints: in the practice of singing songs during what is known as Testimony and Tarry Service, in the practice of singing and praying, but more in the practice of cooking food and visiting homes of others, in the practice of everyday life, the quotidian, mundane, ordinary life, always the possibility for the encounter with God. *Cipriré* communities engaged in hermeneutics: to study the swamp, to survey the interior, to know when to let and to recede into the background. The Saints engage in a likewise hermeneutics: to study a way of life, to survey the interior of the soul, to know when to move the flesh and let it recede in praise and prayer. Both hermeneutics centered on the preparatory steps, a choreographic-sonic shout, for the encounter of surprise.

I am concerned with the critique of theology and philosophy that Black-pentecostal aesthetics posit, vivified and quickened by a "politics of avoidance."[10] The politics of avoidance is the performance and performativity of the *atheology-aphilosophy* of blackness, aestheticized in and through "shouting," a tradition of dance performance linking the Afro-Indigenous and Afro-Islamic to the (New World) Afro-Christian. The *a*theological and *a*philosophical, it will be demonstrated, are necessary markers for what is produced through Blackpentecostalism—the recovery of flesh from which "the body" is a conceptual abstraction produced through normative theological and philosophical discourses.

Consideration of spatial movements upon the ground is but one interrogation into the aesthetic value of Blackpentecostalism, a creative commons and sociality against which theology and philosophy denigrated. I consider both Calvinist theology and Enlightenment philosophy as simply figurations of a more general tendency to not-think blackness, to avert it and to create of it something by way of such aversion. More than mere denigration, normative theology and philosophy are produced through aversion, through a shuddering look and look away, a muted, mutated hearing and hearing away from Blackpentecostal aesthetic performance. Calvinist theology is exemplary because of its relation to the Great Awakening revivals of the eighteenth thru nineteenth centuries. Camp meetings, soul feasts, and the weeping and gnashing of repentant teeth are the primary mimetic structure for "revival," and the gatherings of the Great Awakening are remembered as specifically aesthetic employments of "enthusiasms" that bear a genealogical—if not anthropological, musicological, axiological, and sociological—relation to the twentieth-century Pentecostal movement. Enlightenment thought is exemplary because of the ways theologies were articulated both along its flows and sometimes against its currents. The category of blackness is relational as an oppositional force, engaged through aversion, and this aversive turn and turn away is theological-philosophical choreographics.

Within Calvinist theology, I elaborate upon George Whitefield[11] and Jonathan Edwards as two exemplar figures. And within Enlightenment philosophy, I utilize Immanuel Kant's anthropology. Both theology and philosophy will bear out how aversion is the structuring logic, aversion specifically to blackness, to Blackpentecostal aesthetics. And this because these aversive modalities of thought are, collectively, a *choreographic protocol and itinerary*. The choreographic is set loose through thinking the concept of aversion that sparks these interconnected theological and philosophical traditions. To say that Calvinist doctrine and Enlightenment thought are structured through a choreographic protocol and itinerary announces the ways through which the relationship of the secular and the religious, the interior and exterior, the moving and stilled are necessary for the creation of race as an organizing logic and teleological principle.[12] It is also to consider how these secular and spiritual thought exercises necessitated multiple leaps, splits, displacements, varied pirouettes, pliés, and postures, that followed or averred a path, both with and against each other but, most profoundly, always away from the concept of blackness. The choreographic protocol and itinerary is about making distinction categorical, and keeping such categorical distinction pure, in order to produce thought. It is an enclosure against thought, a cognizing that occurs through by excluding sensual, material forms of life.

Both Calvinist and Enlightenment thought make present—like the Africanist presence Toni Morrison describes: "Through significant and underscored omissions, startling contradictions, heavily nuanced conflicts, through the way writers peopled their work with the signs and bodies of this presence—one can see that a real or fabricated Africanist presence was crucial to their sense of Americanness"[13]—a concept of blackness embodied in the figure of the black, negro, racial/ized figure. Crucial to the *sense of theology*, to the *sense of philosophy*—crucial to, that is, the would-be theologian, the would-be philosopher—is a black presence, and this through an aversion to blackness. The sense of theology, the sense of philosophy, occurs by averting blackness, by categorically distinguishing the choreographic from the sonic, by cognizing through placement. As a critique of and break from the episteme that produces the normative sense of theology and sense of philosophy, in this chapter I consider the specifically choreographic aspect of what I call the choreosonic, the always attendant and interconnected concept of movement and sound, as the *a*theology-*a*philosophy of blackness, how Blackpentecostalism utilizes choreosonics as a politics of avoidance that exists previous to aversive theological, philosophical thought. Thus, the spirited, energetic, expressive Blackpentecostal dance tradition called "shouting" at the turn of the twentieth century. But we've gotta get there first, so I explore the tradition of expressiveness of this choreosonic dance, found in the "Ring Shout" that precedes Blackpentecostalism, and within the Afro-Arabic *saut* tradition of Sufi Dervish tradition that precede them both. (What I will, when speaking of the three together as a unit, term "shout traditions"). Not only the physical movements of such counterclockwise itineraries, there is also a homophonic substance—the reiteration of the sound of the word, of the concept pronounced "shout" in New World English—of this choreosonic tradition. The splitting of the choreo from the sonic, however, is illusory at best. The split is only momentary, not categorical. And this because the shout does not take place without making, taking, and breaking sound; the shout traditions are choreographic insofar as they are sonic, and are sonic insofar as they are choreographic. This portmanteau thinks the concept of choreography and sonicity together by breaking them apart.

Choreosonics are ephemeral performances and Ronald Judy's *(Dis)Forming the American Canon* gives concrete ground from which to begin an analysis of theology, philosophy, and the multiple modes of placement and spatially organized ideas and bodies, as he is attentive to the question and problematic of canonizing ephemera. He urges against the ways in which the very notion of a literary tradition redoubles the unnecessary opposition of theoria—the "abstract and cognitive contemplation of the invisible, indivisible Being," the "order of rational discourse built on the principle of noncontradiction"—to aesthesis—the "field of the sensible as illusion."[14] The historic split between theory and aesthetic is a crucial to consider because it seems to be simply another enactment of creating categorical distinction. For Judy, the split of theory from aesthetics was a crucial factor in the constitution of an American canon generally, and an African American black studies canon particularly. Judy engages the work of John Blassingame's *The Slave Community*, to highlight the ways in which Blassingame finds the autobiographic writing to be most useful for understanding the historiography of black people during enslavement. Judy contends that Blassingame had an attachment to autobiography as a "deliberative discourse," which "provides information about the psychology of the slave, how the slave experienced reality as given" even when there are shortcomings to such narrativizing.[15] It is the question of the verifiability of the slave narrative, of the slave autobiography—which becomes a general concern about verifiability of blackness—that for me makes the urgency of thinking Calvinist theology and Enlightenment thought as a choreographic itinerary and protocol.

The material, on-the-ground movements of the shout traditions are ephemeral, once foot shuffles upon ground, once vibration and friction literally sound out, its graphesis dissipates. Performance allows us to think with Judy and around such autobiographical necessity for verifiability and reliability: Austin's performance of the everyday is not about the truthiness or falsity of any such claim, but rather about the efficaciousness.[16] Does the performance do something in the world? What is, and what is the result, of such doing? Can the performance of movement, even in its repetition, teach us something about Blackpentecostal aesthetics? Can performance present a different "documentary history of the collective African American experience of America in slavery," in general?[17] How is the shout tradition an aesthetic prompting for imagining worlds otherwise? And what does the performance of the shout tradition prompt in the performers and the onlookers, onhearers of such aesthetic practices? Does the performance disrupt the epistemology of normativity such that we can imagine otherwise possibilities in their plentitude?

How to understand that tradition of movement, a particular politics of avoidance for the aversion to and for blackness and the enfleshment of such a concept in the figure of the black, raced, negro is what I seek to perform.

> Often the John Brown song was sung, but oftener these incomprehensible negro methodist, meaningless, monotonous, endless chants with obscure syllables recurring constantly & slight variations interwoven, all accompanied with a regular drumming of the feet & clapping of the hands, lake castinets; then the excitement spreads, outside the enclosure men begin to quiver & dance, others join, a circle forms, winding monotonously round some one in the centre. Some heel & toe tumultuously, others merely tremble & stagger on, others stoop & rise, others whirl, others caper sidewise all keep steadily circling like dervishes. . . . At last seems to come a snap and the spell breaks amid general sighs & laughter.[18]

Shouts—Afro-Arabic, Ring, and Blackpentecostal—are the itineraries for the lines of force animating an architectonics of resistance; they perform protocols for movement that always counter and intuit; they are intentionally agitational and nuanced. Barely perceptible auralities of the flesh, given by the jerked movements and the feet scarcely lifted off the ground, given by spin and twist, what I call centrifugitivity. Thomas Wentworth Higginson's recounting the shout choreosonics of the army regiment is notable for his attention to nuance, his attention to the way flesh trembled, almost barely noticed, and such ephemeral movements were the foundation for a tradition. Quiverings and tremblings, whirling and sighing, all part of the choreosonic mood and movement. To arrive at an analysis of twentieth-century Blackpentecostal shouting as dance tradition that carries the vital acts it transfers,[19] I begin with Afro-Arabic *saut*, of which one such possibility for pronunciation in New World English is "shout," though it's a bit difficult to determine. This resistance to determination, it turns out, will be the rickety bridge upon which blackness and performance converge.

SAUT PROVIDES FOR us a bridge between Sea Costal Ring Shout and Blackpentecostal Shouting, though such bridging existed prior to the Middle Passage's situation, a bridge of desire, avoiding the marginalizing practices of transatlantic stolen flesh. That bridge is choreosonic, echoed by way of an irreducible indeterminacy for and refusal of meaning, a translational hesitance that compels our own relation to the apprehension of such a word, such a performance; of any word, of any performance. Lorenzo Dow Turner insisted that the term *saut*, when imported to the Georgia/South Carolina seacoast, referenced the Afro-Arabic circumambulatory movement for Islamic practices, the circumambulation around and about the Kaaba.

> "Dr. L. D. Turner has discovered the Arabic word saut (pronounced like our word 'shout'), in use among the Mohammedans of West Africa meant to run and walk around the Kaaba." Turner's remark concerning the term is particularly interesting owing to his association of the ring shout with the ritual in which hundreds, tightly assembled, move around the Kaaba in a counterclockwise direction.[20]

In Islamic tradition, if one is able to make the journey to Mecca where the Kaaba is located—the cubed, most sacred site of Islam—the circumambulation is to occur seven times. Turner briefly noted how one could either walk or run in order to perform this sacred movement, and how the spatial organizing of persons—tightly assembled flesh, objects among other objects, together—are of import. Implied is that the sociality that emerges by performing this circumambulatory movement together with others is dependent equally upon the uniqueness of individuals choosing both to enter into claustrophobic conditions as an act of praise as well as the pace, speed, rhythm with which they would perform such sociality. Turner linked *saut*, with its counterclockwise circularities, to Ring Shouts, that he noticed in Sea Coastal Georgia and South Carolina in the continental

United States. Though there was—and still is today—contention about the pronunciation of *saut*, what intrigues is the imagined, the thought, the perhaps unverifiable relation *between* as the foundation for tradition. The relation between *saut* and shout, when spoken, underscores the ways in which all we have, all we ever are in, is relation between. Like a bridge.

The presence of Islam as religious, ethical, and political formation of social life on the Georgia and South Carolinian seacoasts resulted from the reverberation and echo of choreosonics, of black flesh, of the importation of enslaved peoples who were Muslim. In fact, "slightly over 50 percent of Africans imported to North America came from areas in which Islam was at least a religion of the minority."[21] Certain, then, the energy and vitality of Islam was felt as a fundamental resource for resistance of the object of black social life. There is

> convincing evidence that the Muslim presence among African slaves was particularly evident on the Eastern Seaboard, including Georgia. Not only was the Muslim presence evident among new slaves—however secretive the practices might have been—but during the period 1730–1860 proof of the Islamic presence is documented . . . However small their number, the fact that Islamic converts had lived in the ancestral West African regions before the slave trade to the Americas lends some credence to the influence, not origin, of the *saut* (Arabic-Islamic) theory behind the ring shout. . . . Were one to assume that elements of Muslim musical practice entered the highly syncretistic nature of counterclockwise religious ritual dances of slaves, and that remnants of such a practice are still evident in the coastal regions where the ring shout survived, examining the influence of Islamic practices might be a logical step to take. Upon closer examination, the term *saut* presents problematic etymological description. The common use of this term today simply is to mean "sound."[22]

This passage compels a journey into the relation between—the nearness of—sound and ground given with each enunciation of *saut*. This in-betweenness of possible pronunciations, of possible definitions, is an excessive force that constitutes the very possibility for meaning. And this would be true for any translation, any word. The enunciation of *saut* is the bridge—the possibility for movement, crossing, leaving, and arrival.

> When I got to Turner's idea that the use of the word 'shout' to refer to circumambular movement derives from the Arabic word *saut*,

Djamilaa said no, that couldn't be, that *saut* isn't pronounced like 'shout' and that it doesn't mean to walk around the Ka'aba, it means voice, sound. I thought about it a while and then said it was no problem, that *saut* not being pronounced like 'shout' actually made the point I was trying to make, albeit differently, that *saut*, not sounding like 'shout,' implies the turn toward unsounded shout. . . . I said that the meaning bent toward movement rather than sound was what whatever shout the piece calls for wants—an arced, inostensible shout, inostensible decree. Inostensible decree, I went on, was a proviso issued at the heart of sound which allowed fertile mistakes like Turner's *saut/* shout derivation, the phonic license which made it possible to imagine *saut* might have been (mis)pronounced 'shout.'[23]

The bridge between—*saut*—forces the consideration of the ongoing relation between choreographics and sonics, how they are constitutive of the other, how the distinction cannot ever be maintained, cannot ever be made to be pure, cannot ever be made to be categorical.

Anne Taves discusses "Shouting Methodists" as a precursor to twentieth-century shouting tradition. Weaving together the various ways in which "shout" was used and critiqued, particularly as a Methodist religious practice, it becomes apparent that many of the injunctions against shouting were, in fact, not about choreography but regarded falling out, fainting, swooning, and loud vocalizations. Taves writes about how people would lose strength, restrain from leaping, would melt into tears, weep aloud, or appear concerned. John Fanning Watson noted as much in his anonymously written *Methodist error; or, Friendly, Christian advice, to those Methodists, who indulge in extravagant emotions and bodily exercises.*[24] He said of black noise that "at the black Bethel church in Philadelphia, it has been common to check the immoderate noise of the people," and of the performance of enthusiastic public worship generally, "it began in Virginia, and as I have heard, among the blacks."[25] The choreosonic interplay is a black thing—Fanning Watson just didn't understand—as the black choreosonic brought with it an irreducible indeterminacy. The indeterminacy of meaning blacks carried with them about the meaning of *saut* and shout, it appears, was a vivifying impetus for the "Methodist error"; black participation in Methodist prayer meetings and Awakening revivals necessarily forced a critique of fleshly extravagance.

Saut, as bridge, illustrates the fact that directionality matters. The dance around the Kaaba is a counterclockwise counterclaim for counterinsurgency that is always and at every performance the possibility for social ecstasy, of being beside oneself together with others, wherein the besides are, phonographically we might say, the B-sides of the record, the underside and the underground of the emergence of an emptying of oneself out toward others. Social ecstasy is not about the becoming undone of the subject when confronted with an Other that assumes that doneness is what exists "naturally."[26] Rather, social ecstasy is the conception that the condition of possibility for life is undoneness as ontological priority, an irreducible, unreachable doneness, a horizonal undoneness. The emptying of oneself through spiritual performance of peregrination underscores the capacity to give and receive, to disperse and hold, and lays claim to this undoneness as a way of life. To say that direction matters is not merely to make an assertion about the spatial organizing of movement from one point to another as if following an arrow from bow to target. Rather, it is about the recognition that that which we call "path" is an after-the-fact effect of one possibility being taken out of many; it is the recognition that previous to situation, infinite possibility is a fact of life, infinite possibility remains after-the-fact of chosen path. Social ecstasy as the emptying out of oneself toward a social produces and is produced by infinite possibility.

Direction is one grounding of choreosonic performance and performativity, taking us to sea coastal South Carolina and Georgia generally and to Sapelo Island, GA, the home of Bilali, particularly. This latter island and this figure are both important for our understanding of a politics of avoidance found in the performance of the shout tradition when we consider the purposiveness of directionality on such a small piece of land just off the coast of Georgia.

> If you had been standing on the white sands of this island [Sapelo Island, GA] at dayclean in 1803, or a little later, you might have seen a tall, dark-skinned man with narrow features, his head covered with a cap resembling a Turkish fez, unfold his prayer mat, kneel and pray to the east while the sun rose. This was Bilali, the most famous and powerful of all the Africans who lived on this island during slavery days, and the first of my ancestors I can name.[27]

Born approximately 1760 in Timbo, Futa Jallon, Bilali was stolen into laborious conditions as a teenager and taken to Middle Caicos before being sold to one Thomas Spalding of Sapelo Island in 1802. A collection of writings, known as *Ben Ali's Diary*, was at least partially written by Bilali in Arabic script.[28] On a general level, the movement of Arabic scripting is a counterwestern orientation toward the word, the statement, the phrase, the sentence. Writing occurs from right to left, which may share some resonance with the counterclockwise movements of Kaaba circumambulation. If *directionality matters* is the foundational claim regarding the politics of avoidance; let the direction of script serve as one such alluvial element.

Sapelo Island residents even today show the influence of Bilali that resonates through the performance of direction even in decidedly Christological spaces. Of note is the following passage of Cornelia Bailey, a woman born and raised on Sapelo Island who cherishes the traditions of the land:

> When I'd go to say my nightly prayer, I'd better not, I repeat, I'd better not let Mama catch me with my head turned to the West. I was up for a good fussing at if she did. (. . .) The first thing I learned when it came to directions was East and West. Forget the South and the North. I knew at an early age that the sun rose in the East, so it was easy to pinpoint, and I knew the West, because the sun sets there and the darkness begins. So I knew my directions and who I was supposed to be praying to and who I was supposed to be avoiding. It was God resides in the East. Pray to God, not the devil. We had Muslim and Christian beliefs blended in our religious rituals and praying to the East was the most important Muslim one.[29]

Directionality matters, and it carries the material trace of the purposiveness of movement—turning, tuning, torque—toward social ecstasy. The posture of the flesh has spiritual and spatiotemporal consequences, has particular force when engaged with a social choreography. And the politics of avoidance is enacted at the level of this social choreography that is the reservoir of memory and dissent. Perhaps we can imagine how the eastward orientation, in prayer and praise, in the New World after the fact of the Middle Passage became a moment of acknowledgment for the ancestry, life as stolen flesh. The western world—the direction toward which the enslaved were brought and newly inhabited—was animated by the theological and philosophical aversion for the objects, for the materiality of things, for the persons found in the East. Eastward orientation speaks before, anti- and ante-, this rupture.

Directionality serves as memorial performance. As the first of her ancestors that she can name, Cornelia Bailey bespeaks how Bilali and his posture toward the east are important facts of memory. That memory is a fact of the materiality of the flesh; memory is enfleshed and remembrance is prompted at each performance of the *turn* to the east. Sapelo is the ground upon which the convergence of influences occurs. But is there a relationship between the circumambulation around the Kaaba and the Ring Shout that Bilali and his descendants index? The relationship might just be borne out on another excess, another accouterment, another throw-away material trace: the Turkish fez. I consider the efficacy of the performance of sartorial stylings as bound up with a more general religiocultural way of life. The fez or hat, always remembered as Turkish, functions as a bridge not only to Islam in general, but Sufi Islam in particular and the circular dance of Dervishes, whirling or spinning.

Fourteenth-century Sufi practitioner Ahmad Zarruq described Sufism "a science whose objective is the reparation of the heart and turning it away from all else but God,"[30] and this turn and turn away is evident with Bilali and his descendants' eastward prayers, as well as the counterclockwise moves of the Ring Shout. Sufi whirling or spinning is meditative and Sufi Islamic practices reached Timbo, Futa Jallon by the seventeenth century. It is probable, or we can at least speculate, that Sufism at least in part influenced the Islamic practices of Bilali. Sufism is defined by its doubled choreographic: to draw close to and experience the presence of Allah most intimately in this life as well as to experience *tawhid* (Divine Unity). The aesthetic practice of whirling or spinning allows one to experience this intimacy and presence of divinity, and this experience is prompted by a circularity that is counterclockwise, enacted by the individual but performed as, and is the creation of, a social.

Importantly, I am not making an argument about linearity or causation that leads us from whirling to *saut* to Ring Shout to Blackpentecostal shouting, as that would present a simple teleology created by a unidirectional path toward a proper, normative ecstatics and response. And we just don't have "proof" or "evidence" of such an easy set of causations and effectations. Rather, I argue that Blackpentecostalism's energetic field set loose in the twentieth-century United States existed before that historic 1906 Azusa

Street moment in various commons, various traditions and performances of sharing, of being together tightly in space and moving together. Black-pentecostalism simply brought into relief an enactment of radical openness and sociality that has been of fact of life, "evading each and every natal occasion,"[31] and as such, it is irreducible and anoriginal.

Bilali and his descendants' performances of the Ring Shout on Sapelo Island, GA—called simply "shouting" in the religious context or given various names such as the Buzzard Lope as a "secular" example—allow for a more robust analysis of this antebellum practice generally.

A space is cleared by moving the benches, and the men and women arrange themselves, generally alternatedly, in a ring, their bodies quite close. The music starts and the ring begins to move. Around it goes, at first slowly, then with quickening pace. Around and around it moves on shuffling feet that do not leave the floor, one foot beating with the heel a decided accent in two-four time. The music is supplemented by the clapping of hands. As the ring goes around it begins to take on signs of frenzy. The music, starting, perhaps with a Spiritual, becomes a wild, monotonous chant. The same musical phrase is repeated over and over one, two, three, four, five hours. The words become a repetition of an in-coherent cry. The very monotony of sound and motion produces an ecstatic state. Women, screaming, fall to the ground prone and quivering. Men, exhausted, drop out of the shout. But the ring closes up and moves around and around.[32]

This dance tradition, performed on the seacoasts of South Carolina and Georgia, presents the convergence of sacred practices on the ground, a choreosonic performance that rose to the occasion of enslavement's desire to make of them socially dead subjects, without honor, alienated through natal practice.[33] With the performance of the Ring Shout, the formation of the circle produced the occasion for excitement to spread from person to person. Some danced a heel-toe maneuver with tumult, others trembling with staggered movement, others still stooped and rose, some whirled, some twisted side to side. These variegated movements produced the circle in which the performance occurred. The variegation did not only occur on the level of the movements. The movements, the choreography, were always also the production of sonicity: a trembled foot upon the ground vibrated, and thus sounded out, differently than a heel-toe tumult. Ending often with sighs and laughs, shouters audibly breathed responses—breathed strange utterances—attendant to such movements and motives, sounding out together while simultaneously marking the individual's enfleshed performance of sociality as dissent.

The Ring Shout is but one performance of centrifugitivity: within the circumambulatory counterclockwise movements as a social form, individual twists and turns of individual flesh. Centripetal and centrifugal movements at one and the same time, the secretion of aesthetic modes of existence as preparation for battle is centrifugitivity. Centrifugitivity illustrates the assertion of uniqueness and divergence, dissent and descent, as the grounds for a social gathering of thought. The possibility for social form here is dissent, dissent that is anoriginary. Each shouter intentions their own motives and movements in concert with and as relation between the social form created at the moment of danced encounter. Perhaps this is an Enlightenment grounded in social relation between, where what the dancers escape into is the social world against the conditions of being shored up against sensory deprivation, where they enter into the social space in order to perform otherwise organization. These persons moved their flesh with intentionality of the social form they were in process of creating in mind; they had to think the social to make the social.

Whether whirling, *saut* or ring, shouting occurs in the circle—a geometric, spatial form that allows the irruption for centrifugitive irruption while concurrently being such an irruption—dispersing vitality such that the individuals could reach fatigue. Lorenzo Dow Turner, in his *Africanisms in the Gullah Dialect* writes that *saut* means "to move around the Kabaa . . . until exhausted" and that *sauwata* means "to run until exhausted."[34] Until exhausted. Even if the object of concern—is it a choreography or sonicity, is it dance or sound—is under dispute, the consistency of vibrating the flesh as dance, as sound, until exhaustion is important. What does it mean to push the flesh to exhaustion, what is it about exhaustion that is desired for performance? What does exhaustion mean for the flesh that is supposed to produce continually for others under duress? How does exhaustion recover, how does it speak back, against the degradation of the flesh? This is particularly striking for the enslaved, many of whom after having worked sunup to sundown, would steal away and perform such dances into the early hours of the morning. The geometric circle, the spatializing loci of such dance, lays bare the ways in which centrifugitivity is the desire for spontaneous, spirited dispersal of love, life, after the point of possibility, when possibility has been fully realized and exasperated.[35] These performances of Ring Shout were figurations of sociality: that what occurred with sighs, laughter, perspiration, and exhaustion while being together, in one place, on one according, waiting for, while at the same time producing, the sound of a rushing mighty wind of change and dissent with each jerked foot, snapped body was a politics, a form of life, a critique of the given, violent, violative world. The Ring Shout as a social form of centrifugitivity carried the indeterminacy of meaning, and this indeterminacy was the condition of its possibility.

At the turn of the twentieth century, William Seymour and Charles Harrison Mason—both key figures of twentieth-century Blackpentecostalism—began peregrinations and a holy vagrancy of sorts in order to find experience, "an experience [which] is something you come out of changed."[36] William Seymour was founder of the Azusa Street, Apostolic Mission Church where the global Pentecostal twentieth-century movement was "birthed" in 1906. Previous to his arrival in Los Angeles, he traveled the country continually seeking a deeper, more profound, material experience of God. Charles Harrison Mason, founder of the Church of God in Christ also traveled the country seeking a divine encounter, an encounter of experience. Having met Seymour previously in Mississippi, Mason traveled to the Apostolic Mission in 1906 to learn more about the Holy Ghost experience people were proclaiming and likewise had the "baptism in the Holy Spirit" with the experience of speaking in tongues. The varied directions—from Louisiana to Indiana, Ohio, Mississippi, Texas, and California in the case of Seymour, and from Tennessee to Arkansas, Mississippi, and California for Mason—set the grounds for an experience of spirituality that was about the aesthetics of spatiality, the aesthetics of directionality, the aesthetics, that is, of choreosonic performance. Seymour and Mason were continually on the search, involved in seeking out, through extension and critique, for what some of John Wesley's followers called "experimental religion."[37]

And the experimental had everything to do with the experiential. Seymour and Mason went in search of experience, and that search was a kind of inventiveness, the creation of velocity force field, centrifugitive desire. What they discovered, perhaps most profoundly, was an ongoing need for discovery: the continual invocation of dissent as descent, further below, deeper, underground. They knew that they wanted something deeper and more profound than Wesleyan-Holiness sanctification. They literally traveled all over the country in search of experience, seeking something through which they would enter, and come out, changed. This search was generative and profound.

Zora Neale Hurston performed anthropological, sociological studies of this religious movement.[38] Her analysis is important because she understood the class struggle that this seemingly new religiocultural movement articulated: "The Sanctified Church is a protest against the high-brow tendency in Negro Protestant congregations as the Negroes gain more education and wealth."[39] She stated that this sect was "a revitalizing element in Negro music and religion" and that this collection of groups was "putting back into Negro religion those elements which were brought over from Africa and grafted onto Christianity."[40] Grant Wacker corroborates these pronouncements, stating, "pentecostal worship oscillate[s] between antistructural and structural impulses. Planned spontaneity, we might call it."[41] Hurston noticed and extended a discourse regarding this revitalizing element in negro religiosity, the choreosonics of such a movement, the ways movement was integral to the enunciation of social life:

> There can be little doubt that shouting is a survival of the African 'possession' by the gods. In Africa it is sacred to the priesthood or acolytes, in America it has become generalized. (. . .) Broadly speaking, shouting is an emotional explosion, responsive to rhythm. It is called forth by: (1) sung rhythm; (2) spoken rhythm; (3) humming rhythm; (4) the foot-patting or hand-clapping that intimates very closely the tom-tom. . . .
>
> There are two main types of shouters: (1) silent; (2) vocal. There is a sort of intermediary where one stage is silent and the other vocal. The silent type take with violent retching and twitching motions. Sometimes they remain seated, sometimes they jump up and down and fling the body about with great violence. Lips tightly pursed, eyes closed. The seizure ends by collapse. The vocal type is the more frequent. There are all gradations from quiet weeping while seated, to the unrestrained screaming while leaping pews and running up and down the aisle. Some, unless restrained, run up into the pulpit and embrace the preacher. Some are taken with hysterical laughing spells.[42]

The class struggle internal to black social life was aestheticized and shouting was one such articulation to the resistance for certain social forms.

Aesthetic form, then, was not the merely aesthetic—aesthetic as, through modern thought, separable and distinct from theory—but an aesthetic practice that was the announcement and elaboration of collective, improvisational, intellectual practice. This collective, improvisational, intellectual practice took as its target class as a modality that produced difference and worked fundamentally against it. It was a labor practice in the service of producing otherwise possibilities for thought. What showed up for Hurston as "survivals" of African forms of "possession," Blackpentecostal shouting—after the Ring Shout had all but been stamped out of most communal practices—rose to the specific occasion of its occurrence. Blackpentecostal shouting Hurston documented enacted centrifugitive performance, the force necessary to produce multiple movements that have within them the capacity for descent and dissent. The shouting Hurston documented evince what Frantz Fanon called the refusal of positionality wherein "no strategic position is given preference" as the creation of, the grounds for, social form.[43] Blackpentecostal shouting creates a social and though it can be performed alone, it is the being together with others at the moment of such performance that is privileged. The individual shouter creates social form by mixing in an irreducibly already available individual styling. It makes the kids laugh and learn. It makes the elders happy to see spiritual change. This feeling of joy disperses through the congregation.

Rhythm is centripetal force—hovering overhead, in ears, vibrating within flesh—pulling toward its sonic, resonant center, but while it pulls others in, rhythm must act as its antithesis, centrifugally sending out signal from its varied centers. Centrifugitivity is the enactment of centripetal and centrifugal force spontaneously, simultaneously. But importantly, centrifugitivity is against the notion of centering.

Lambert stared at them a moment, then began by saying that all the talk of being 'more centered' was just that, *talk*, and had long ago become to easy to throw around anymore. He then asked what, or where, was this 'center' and how would anyone know it if it were there. He went on, tilting his chair back on its hind legs, folding his arms across his chest and saying that he wasn't sure anyone had anything more than the mere word 'center,' that it didn't simply name something one doesn't have and thus disguises a swarm of untested assumptions about. Then he shifted his argument a bit, saying that if our music does have a center, as he could argue it indeed does, how would someone who admits being 'somewhat uninformed' recognize it, that maybe the fellow from the radio station wasn't saying anything more than that our music churns out of a center other than his, one he's unfamiliar with.[44]

As with the Ring Shout, exhaustion after the snap, after the break, might be what is most desired with Blackpentecostal shouting. In Hurston's description, one sees the ontological edge she gave to the shout traditions. They are emotional explosions that are responsive to conditions of their possibility, but they are, likewise, called forth from some such submerged underground, inexhaustibly dense space. Called forth and responsive to, the shout tradition of our concern existed prior to its being hailed, the tradition is not just hallucinatory of sadness or melancholy but was used during enslavement to occasion resistance as well as create otherwise words, otherwise worlds, in the midst of the centering gravity of violence and violation. The centrifugitive force of shouting was sent out to destabilize, to decenter, the seeming totalizing force of centralizing violence. Seeking exhaustion, this falling out, this snap and laugh, choreosonics of Blackpentecostal aesthetics are about being and sustaining undoneness. As undone, these aesthetic practices are about the refusal of being centered, about dispersing with the spatiotemporal geometric logics of western civil society, a search, a performance, of otherwise directionality.

Charles Harrison Mason, COGIC's founder, wrote about the efficacy of shouting. In his pamphlet "Is It Right for the Saints of God to Dance?" he answered with an emphatic "yes."[45] But it is the extrapolation, the explication, the experience that moves beyond the "yes" that is moving:

> The children of God dance of God, for God, and to the praise and glory of his name. They have the joy of the spirit of the Lord in them, they are joyful to their King—the Christ. At times they may be dancing Christ is all, or none but Christ. How sweet it is to dance in Him and about Him, for he is all. So to dance in the Spirit of the Lord expresses joy and victory.[46]

Mason's description of shouting intrigues because of the way a centrifugitive architectonics structures his rendering of the dance within this Blackpentecostal sect. This centrifugitive structure occurs at the level of rhetoric, particularly the prepositions of, for, and to God, in and about Him.

This centripetal, centrifugal set of prepositions sets up, and maybe steals a-way, the *a*theological "space" in which the Blackpentecostal choreosonic performance not only took its place but also thrived and flourished therein. Mason's rhetoric was consistent with Ring Shout practices insofar as centrifugitivity was the grounds for making a way out of no way, grounds upon which sounds could emanate needed clearing.[47] But also with his rhetoric is the reinstantiation of directionality. Prepositions are "pointing" terms; they bespeak spatial orientation and positionality. At the moment of the enunciation of the dance *of*, *to*, and *for* God, *in* and *about* Him, Mason also rehearsed a particular hesitance with positionality that would have him stilled. No position was privileged, but each had the capacity to be broken and breaking. With the centrifugitive prepositionality—with each motor behavior—the *of*, *to*, and *for*, the *in* and *about*, were resourced simultaneously. Mason's pamphlet gave an *a*theological-*a*philosophical response to folks who deemed enthusiasm too moving and dance too erratic. He was cognizant of the critique of shouting as "dance," and he rose to the occasion of its response.

There is more, of course. There is the word itself, "shout/ing," and the problematics that come with its enunciation. The performative utterance shout/ing carries the trace of *saut*'s internal indeterminacy with regard to meaning. When one declares "the people were shouting today at church," for example, one would do well to seek clarification: Were these vocal utterances or movements of the flesh? Reading through several turn-of-the-twentieth-century Pentecostal periodicals—*The Apostolic Faith*, for example—when confronted with the word shout/ing, I each time wondered what was the nature of the shout. Was it the vocable, or the choreographic? For example, *The Apostolic Faith* records the following:

> Holy quietness does not mean to hold your mouth shut and not praise God. It means that the spirit hushes all the flesh. The Lord is in His holy temple and let all the flesh be silent before Him. This quietness will let the Spirit speak out in praises and shouts and song. It is holy quietness in heaven, when the praise is like the voice of 'many waters' and 'mighty thunderings.' (Rev. 19:6) We want this holy quietness all the time, so we will get used to heaven before we get there.[48]

What were the "shouts" about which the preacher—likely Seymour himself—briefly testified? Were they the choreographic, or the sonic? We will not, unfortunately, ever know, and it is this indeterminacy of meaning that undergirds such testimony. One would need to go there, experience there, feel there, hear there in order to have knowledge of such a field, such a moment. But even the question—was this choreographic or sonic—veils the truth of the choreosonic. Even if these were merely movements, those movements of flesh would have their attendant sonic registers. And if only merely vocalizing, such vocalizing would have its necessary choreographic resonances. The knowledge of shouting is the knowledge of hesitance, the knowledge of the very possibility of indistinction, the knowledge of indeterminacy.

The distinction, the categorical difference, of choreography and sonicity becomes undone. This is knowledge that is produced through the materiality of dwelling together with others, awaiting sounds and movements as the spirit gives utterance. The article from the *Los Angeles Daily Times* also gave a clue as to how shouting was first performed in this earliest moment of the movement: "Undismayed by the fearful attitude of the colored worshipper, another black woman jumped to the floor and began a wild gesticulation, which ended in a gurgle of wordless prayers which were nothing less than shocking."[49] She jumped to the floor and gesticulated. This was an eruption into and disruption of the service itself. Though someone had fallen out, "slain in the spirit," Blackpentecostals might say, worship continued undeterred. Such eruptions and disruptions are the yielding to surprise. The dissent apparent with the "undismayed" attitude was the yielding for others to worship "in their own way," originally differentiated, as the formation of the ring, of the circle, of the social way of life. Shouting no longer takes place within the circle, but the energy of whirling, of *saut* and Ring Shout, are dispersed, generalized, made available to all. All this from walks and runs and journeys in small compact spaces, on streets, across the country. Shouting, then, is but one choreosonic *a*theological-*a*philosophical way of life. It is one enfleshment of what a choreosonic performance and its tradition appears like in the world. But what then can we say of philosophy and theology as abstractions against which Blackpentecostal aesthetics evade? That is, how is blackness, black flesh, cognized within these two modalities of thought?

To GO FOR a walk everyday. For this walk to bespeak something of desire for knowledge, to think, to breathe, to get fresh air. Immanuel Kant's place in western philosophy, his residence in Enlightenment thought, cannot be understated. His place, his residence, can be analyzed if we give attention to the walking he did everyday. And such analysis gives us tools to both elaborate upon and critique how philosophy assumes thought can be hierarchized and how such hierarchy are racialized.

> When he had a house of his own, he had every day a few friends dine with him. He liked to have a mixed company—merchants, professional men, and especially a few younger men. After dinner followed regularly his daily walk for an hour or more, along what was from him named 'The Philosopher's Walk,' until he was driven from it by the number of beggars whom his habit of almsgiving had attracted there. Even the severest weather did not interfere with this daily walk, in which his earlier years he usually had companions; after sixty years of age he walked alone, for the reasons already mentioned.[50]

Offered here by Kant's daily programmatic is not an argument that choreographic, spatial language is used merely to metaphorically think about concepts, logic, reason, and judgment. Rather, this is an argument that what Kant calls philosophy, that the particularly strained mode of thought he produces, is made possible by the choreographic as a field of place and movement, his own quotidian peregrinations as an embodiment of such philosophizing. Daily walking to ruminate, to think, to go over, to ponder, to consider, daily walks to linger, to wander. Kant's thought had to be worked out *in the flesh* but it would be an experience of Blackpentecostal practice that he would come to suppress in the service of producing his *philosophical* thought.

What I'm saying is Kant desired to shout, to work out in the flesh, what he thought about. Yet it is the desire to shout, to be part of shout traditions that ran in him that was made felt, known through the refusal, the repression, of sociality. His desire was evinced by his sociability, his invitation to others to come to his home—as a gathering space for thought—in order to ruminate on a variety of topics. But where Kant falls short of shouting, while moving in its direction against his intentionally pronounced choreographies, is by his aversion to beggars. Beggars are those in need, those who make a request with consistency, urgency. What drove Kant away from the walkway he so named after his quotidian journeys was an aversion, not for the capacity of the street to carry and be sociality, but the material emergence of this fact. So many beggars. Too many beggars. It is not that beggars were an impossibility for his thought; indeed, he was an almsgiver. Rather, it was the number that surprised him, and this number was made possible by the street. Unlike his home, the street was a space of social gathering where all types of unavoidable, improvisational choreosonic modes of life relayed and interplayed. The street could not be rationalized, could not be controlled. The choreosonics of the street depended upon being open and available, vulnerable, to otherwise possibilities for movement.

The street is not a place where choreography happens as opposed to sonicity, or vice versa. The street is what makes intensely felt the confluence—which is to say the irreducible interrelation and resistance to categorical distinction—of the choreosonic as a way of life. It is a space, in other words, where Blackpentecostal shouting happens all of the time. Engaging in a walk at the same time each day along the same route is a choreographic itinerary and protocol for movement. Such that the very thing that drove Kant from the daily journey is the thing that drove his philosophic engagements, worry over the choreosonic materiality of the object. The aversion to beggars was simply the presencing of aversion as general philosophic performance. Not a ruse or a metaphorical flourish, aversion was a material way to be, and thus to think about being, in the world. If only those objects of aversion would move out the way:

> The knowledge of bodies as substances, and as changeable substances, is transcendental when it states that the changing must have a cause; but the principle is metaphysical when it asserts that the changing must have an external cause. In the first case, bodies need only be thought in terms of ontological predicates (pure intellectual concepts), i.e., as substance, for the proposition is to be understood a priori. In the second case, the empirical concept of a body, as a movable thing in space, must be introduced to support the proposition; although once this is done it may be seen quite a priori that the latter predicate, movement only by means of an external cause, applies to a body.[51]

A body is a moveable thing in space, in time. But the materiality of the thing is itself discardable in the service of producing philosophical thought. Kant preferred the amateriality of the physical object, as its realness had the capacity to be the very hindrance of thought. Nothing's got to be real for Kant, he's no Patti LaBelle.

In Kantian aesthetics, materiality that prompts aesthetic thought is immediately discardable once theorizing has commenced. Pure judgment relies upon the object's dematerializing while also claiming that the very materiality that prompts thought was never necessary. The materiality is not an a priori principle. Rather, aesthetic judgment is a detachment,[52] which can be organized, choreographed, without bodies. Kant's encounter with the overwhelming presence of beggars on the street, relinquishing his walk because of their bodies, was an anticorporeal choreographic itinerary. Materiality—any object itself—must be thought as an impenetrability (as that which can be grasped, held, and captured), after which thought as categorically distinct, after which thought choreographically (placed to the side, set at remove) in order for its contemplation. It is only after this threefold discarding of *other* thought that the possibility of the beautiful is enacted.[53] The beautiful emerges as the dance of the choreographer. The object of concern must be set at remove—at critical choreographic distance, at categorical distinction—for pure judgment. The materiality, then, is the impurity previous to choreographic philosophy. Yet there is a utility of impurity. Blackpentecostal aesthetic production bears this utility out. Yet there is a utility of impurity, it has a use value; it can be exploited. It shows up in philosophy as the object of aversion.

AVERSION. IT IS a turning and turning away of the flesh, of the mental faculties, from objects. Aversion is enacted in such a way that in Kantian aesthetics, such objects that produce aversion cannot produce the sensation of beauty. Yet, from where does the aversion emerge? Is it within the object, the abject thing, or in the one refusing such engagement? Aversion leaves a space open—a zone of choreosonic possibility—such that the one who feels aversion, whose flesh shudders and eyes shutter off and away, simply reflects on their own process of hermetically sealed thought. To be precise, the disgust that the subject feels is the disgust of and with the *self,* not with the object. The object becomes the ruse of philosophizing; it is the scapegoat.[54]

Enlightenment, Kant answered the question in 1784, is "the emergence from (one's) self-incurred minority" and minority, accordingly, is the "inability to make use of one's own understanding *without direction from another.*"[55] Enlightenment thought is the aversion to choreosonics, it is movement of the mind, of the faculties, of one's own accord without considering the space placement of another. Enlightenment is the emergence—the becoming, the bursting forth and free—into an antisocial, amaterial, way of knowing, thinking, doing, moving. It is the emergence of a different epistemology that assumes categorical distinction through discarding the materiality of objects. Of course to become, to burst forth and free are not, of themselves, problematic. This is not a critique of movement, emergence, or escape. Harriet Tubman burst into New York, having escaped by herself only to find her freedom anything but sweet because she was lonely. She returned to Maryland in order to have others abscond with her. If liberation were to mean anything, it would have to be a social thing, done together with others, a meditative, contemplative practice of sociality.[56] Kant's Enlightenment thought, however, is a desire to dance by oneself on the dance floor and to be unbothered by the sweat of another, nor their rhythms, nor smells. And not only dance but to move without such movements sounding out. It is a retreat from choreosonic possibility in order to produce knowledge. His thought presumes that such distinctions could be made and, as such, maintained. And the maintenance of the distinctions would be in the service of an analytics, an epistemology, a way of life. So what had to be suppressed in Kant's thought is the sounded movement, is the moving sound, that occasioned thought.

In order to think Enlightenment philosophy, the general choreographies of bodies, of objects, of things as well as the enactment of aversions in particular must be considered. For Kant, thinking was the enterprise of the individual; he did not allow for the masses to be thinking together, for there to be social thought. Yet to be considered, then, is the type of liberatory practice that can exist as a function of sociality. The beginning of Kant's Enlightenment thought is found in the averted posture toward, and thus against, the social, and the choreographic is the heart of aversive matters. Aversion, as the foundational claim for such movement, is a choreographic philosophy while likewise it is a philosophical choreography. To avert is to turn away, it is to withdraw, it is to alienate and estrange. To avert is to refuse to see, feel, experience an object because of the impulsive recoil away from that object, leaving the object intact. Such that the issue of what is theorized, what is cognized, what is thought through Enlightenment's aversion remains to be elaborated. That is, how does Enlightenment thought, how does philosophy in general, cognize the object from which it averts its gaze, its ear, rendering the materiality and material reality of such an object inconsequential?

Denise Ferreira da Silva, when writing about Kant's relationship to epistemology, says:

> By locating the conditions of possibility of knowledge before and beyond sense perception, postulating that terms such as time, space, substance, totality, and so on are the tools 'pure reason' provides to the understanding, (Kant) establishes that now scientific knowledge could progress independent of subjective (psychological) and purely empirical concerns and without principles derived solely from either of them.[57]

Thus epistemology, knowledge of reason, knowledge of purity, are the before and beyond; an assertion of its being otherwise than sensual perception. This before and beyond is spatial, the choreographic itinerary of aversion itself. To know "before and beyond experience" is to have aversion *for* sense perception and that which allows it, experience.

Experience is a problem. W.E.B. Du Bois's now infamous question—how does it feel to be a problem?—carries within it the trace of other attendant queries: How does it feel to be the object before and beyond sense perception; how does it feel to be experience? How does it feel to be specifically experience that produces averted gazes as the grounds for philosophy? And when inflected through the Awakening revivals that were occurring at the same time of Kant's writing, participating in a similar configuratory project of averting blackness, we might ask Du Bois's question anew: How does it feel to be enthusiastic (about which more below)? So we shuffle and leap toward Kant's theorizing aesthetics, time, and space because of his influence, both in assisting to constitute and understanding of Enlightenment thought but also because of the ongoingness of his status within the western philosophic tradition.

In his *Critique of Judgment*, Kant gave a method for considering the type of reflection that makes Enlightenment philosophizing possible as a choreographic itinerary and protocol.

> Hence philosophy is properly divided into two parts quite distinct in their principles; a theoretical part, as Philosophy of Nature and a practical part, as Philosophy of Morals, and this last is what is called practical legislation for the reason based upon the concept of freedom. However, up till now these expressions have been grossly misused in dividing the different principles, and through them, philosophy. . . . Now, in

the division of a science of reason, everything turns on the difference between objects requiring different principles for understanding.[58]

Evident are the divisions, the splits, the displacements that make the possibility for the discovery of rationality. For Kant, "everything turns on the difference between objects," and this turning is a turning away, an aversion for the materiality of objects, of things in general and an averse corporeal-metaphysical reaction to certain anthropological bodies, objects in the particular. Like the racial emphysema causing heart palpitations and triggering heightened, excited breathing, excited breathing that produced lynching violence. Kant's epistemic production was necessarily divisional among space and time, among concepts, among objects. This is choreographic. It is about the division of labor, about the transformation of *potentia* to *kinesthesia* of the theoretical, of the concept, that made the material body inconsequential. The interior thought processes yield a certain ordering of the world, of experience. And if philosophy can be (im)properly divided—sectioned, cornered, moved—we must consider the objects of such divisional labor. And more, philosophy in general is divided up, it is produced through the capacity to make a claim that categorical distinction is not only possible, but that distinction can remain pure. Nature and morals, he says, are the categorically distinct zones into which one properly divides to produce philosophical thought.

Kant also elaborates the concept of the sublime and here, too, is a choreographic modality of thought, sullied by an aversion for objects, an aversion for materiality and sociality. The sublime in Kantian philosophy—a fact of quantity—leads to "an outrage of the imagination" because it refuses apprehension. This refusal of being apprehended, grasped, held, however, does not mean it can't be contemplated.[59] This refusal of apprehension, because of quantitative fact, overwhelms the possibility for thought. Yet, this refusal of apprehension does not mean the sublime cannot produce pleasure. The sublime presents infinite possibility as it cannot be "contained in any sensuous form."[60] Its irreducibility and originary displacement is a problem for philosophic thought. The apprehension in the mind as sublime is a ruse since the sublime is the resistance to apprehension, existing as open-ended. This presents the impossibility of the object's material existence. Yet the attempt is still made to "know" philosophically the objects that produce the sublime. And this knowability is based upon what Foucault believes is the Enlightenment's assumption of the impenetrability of objects. This impenetrability becomes the occasion for the assumption of the possibilities for *any* object by way of the lack of interiority of *some* objects.

Enlightenment as the staging of rationalist discourse assumes the impenetrability of objects as the foundation for knowledge.[61] Impenetrability conceptually precludes the possibility of solicitation and invite. Kant's judgment of taste elucidates: "The judgment of taste does not depend upon a concept (namely that of a general ground of the subjective appropriateness of nature for the power of judgment), but one from which nothing can be known of the object, and nothing proved, because it is in itself indeterminable and useless for knowledge."[62] How does one have a knowledge of that which is useless for knowledge; what extends outward from such an object of impossible epistemic possibility? Impenetrability functions as *telos*, as the grounded assumption of the object that allows for the grasping or aversion of, to, and for, in and about things. Impenetrability of the object is transformed through rationalist discourse from the circumstance of the philosopher lacking of knowledge to the very possibility for having knowledge. Rationalist language of Enlightenment thought is a posture toward the ground and production of knowledge by positing the impenetrability of the object (and quite possibly a more general antifeminist, antiqueer, worry over the penetrability of things, where what is supposed of penetration is denigration rather than the possibility of and for pleasure). After such impenetrability is established in *philosophical* thought, the philosopher then posits that the object must be assumed, taken up into his grasp, captured, stolen. This belief in impenetrability is grounded in the concept of categorical distinction as axiomatic, this belief presumes that the possibility for discovery has been exhausted, exhaustion as an endpoint rather than a place from which to begin. How is it possible for that which is open-ended and resists enclosure, that which is resistant previous to thought, to be thought? The mind must exceed its only capacity for thought and exist—think, dance, leap—in that otherwise spatiotemporal zone.

Kant theorized, in his Transcendental Aesthetic, concepts of space and time. Written in 1781 before "Answer to the Question: What is Enlightenment" (1784) and *Critique of Judgment* (1793), Kant's writing about the Transcendental Aesthetic literally cleared the spatiotemporal ground for the dance and play of his philosophical reasoning.

The effect produced by an object upon the faculty of representation (*Vorstellungsfähigkeit*), so far as we are affected by it, is called sensation (*Empfindung*). An intuition (*Anschauung*) of an object, by means of sensation, is called empirical. The undefined object of such an empirical intuition is called phenomenon (*Erscheinung*). In a phenomenon I call that which corresponds to the sensation its matter; but that which causes the manifold matter of the phenomenon to be perceived as arranged in a certain order, I call its form. Now it is clear that it cannot be sensation again through which sensations are arranged and placed in certain forms. The matter of all phenomena is given us *a posteriori*; but their form must be ready for them in the mind (*Gemüth*) *a priori*, and must therefore be capable of being considered as separate from all sensations. I call all representations in which there is nothing that belongs to sensation, pure (in a transcendental sense). The pure form therefore of all sensuous intuitions, that form in which the manifold elements of the phenomena are seen in a certain order, must be found in the mind *a priori*.[63]

The materiality of objects corresponds to sensation and is only felt after the fact of encounter, but the form of the object exists erstwhile situations, form is always already "ready" in the mind, waiting for objects to be assumed— taken up in, subsumed, and captured—in philosophical thought. Spatial organizing for thought occurs here, a choreographic itinerary and protocol for the ordering and movement of, to, and for, in and about representation, sensation, intuition, and phenomenon. It is the grounds of thought, the matter, that becomes unnecessary for philosophical pondering, as it is form that, for Kant, exists a priori. The order for thinking objects is an ordering that seeks out verification for some preexistent arrangement. Sensation is "arranged and placed in certain forms," and this choreography of sensation is an interplay of movement that produces sensible, pure knowledge. The ordering of form "must be found in the mind *a priori*" as an irreducible purity. But this purity is the aversion to thinking the impure. Philosophical choreography of turning away from the object is the way to produce the proper intellectual, scholar, thinker, philosopher, the subject. "In general these conditions pertain to that specific conception of identity—here that particular construal of philosophical identity—in which identity is both established and secured as a result of initial differentiation."[64] The philosopher establishes the identity as philosopher through an initial differentiation, the assumption that differentiation exists, that distinction, categorical, is possibility.

Alas, Kant shored up against materiality and ended up with a theory of thinking the self, himself, the human subject as the reflection of an *a priori* fear of the matter of things. In Kant's elaboration of Enlightenment and aesthetics, space is not a thing of itself but is the displacement created by the movement of an object.[65] Space confers upon objects form, size, and position, but elsewhere, when Kant discussed the beautiful and the sublime, they each depend upon the abstraction and discardability of the materiality of the object. So what type of object takes up space for Kant? It appears that they are objects of the mind; they exist as a priori concepts and are reflections of the antisociality of thought, the escape from self-incurred minority into the release of seclusion and aloneness that is productive of the scholar, of the thinker. Kant produced his argument about the nonnecessity of the materiality of objects by stating that difference, and difference as placement, emerges previous to the actual arrangement and placement. The arrangements and placements of representation occur in the mind of the philosopher and *produce* the objects of concern. Such that what is noticed, seen, felt, is an effect of what the philosopher wants to notice, see, feel.

The representation of the object by the displacement of materiality before encounter is constitutive of philosophic thought. And Kant grounds the possibility of space in the concept of the subject; only the subject can have a sense of space. The proper subject is the one that adheres to the separation, the categorical distinction, of the materiality of the object from the thinking its ground of possibility. The possibility of subjectivity is given by the multiple shifts, movements, and displacements of materiality. The very concept of the subject, grounded in the Transcendental Aesthetic of space, is a displacement and, as such, articulates the choreography animating a mode of cognition antagonistic to Blackpentecostal aesthetic performance.

Of the Transcendental Aesthetic of Time, Kant says, "Time is not an empirical concept deduced from any experience, for neither coexistence nor succession would enter into our perception, if the representation of time were not given *a priori*. Only when this representation *a priori* is given, can we imagine that certain things happen at the same time (simultaneously) or at different times (successively)."[66] However, this *a priori* necessity establishes for Kant that "time has one dimension only; different times are not simultaneous, but successive, while different spaces are never successive, but simultaneous."[67] Though Kant could *imagine* that things could happen concurrently, simultaneously, at the same time, he almost immediately qualified his statement saying that after the a priori principle of time as representational is established, that time cannot exist in simultaneity. As a philosophical concept, time for Kant is the gathering and discarding of imaginative excess. Imagination is that which makes simultaneity possible and also that which is ungrounded. It is this ungroundedness that makes it necessarily discardable. Philosophical thought, so construed, is a failure of imagination; it refuses to think *too much*, it is a refusal to think alongside, think aligned with, excess. To restate differently, categorically distinct, categorically pure philosophical thought is simply another enclosure of and on thought in order to produce and perform a unique, intellectual self. Philosophical thought is produced through the enclosure on and discarding of imaginative excess, an excess that exists previous to situation. Such thought is produced by the aspirational tendency for and desiring of an enclosed, bordered, coherent, stable subject position, place in space and time. This desire to be a subject, to be Man, to perform the coloniality of being/power/truth/freedom, subordinates and closes off thought from its being irreducibly, anoriginally open.[68] The enclosure of and on thought is what produces the categorical distinction wherein some thought matters and other thought is discarded. And this as the grounds for philosophizing. Imagination is forced to fail, to not exceed its delimitation, to withdraw itself within predetermined borders.

Yet simultaneity, which is sociality, is what makes polyrhythm possibility. *Ekstasis* is the state of being enraptured, being beside oneself, and such being is a spatiotemporal disruption. The choreographic that informs the grounds of Enlightenment thought is the likewise discardability, of sonicity, the sound, the imagination. The choreographic as severed from the sonic that is the grounds for Enlightenment thought privileges time as succession, as teleology. But what of the sociality of polyrhythmia? Afro-Arabic *saut*, South Carolina and Georgia sea coastal Ring Shout, and twentieth-century Blackpentecostal shouting offer something of a rejoinder to such choreographic itinerary and protocol, to such categorical distinction. The shout traditions offer a collective, social intellectual practice that is *a*theological and *a*philosophical.

Polyrhythmia contradicts the philosophy of aversion through a politics of avoidance; it voids time as a succession with purposive "ends." Kant's subject is produced through "bad timing." Kant's subject is produced by the desire for simultaneity that is achievable spatially but not temporally. And this is a problem because the kinesthetic force that produces the subject in Kant's Transcendental Aesthetic is centrifugal, making the subject a spatiotemporal movement away from itself. The very concepts of time and space, temporality and spatiality, are split, categorically maintained as distinct, and ordered according to a choreographic arrangement in the service of placement and constraint, grounding the very possibility of the utility of imaginative excess. "The field for observations of these peculiarities of human nature is very extensive and still conceals a rich lode for discoveries that are as charming as they are instructive. For now, *I will cast my glance* only on several places that seem especially to stand out in this region, and even on these more with the eye of an observer than of the philosopher."[69] To glance is to avert the gaze previous to encounter with an object, with a thing. This glance, this averted gaze, carries with it the material content of the choreosonic politics of avoidance that Blackpentecostal aesthetics employ.[70] And what is the differentiation between the observer and philosopher except what has been determined by the would-be philosopher as distinct?

The fourth section of such "observations" is where Kant explicitly spoke about race and racialization, about the black. He spoke in consistently problematic—but certainly, programmatic, choreographic—ways.

The Negroes of Africa have by nature no feeling that rises above the ridiculous. Mr. Hume challenges anyone to adduce a single example where a Negro has demonstrated talents, and asserts that among the hundreds of thousands of blacks who have been transported elsewhere from their countries, although very many of them have been set free, nevertheless not a single one has ever been found who has accomplished something great in art or science or shown any other praiseworthy quality, while among the whites there are always those who rise up from the lowest rabble and through extraordinary gifts earn respect in the world. So essential is the difference between these two human kinds, and it seems to be just as great with regard to the capacities of mind as it is with respect to color. . . .

In the lands of the blacks can one expect anything better than what is generally found there, namely the female sex in the deepest slavery? ... Indeed, Father Labat reports that a Negro carpenter, whom he reproached for haughty treatment of his wives, replied: You whites are real fools, for first you concede so much to your wives, and then you complain when they drive you crazy. There might be something worth considering, except for the fact that this scoundrel was completely black from head to foot, a distinct proof that hat he said was stupid.[71]

The capacity of Kant's Enlightenment thought to understand anything about the negro, anything of the black, was immediately inhibited by the aversion, the choreographic gathering and placement to the side, of thought that undergirded Kant's rendering of some others' thoughts. What does that mean? It means Kant first acquiesced to Mr. Hume and then to Father Labat, they acted as the verifications for and the grounds of his philosophic thought. What was coordinated there, in time, in space, as a choreographic arrhythmia at the heart of his theorizing? Kant's theory of Enlightenment was founded upon the escape from sociality and sociability in order to think oneself alone. The scholar, the philosopher, the subject would emerge when that individual thinks for himself without the aid of others. Throughout the whole of his observations, Kant's glance alone was enough to think the various peoples of the world, prejudicial though his thoughts may have been. But when it came to the negro, to the black, to the concept and ground of thinking such being, Kant deferred to others, he entered into the very conditions that Enlightenment would escape.

Color, for Kant, came to stand in for the set of mental incapacities of the black. The incapacity to think, the inability to be anything other than stupid, Kant would find on the epidermis. The epidermis was useful insofar as it made it acceptable and expedient to necessitate a social project of thought in order to declare a truth, a social project that was the antithesis to the formation of the scholar, of the philosopher, of the subject. Kant's thought about race was constituted by the fundamental incapacity to think a certain set of objects as a function of enlightened, aversive choreographies. Kant's Enlightenment thought, we might say, is not yet begun. An enlightened philosophy of blackness was not achievable for Kant. As the skin stood in for a certain incapacity to think, this philosophical tradition was constituted by that impenetrable incapacity. But lingering is a question of the meaning of the object that resisted the glance, the object that required thought to be social. The "logical" possibility for Enlightenment and for a universalism is broken down before its enactment by the concept of blackness, the figure of the black, the negro. To establish an Enlightenment depends upon a glance at, which is at the same time an aversion for, blackness wherein the object of the glance, of the averted gaze is placed off to the side of, and is made the peripheral to, thought.

Enlightenment, so construed, is the coordination of such displacement; it is the choreographic itinerary and protocol for claiming an object by refusing its counterfactual. We must think the grid created by such thought and what slipped through the cracks. This grid is the zone of articulation for the irreducible unrepresentability of blackness as "proper" and property. This zone lays bare blackness as "irreducibly disordering," as the resistance to being owned even in the place of the mind. Blackness and subjectivity are constantly at odds, and Kant rightly stumbled upon it as an emergence of the social. His vulgar dismissal of blackness still instantiated the constitutive nature of blackness: the production of a sociality. This is not to claim that sociality, of itself, produces only good things but rather to highlight the inescapability of sociality. Sociality is otherwise possibility enacted in the flesh. This otherwise possibility thwarts epistemological projects based on pure reason, purity itself, categorical distinction. The negro as character and the black skin as color serve as the giving of general, natural purpose in the world.

> The purposive character in an organization is surely the general reason for inferring a preparation that is originally placed in nature of a creature with this intent, and for inferring created germs, if this end could only be obtained later on. Now with respect to the peculiarity of a race, this purposive character can be demonstrated nowhere so clearly as in the Negro race. . . . Thus it was an arrangement very wisely made by Nature to organize their skin such that the blood, since it is does not by far sufficiently remove enough phlogiston through the lungs, could depholistize itself much more strongly through the skin than is the case with us. It thus had to transport a lot of phlogiston into the ends of the arteries, thereby becoming overloaded with it in this location, that is, under the skin itself, and so shine through black, although it is still red in the interior of the body. Moreover, the different organization of Negro skin from ours is already noticeable through touch.—As far as the purposiveness of the organization of the other races is concerned, to

the extent that it can be inferred from their color, it is indeed not possible to demonstrate it with equal probability.[72]

Kant's logic *danced around the subject* by an insistent centrifugal force that created distance—space—between the subject of philosophy, and the thinker that begs, between the subject of philosophy and the thinker that dances. What Kant desired was a choreographic itinerary and protocol for thought protected from external obstructional circumambulation but he encountered the choreosonic noise of beggars, with their insistent pleas and complaints. There was an arrhythmia at the heart of Kant's initial movement—a resistance to the materiality, his escape from self-incurred vibratory force—where what he dispensed with was a sociality that would balance, centripetally recalibrating his position. Turns out, further still, that the "subject" of philosophy is the reflection of the "thinker" of philosophy. And this is found most emphatically with his anthropology of race. Kant did not think Africa or the Negro or the black; rather, he thought his relation to Africa and the negro and the black that was simply the choreographic forceful turn and turn away from the possibility of sociality, from the production of knowledge that would not only endure but desire to deepen self-incurred minority. His relation to Africa, the negro and the black was his relation to the grounds of dancing around a subject that set into motion his antisociality as the production of the concept of subjectivity, of himself as subject. His aversion, as racialization, was an aversive reaction to himself as subject, choreographically displaced into an othered spatiotemporal field and body, of dark continents. The confrontation with the negro, with blackness, produced within Kant a compulsory consideration of the meaning of things having a purpose grounded in nature. This grounding is organizational; it bestowed a general understanding of difference. But if, as I have attempted to demonstrate, Kant had an aversion for negroes, for blacks, for blackness as a concept, aversion operated as a natural and generalizable aversion for things.

Blackness serves a purpose in intellectual projects, philosophical *and* theological both. The "purposiveness" Kant ascribes to negroes in his philosophic thought shared a conception of the utility of the "other" during the Great Awakening revivals. A racial/ist logic—based on New World subjectivities of discrete purity of difference, of categorical distinction—was the lifeblood of much of the preaching during the Great Awakening revival moments.[73] "Indians" and "Blacks" were utilized as the most marginal, peripheral test case scenarios for the possibilities of God's saving grace. Believers—white—would come to know the power of their god by how he'd consider and save those *they* considered savage. The Awakening revivals, like Kant's "purposiveness," created a categorical distinction—the negro, the savage, as categorically different from the white—in order to consider the nature of objects and teleology *as natural and general.* Dreadfulness, sadness, and fear—particularly, of death and hell—were foundational claims for prompting majorities toward salvation with the Awakening revivals. Salvation, as a "new and living way," was a gathering around the concepts of scarcity rather than abundance, terror rather than pleasure, contempt rather than joy. People converted through these revivals spoke of pleasure and joy. However, the grounds for such pleasure and joy were only after-the-fact of such *theological*—constrained thought, thought that assumed categorical distinction as anthropological truth—claims.

Jonathan Edwards is important for this discussion because of the legendary place he holds in an American imaginary of religious intrigue. His famous sermon, "Sinners in the Hands of an Angry God,"[74] is thought to have been preached in response to the "New York City Plot" wherein negroes were charged with setting fires in the city and burglarizing in 1741. Considering this sermon is productive for larger claims about theology as enacting an aversion for choreosonic possibility, an aversion for blackness.[75] Though preached before Kant's critical writings, the Awakening revivals spanned a temporal measure that was both in response to the beginnings of Enlightenment thought and was a residue of its aftermath. The Awakening revivals and Enlightenment thought, when considering blackness, was a *tradition*, was the performance of choreographic moves, shuffles, and leaps. The tradition cohered around the aversive object, the fact of blackness. Edwards preached an anthropology and theology of blackness. "Sinners" is particularly symptomatic. Not only were the sermon's imagery and force constituted by the revolutionary insurrectionist fugitivity of enslaved blacks and poor whites in Manhattan, but the sermon was a direct reflection of the a general paranoia and worry about the capacity for black radical resistance to enslavement practices, given the fact that no white person was killed during the insurrectionist episode. The disproportionate response to the "plot" has been compared, in magnitude, to the Salem Witch Trials of 1691, given the fact that 150 persons had to stand trial between April and July 1741 and because 32 persons were convicted and sentenced to death.

In the sermon, Edwards pontificates:

> There is nothing that keeps wicked men, at any one moment, out of hell, but the mere pleasure of God. By 'the mere pleasure of God,' I mean his sovereign pleasure, his arbitrary will, restrained by no obligation, hindered by no manner of difficulty, any more than if nothing else but God's mere will had in the least degree, or in any respect whatsoever, any hand in the preservation of wicked men one moment. . . .
>
> The misery you are exposed to is that which God will inflict to that end, that he might show what that wrath of Jehovah is.[76]

Thinking Edwards's words with relation to the New York rebels, his concerns become peculiarly quickened by the prospect a *becoming black* of the unconverted. This *becoming black* is evinced through the loss of sovereignty, by being—so thought—totally controlled by the will of another, one omnipotent. This *becoming black* would be the material, corporeal embodiment of remaining sinners at the hand of a sovereign that can at will put to death those who may rise against such a divine figure. This *becoming black* would be punishment. If Toni Morrison is correct about there being an Africanist presence in American literature generally, this would likewise be true of American sermonizing.[77] The condition elaborated for sinners in Edwards's sermon was the generalized condition of the enslaved as a juridical, theological, and philosophical preoccupation. The hearers of Edwards's sermon were cognizant of the happenings in New York and, thus, had the example of what was done to the enslaved as a matter of material fact and historic condition. The more than thirty were hanged for their purported capacity to kill, for a general insurrectionist sociality, their feet were on slippery ground as they existed in a situation and institution that could, at will, choose a variety of aesthetic productions for death.

That Edwards invoked fire is notable because poor whites and the enslaved conspired together to perform a series of fires throughout the city and those sentenced to death were burned at the stake. Sinners in the hands of an angry deity could just as well be paralleled to consider the enslaved and their co-conspirators in the hands of an angry nation-state. And perhaps that was the point. We must consider the pleasure of the sovereign—both a deity and the nation-state—and how that pleasure comes about. Edwards's deity had the power to condemn and kill at will but exercised restraint as a mode of pleasure and enjoyment because, according to him, the sinners deserve their demise. This was Calvinist theology-philosophy, and the institution of enslavement bore that out. The enslaved people and poor whites that incited insurrection in 1741 against the capitalist class struggle and enslavement were sinners by way of birth, through the choice of the all-wise sovereign of the heavenlies and of the state. They were, already, upon slippery ground and at the mercy of a kind and restrained deity. The ends that these sinners of a motley crew met, of course then, was divine justice. But this justice depended upon a system already set in place wherein they would not be able to ever win, an inequitable situation wherein they would always be cast as other, as material representation of objects of knowledge. They were predestined for such failure.

Similar to Kant's Transcendental Aesthetic of space, this would be an a priori ordering of the divine world, an order not dependent upon flesh at all. This ordering preceded flesh, preceded materiality, and simply sought out bodies to fill Christological salvific space and time. However, the velocity of such sermonizing against sinners was set by those that produced infraction, not the sermonizer. Those that supposedly had—according to theological and philosophical thought—no will nor volition had to have such will and volition recognized and contended against. Such will and volition was so worrisome because of its revolutionary impulse, how it would spread outward from those enslaved to poor whites, creating otherwise modes of sociality, otherwise modes of resistance. These "sinners" were generative because they set the pace of Edwards's sermonic moment. Fugitivity is not determined by an external set of values but sets the necessity for response to it. Edwards sermon, it appears to me, is in the tradition of the desire to capture for the sovereign. Even the language of being in the hand, captured, is most pronounced for his congregation. But the insurrection in which people partook was in a long tradition of fugitivity against the nation-state and against the divine sovereign's hand, set free by way of choosing another way to live. And to engage in insurrectionist plots at least implies the idea of sovereignty, of a deity that has predestined them for death and destruction, has been rejected. Such rejection through insurrectionist plot is an ethical demand, to reject such theology in the cause of justice, in the cause of equity. Edwards's sermon attempted to chase and capture the fugitive spirit of blackness, to repress this fugitivity in the service of a proper religious subjectivity. There is no wonder, then, that he was radically against enthusiastic, embodied, response to the divine. That is to say, there is blackness running through and animating the very grounds of his critique, a blackness that he necessarily disregarded and discarded through averting his gaze from "sinners" while glaring in the direction of the metaphysical so-called elect.

The marginalizing excesses and flourishes—excesses that, according to a Calvinist Christology, separates humanity from the divine figure— are that which make and form a Christologically converted, a theologically proper, subject position. The "elect" as a community, as those predestined according to this racial/ist logic function both as an amorphous mass, a grouped articulation of what Denise da Silva calls "transcendental poesis" that depends upon coherence, regulation, and removal of difference.[78] Calvinist doctrine, which was the quickening power for the Awakening revivals, was the actualization of whiteness against enthusiasm, embodiment, experience. To actualize a set of behaviors in the service of a normative striving that was regulative of difference, born out of fear and loathing, is the process of transcendental poesis, even as sometimes the rhetoric of community is used, violently replacing the anoriginal difference, marking community through a purity, that is, the static "I." There is an excess of imagination that is the spatiotemporal relay between Calvinist predestination and the status of the negro, the slave, the black. This excess is the problem of thought that blackness occupies in the theological mind. This problem of blackness poses the problem of thinking theologically: What to do with a seemingly justice-oriented deity when the material condition of negroes, an effect of the sovereign's pleasure, seems to go unnoticed, seems to be averted? What when there are recognizable zones from which this sovereign seems to insist averting? The question of the negro and salvation is the problematic of relationship—in general—to a sovereign, and an atheism must lie at the heart of such problematic thought.

Black flesh, in theological-philosophical thought that was critical of enthusiasm, came to be the periphery and served the purpose of millennialism's potentiality. The conversion of negroes and Indians were noted by figures like George Whitefield and Edwards because of the general assumption of their fundamental, categorical, difference. Nahum Chandler puts forth a set of concerns that are useful for thinking the "place" of the black in theological thought:

> At its infrastructural core, the eighteenth-century discourse was organized around one titular question: are Negroes human, and, if so, are they "fully" human? On the basis of what criteria should their status in relation to (other) humans be judged? And, is that relation one of fundamental, or relative, sameness or difference? And, of course, the question, what is human? (or, what is man?) is always and everywhere at issue, even if only implicitly. This question was especially articulated as a discourse concerning the humanity of Negro slaves. . . . Yet, hidden within both of these questions, and essentially the corollary of the question concerning the humanity of the Negro, even as it is in all truth not less fundamental, was a question about the status of a putative European American or "White" identity.[79]

The problem of "full humanity" was not limited to the domain of the philosophical or the juridical but found its own vivification in theological discourse and material practice as well. There is a parallel set of concerns about the capacity to be human, notions of nature and whiteness in which Calvinist doctrine participates. Yet Calvinist doctrine also extended those concerns to questions regarding the nature of God as all-knowing and justice-oriented, the concern about theophany. The negro as a category of thought, enthusiasm as a category of ecstatics and bodily movement,[80] and the black flesh as the "natural" materiality of such pondering are exemplary for the articulation of these concerns.

The surprise with which figures like Whitefield and Edwards spoke about Indian and negro conversion as evidence of the coming of the kingdom of God, as a millennialist orientation implied that negroes, black flesh, and state violence should be articulated together as a relation of continual violation against peripheral flesh. That flesh came to stand in for a general capacity of the state and God to inflict harm on the one hand, and the general capacity to receive harm of the state and God on the other. Blackness—when thought within the bounds of pure reason, which is to say when thought theologically—calls into being the violence of the state, of the divine. To riff on Hortense Spillers, theological reflection—as a categorically distinct modality of thought—needs this construal of blackness, and if it were not here, it would have to be invented.[81] In fact, however, it *was* invented. This calling into being the violence of the state and of God radically calls into question the concepts of nationhood and a divine world. The focus on the presence or absence of black and indigene flesh conceptualizes a specific relation of the peripheral to the nation-state, to citizenship and to violence. And the peripheral only comes to matter in a choreographic itinerary and protocol that grounds normative spatial organizing in the concept of the center.

The desire for particular flesh-as-other is consistent with theological notions of purposiveness, where particular marginalized figures come to stand in for the limits of availability for conversion theologically. Both George Whitefield and Jonathan Edwards owned slaves but were "encouraged" by the fact that their blacks could receive "salvation" by their powerful preaching on behalf of the sovereign deity. And though Ann Taves questions the efficacy of preaching, as opposed to small group meetings, for conversion,[82] it is the narrativity of the relation of preached word to conversion of the marginalized, racialized others that is of intrigue. Whitefield's and Edwards's ideas about the purposiveness of these marginal characters set into motion their astonishment, shock, and eventually, pleasure gained from the "even these" being converted. What leaps out is how the conversion of Indians and negroes verified the rightness of the sovereign. And for Kant, the color of blacks verified the rightness of nature and her hierarchizing. Kant is important given his anthropology that was spatially organized because his theorizing elucidates the way that the theology of the Awakenings, theology generally as a categorical distinct thought process—were foundationally anthropological. Not a "theological anthropology" but an anthropological project that produced theology as a mode of reflection, justified by a comparison and scientism of racial/ized peoples and their capacities for relating to a divine world.

from: a
to: a
Wednesday November 25, 2009, 11:34am
Subject: Re: . . .
moth's powder,
There are two types of churches: ones with low-ceilings and others with high. Think about it. Aren't those the only type you've ever

attended? This is to say nothing of how big the church is or how many people it can seat. But rather, the space between floor and ceiling creates some amazing room for the sound to bounce around, from what I've experienced.

Low ceilings, of course, mean everything will sound out with a bit of a muffle on it: think of a trumpet mute. Or maybe something akin to the antithesis of a noise filter, where all this stuff stands between your ears and the "pure" or true sound itself. It doesn't matter how loud the sound is in the church, the low-ceiling will compress that sound, make it less angular and things will sound—accordingly—more insular, will sound more pressing. Imagine listening through something like Harriet Jacobs crawlspace, if you will.

Growing up, one bishop's church building we often visited might be the very definition of low ceiling. It was an old supermarket, a converted A&P or Pathmark or Shop Rite, now for the Master's use, with the purpose of the up building of the kingdom. And the sound of that church was so very different from the sound of other churches and i suspect it is because when sound would ring out—from the Leslie speaker to the tambourines to the hand-clapping to the preacher in the microphones—that sound would only be able to go up but so high until being dispersed. The sound had to travel horizontally much more than vertically so stuff happening in the front of the church didn't reach the back until maybe beat or two later, so much so that if you sat in the back of the church, you were already behind the move of spirit that took place in the front [the two Leslie speakers, of course, were in the front of the church and not the back]. This is why, I think, most of the people who sat in the back were more spectatorial in their engagement with the church. Not because they didn't want to feel anything but, because of the sound, their arrival was always late a bit. And I can't even tell you how sad they looked when folks in the front were shouting [today, people call it dancing but we called it shouting; the *ring shout*, of course, with the shuffling feet, could be thought as the predecessor to pentecostal shouting. anyway.] syncopation indeed.

But then there is, then and of course, that other type of church building, one where the ceiling is high and the sounds have to travel vertically as much as horizontally, so sound circulates differently, it literally *circulates*, creates a circle by its centripetal and centrifugal force turning

turning turning around and around and around, sound going under over and above you. In this high-ceiling church, sound "rings" a lot more, it remains in the air and is heard thereafter, it strikes everyone much more at almost about the same time [but, still, a ruse, really]. If the low ceiling muffles, the high-ceiling releases and sounds tremble with treble. Everything seems clear in those types of environments.

If you had ever paid attention at all, you would have noticed in the low ceiling church the organist playing in the high register a lot more [at least an octave above middle c] to invoke the spirit and in the high ceiling church, this same organist might very likely muddy the waters by playing dark bass notes. I think, in both instances, the musician would feel the difference created by the architecture, by the acoustic environment, made possible by the height of the ceilings. Without knowing it but certainly feeling it, they'd play in ways to create as much balance as possible in the space.

Would you be surprised to know—I think I can be a bit more candid with you after all this time and after all of these emails; I should really stop doing this . . . really—but would you be surprised to know that my first time really, really touching Derrick was in a high-ceiling church? It was the second week in august right before I was to leave for college, so I was eighteen years old and we were having convocation in one of those churches. This church, of course, was a converted synagogue made possible by white flight from inner cities years and years ago [and I think there might be a relationship between pentecostal sound, white flight and synagogues: think Detroit—Bailey Cathedral is pretty famous for its sound, a former synagogue—there are, of course, too many examples; there are others, of course]. In any regard, this synagogue-turned-cathedral became the home to many a pentecostal service where the power of the Lord came down. But when—and this is true for lots of synagogues-turned-churches—when services weren't big, or there just weren't enough people or not enough money to pay the electric company to light the full sanctuary, services would occur in the basements of these large tabernacles, cathedrals, temples of the most high. And in those basements are the perfect mix between the high and low ceiling, at least in terms of sound. Thus, the organist has the best possibility of balanced sound and, subsequently, moving the congregation.

And it was then in august. It was a Monday night so not a lot of people planned to be at the service anyway but Derrick and I both sang with the convocation choir and he had just directed some song and winked at me ever so faintly, bravely, sinfully and erotically while directing and nobody saw it but me and I was astonished and shocked and scared shitless because the Lord was certain to strike us down at any moment, given his display. But nobody saw it and we had never had sex, only'd lay in the bed next to each other and touch ever so slightly but I already told you about that. It was in August after we sang that I first noticed the grace of his body when he was shouting.

And you know when someone is gonna shout. Vanessa was playing the organ—can I tell you how much I love a girl organist? Nineteen years old, killing the bass and the drive and the changes. Augment, suspend, seventh, minor: go! She did it all. She was playing and we marched our happy asses back to our seats—metal chairs in the basement, so you know the sound just bounced off everything and sounded so good—and we began to clap. The song was an up-tempo tune where we sang about climbing mountains or knowing what prayer can do or some other song where the only thing that really mattered in the song was the vamp—or the drive, or to be really throw-back, the *special*—and once we were done and back in our seats and Mother Jackson was encouraging the saints to *praise the Lord, church!* Vanessa began playing ever so faster and ever so faster and ever so faster and eversofaster until it was at full shout speed. Brooklyn pace. So you know it was quick.

And it was in that Monday in august when i noticed Derrick's grace. So he was gonna shout and I knew it. At first, he was seated [he was tired from directing]. But then as the music swelled and sped, he stood and began to clap a bit hesitantly . . . elegantly, looking about him and smiling at the saints dancing but—you could almost hear the commentary in his head—not himself dancing. Then, he put his right hand in front of him on the metal chair. Then, he put his head down. And, you know what happens when the hand is gripping the chair or pew in front of you and the head is down? He had his program in the left hand and he began to dance *playfully*, eyes still open, head down but looking around a bit. But then Vanessa hit the chords that everyone was waiting for, some chording that Twinkie's been doing since at least 1979 before I was born—*dun dun dun dun dun, dun dun dun dun dun, dun dun dun dun dun-dun dun dun dun!*—And he let out a little yelp and by then, his feet were moving and he threw the program down and he moved from out of the row into the aisle and had both his arms bent at the elbow but tight next to him and his head was down and his eyes were closed and his feet did some hop-scotch shit.

The pit of my stomach dropped because Vanessa did it again and this time more people were screaming and the sound was a bit more clear and more people were dancing and I knew that if someone as young and beautiful as Derrick could dance in public—I didn't do such things very often, I always felt the display too public and I never wanted people to look at me—*dun dun dun dun dun!*—and I ran up next to Derrick and it was the spirit moving me, I promise, I had no idea what was occurring— and grabbed his left hand and we shouted together. My stomach always dropped right at the border between playful dance and full out shout, holy terror, I suppose. Our feet did not cross, we did not step on each other's toes. And he didn't fight me but—and I don't know how I knew this—but he knew it was me, though his eyes were shut tightly.

We were sweaty after it all. The preacher got up and because we were still a bit young and people would not ogle us leaving the basement sanctuary for some air—or to pee—after such a display, we went to the bathroom. Vanessa was backing up the preacher who, I'm sure, wasn't making much sense but used the high energy from the high-low-ceiling sound to animate his sermon. He was, if anything, smart. Folks were already praising so he just kept a spirited engagement with the congregation so, in the bathroom, we heard a combination of *Yes! Thank the Lord! Praise Him! Bless me! Fix me! Do it Lord!*

Anyway, we both peed. In separate stalls. Went up to the sinks to wash our hands—*shhhhhhhh*—the water said and then we turned off our faucets. I was drying my hands. He was drying his. We'd said nothing. He was so graceful and that was all i could think about. We were both sweating. He took his brown paper towel—the rough ones that, when you fold them, have rough edges and corners and aren't too soothing—he took that paper towel and brushed it over my brow. I said *thanks*. I took mine, smirked a bit, and brushed it over his brow. He said nothing. He took his paper towel—he was standing to my right—placed it in his right hand and put his left arm at the small of my back and I sorta knew to turn to him. He brushed it against my brow again but my right arm was caught and could not move between our bodies and his left arm; and my left arm was caught between his upheld hand brushing my brow. i turned around. Someone could have walked in. I was terrified. Terrified. Simply terrified.

The sound from the basement sanctuary of that former synagogue forced its way through the door but was muffled. We—in the bathroom—said nothing. He dropped the towel and took my right hand and took me to the handicapped stall. Undid my pants. Undid his. We stood there, shirts on, pants and underwear at our ankles. He kissed me. We rubbed against each other for nothing more than a minute. We said nothing. We pulled up our pants, washed our hands again and sat apart from each other in the sanctuary. He would not, of course, take my phone calls for weeks after that, not until I left for college. Maybe the music caused us to act out of ourselves, or to be more fully human. It, of course, felt good.[83]

THE DAY OF Pentecost has fully come. Blackpentecost, however, has and is yet and still to come. The aesthetic practice prompted by tightly being together in one space—enacting difference transferring vitality—is perpetual and everywhere around us. Shouting in Blackpentecostalism at the turn of the twentieth century is not the same as the *saut* or the peregrination around the Kaaba in Mecca; neither is it the same as the Ring Shout dance that was prominent on the seacoasts of Georgia and South Carolina. Rather, like the *tradition* of Enlightenment thought and Awakening revivals—a tradition aversive to blackness—these various choreosonics are a tradition in the service of explicating blackness. In this choreosonic shout tradition, vitality transferred, a way to create a social form was carried to and then dwelt within this particular way of life. What sorts of injunctions existed against certain modes of social life and how were the aesthetic dances of Blackpentecostalism in response to such injunctions? Is Blackpentecostal shouting but one other example of "stealing away" to produce an old form otherwise? Possibly. Exhaustedly? Certainly. To steal away is the topical thrust, the undergrounded verve of black performance; it is the unceasing theme around which black performance varies. It is a different relation to time and space, the grounds for, without being educated into, modernity. The shout tradition is an ethical demand to vary and antagonize, to be restless and restive against the dominant political economy and its ordering of the world.

Edwards's "Sinners in the Hands of an Angry God" is exemplary of the type of sermonizing that the Great Awakening Calvinist preaching was known for: hell, brimstone, dread, fear, loathing. The itinerant movements and motivations to cross the Atlantic and to travel the colonies were to spread a particular fear of God in order to convert. The converted responded to these theological proclamations, and if there were joy to be found in life, it would come after the enthusiastic, embodied tears, swaying and vocal shouting as prompted by terror. But what if there were a gathering around abundance, around pleasure, around joy? Not as an after-effect of conversion but as the grounds, as the foundational claim, for sociality? I have specifically used the word "itinerary" to discuss the choreographic nature of aversion because the word is useful to consider how twentieth-century Blackpentecostalism was prompted by itinerancy, wandering, what Louisiana law at the same time would call vagrancy.[84] Whereas Whitefield and Edwards both itinerated as a way of theological life, the direction of such itineration was clearly to continue a pronouncement of dread.

Margaret Washington Creel writes that participation in the Gullah Ring Shout was limited to those persons who joined the local praise house, those who were baptized: "Only members of the Praise House could join in the Ring Shout. Children were taught the shout at a very early age but never allowed to participate in or attend religious gatherings where the shout was performed until they became Praise House members."[85] However, Charles Harrison Mason had a much more expansive understanding of the possibilities for shouting. Mason's shouting was voluntary, an act of worship that did not necessitate conversion, democratized and made the aesthetic practice available to all without secularizing it.[86] Shouting functioned as an "inculcation" of piety, the performance of shouting allowing the congregant to go further and deeper still in a possible encounter with the divine.[87] This inculcation also presented the possibility of repetition as a means to having the "Pentecostal experience."

The Ring Shout was explicitly relegated to a specific time—after the "official" service (in whatever capacity decided upon by the congregants), a specific space and time or during a prayer meeting—benches pushed to the walls. An area, literally, was cleared in order for shouters to dance during antebellum practices. This, no doubt, was at least in part related to the necessity for shouts to occur as clandestine events, many times in the woods far away from plantations and earshots of those who sought to inflict violence upon the shouters. But even with the more official praise houses—small, compact spaces sometimes constructed, other times the home of a particular individual—the space in the center would be cleared in order for shouters to dance.

The case was different with Blackpentecostalism. Interruption was aestheticized, the moment of encounter with the divine could occur at any moment during (and sometimes even before or after) the service, and if one so felt led, they could erupt in corporeal praise, shouting. With many descriptions of the Ring Shout as well as those regarding Blackpentecostal shouting, longevity is a main feature: the ability to shout all night long, into the early morning. Bishop Daniel Alexander Payne of the African Methodist Episcopal Church critiqued shouters he encountered because they would be fatigued and, thus, ineffectual during their work hours.[88] The *Los Angeles Daily Times* article noted, "One of the wildest of the meetings was held last night, and the highest pitch of excitement was reached by the gathering, which continued to 'worship' until nearly midnight." This to note that shouting can take place for hours and move about the congregation from member to member, energy flowing until each one reaches a level of exhaustion. But for this exhaustion to be reached, there must be—as a sociality—inexhaustible breath, inexhaustible spirit.

Shouters continually draw from breath—in their flesh—as a resource from which to continue. With Blackpentecostal performance of shouting, gone are the formal, organized rings, though one shouter may be held within a small ring of a few persons to ensure safety. Instead of shuffling the feet across the ground in a ring formation, a Blackpentecostal shouter may jump up and down, or hold arms up, bent at the elbow with feet moving to the rhythm of a repetitive song or chant, or they may bend their body—rather than at the knee bone, prominent for Ring Shout dance—at the waist, hunched over just a bit, arms bent at the elbows and the fronts of their hands resting on their lower back. Moving to the rhythm: of the drum, of the clapping hands, of their hearts. Shouting feels good. It is erotic. And that because it is fleshly. Looking at the flesh dance and move and sway prompts otherwise than a sacred possibility. Or, more precisely, sacred possibility is found in what is thought the categorically distinct and pure zone of eros. The gestures, the movements, have within the capacity to destabilize us, watching and becoming destabilized, energized, desirous of the flesh that moves. Such dancing flesh, such shouting, extends outward and reaches for flesh, for feeling, otherwise.

Beautiful. Like marronage escapees existing in swamps. Creating worlds there, other modes of inhabitation. Such creation—together with others—is the performance of a general critique of the places from which they escaped and absconded. Breathing itself, dance, eating itself, pottery. All such things were performative irruptions against strained modalities of thought, the befalling of understanding on imaginative excess.[89] Marronage illustrates that worlds could be fashioned from having been excluded, though those excluded never presumed categorical difference. They were, in effect, open to others coming and dwelling with them, making a world with them, *in exclusion*. One form of Enlightenment thought—and in this it shares with Awakening revivals—emerges from a general incapacity to consider the irreducibility, emerges by grounding the very possibility for knowledge in the impenetrability of objects. Impenetrability—in the name of transcendental aesthetics *or* predestined itinerary—is produced through a black presence, the presence of blackness, that is engaged through aversion. Impenetrability makes of Enlightenment and Awakening thought the flip sides of the same coin. Transcendental aesthetics of time and space, Awakening theologizing of predestination of souls, both rely on the presupposition of the impenetrability of and an aversion for black objects. Thus, knowledge production is based on a misunderstanding of blackness. This impenetrability becomes the occasion for graspability, for assumption, for the literal taking objects up into the hand and placing them off and to the side. Impenetrability might be the animating underside of theology-philosophy, aversion its core logic. But there is otherwise possibility, choreosonic possibility, which does not assume impenetrability. Rather, choreosonic performance is grounded in irreducibility, a celebration of a general agnosticism that causes one to go further and further deeper still. This is an agnosticism, a black disbelief that is at the heart of blackness as *a*theology: even in the situation and condition of not knowing what one is after, one still searches, one still travels to cypress swamps, to the South Carolina-Georgia interior, to California for experience, one still shouts *of*, *to*, and *for*, *in* and *about* joy. This is a social choreosonics, a social project. Another Enlightenment—a luminous blackness, illuminating darkness—given as the constant and ongoing performance of escape into the secret, the secretion into the interior, the interior of the plentitude, the irreducibility of otherwise. They are dancing there.

They are shouting there. Sonically. Choreographically. In theology, in philosophy—through aversion—blackness remains, blackness exceeds, blackness is yet to be thought. It is there in otherwise possibility, as choreosonic performance—which is another way to say *a way of life*—that thought is *of, to,* and *for, in* and *about* blackness.

3

NOISE

That vibration can be thought, cognized, practiced through its being gathered and organized along the line of, and against being relegated to, joy is a radical disruption of western theology-philosophy. And not because Christian theology, which is always and everywhere Christian philosophy, implores believers to make joyful noise. Rather, it is a disruption because theology-philosophy that emerges from within the western epistemology of categorical, absolute difference as its operating ground considers noise as always in need of abatement. Noise is that ephemeral movement that cannot be pinpointed, separated, individuated. Noise *is*, only insofar as it is irreducibly social, irreducibly formed by vibration off other surfaces, through and against air such that vibration, movement, begs its being heard, its being listened to. Noise has been a problem for technological innovation at least since the 1920s,[1] but the idea of noise as a problem for theological-philosophical thought takes us back further still to Enlightenment discourse.

The audiovisual encounter of problems—whether of the inanimate kind, or of sounds, or of negroes—has been a concern of the western theological-philosophical tradition at least since the writing of Edmund Burke, though no doubt, previous to him as well. In *A Philosophical Enquiry Into the Origin of Our Ideas of the Sublime and Beautiful*, Burke wrote about color's ability to induce one's experience of the sublime, how color can be all-consuming in its magnitude and force, how color can be irresistible power that inspires awe and reverence. The sublime—in terms of color—is produced, not by white or light color, "but of sad and fuscous colours, as black, or brown, or deep purple, and the like."[2] Immediately after describing dark color's relation to the sublime, Burke describes how sound also allows entry into a zone where time and space are indistinct, the space of blackness. He says about in such a zone: "Excessive loudness alone is sufficient to overpower the soul, to suspend its action, and to fill it with terror."[3] He continues, "The noise of vast cataracts, raging storms, thunder, or artillery, awakes a great and awful sensation in the mind, though we can observe no nicety or artifice in those sorts of music," and human crowds shouting together "so amazes and confounds the imagination, that, in this staggering, and hurry of the mind, the best established tempers can scarcely forbear being borne down, and joining in the common cry, and common resolution of the crowd."[4]

Fuscous color coalesces with loud sound; blackness is noise. The conflation of darkness/blackness with noise, with need for abatement, was also an ideology germane to American coloniality: "If colonial elites agreed on what produced sound, they also agreed on who produced noise. Native Americans, African Americans (slave and free), and the laboring classes generally were among the greatest noise-makers in colonial America. . . . African Americans, like Native Americans and other nonliterate groups, 'defied the surveillance of writing' and made sounds that threatened to fracture the acoustic world of English settlers."[5] Sound as distinct from noise, and this categorically. After such categorical distinction, noise, in general, became racialized as the other of Europe, as the other of rationality, as the other of the proper. The other of Europe was not just spatially located in Europe but was a way to think one's place in the world. Such that the very same constitution of noise as racialized that grounded Burke's thought could likewise be an American colonialist project. Theological-philosophical thought traveled, created the spatial and temporal logic through racializing aesthetics, through racializing sound. The ability to racialize aesthetics depends upon an ongoing distinction of sound from noise.

Burke's argument about the beautiful and the sublime advances by stating that darkness is "terrible in its own nature" and that blackness is unique form of terrible darkness, "a more confined idea."[6] Blackness for Burke is the natural operation of a disagreeableness without association, an irreducible confrontational state. When a young boy received medical treatment for cataracts and was finally able to see, upon his first visual encounter with a negro woman, he was filled with terror. Burke argues that the terror was because of the encounter with darkness, with the enfleshment of categorical distinction through raced, gendered substance.[7] Burke attended to the audiovisuality of the sublime's graspability; the force of the sublime is granted by and grounded in the expansiveness of darkness and the overwhelming of noise. Darkness (and its attendant, confined form, blackness) is terrible in that it causes physical spasms of the eye "produced by its own efforts in pursuit of its objects" wherein "one will find, if he opens his eyes and makes an effort to see in a dark place, that a very perceivable pain ensues."[8] Burke says of blackness that it is a "partial darkness" that "derives some of its powers from being mixed and surrounded with coloured bodies. In its own nature, it cannot be considered as a colour. Black bodies, reflecting none, or but a few rays, with regard to sight, are but as so many vacant spaces dispersed among the objects we view," and is a "convulsion as is caused when any thing happens against the expectance of the mind."[9] And, finally, "Black will always have something melancholy in it, because the sensory will always find the change to it from other colours too violent."[10]

Recounting Burke's ruminations on blackness confirms for us the ways blackness—for Burke and in the western philosophical tradition of which he is part—opens up as it closes down upon the mind, upon the senses. And we must keep in mind that it is this Mr. Burke that Immanuel Kant references regarding the blacks of Africa. Blackness is an ongoing, anoriginal assault on desire for normative beauty, normative form. It is both a color and exceeds the colorful. It resonates sonically and bothers the mental faculties. Blackness terrifies because it is ungovernable, it is anarchic in its deformation, is not given to control. It is, literally, a hell of an encounter. Anoriginal, irreducible, audiovisual encounter is a preoccupation for Burke's thoughts on the sublime and the beautiful. The terror of the encounter with the black object is by way of its transformational force: from the real to the sublime, from quietude to shouts with a crowd, from rest to convulsion. Going through Burke produces questions about encounter and enquiry: (1) What about blackness produces the concept of encounter itself, how is blackness the encounter, the irreducible mode of sociality? (2) What emerges in the concept of enquiry that disperses itself by the confrontation with blackness? (3) And what when we acknowledge that this encounter is one produced through an aversive logic, a logic that leaves intact the thing itself, that the blackness so elaborated through theology-philosophy is the reflection of the one that theologizes, the one that philosophizes, the one that is otherwise than the black object? Burke was correct to assert that the feeling prompted by the sublime is reflective of the subject of philosophy; the sublime is not in the object but in the observer, the philosopher. Such that the way Kant dances around the subject is coterminous with the way Burke elaborates the resistance, the terror, the pain of the subject. But these elaborations of the subject are grounded in an initiatory distinction of categorization of object and subject. And it is that distinction that needs interrogation.

Western epistemology assumes categorical distinction as the ground of its operation, producing an enquiry that abstracts the concept of origin (which is to say the concept of purity, of metaphysical difference) from (the effects of) blackness that precedes it. In other words, the concept of origin—or, originarity—is the consequence of abstraction from blackness and not previous to it. Consider the following:

> While walking in New Orleans on a Sunday afternoon in 1819, the architect and engineer Benjamin Latrobe suddenly heard "a most extraordinary noise, which I supposed to proceed from some horse mill, the horses tramping on a wooden floor." Following the sound to its source, Latrobe came upon an area of open ground adjacent to the city, on which some five or six hundred blacks were "formed into circular groupes in the midst of four of which . . . was a ring." Within these rings, slave instrumentalists were playing while African Louisianans danced. The sounds emanating from the dancing rings at Congo Square, as this open area near the city had become known, evoked in Latrobe an overwhelming sense of cultural alienation. The drumming was "abominably loud"; the singing "uncouth" and "detestable." "I have never," the traveller announced, "seen any thing more brutally savage, and at the same time dull and stupide than this whole exhibition."[11]

Latrobe experienced the vibration as noise, and as noise, and such noise produced in him alienation. What if he had let the rhythms move him, if he had consented to the noise of the encounter? His self-regulation, hinted by his rhetorical dismissal of the sounds as brutally savage as well as dull and stupid, was the same movement of flight and escape that structured Burke's philosophy of the noncolor of blackness. The encounter is the occasion for givenness, for transcendence, for movement. The black figure is the manifestation, the *embodiment* (against enfleshment) and sonic materiality, of such purposiveness, of such transformation, of such movement. To consider the onhearers—those who would overhear, mishear, hear into—blackness and attempt to control it and the objects called black through theological-philosophical thought compel an analysis of the *sonic* aspect of the choreosonic, to think noise, joyful noise, Blackpentecostal noise, against abatement. The noise produced alienation and, as such, was the production of the logic of aversion for the one that experienced alienation. Such that the noise of blacks, of black objects, is otherwise than what is recounted in theology-philosophy. That which is averted remains to be elaborated. Such an elaboration and analysis, here, will consider how noise is taken up within the social world of blackness, of black objects, and considering it, thinking it, otherwise.

There is an impurity that runs through the hearing and listening practices of theology and philosophy, an impurity that normative thought seeks to discard. Such discardability is about the hierarchizing of sound *as* the hierarchizing of social forms, making discardable certain social formations, though the socialities thus discarded are the very grounds for such thinking. Leigh Eric Schmidt discusses how Natural philosophy desired a purification of listening practices—what we might think of as the removal of grit and noise—which would represent "the end of the credulous acceptance of all the hearsay about the miraculous, the marvelous, the revelatory," and this would ultimately mean philosophy would have achieved "the quieting of all those heavenly and demonic voices by which 'superstition' had for so long impeded the advancement of knowledge."[12] And the category of "enthusiasm"—critiqued by both theologians and philosophers—regarded the possibility of hearing God with immediacy, an unmediated hearing.[13] This chapter turns to Calvinist doctrine as one example of the ways theology itself is a delimitation of thought, how theology is a categorical distinction grounded in the same western logics of race and purity. And this to demonstrate the ways theology and philosophy depend upon the removal of a certain sonicity, a sonic materiality, that was cathected to the religious, the spiritual.

Enlightenment philosophy was averse to hearing and listening practices in general. The invention of the stethoscope, a device that made hearing the interiority of the body more pronounced, was first imagined by Robert Hooke during the height of Enlightenment thought, though only later realized in the early nineteenth century.[14] The intention of this device was the scientizing of hearing, of hearing's being made precise and not given to the religious, the spiritual, the ceaseless imprecision noise produces and is produced by. Schmidt described this invention as the mediation of sound by way of "penetrative discernment that embodied reasonable ways of hearing, the trained ear with its careful acquired perceptions."[15] That hearing could be made precise, that it could be scientized, that noise could be controlled, all operating through the logic of pure distinction, of categorical difference. This chapter considers the noisiness of blackness, the joyful noise of Blackpentecostal aesthetics. And this by considering the noisemaking during Testimony and Tarry moments of Blackpentecostal church service. And this to ask: What when one is the black object that prompts theological-philosophical—that prompts aversive—thought? What can be heard, felt, experienced from the position of that object? What is the status of its thought? How does that object—of one other's theological-philosophical inquiry—produce knowledge? I am concerned with what the black object hears around itself, how the black object moves about itself, that creates the social/sexual/sonic zone that both terrifies and solicits thought. What is the intentionality of the object conceptualized as reducible to the given capacity for one other's thought? I consider the capacity of the background—by raising a few characters who would make joyful noise, who heard joyful noise, by their modes of inhabiting the world with others—to reassert that the categorical distinction between background and foreground in blackness, because of black performance, because of Blackpentecostal aesthetics is obliterated. The *a*theological-*a*philosophical force of Blackpentecostal aesthetic performance produces a "politics of avoidance" against the aversive logics of categorical distinction. Focusing on two particular moments of the Blackpentecostal church service—Testimony and Tarrying—shows how Blackpentecostal choreosonics manifest resistance that exists *before* and *against* the power and force of aversion.

Joyful noise. This joyful noise is fundamentally a critique of the given world, a political economy of austerity and exploitation. Blackpentecostals are sounding out a way, rehearsing a mode of sonic production that refuses origin and purity, utilizing melismatic, melodic irruption, irreducible noise. That noise can be joyful is an important claim to make. Noise is a fundamental feature of Blackpentecostal aesthetics and, as such, is a likewise illustration of the choreosonic itinerary and protocol of blackness. Violating ordinances, "polluting" the air with praise,[16] Blackpentecostal aesthetic practice is a critique of western law, grounded as it is in the liberal subject with all the attendant rights that accrue to such a landed "man." "In June 1906, the Los Angeles Ministerial Association attempted to silence [William] Seymour and the revival. It filed a complaint with the Los Angeles Police Department against the 'negro revival' (thus injecting race into the complaint) on the grounds that it was disturbing the peace. The police investigated the charges and decided against their request because it was located in an industrial, not residential, section of the city."[17] Though this first call for police to investigate the noise of Blackpentecostals turned out negative results for the Los Angeles Ministerial Association, notable is the way the Association thought the noise in need of remediation through invoking police power and authority. That the police were called as a modality of control illustrates the ways policing the boundaries of blackness was an aesthetic concern. To rid the area of such noise would have rid the area of the flesh—black, white, indigenous, Mexican, Korean—that gathered together at 312 Azusa Street for their revival. To be proper and decorous was to be ceaselessly noiseless, to be devoid of vibratory force. Also highlighted by requesting a police response is the notion of protection and belonging the LAMA assumed was their rightful claim. This noise had all sorts of resonance and produced all sorts of problems.

Such noise is called joyful. And the Saints often call such joy "unspeakable." That noise can be joyful and joy can be unspeakable produces another way to analyze and interrogate categorical distinction. And that because the unspeakable is vibrated and sounded out, and such vibration and sound is produced from, and emerges from within while producing, joy. Joyful noise, the noise of Blackpentecostal aesthetics, operates from a different epistemological decentering, a centrifugitive refusal of centeredness.

The logics of racial capitalism have radically, fundamentally imposed categorical distinction on us. Theology and philosophy are two such modalities of delimited thought, such that to operate within the delimitation of thought as rule and practice is to produce anew the very logic of exclusion and hierarchy, the very logic of racial capital. Liberation cannot come from reworking the already given epistemology by *centering* blackness, by centering black performance, by centering Blackpentecostal aesthetics. We must think—which is to say, imagine, perform—against such "logical" distinction, and such geometric spatial and temporal organization. We must think the question of who we are, what blackness is, from the dispossession of having displaced the episteme germane to western thought. Dispossession only insofar as a unique aspect of blackness and indegineity in western civilization is displacement and dispossession from ground such that whiteness could place, center itself on, own ground.[18] And with how the shout tradition calls into question the distinction of choreography from sonicity as an explicit example of calling into question a general production of absolute distinction, the Saints' joyful noise—in the guise of song, in the guise of praise—sharpens the analysis, gives it clarity, through the ephemera of noise. Noise-making from within the Blackpentecostal episteme is choreosonic; it is always about metaphorical and material movement. All sound is motion, all motion movement, all movement choreosonic. Such choreosonic breakdown also produces a radical question of being, of historical being, of the way blackness, of the way Blackpentecostal aesthetic performance, is an intervention into what is colloquially called the "historical moment." And this through noise's movement against being stilled, against its being captured, against its being reducible to western theological-philosophical "man's" conceptions.

The sense of historical being elaborated in western thought—theology and philosophy—assumes time as teleology, as forward moving.[19] And this sense of historical being would assume possessive individualism—that time and energy are disposable, that time and a sense of its moving can be possessed, that time and its passage can be subject to the right to use or exclude from its boundary—as the ground of its operation.[20] And western musicology fits squarely within this modality, music moving in similar fashion. Blackness, Blackpentecostal aesthetic practice, disrupts the logic of linear time and space, and this chapter will attend to the ways black objects heard things, the ways black objects were heard, and how such hearing was the grounds for being moved, how such hearing was the grounds for sociality, social life.

What was gifted by the brutal violence of Georg Wilhelm Friedrich Hegel when he claimed that Africa has no history, that Africa—and negroes therein—were not part of History?

> At this point we leave Africa, not to mention it again. For it is no historical part of the World; it has no movement or development to exhibit. Historical movements in it—that is in its northern part—belong to the Asiatic or European World. Carthage displayed there

an important transitionary phase of civilization; but, as a Phoenician colony, it belongs to Asia. Egypt will be considered in reference to the passage of the human mind from its Eastern to its Western phase, but it does not belong to the African Spirit. What we properly understand by Africa, is the Unhistorical, Undeveloped Spirit, still involved in the conditions of mere nature, and which had to be presented here only as on the threshold of the World's History.[21]

It is not that Africa, for Hegel's philosophical thought, had no movement but that such movement and development were not for *exhibit*. Exhibit, of course, has all sorts of juridical and theological resonances: a document or object presented in court and considered official evidence; the documents (letters of orders, institution and induction, and so on) that a beneficed or licensed clergyman may be required to produce at the first visitation after his admission; or simply, producing evidence. In Hegel's thought, such an analytics of Africa is not worthy, does not exist in the zone, of the juridical nor the ecclesial; thus, the nonnecessity of presenting evidence of that which he claims. And such claims would constitute a categorical distinction.

How is such categorical exclusion, categorical distinction, the very possibility of producing History? Such that we must ask: What is the problem with the urgency "to make history," to "be a part of history," to desire to be historical being? All this to ask: How does a people—whose fundamental aesthetic practice is a critique of Newtonian time and space, a critique of Kant's transcendental aesthetic, whose performance is against predestined theology, against spatial and temporal coherence[22]—how does such a people critique also and likewise the very concept of "historical being," of existing in particular "historical moments"? What is history, what is the historical? And as historical being, who is allowed to nominate oneself, or one's moment, to the status of "the historical"? This is to ask again, in a different register and key, how is one nominated to the role of philosopher, theologian? How does the historical operate through categorical distinction, through the abatement of choreosonic noise, through the abatement of the joyful noise of Blackpentecostal aesthetic practice? What must be conceded in order to gain a sense of *historical* being, a sense of self, that only reiterates the western theological-philosophical sense of being, an existence that Sylvia Wynter asserts emerges from "coloniality"?[23] Denise

Ferreira da Silva says, "The descriptor *historicity* presupposes an ethical principle, transcendality, the foundation and end, actualized in a collectivity's temporal trajectory."[24] What to do, however, when one is—when ones are—not only not within the trajectory of such an ethics but the sociality that one bears, the trace of otherwise possibility, is a critique of such a teleology, such a temporal and spatial zone?

I want to think the otherwise historical, the *disruption* of the historical—and as such, historical being. Steven Salaita says that this sense of western history emerges from settler colonial logic, through its being quite literally "settled," and immovable, unchangeable.[25] Such that what happened *happened*, that what violence that attended past events have created for us a condition of current immobility. Such that white supremacist capitalist heteropatriarchy is, in other words, a settled case, settled in the alluvium of shed blood, sweat, and tears. Yet John Mbiti's *African Religions and Philosophy* is important here and not because the work makes African thought iterable and coherent to western theology-philosophy. Rather, his work is important because Mbiti elaborates a different relation to temporality, narrativity (grounded in myth, for example) and, also then, to space. For example, Mbiti writes:

> The linear concept of time in western thought, with an indefinite past, present and infinite future, is practically foreign to African thinking. The future is virtually absent because events which lie in it have not taken place, they have not been realized and cannot, therefore, constitute time. If, however, future events are certain to occur, or if they fall within the inevitable rhythm of nature, they at best constitute only *potential time*, not *actual time*. What is taking place now no doubt unfolds the future, but once an event has taken place, it is no longer in the future but in the present and the past. *Actual time* is therefore what is present and what is past. It moves 'backward' rather than 'forward'; and people set their minds not on future things, but chiefly in what has taken place.[26]

Mbiti's elaboration of time and history highlights the fact of other epistemologies of operation, other modes of collective, improvisational thought that are not theological-philosophical, are not grounded in categorical distinction of linear time with its past, present, and future tenses that are separable and hold each other in abeyance. The fact of other epistemologies is the fact of otherwise possibilities, otherwise means to organizing thought regarding time and space. As such, there are other ways to think the world and relation to such a thing, such a place. With Mbiti's formulation, it seems the *event* serves as the primary object through which life occurs, the eventuality of now, the succession of *actual time* moving backward, not forward. Counterclockwise, perhaps? Centrifugitive, certainly. Such centrifugitive time would cause us to rethink the noise in praise houses and hush harbors, the joyful noise of Blackpentecostal practice, because the rupture of liberation and freedom so desired by enslaved peoples then and those of us marginalized through racialization today can now be considered *potential* time. Potential time because performance practice of blackness is about the certainty, the spiritual conviction, of the to-come liberative possibility, and is the living out of liberation as *belief in the flesh*. Such enfleshment of a break, some out from time and space itself such that it can irrupt, erupt, at any moment, and any *past* can be reconstituted.

Cedric Robinson in *Black Marxism: The Making of the Black Radical Tradition* wrote about the "ontological totality" of black being, which is its collective consciousness and capacity for thought and performance. Though he used the phrase "historical being," his seems to run counter to the critique of a *sense* of being historical that I am engaging here because the historic he elaborates emerges through the ontological totality, through the collective, improvisational, choreosonic performance of blackness. Ontological totality is the rejection of the very "terms of order"[27] from which western man, the coloniality of being, emerges. Such that when Robinson wrote of the Black Radical Tradition as "the impulse to make history in their own terms,"[28] what is elaborated is an impulse to make an otherwise historical, an *a*historical, against the imposition of having to be in "History" and the transcendental being that such History implies.

Joyful noise, black praise noise, the Blackpentecostal sense of being is an enactment of the ante-historical, is an enactment of the ante-History. The foundational vibrational noise, joyful noise, black noising—to borrow a bit from Hortense Spillers—is to be before as vestibular to not only culture, but also vestibular to the historical and History, the modality of theological-philosophical thought that produced such distinctions.[29] And if Walter Benjamin is right[30]—that history is that which flashes before us in a moment of danger, of crisis—then how can one make a claim for the historical moment when we have been in this particular flash since at least

1492?[31] The modality of the historical, of historical being, of transcendental History I here critique emerges out of a logic of aversion. To say, for example, "I'm going to make history" or "this is going to be historical" is a claim on *events to come* regarding how they will register in some future's past. The same would be true for any dissection of a past event as historical over and against other moments. These claims, in other words, are fundamentally about the claimant, not events in the world, claims about how one will position oneself in time, in space. And this time and space is not distinct from Kant's transcendental aesthetic, not distinct from Newtonian physics. This time and space conferring historical being occurs by having an aversion for all the other moments that are not deemed worthy enough to be, or proper to, History, to the historical moment. To make a claim for the historical, then, is to make a claim about oneself as the theologian-philosopher-historian that *produces* the moment of history. As aversive logic, this modality of historical being is produced through categorical distinction and absolute categorical distinction is grounded and based in Kant's categorical imperative, the idea of a universal, unconditional requirement that is an end in itself.[32]

This mode of the historical, of History and historical being, is one that Valentin Mudimbe engages as the creation of the power-knowledge couplet of modernity at the momentary epistemological "invention of Africa."[33] He offers, "The problem is that during this period both imperialism and anthropology took shape, allowing the reification of the 'primitive.' The key is the idea of History with a capital H, which first incorporates St. Augustine's notion of *providentia* and later on expresses itself in the evidence of Social Darwinism. Evolution, conquest, and difference become signs of a theological, biological, and anthropological destiny, and assign to things and beings both their natural slots and social mission," and "From this point, various schools of anthropology developed models and techniques to describe the 'primitive' in accordance with changing trends within the framework of Western experience."[34] The Blackpentecostal aesthetic is an intervention into the concept of categorical distinction and is a tradition that produces a fundamental critique of the very possibility of History that rests on, and indeed needs, the transcendental subject. Blackpentecostal choreosonics critique the concept of origin—"A starting point is not necessarily a beginning, not in the sense of coming into being; the starting point already situates and is situated in a large configuration, in the field of becoming, in its constitutive comings/goings"[35]—and they move along various starting points, recognizing each as anoriginal, as tenuous, as having an irreducible "insistent previousness,"[36] an insistent before, an insistent choreosonic vibration that exists prior to such a thing called History. And if ontological totality is about collective being, then perhaps what we're after is the tradition of the performance of the critique of the individualizing, subject-making nature of History, of historical being, of the historical moment.

If we follow Sylvia Wynter, the coloniality of being/power/truth/freedom would also have its historical resonances: the coloniality of History, of historical being, of being historical, of the historical moment, of making history. The coloniality of being/power/truth/freedom is assumed in each and every assertion of the desire to produce the historical. The Blackpentecostal tradition does not make so much as it unmakes History, and an analysis of the noise, the joyful noise, emerging from varied spaces will elucidate such claims. Noise is the critique of the proper including proper History, proper historical memory, proper historical moment. Noise is that which is purported to *not* belong, that which supposedly waits in need of abatement. To make noise, to make it joyfully, is to criticize the epistemology of western civilization, to critique the coloniality of being/power/truth/freedom, to perform an intervention into the object, the theme, and the transcendental subject of History. Harriet Jacobs heard noise. Such a hearing will have been the occasion for joy. In compressed space and time, such joy had to be unspeakable.

WHAT CAN ONE hear in confinement, and how can that hearing be connective lineament? In her grandmother's crawlspace for seven years—compressed as a means to escape, confined with access only to shallow air as a means to flight—Harriet Jacobs was both discarded and discardable.[37] What did it mean to be discarded, for discardable materiality to bespeak an ontological condition? What can we learn from Jacobs's existence in the crawlspace, of her throwing herself into claustrophobic conditions to stage her eventual scurrying away? Her discarded flesh bodied forth socially and a sociality. What is the social life of the discarded? Her existence in that crawlspace, as an object that was thrown and thrown away, is cause for celebration. Not a celebration of the conditions of emergence that demanded her being discarded—that would be quite vulgar—but a celebration of the love that the peculiar institution was to have interdicted, a love she was not to have or hold that prompted her desire for escape, a love as the grounds for her desire to give care. Harriet Jacobs—before any such twentieth-century Bonnie Brae Street or Azusa Street moment—knew something about Blackpentecostal aesthetic performance. What she did with her flesh, as care for her own and the flesh of others, is a frame for how we might want to think about care and concern generally. The choreosonic, for Harriet Jacobs, was an important resource for allowing her thriving, even in the most horrific of conditions.

> A small shed had been added to my grandmother's house years ago. Some boards were laid across the joists at the top, and between these boards and the roof was a very small garret, never occupied by any thing but rats and mice. It was a pent roof, covered with nothing but shingles, according to southern custom for such buildings. The garret was only nine feet long and seven wide. The highest part was three feet high, and sloped down abruptly to loose the board floor. There was no admission for either light or air. . . . To this hole I was conveyed as soon as I entered the house. The air was stifling; the darkness total.[38]

Jacobs's escape was grounded in the irruptive force of Blackpentecostal choreosonic practice. She wrote about the sound she heard in confinement, and that hearing was foundational for the telling of her narrative. Sound reverberated throughout Jacobs's text and is the residue and materiality of thought that her memory refused to forget. Severed sight, eclipsed connection: "And now came the trying hour for that drove of human beings, driven away like cattle, to be sold they knew not where. Husbands were torn from wives, parents from children, never to look upon each other again this side of the grave. There was wringing of hands and cries of despair."[39] Sound remains. Her text is a choreosonic performance.

> When I had been in the family [of Dr. Flint, the man who purchased and subsequently harassed her daily for sex] a few weeks, one of the plantation slaves was brought to town, by order of his master. It was near night when he arrived, and Dr. Flint ordered him to be taken to the work house, and tied up to the joist, so that his feet would just escape the ground. In that situation he was to wait till the doctor had taken his tea. I shall never forget the night. Never before, in my life, had I

heard hundreds of blows fall, in succession, on a human being. His piteous groans, and his "O, pray don't, massa," rang in my ear for months afterwards.[40]

To consider the sounds, those piteous groans, is to think about how sound can prompt movement toward escape. But more, sound compelled the movement of pen to paper. The sounds Jacobs heard "rang in her ears for months," so much so that she not only remembered the sound but also retold the sound to her audience. That ringing sound, that emanatory vibration, was the ground for the narrativity of the slave girl's incidents. Sound—what was heard—thus, was the residual materiality of enslavement. There appears to be, embedded in the text, an attempt to transfer the knowledge of enslavement to readers by way of recalling and retelling how the institution sounded, how the institutional force of enslavement reverberated, because sight was impossible.[41] Sound, then, was the *basis* for sight. Noise, the basis for writing. For Jacobs, sonic vibrations were a mnemonic reservoir that produced the very occasion to recall sights, sounds, smells, touches. Sound not only recalled memory but was the memory itself. The sound in Jacobs's text underscores how she cognized enslavement and she encouraged her audience—through the reiteration of sound events—to literally and colloquially *hear her out*, to listen to the text as it performs rather than simply reading it.

In Jacobs's recalling, the antebellum soundscape compelled thoughts of fear as well as excitement, terror as well as joy. She told of how slave codes were read aloud on ships: "Every vessel northward bound was thoroughly examined, and the law against harboring fugitives was read to all on board."[42] Throughout the text, Dr. Flint would read letters aloud to his family and to her grandmother. She described how sound technology was used to facilitate flight and escape: "It was not long before we heard the paddle of oars, and the low whistle, which had been agreed upon as a signal."[43] Having spent time under floorboards, in a swamp and years in a crawlspace, Jacobs's text continually "hears" sound through spaces of darkness, spaces where sight was at best compromised and, at worst, impossible. That sound is noise. What materializes is a theory of memory, recall, and narrative that depends upon lost sight, amplified noise. The creek of wood floorboards. The sound of sweeping. The voices of children playing. The sonic in her text functioned in the service of elaborating the experiences of enslavement without allowing a reader's slippage into mere empathy, which, Saidiya Hartman says, dovetails in a "too-easy intimacy" that effaces the enslaved and "fails to expand the space of the other but merely places the self in its stead."[44] But the sonic was always of movement. The creek of wood floorboards announced the movement of flesh overhead; the sound of sweeping the movement of flesh cleaning floors; the sound of children playing the flesh of still living family moving, living, having their being. The sonic, in other words, was always the enunciation of choreosonic performance.

The thrust of Jacobs's text comes from the unbelievable: she dwelled seven years in the crawlspace of her grandmother's home. Near suffocation, Jacobs had very little room to maneuver her body, very little air to breathe and very little light through a crack in the wall. Nathaniel Mackey in *From a Broken Bottle Traces of Perfume Still Emanate* explicates the generativity of compression:

> I've come up with a very dense form of writing, brief blocks of which are to be used to punctuate and otherwise season the music. Compressed Accompaniments I call them. I'm enclosing copies of the ones I've written for this piece. . . . What happens is that each station is presided over, so to speak, by one of the Accompaniments, and in the course of the performance each player moves from station to station, at each of which he or she recites a particular Accompaniment which "defines" that station. (I put the word "defines" in quotes because the point is to occupy a place, not to advocate a position. The word "informs," it occurs to me now, might get more aptly at what I mean.) . . . Some would say it's not my place to make comments on what I've written, but let me suggest that what's most notably at issue in the Accompaniments' he/she confrontation is a binary round of works and deeds whereby the dead accost a ground of uncapturable "stations." The point is that any insistence on locale must have long since given way to locus, that the rainbow bridge which makes for unrest ongoingly echoes what creaking the rickety bed of conception makes. I admit this is business we've been over before, but bear with it long enough to hear the cricketlike chirp one gets from the guitar in most reggae bands as the echoic spectre of a sexual "cut" (sex/unsexed, seeded/unsown, etc.)—"ineffable glints or vaguely audible grunts of unavoidable alarm."[45]

Having dwelt in the crawlspace for seven years, she can be said to have defined—to have informed—that small, compressed space by her absence, a position she occupied without advocating for its health or safety. Mackey's text demonstrates the ongoing preoccupation with movement and compression, antiphony and texture, which vivifies black performance traditions from spirituals to gospel, from blues to jazz, a preoccupation that animated Jacobs's text likewise. Jacobs's ability to recall life that transpired while she was in the crawlspace—her mode of escape—depended on a forced looking away that heightened her awareness of the sound in and around her. The sound heard, generally considered "noise"—of children and horses and wind blowing, for example—was differently intentioned, through imagination, in Jacobs's text. Jacobs was compressed, indeed, but also accompanied, which is to say in existence with others, pointing us toward the ways in which compression and constraint do not ever remove possibilities for movement, flight, and escape.

Jacobs's attunement to black performance—which is to say the transfer of resistance as the force for life, the transfer of resistance as energetic field, through the reiteration of motions, migrations, flights, fleeings, abscondings, escapes—through Jacobs's own stilled flight, stilled escape in the nearly suffocating crawlspace concerns, quite literally, breath and movement, giving and withholding. Giving herself over to conditions of confinement, withholding as much sound as possible in order to remain undetectable, those movements were held together in her performance of/ as escape. Jacobs's life and escape anticipated and pre-performed Martin Heidegger's later theory of being, time, and the given, his theorizing giving and withholding.[46] Heidegger reminds readers that Being and Time are not actual, but their givenness, their gifting, their extending outward and manifesting a sociality, a relationality, are real. "Being is not. There is, It gives Being as the unconcealing; as the gift of unconcealing it is retained in the giving."[47] He continued, "Time is not. There is, It gives time. The giving that gives time is determined by denying and withholding nearness."[48]

Jacobs anticipated and performed this. She unconcealed herself as a gift by enclosing herself in tight quarters; she discarded herself because of the discarded nature of the enslaved. That discardedness, or following Heidegger, "self-withdrawal," was a giving, it was a gift that operated in a different spatial and temporal measure than western thought allows. Her self-withdrawal could be thought as a secretion into the interior, a letting out into the crawlspace for protection. Temporal presencing depended on the gift of unconcealment. To be attuned to the gift and the given is to consider an irreducible relationship of giving, blackness, and the discarded. Daphne Brooks thinks through issues of approach and proximity—and, thus, giving and withholding—in her theorization of black cultural production and performance. Brooks's idea that "motion, migration, and flight" as an "operative trope in the black abolitionist cultural production of the slave's narrative" underscores how being discarded and discardable created the occasion for Jacobs to critically intervene into a system, an institution, a given and known world that would have her, her progeny, her peoples, in such conditions of violence and violation.[49]

While the "piteous groans," one form of screaming, quickened Jacobs's knowledge of the distasteful, doleful nature of enslavement, we must also consider what it means to occupy the space of a scream, what it means to position oneself within sonic materiality that bespeaks burden and pain but also allows for the protection against burden and pain.

> When you yell/scream, you take a deep breath and basically hold it to get the sound out . . . so you are not breathing. This leads to decreased oxygenation to the fetus. Oxygenation to the fetus is always important, but becomes critically important during the labor process. The contractions associated with birth have the potential to lead to decrease oxygenation to the fetus, leading to a certain type of heart deceleration, leading to a possible urgent/emergent situation. So yelling in labor can be like a double whammy.[50]

An OB/GYN colleague of mine sent me a personal communication concerning the nature of screaming when giving birth. It was on the occasion of the birth of my godson at a natural birthing center in Philadelphia that whet my appetite for thinking the relationship of sound, and breath, to screaming. The midwife told my friend that screaming while in labor merely restricts airflow into and out of the body, whereas moaning would allow her a bit of physiological reprieve, how moaning would, indeed, let her labor with less discomfort. Though the pain is sharp, screaming blocks airflow, it is literally sound without the exhalation of air, *sound without the operation of breathing*. Such that the screams of the man that rang in Jacobs's ear were a withholding of breath and the giving of sound. In this instance, the discarded and the discardable is the emission of sound, the scream itself. The discarded and discardable materiality of scream is art; art insofar as in its presencing, it quickens in the hearer a response, whether an averted hearing so as to not respond or as a desire to listen more deeply, more intently.

The scream is an aesthetic object that carries the trace and weight of its source of emanation. Jacobs—within the hold of the crawlspace—"informs" rather than "defines" the sonic materiality, the choreosonic reality, of noise, of joyful noise, of Blackpentecostal aesthetic performance. She made herself discardable; she made herself noise. And this for love.

> Morning came. I knew it only by the noises I heard for in my small den day and night were all the same. I suffered for air even more than for light. But I was not comfortless. I heard the voices of my children. There was joy and there was sadness in the sound. It made my tears flow. How I longed to speak to them! I was eager to look on their faces; but there was no hole, no crack, through which I could peep.[51]

> "I was standing under the eaves, one day, before Ellen [Linda Brent's daughter] went away, and I heard somebody cough up over the wood shed. I don't know what made me think it was you, but I did think so. I missed Ellen, the night before she went away; and grandmother brought her back into the room in the night; and I thought maybe she'd been to see you, before she went, for I heard grandmother whisper to her. 'Now go to sleep; and remember never to tell.'"

> I asked him if he ever mentioned his suspicions to his sister. He said he never did; but after he heard the cough, if he saw her playing with other children on that side of the house, he always tried to coax her round to the other side, for fear they would hear me cough, too. He said he had kept a close lookout for Dr. Flint, and if he saw him speak to a constable, or a patrol, he always told grandmother. I now recollected that I had seen him manifest uneasiness, when people were on that side of the house, and I had at the time been puzzled to conjecture a motive for his actions.[52]

The noise of these scenes produces an audiovisual encounter for readers. The noise Jacobs heard, at the moment of their emanation, had to go unspoken. But the noise Jacobs heard was also cause for great joy. Further still, the noise her son heard about him—the cough above him near the wood shed—became an occasion for joy. And for him, as for Jacobs likewise, such joy was unspeakable. Joyful noise. What does it mean for him to hear noise, to hear coughing, and have knowledge of mothering that was thought to not exist for black women in the antebellum period? What does it mean for him to hear noise and recognize life therein?

His mother Harriet made herself noise, and made noise, and such performance, such making, was a moment to enact radical care through radical sociality. This radical care and sociality was established through another epistemology, an epistemology that did not assume the discardability and uselessness of noise. This radical care and sociality was established through another epistemology, an epistemology that did not ground the capacity for thought in the capacity to *see* at the expense of other sensual capacities. Rather, this radical care and sociality was established through a choreosonic itinerary and protocol, through thinking ceaseless noise as productive of otherwise possibilities for existing together with others. Noise had a hearing that was generative for understanding life, both on the inside of the crawlspace where seeing was nearly impossible and on the outside where only sound could tether those lines of kinship. Noise was a critique of historical being, the historical moment. Noise heard, making noise, both illustrate the necessity of abiding, abiding against thinking categorical distinction as the grounds for producing History. They operated from a different hermeneutic altogether. Joyful noise.

LIKE A REPETITIOUS testimony service chorus, I return yet again to Karl Marx's "On the Jewish Question," as it is a useful means to anchoring the relation of class aspiration to religiocultural aesthetic performance. Marx wrote in reply to Bruno Bauer, resisting Bauer's claim that, for Jews, "you cannot be emancipated politically without emancipating yourselves radically from Judaism,"[53] because implied in such a claim is the idea that there exists persons who are "more capable of emancipation" than others.[54] Marx's concern about the possibility of emancipation for the Jew takes a more general form as the possibility for emancipation for the person through politics, through the state, through the performance of propriety, normativity, in the service of the state. The refusal to perform religiosity in order to gain political freedom is a ruse. One would need leave behind their primitivity, always interarticulated with a backward superstition and cultic behavior, in order to be secular and, thus, enlightened. But Marx demonstrates how this leaving-behind is no emancipatory process at all, but a new submission that radically buttresses the inequitable distribution of power that the state needs for its ongoing operation. I think Marx would perhaps think something like a politics of avoidance would produce abolition and emancipation in excess of, and as an antagonism to, the state, to political emancipation. And Marx, like Zora Neale Hurston after him, realized the ways class aspiration had lots to do with the aesthetic practices that are thought to be in excess of, discardable to, ways of life.

So what would it mean to give the politics of avoidance a hearing? How does the choreosonic performance of the politics of avoidance offer a critical analytics for contesting theology-philosophy as categorically distinct modalities of thought? Enlightenment thought, following Ronald Judy's analysis of the separation between theory and aesthetic—where the aesthetic is the discardable immateriality, the excess that is not only unnecessary but a fundamental flaw in the history of thought and Being—was a problem of the literary, by way of representation of verifiability and reliability.[55] That is, it sought to create and understand the notion of culture by way of the written word. I would like to extend Judy's analysis of the rupture of theory from aesthetics by considering the separation as a moment of the enactment of the aversion that I believe blackness, as a resistance that is prior to power, calls into being. The *a*theological-*a*philosophical choreosonic performance—performance that is willfully unreasonable for the untrained ear, performance that gathers and disperses noise—is excess, is the Blackpentecostal aesthetic. I consider the excess—song during Testimony Service, praise during Tarrying—as resisting the spilt between theory and aesthetic. The split and subsequent opposition of theory to aesthetic, wherein theory was privileged as dematerialized and the result of the process of thought, the aesthetic is that which is so averted. Enthusiasm found a similar split and critique as a bodily manifestation. The enthusiastic and aesthetic, then, were victim to the aversion, a turn and turn away, a shift and displacement, a split and division.

What the Saints call Testimony Service doesn't so much begin as much as it happens, as it eventuates, as it anoriginarily opens. Someone might sing a song or lead a prayer, but the service doesn't "begin," because such a concept would presume that the work of Spirit is in need of being convoked. But the Blackpentecostal belief that one *carries* the Spirit with them on a daily basis, that one does not "catch" but instead one will "have" the Spirit indwelling is important. This belief in indwelling means that one does not need to conjure up Spirit, but rather Spirit is the indwelling force in which

Saints participate ongoingly. Without borders. Without enclosure. Like a dream state, Saints just end up in the middle of—they slip into—the event of encounter called Testimony Service. Such slippage happens through a choreosonic itineration and protocol. The Saints take up the *potential time* of otherwise temporalities and spatial zones, the potential time marking the fact of an immediately to come, a soon-to-come, encounter with the divine.

Reverend Ford Washington McGee recorded various live albums produced by Okeh Records and Victor Records, spanning the years between 1926 and 1930. Born in Tennessee, McGee joined the Church of God in Christ in 1918, a group that was at that time twelve years old, in its adolescence. In his various recordings are sermons, exhortations, and testimonies of Saints interspersed with song. Titles such as "From the Jailhouse to the Throne," "Shine-Drinking," "Women's Clothes (You Can't Hide)," and "Everybody Don't Know Who Jesus Is" give a round picture of the types of things he was wont to discuss in his sermonizing.[56] But there is one recording in particular that is useful for thinking about the choreosonic atmosphere created by Blackpentecostal testimony service.

In the recording titled "Testifyin' Meetin'," one is immediately drawn in by the sonic environment the Saints created for critical reflection on life, a space for praise. McGee commenced the first song, low voice full of gravel and conviction, along with the strum of a guitar and the sound of women Saints follow after. He then asked for Sister Griffin to "give us a good testimon-ay!" I imagine her jumping up from her seat, because, as she says, she "thanks the Lord for Jee-suuus! And the power of the blood!" The excitement of her voice, no doubt, was matched with a choreographics of the body, the animation of praise. The gesture, the posture, of the flesh has to meet the performance of voice, the performance of breath. This is the choreosonic performance of Blackpentecostal aesthetics. Sister Griffin continued, briefly, until she sat, and McGee began a rousing chorus of Johnson Oatman's 1903 hymn, "Lift Him Up." After they sang one round of the chorus, McGee called on Mother Hooks to testify about the goodness of the Lord. And she was simply happy for "this wonderful way of salvation!" Following her testimony, yet another song, "I found Him, and I'm Glad!"

The testimonies are song's punctuatory irruption. The testimonies do not necessarily interrupt but introduce a new path by which the Saints could flow; they are integral to the improvisational structure. The testimony serves as a point of transition between songs, between affective moods, where rhythm and intensity ebb and flow. Each testimony—between song and sentiment—is both cutting and being cut, is both grounding and being grounded, by the Spirit. The point is not to begin and end songs, to begin and end testimonies. One is not in one song then another, in one testimony then another. Rather, the entire performance is to create a mood, to create an atmosphere, to create an environment where interruption is desired, where sporadic, spirited encounter happens. The transitions between movements, when thought through normative, western theology-philosophy would be categorical imperatives, endings calling for new beginnings. But the transitions, when conceptualized through Blackpentecostal aesthetic practice, are joyful noise, full of glory; these transitions are not discardable but create *together* with song the entire choreosonic mood and moment.

Jon Michael Spencer explains the testimony song as such:

> [Testimony songs] are used by the "saints" to commence their testimonies during testimony services. Opening one's testifying in this way is a longstanding tradition that flourished in the postbellum black Protestant and Holiness churches, later finding its way into Pentecostalism. In testifying, a worshiper stands, sings a verse or two (of the chorus) of a favorite hymn, and then gives her or his spoken testimony using the theme and language of the song. The fact that testimony typically begins with and is built thematically upon a hymn illustrates what an essential source of theology these songs have been for laity over the years of struggle.[57]

The praise song and chant "Yes, Lord," as performed by Pentecostal Temple Church of God in Christ in Memphis, Tennessee (1990), is a primary example of what Blackpentecostal noisemaking can do, what it can produce.[58] A point that produces transition while also being the transition itself, a seven-line song that cuts and is being cut, that grounds and is being grounded, this song, this chant, is an arrival and rupture through a word, yes. Pentecostal Temple singing "Yes, Lord," one hears the seven-line chant, beginning with the single word "yes." This word, this "yes," chanted seven times, descending up and down the scale to the key's resolve only to begin again. Then a break, from "yes" to "yes, lord." Punctuating the chant are hand claps, are the sounds of the bass and snare drum, of the cymbals, of Saints praising noise-like together. Such breaking of the "yes" to "yes, lord" to the shout, the dance. The song is, and is about, praise. It is noise made in the service of, with the purpose for, being joyful, bespeaking the unspeakableness of joy.

"Yes, Lord," has a storied and murky narrative. The authorship of the song often is attributed to Charles Harrison Mason, and it is certainly true that Mason was known to say, and to enjoy such saying, variations of the theme "yes, Lord!" often in his praying and preaching.[59] Though he never claimed to first sing this song, many in the Church of God in Christ consider it his writing and melodic pattern. However, biographer for Arenia C. Mallory—another of COGIC's famed members—claimed that she was the first to sing the praise in New York City as a means to public repentance for what the Saints conceived to be her act of "sin"—divorce.

> Certainly, the Lord was with Arenia Mallory on that day as she stood before the congregation in New York City. When she rose to speak, she repented and confessed her sin according to Acts 3:19. The presence of the Lord came upon her as she lifted her hands to God. Suddenly, the Lord spoke through her with a praise of "Yes, Lord." The whole church caught on fire and started singing the praise—"Yes, Lord"—speaking with others tongues as the spirit gave them utterance according to Acts 2:4.[60]

What we have, even at the level of the narrative about this chant that has come to stand in for the sound and anthem of COGIC, is an incoherence at the heart of the song. The incoherence has everything to do with the question of authorship if we operate from the episteme of modernity, from the cognized distinction of theoria from aesthesis. Yet, from a Blackpentecostal hermeneutic, authorship becomes unimportant. Unimportant because authorship cannot write one into being, being is not grounded in the capacity to be author. More important is the fact of its being sung in such a way that the song spread throughout not only the COGIC group but also several Blackpentecostal groups. The "Yes, Lord" chant is but a crystallization of thought, of an *a*theology-*a*philosophy grounded in a politics of avoidance. The chant "yes" is the kernel that has within it the whole and hull of the testimony song and tarry praise noise in its intensity and repetition. It is choreosonic in its centrifugitive force, culmination and commencement, agreement and dissent in the same tonal breath, harmonic utterance, polyrhythmic hush.

Seven lines that are repetitiously chanted, Saints begin, usually with singing the single word "yes." As they continue, Saints add to "yes" with "yes, Lord," and they sometimes sing vocables "oh!" or "mm!" They can also make earnest pleas, "have your way!" "in this place!" All these words, all these varied themes are crystalized in the one word, the rupturing "yes." Saints might sing this song for varied lengths of time, from two minutes to twenty, according to the feeling trying to be achieved when singing. The point of it all is that the "yes" is not reducible to the words, to the lyrics, but the ways with which the singing occurs. The song "Yes, Lord" is a moment of consent in a world that ongoingly exploits. Such that "Yes, Lord" can be thought to be a critique of the exploitation that is foundational to the political economy of racial capitalism; it can be thought to be the refusal of abstraction and alienation by the proclamation of a "yes" found in worlds of otherwise possibility. The "yes" functions as a "no" to present conditions, a comment on how "yes" is possible and—yes, even—desirable but not within the strictures of the known and given world's epistemology. "Yes" is for otherwise possibilities. "Yes" is holy.

Whether McGee's "Testifyin' Meetin'," Oneness Pentecostal refrains of "I've Been Down in Jesus' Name," or COGIC's "Yes, Lord," repetition during testimony service—of lyrics, of song patterns (AABA and 1–4–1–5 major chord progression, as examples), of sentiments—is of necessity. Repetition elucidates the catechismal nature and meditative quality of Blackpentecostal choreosonic performance. This catechismal nature and meditative quality is also, at the same time, a disruption of grammar, a disruption of an enclosed form. During the antebellum period, scripture catechisms were written specifically for negroes, for those enslaved—Cotton Mather's pamphlet "The Negro Christianized. An Essay to Excite and Assist that Good Work, the Instruction of Negro-Servants in Christianity"[61] and Robert Ryland's *The Scripture Catechism for Coloured People*[62] as two examples—encouraging white capitalists to care for the souls of these pieces of property. What intrigues in these catechisms is their grammatical nature, the ways in which there is a call and response that refuses extemporaneous utterance, that resists improvisation, that reduces the irruption of noise.

Catechisms written by missionaries for the instruction of slaves were adaptable to use in the teaching of reading and were used in that way, despite the claim that they were written for oral instruction. Most were prepared in simple, clear, short questions and answers, a method also used in primers. . . . The content of the catechisms emphasized salvation, not subordination, though most did include lengthy sections on duties of slaves to masters—after all, they had to be approved by masters in order to reach the slaves.[63]

The person is supposed to respond to queries with an affirmation or negation, and then the correct scriptural justification for such a position. Catechism—in this way—was a rote exercise, not about the change in heart and mind, but about the ability to respond correctly within the strictures of normative form. Peter Linebaugh in *Ned Ludd & Queen Mab: Machine-Breaking, Romanticism, and the Several Commons of 1811–12* wrote about "enclosure" of land, of family and of language as a problem of wealth and resource distribution: "The world was being enclosed, life was being closed off, people shut in. In 1795 before he was silenced by government the English Jacobin, John Thelwall, referred to 'the inclosing system' which he defined as 'that system of enclosure by which the rich monopolize to themselves the estates, rights, and possessions of the poor,'" and that "the system of enclosure applied to land where enclosure became commodification."[64] The concept of enclosure was not merely about land but also included the division of labor, transportation, and "in cultural expressions, too, we find several forms of closure, such as the dictionaries and grammars of language, the censorship of press and speech, and the silencing of Thelwall, who spent the rest of his life relieving stammerers by teaching 'elocution.'"[65] I consider the negro catechisms to enact the same logic of enclosure, the reduction of choreosonic possibility, the repression of joyful noise, the gathering up and discarding of speeched difference for the enunciation of spiritual coherence. Catechism is repetitious but in this instance is about reducing the improvisational impulse internal to repetitious function and form. Negro catechisms were a mode of noise abatement.

Negro catechisms were to be performed through repetition in such a way as to inculcate a certain reflexivity of yielding to being controlled, in such a way as to reduce the possibility for excess movement, excess thought. The catechisms, with their inclusive exhortations for enslaved peoples to obey masters, were a solicitation of acceptance of lot and station in life. They were not to allow for the flourishing of joyful noise and imaginative flight but were the production of theology-philosophy as delimited modalities of thought. Yet even such a theology-philosophy attempting to control black flesh failed in its very enunciation. In Ryland's catechism, one finds the breakdown from Standard English in the queries, beginning questions with the word "and" from one declarative idea to the next:

9. Does the happiness of the righteous consist in freedom from sin?—...
10. And in a discharge from all sufferings?—...
11. And in a state of perfection?—...
12. And of complete glory?—...
13. Are they admitted to a glorious abode?—...
14. And to a glorious employment?—...[66]

This "and" operates as a rupture, as an arrival, similar to the "yes" that COGIC Saints would sing almost a century later. That is, the "and" in Ryland's catechismal rubric is a point of transition; it breaks down standard and form even while purporting to create standard and form. His catechismal formula breaks its own theological-philosophical force at the level of rhetoric, at the level of grammar. And that is but the gift of black performance, of Blackpentecostal choreosonics. That the one undergoing catechism would need to respond "yes" to these posed questions does not, however, mean an affirmation of the system, of the institution, of the world created upon and predicated on the discardability of blackness. "Yes," in other words, needs to be understood as emerging from within its epistemological grammar, its own epistemological spatial and temporal zone. Such that if blackness otherwise than Kant's transcendental aesthetic, otherwise than the predestined possibility for liberation before and against being racialized black, a "yes" that emerges in black is an affirmation of such a zone, a critical intervention into and comment against the space of purported coherence. It is a "yes" that avoids the very encounter produced by aversion for blackness, for black social life.

Within the "Yes, Lord" chant is the resistance to such catechismal desire to produce categorical theological-philosophical distinction of a racialized salvation, a negro salvation that would have at its core the necessity of black subservience. Though it produces a catechismal affirmation, the chant at the very same moment of sung, moaned, breathed utterance, is the straining and striving against such normativity and form. The seven-line plea of "yes" with its variants are arrhythmic, and the Saints decide together at the moment of its singing how long the "yes" will stretch. Once "yes" is given over to melismatic disruption and elongation, to falsetto and yodel, over to growling and howling, given over to choreographics of gesturing flesh with hand claps, foot stomps and bowed heads, the word both is and exceeds the bounds of its linguistic enunciation. As such, the singing of the "yes" is about desire, desire for a new and living way, desire for horizonal thrust of otherwise.

To TARRY.[67] WHAT the congregants at Butts Miracle Temple COGIC in Daytona Beach, FL (2009) enunciate through voice, through flesh—screams and yelps, orations of "Jesus!" and "Hallelujah," the handclapping and murmuring—is anything but easy to recount through writing. This joyful noise, this tarrying praise, is not fully representable through writing; it avoids its own representation. Lindon Barrett wrote about how within western figurations for what it means to be human—and this would necessarily include theological-philosophical renderings of the question of humanness—that "those who master literacy defined in Western terms stand within the circle of language-consciousness and, accordingly, full humanity. Those who do not, stand without."[68] This is consistent with the lettered accumulation that catechism was supposed to produced in the enslaved, the ability to "read my title clear,"[69] that they would learn the Word by rote, that they would learn the Word and allow for the theological-philosophical question about the limits of humanity to be tested upon them.

There is an excess that joyful noise produces while producing excess, another mode of sociality and intellectual practice that is not reducible to language-consciousness, but one that, rather, abandons such easy representation. Of course, the possibility of the enslaved achieving "full humanity," according to western theological-philosophical constructions, would always be a question, never answered. Some scholars believe that Africans quickly acknowledged the necessity of learning letters as a means to freedom: "Africans who were enslaved quickly recognized the value of reading and writing—not only for their practical uses (from the beginning of slavery, slaves used reading and writing skills to run away) but because literacy, especially the ability to write, signified an establishment of the African's human identity to the European world."[70] However, this assertion assumes that the "African" wanted to establish something called "identity," and that to the "European world." The foundational principle to such a claim is that whatever would come to be called a Europe/an, an Africa/n, an America/n was not in flux at the time of the stealing flesh for capital trade; it presumes that not only was a Europe/an a coherent idea but that that called Africa/n was also, at the very same time, coherent and that the African would recognize such coherence and aspire toward that identity. Lettered accumulation would amount to nothing other than an aspirational tendency toward whiteness, the desire to own property.

What the joyful noise of tarrying highlights, it seems, is the intentional refusal to produce coherence, the intentional standing outside the circle of language consciousness, the intentional celebration of Spillers's vestibularity. This necessarily means, then, that the choreosonic performance of Blackpentecostalism is always a critique of normative function and form that is the grounds for the western theological-philosophical epistemology, including the way this episteme produces race, gender, sexuality, class, ability, nationality as categorical distinctions. Noise—joyful as it is—gets in the way of such smooth, easy conceptualizations. Joyful noise is the choreosonic resonance and reverberation of being "vestibular to culture," wherein this condition is not denigrated but celebrated as yielding the possibility to see, feel, experience, to know worlds, to see both within and beside Du Boisian veils, varied consciousness that are produced through choreosonic sociality. And when not critiquing normative function and form, Blackpentecostals relinquish their birthright, they relinquish the very force of otherwise possibility that made and makes them possible as an intervention into the marginalizing violent world. Blackpentecostal aesthetics, to assert again, do not *belong* to Blackpentecostals but can be enacted. Blackpentecostals simply carry the tradition in secreted and clandestine modalities.

What is heard during the tarry service is not easily translatable, such that writing about it necessitates a different—a Blackpentecostal—relation to language, to literacy, to linguistics. Joyful noise found in tarry praise is unlike the "Yes, Lord" chant in that the praise noise is not reducible to linguistic representation; even when one hears exclamations of "yes!" and "Jesus!" and "oh!," apparent is how there is a "noise under the noise,"[71] how there is a hum, a persistence in intensity that is dynamic—at once loud, at once quiet, always reflective. David Daniels has this to say about

Blackpentecostal sonority: "The syntax of early Pentecostal sound contained 'more non-verbal sounds' than its Protestant counterparts on the American religious soundscape. There was a place for 'sporadic, unpredictable' sounds."[72] And there is, according to him, a liturgical role that silence enacts: "According to various accounts the early Pentecostal soundscape privileged silence, especially in tarrying and other forms of prayer. Silence was more than a gap in worship; silence played a liturgical role."[73]

The *Los Angeles Times* 1906 article that "announced" the first sounds of this movement on Azusa Street made this audible. "Colored people and a sprinkling of whites compose the congregation, and night is made hideous in the neighborhood by the howlings of the worshippers who spend hours swaying forth and back in a nerve-racking attitude of prayer and supplication. They claim to have 'the gift of tongues;' and to be able to comprehend the babel."[74] The utterances were not spoken but breathed, and the energy the congregants accessed and produced worked them into a frenzied state. The noises of "howlings" interrupted the restfulness and quietude of Azusa Street neighborhood, though it was intentionally chosen because it wasn't residential. Consistent with the Acts 2 accounting of Pentecost, there were sounds that changed the soundscape of Los Angeles so much so that everyone took notice. And if Daniels is correct in his assertion about the liturgical role of silence during tarrying, it becomes important to note that the aesthetics of Blackpentecostalism are not merely about loudness but are about the use and deployments of volume, the leveling and leveling off of such vibrational sonic velocities. Normally considered simply "loud," what is apparent is how Blackpentecostal aesthetic practice is dynamic, how the practice plays with volume, intensity, control, how the practice modulates and undulates.

What the joyful noise of tarrying praise and testimony service songs both produce is, not the reunification, but the performance of the inseparability of aesthesis and theoria, the performance of the ongoing irreducible interrelation that exists before western theological-philosophical thought performed an operation of categorical distinction. What joyful noise, what Blackpentecostal aesthetic practice is, is the reckless abandonment, an escape and secretion *into* the flesh, a choreosonics that decidedly pronounces the sacredness of the black flesh. Aesthetics, here, are always a political, economic project; they are always the practice of theory inseparable. Of tarrying particularly, Daniels states, "Tarrying parallels contemplative prayer forms that seek communion with God rather than those that seek union with God. . . . While most contemplative prayer forms limit bodily involvement and movement, tarrying incorporates active, bodily participation. Finally, tarrying is not a private experience of an individual directing him- or herself; it is a communal event with the encouragement of altar workers and a prayerful congregation."[75] Daniels points in the direction of the present writing; he sets the ground for considering the choreosonic dimensions of Blackpentecostal aesthetic practice. If the shout tradition is an enactment of centrifugitivity with its centripetal and centrifugal force at each turn in ways that Blackpentecostal sounds are likewise, then there is ample ground upon which to begin thinking about the sound of tarrying and testimony service singing, the sonicity and its tradition. This sound, this intensity we find in the soundworld of Blackpentecostalism has its tradition performed in the meditative resistance, restive love, against marginalization and oppression, to being stolen and sold as chattel. This tradition is not the establishment of historical being but its obliteration. We turn to the soundworlds of the enslaved during the antebellum period.

It may appear a bit strange to connect the joyful noise of Blackpentecostal testimony service songs and the tarry praise to the seemingly "secular" work songs performed on plantations during the antebellum era, but the performance forms of the sounds, of the choreosonicity, is what I believe make the relation something other than tenuous. Samuel Floyd stated that work songs "were characterized by regular meters and rhythms, contained grunts and moans as part of their expressive vocabulary, and made use of overlapping call-and-response constructions."[76] And as Anthony Heilbut argues, "The essence of the gospel style is a wordless moan."[77] Moreover, Shane and Graham White's research into the sonic environment of New World slavery assert that calls and hollers could be used to enunciate "loneliness, pain, or despair," but at other times, such sounds could be used to measure distance.[78] Some utterances were "pure sound rather than . . . vehicles for the conveying of information."[79] Also included were "vocal leaps, glides, moans, yells, and elisions";[80] a "tendency of black singers (and instrumentalists) to 'play' with pitch, to worry, for example, the third and seventh degrees of the scale" and the "practice of extending the number of syllables in a sung word in order to give greater scope for melismatic play."[81] "Bent" notes assume a western episteme; it assumes there is a pure note, a pure sound, and its being bent. Yet each tone in such bending is its own note simultaneously. Such that each tone within the range of what is it is initially thought to bend is both note and intervention. And this relationship, this relay, is irreducible. The distinction of note from its bending obtains only after one assumes a modality for cognizing sound and hierarchizing some of it as pure.

These various sounds—found at the plantation—were themselves a form of labor; they were work produced in excess of the chopping of wood, the hoeing of crops, the suckling of children. These sounds were a practice that both allowed for the persistence of the object, of the analog-organic machine to live—which, also, was the capacity for the analog-organic machine to produce work for another—while concurrently sounds that critiqued the conditions under which such labor was produced. A yes to life, a no to the conditions of living. The sounds were a choreosonic Luddism, breaking the machine while allowing for its perseverance. Enslaved persons were to be machines, analog-organic cyborgs that were to merely produce labor—the harvesting of cotton, coffee, sugar, and tobacco, for example—and anything in excess of that production was discardable. The work, the labor, functioned as catechismal; it was to inculcate a "pious disposition"[82] toward the rote exercises of chopping, planting, and hoeing. But this choreosonicity, this excess, was hallucinative of another life, another zone of inhabitation upon which to perform an intellectual practice. Choreosonic vibration broke—while giving—form. Otherwise form, otherwise forum. That is to say, otherwise shape and otherwise space. "They could send a signal through drums . . . and they used to holler to each other through codes. . . . They would holler. And even the ladies, when they would be going to work, they would signal each other. Just holler, tell'em we ready. . . . They had strong voices, their voices just carried. I don't know why your voice don't carry like that now. But they could holler."[83]

The vocable, the rhythm: both audible, both resonant, both vibratory, felt in the flesh, heard. The sound of the drum, the sound of the voice, the sound of the flesh when clapped, slapped, carries. But what is being carried, carried underneath and above the vibratory frequency that can be heard? Is there a presence in the sound that bespeaks the condition of life, abundant life, that emerges within the crucible of enslavement, that is not created but rather rises to the occasion of brutal violence and violation? What is carried, it seems, is the sociality of otherwise form, otherwise forum, grounded in the reality of its present moment, open to the possibility through the improvisatory use of imaginative faculty. And it was this imaginative faculty was integral to the critique of the economic system of exploitation that needed their analog-organic flesh.

For Karl Marx,

> *Labour* is the activity of the worker. It creates all value, and is itself invaluable; its only measure is time. The commodity the worker sells the capitalist is his power to labour, or, yet more accurately, the "right of disposition" over his (or her) labour power . . . that is, the right to determine how this power will be used. The sale of disposition over labour power is therefore not only a 'purely economic' but also a political act. During the period of work, the worker does not have the right of self-determination, but becomes an unfree person, little distinguishable from a slave. With this concept of what it is the worker sells the capitalist, the term 'political economy' acquires its full meaning.[84]

And Cedric Robinson extends Marx by engaging labor in black. He says, "The creation of the Negro was obviously at the cost of immense expenditures of psychic and intellectual energies in the West. The exercise was obligatory. It was an effort commensurate with the importance black labor power possessed for the world economy sculpted and dominated by the ruling and mercantile classes of Western Europe."[85] He goes on to say:

> This "Negro" was a wholly distinct ideological construct from those images of Africans that had preceded it. It differed in function and ultimately in kind. Where previously the Blacks were a fearful phenomenon to Europeans because of their historical association with civilizations superior, dominant, and/or antagonistic to Western societies (the most recent being that of Islam), now the ideograph of Blacks came to signify a difference of species, an exploitable source of energy (labor power) both mindless to the organizational requirements of production and insensitive to the subhuman conditions of work.[86]

Finally, Robinson offers that "African labor power as slave labor was integrated into the organic composition of nineteenth-century manufacturing and industrial capitalism, thus sustaining the emergence of an extra-European world market within which the accumulation of capital was garnered for the further development of industrial production."[87]

According to Marx's *Grundrisse*, work-time makes an individual unfree, work-time is the condition of enslavement. If this is correct, then enslaved Africans were, of necessity, constantly "at work," "on the clock," punching perpetual timecards without any relief. And this because if enslavement and work-time are coterminous, one enslaved will not have had the ability to "own" one's labor power and would be, thus, in a continuous mode of work. Planting and hoeing? Work. Sleeping and praying? Work. Transatlantic enslavement would then have been the condition that eliminated the possibility of non-work-time; it was, *essentially*, an attack on—through the creation of a violently exclusionary, categorically distinct—temporality. This temporality, the temporality of racial capital—the temporality, then, of western theological-philosophical thought—is always a racialized temporality, a temporality grounded in the capacity to produce racial difference, racial distinction as a timeless timeliness. With such a rendering, it would appear—at first blush, at least—that work-time as enslavement is totalizing. However, there is an excess, an excess in and as choreosonic, an excess that not only resonates—vibratory frequency—as dissent, this dissent, this choreosonic force is a critique of the very conditions under which work-time as enslavement emerges.

What presences itself in the choreosonic force of Blackpentecostal aesthetic performance is the breaking of the concept of "self-determination," a concept integral to the elaboration, to the emergence, of the object of work-time as enslavement. Within this break is a critical space of exploration to reconsider if effects of work, of slavery, on the person that works, on the person that is enslaved, are totalizing. I draw on Denise Ferreira da Silva who analyzes the very quicksand upon which the idea of self-determination is built. She finds that self-determination is a concept that metastasizes in the western philosophic tradition to account for, and theorize about, the ones presumed to be "without thought, will, or volition," and this is most assuredly a racial/ist category.[88] Self-determination, conceptually, is the assumption of European man as a thinker with will, with volition, and both the indigenes of the Americas and the black/negroes of Africa were—and still are today—without such possibility. Though she writes specifically about the creation of race, because of Spillers's "vestibularity"—always about the interarticulation of gender, sexuality, and race—we can extend da Silva toward how gender is a figuration of the same problem of self-determination.

What da Silva writes as the "others of Europe" would, by way of the problem of self-determination, assume a "Europe," a "man" and its "others," all configured through stasis and coherence, with the "others of Europe," always lacking will and volition. Such that these "others of Europe" not only lacked will and volition, but *having* will and volition would also come to mean having normative temporality by having the capacity for non-work-time. Going through da Silva, one finds the very aspiration toward self-determination a ruse—as a moth, once grasped, disintegrates into powder—even while the concept is proselytized in the service toward political emancipation. And so a return to Marx's critique of political emancipation in "On the Jewish Question" that also serves as a likewise appraisal of the concept of self-determination.

For Marx, the political emancipation of humankind would come by the reduction of difference, the removal of accent, the resistance to improvisation: "The state abolishes, in its own way, distinctions of birth, social rank, education, occupation, when it declares that birth, social rank, education, occupation, are nonpolitical distinctions, when it proclaims, without regard to these distinction, that every member of the nation is an equal participant in national sovereignty, when it treats all elements of the real life of the nation from the standpoint of the state."[89] Political emancipation is no abolition at all; it is life subsumed under the state, it is the diminishment of abundance. Political emancipation is submission to normative temporality, to eliminating non-work-time as a possibility for an "other," political emancipation is the creation of the margin through violence. Self-determination, then, is likewise in the service of the gathering up and removal of difference, in this case, of sociality, of commons. What one gives up through the political emancipation in order to gain citizenship is what one effectuates as self-determination.

"Ned Ludd," a mythical character at the dawn of the Industrial Revolution, picked up a hammer and began to smash machines that were replacing person power with automation. Though mythical, several peoples worldwide took up the cause of Ned Ludd, as they believed the Industrial Revolution was an attack on the commons, a desired obliteration of communal land, part and parcel of the enclosure process. Picking up hammers, Luddites "helped make it possible to see machine-breaking as a means of defending the commons. . . . The Luddites were machine-breakers of the north of England who differed from tool-breakers of the past or of other countries by giving themselves a mythological name, Ned Ludd, or Captain Ludd."[90] It was not only important for them to take up the cause of machine-breaking but to have for themselves a name by which they could be known. And so named, "Ned Ludd" became not merely a practice of smashing things, but an aesthetic performance, one that was taken up in poetics and visual arts.

Luddism, according to Peter Linebaugh, should not be relegated to actions taking place in England. Importantly for the present discussion, Linebaugh thinks of the Luddite tradition of the plantation in the Americas: "The destruction of farm implements by those working them on American plantations belongs to the story of Luddism, not just because they too were tool breakers, but they were part of the Atlantic recomposition of textile labor power. They grew the cotton that was spun and woven in Lancashire" and at least in part thinks of enslavement resistance as part of the story of Luddism because the plantation was foundational to and part of the political economy to which Luddites in England were responding.[91] But does machine-breaking need only occur through the hammer against the machine?

If, as Linebaugh contends, "slavery and the machine produce the person as automaton,"[92] a Luddic relation to the enslaved-as-machine would mean the breaking of oneself, the hammering of one's body. Though there are examples of enslaved persons mutilating their flesh in the service of this very possibility of inhibiting work, were there other options?

> Calls, cries, and hollers; call-and-response devices; additive rhythms and polyrhythms; heterophony, pendular thirds, blue notes, bent notes, and elisions; hums, moans, grunts, vocables, and other rhythmic-oral declamations, interjections, and punctuations; off-beat melodic phrasings and parallel intervals and chords; constant repetition of rhythmic and melodic figures and phrases (from which riffs and vamps would be derived); timbral distortions of various kinds; musical individuality within collectivity; game rivalry; hand clapping, foot patting, and approximations thereof; apart-playing; and the metronomic pulse that underlies all African-American music.[93]

This is an exhaustive listing of the "pulse that underlies all African-American music,"[94] according to Samuel Floyd, consistent with what Shane White and Graham White underscore about the choreosonic world of the enslaved during the antebellum era. I want to consider these various sounds, this created sonorous world, as using the verve of voice and noise to break the analog-organic machine, to break the automaton, through evidence of life, by improvisatory performance, through breath, through black pneuma that animates any sonic performance. What if these varied sounds acted as hammer against the condition under which such exploitive labor practices are produced? In this way, the hammer both smashes the ruse of the performer existing only for the service and production of the owner, and the idea that the performer has no will, volition, or thought since the latter comes out, quite literally, through the utilization of choreosonic resources. "It is not surprising to find whites describing such sounds as 'wild and barbarous,' 'uncouth,' 'a dismal howl,' or 'hideous noise.' The African and African American practice of weaving a variety of wordless intensifiers—shouts, cries, yells, groans—into a melody, translating, thereby, these strongly felt emotions into sound, can only have increased whites' sense of alienation."[95]

Marxist alienation "is conceived of as fundamentally a particular relation of property, namely involuntary sale (surrender of ownership) to a hostile Other . . ."[96] What White and White stumble upon, it seems, is the "sense of alienation" that the sonorous world of Blackpentecostal aesthetic performance could induce for its listeners that had a relationship to property and ownership grounded in coercion and hostility. But whereas Marxian alienation is conceived as that which the worker as slave experiences—because work-time is enslavement and enslavement is the perpetual lack of non-work-time, is continuous work-time—here with the choreosonicity of African America, we find that whiteness as property produces its own virulent alienation against itself, here, a hostility befuddled by the inexhaustible resource of resistance found in black performance. That is, when at the moment of performance of the various sounds of African America, phrases such as "uncouth," "wild and barbarous," and "hideous noise," are used, these descriptors come to stand in rhetorically for a sense perception of what the involuntary purchase—through coercion as theft—of a resistant Other sounds like. As with Kant's dancing around the subject that was himself in Chapter 2, what the rhetorics reveal is the alienation produced on the speaker, as the speaker, because of the inalterable, untenable distance the desire, the ownership, the having of private property has produced between the speaker and the objects discussed. In such a way, the object becomes—by existing and abiding within social world even if by exclusion—an instrument.

To DESIRE THAT one "might be used as an instrument,"[97] to objectify oneself for the use of another, this desire has the capacity to produce a critique of a political economy, a mode of theological-philosophical cognition, that exploits based on the one, the object, said to have no will, no volition. To desire to be made instrument, to desire use for meditative, sacred practice as a means of connecting with others, illustrates will and volition that emerges from a different epistemology, a Blackpentecostal epistemology, a choreosonic form and forum. In the words of the testimony given by the Brother Steadfast at Rev. F. W. McGee's "Testifyin' Meetin,'" he asked that the Saints would pray that he would be "used as an instrument in His hand," and the choice of who he would be in service to was the choice to be made an instrument in the service—not for the purposes of "the world"—but as a critique of the world in which he found himself. A yes as a *no* to the current order of things. There is something about the desire to be made an instrument, to be fashioned into something that would sound and sound out, speak and speak against conditions in which one was forced to exist.

Blackpentecostalism, if anything, is an open-ended question, concerned fundamentally with how to strive against "the world." And the choreosonic world of blackness is necessarily an affirmation, a "yes" to the sociality that furnishes forth against the proper and individuation. Rhetorics of the barbarity and wildness of these sounds are the witness and confession of whiteness to the sense of estrangement that is produced by property ownership and cognizing categorical distinction toward self-determination. Such that what is generally deemed, from the side of ownership and propriety as "uncouth," "wild and barbarous" noise, is but the producing of theological-philosophical thought, a mode of cognition that represses the uncouth, wild, and barbarous excesses of imagination. This choreosonic way of life—at once considered discardable and excessive, though also, on the underside of such rhetorical dismissal, were considered moving—is the enunciation of an otherwise world, a world that vibrates against inequities of the one in which labor exploitation foundational. What if joyful noise bespeaks a sociality, a togetherness, that moves oneself and others toward that other world?

The phrase "crisis averted" is useful here. When this phrase is invoked, is the thing-in-itself any longer—and had it ever been—a "crisis"?

Pondering aversion and the (social life of the) thing averted, if theorized as a crisis—a car accident, a slip-and-fall, the lack of structure for Moynihan's negro family—once averted, what does that mean for the object of so-called would-be crisis? Is the thing itself a crisis, or is it the set of capacities to be crisis, to be engaged in crisis as process, as an accrual of those breaks, cracks, and fissures that make something crisis? For something to be an averted crisis, as a category, is to make a normative claim previous to situation, prior to event. It is to make a claim, a historical claim, a claim as historical being. Aversion, thus, names by way of negation, by way of that which is—quite literally—not, what has been obscured, what has slipped away. And when conceived as a making, as a process of accrual, then one would have to think about the structures and forces that go into such making, such creating. If the thing is the set of capacities to be made or created into crisis, we must pause to think about the forces that attempt such fashioning. This making, this creating, thus, is aesthetic, it is about a way to make, a desired form through which analyses occur. Aversion of the thing is about the effects, the affect, of the capacity to be infinity possibility and to quell such energy.

A theology-philosophy of aversion forestalls otherwise possibility, making normative claims on what any set of behaviors, or what any group of people, could and should possibly be. The "crisis" as the thing so believed to be the only future is but one possibility. To name the thing as crisis averted is to strip away the fact that the infinite set of capacities to be otherwise exists alongside the possible crisis, but it is also to refuse the fact that the infinite other possibilities cannot ever be fully named, claimed, or thought. This phraseology lays bare the fact of normative claim and stance of the very consideration of a thing as crisis. Moynihan looked at the negro Family, wrote about its nonnormativity, its resistance to patriarchal structure, as "crisis" that is enmeshed in a "tangle of pathology."[98] But, and of course, the notions of crisis and pathology were thought as such because of the centering of regulative narrative and behavior that sought to refuse the flourishing of life and love, kin and kith bonds that did not seek to merely mirror hegemonic priority. Concern with how the thing-in-itself avoids the claim that aversion produces, the claim that aversion bodies forth, occurs by way of performance, by way of event, that is at once resistant to any normative claim but also a general flow, a general directionality that vibrates, choreosonically moves and sounds out volitionally, with intention, with thought, without regard to the one averting. A politics of avoidance for the theology-philosophy of aversion makes possible the terms of thought, the terms of refusal by and in which the thing, the thing-in-itself, the object, the resistance of the object—which is to say blackness—operates.

We might, for example, contend that there was a particularly classist articulation of the normative behaviors and comportments for black religiosity that were not merely postemancipation, social uplift ideologies. Daniel Alexander Payne, bishop in the African Methodist Episcopal denomination, was very much a critic of the choreosonics of the Ring Shout because it was an embarrassment and the improper way to be Christian. Rather, he felt the dance was primitivist. He is quoted at length:

> About this time I attended a "bush meeting," where I went to please the pastor whose circuit I was visiting. After the sermon they formed a ring, and with coats off sung, clapped their hands and stamped their feet in a most ridiculous and heathenish way. I requested the pastor to go and stop their dancing. At his request they stopped their dancing and clapping of hands, but remained singing and rocking their bodies to and fro. This they did for about fifteen minutes. I then went, and taking their leader by the arm requested him to desist and to sit down and sing in a rational manner. I told him also that it was a heathenish way to worship and disgraceful to themselves, the race, and the Christian name. In that instance they broke up their ring; but would not sit down, and walked sullenly away. In some cases all that I could do was to teach and preach the right, fit, and proper way of serving God. To the most thoughtful and intelligent I usually succeeded in making the "Band" disgusting; but by the ignorant masses, as in the case mentioned, it was regarded as the essence of religion.[99]

And,

> I suppose that with the most stupid and headstrong it is an incurable religious disease, but it is with me a question whether it would not be better to let such people go out of the Church than remain in it to perpetuate their evil practice and thus do two things: disgrace the Christian name and corrupt others. Any one who knows human nature must infer the result after such midnight practices to be that the day after they are unfit for labor, and that at the end of the dance their exhaustion

would render them an easy prey to Satan. These meetings must always be more damaging physically, morally, and religiously than beneficial. How needful it is to have an intelligent ministry to teach these people who hold to this ignorant mode of worship the true method of serving God.[100]

Aversion is not only evident in the Enlightenment thought of figures like Burke and Kant, but also a theology of aversion undergirds the resistance to choreosonic social forms such as the Ring Shout. The words of Payne rather emphatically illustrate the ways in which a theology and philosophy of aversion is a desired repression, a desired dismissal and discarding of the choreosonic performance of Blackpentecostal flourishing. Payne used his preaching in order to prompt into the hearers notions of disgust with their aesthetic practices. Payne gave much grist for the mill: the dances, clapping, singing he saw—and, no doubt heard, because of vibrational resonance, no doubt felt in his flesh—were "stupid," "ridiculous," and "heathenish." These choreosonics were not rational and lacked grace and composure. They were performed by the "ignorant masses," those who refused to enter into something called "intelligence." As well, because of the exhaustion that arises from such midnight dancing, the shouters would be "unfit for labor." James Weldon Johnson corroborated this line of reasoning, stating that it was the "educated" of the ministry, of the church, who endured the primitivity of such choreosonics, such motives, eventually banning the practice altogether.[101] But the ring, with its choreosonics, with its movement and attendant sonicity, is work, it produces labor, it is a new form and new forum through which the *a*theological-*a*philosophical performance of blackness could be enacted.

Based on these articulations of aversion for particular social formations, I argue that western theology-philosophy is aversive in its logic, animated by political economy, animated likewise by grounding the possibility of entry into subjectivity with cognizing an Other's mental capacity. The economic condition is by way of abstraction and equivalence; it is an articulation of the forces of capitalist thought. Theology-philosophy is about positionality, about particular ways of (not) seeing, of (not) hearing. And mental facility is only possible for those who can be citizen-subjects. Subjectivity, then, is what one has when the excesses, the flourishes, the accent has been gathered and removed. Entry into subjectivity is violence and violative.

Maybe the worry Payne articulated is foundationally a claim about, and thus against, the efficacy, productivity, and creativity of centrifugitivity—the choreosonic ability to twist and spin and dip, to vocally glide, leap, and yodel—and utilize dissent as a form of life. Just what does one become, what does one desire, after having discarded the centrifugitive force that kept—and keeps—alive, that is vital? Crisis, indeed.

To name as crisis averted is to bespeak the knowledge of the one naming, the one glancing, the one refusing to gaze, the one turning away attention. Yet, such a knowledge assumes the position of the omniscient figure, of the sovereign; it is the materiality and bodying forth of a melancholy (loosely?) associated with a general, more fundamental, more foundational agnosticism (where agnosticism here indexes the fact of unknowability; where agnosticism indexes the fact of infinite possibility that cannot ever be fulfilled, cannot be fully considered); this agnosticism antagonizes. Thus, the assertion of aversion is to name or claim a thing by way of lack, by way of what withdraws; the assertion is an assumption that forecloses capacity—infinite possibility—of any thing to be; this foreclosure is a general antagonism against the worry of a general agnosticism; as such, the one averting places oneself in the position of one who has liquidated all plurality, has found essence, knows it, has stripped infinite away from possible, but not only the one who has liquidated, but who has created only one possibility.

For performance artist Adrian Piper, aversion and xenophobia—fear of an object previous to encounter—go hand in hand:

> *Xenophobia* interests me because I am the object of it; *self-transcendence* interests me because I want to understand the subject of it, namely you, there, near the center, in the mainstream. I want to understand what it is about certain kinds of subjects, as well as about certain kinds of objects, that makes you flinch, withdraw, or pour forth defensive rationalizations of your impulses to ignore, reject, or annihilate those you perceive as intruders, those who offend and threaten you by their very existence. I want to understand what it is like to be you. I want my work to transcend the limitations you impose on me, so I can better understand those you impose, doggedly, on yourself. I try to do this in my work by voicing you—sometimes unspoken and often unspeakable—thoughts, by depicting your visions and nightmares, by entering into your psyche, in all its variations, and inviting you to consider its contents—our

contents—with me, together. . . . I want you to be able to understand the experience that saturates so much of our lives in this society, of being held at a distance, examined, analyzed, and evaluated.[102]

Such imposed limitation is theological-philosophical, such imposed limitation is a *delimitation* of imagination, a delimitation placed on thought. Piper's theorizing of xenophobia and aversion yield the ways in which self-regulation—perhaps an attendant process to self-determination?—is necessary for the aversion to things, to objects, to persons as objects, to circumstance. Aversion to objects is the buttressing against a possible encounter and what is thus enunciated about the object from the one who has the faculties to judge normative taste is the refusal to think with the object. Piper's words, by "voicing" the desire of self-transcendence, forces the viewer, the hearer, the one who engages Piper's work to dance around the subject, to categorically distinguish choreography from sonicity in order to arrange and place thought, to remediate noise, and this arrangement, placement, and remediation in order to create a path around such voicing in order to sustain their attention to the art/work.

So what is this thing so averted? And what can we claim of such a thing? A "politics of avoidance" is that which exists previous to the claim aversion attempts to make—as a particular sort of crisis—on a thing is undone by the avoidance of such a claim. As a politics, I mean to index the mode of organization, sociality, that avoidance—quite literally, a voiding that is enacted before any claim to aversion—as practice takes. Theology-philosophy as aversion attempts to name as crisis previous to situational encounter, yet the averted thing makes an irreducible counterclaim and counterfactual, the thing enacts a dispossessive force on the scene that would so subject. Thus, with the politics of avoidance is the performance and performativity of the refusal to reduce personhood to subjectivity.[103] It is a politics, simply, because it is a form of life, it is a form life takes; it is a forum for life, and it is the forum in which life occurs.

Where the theology-philosophy of aversion privileges space and time as abstractions—both theoretical and physical—through the dematerialization of the object creating the possibility for intellectuality and subjectivity, the politics of avoidance privileges deepening and gettin' down together as the production of social intellect, the constant escape into "irreducible density" of and into others.[104] As a politics that avoids its own being stilled, stolen, stultified, the generalizability is at the same time the refusal of universality that extracts and abstracts from and discards of materiality, enthusiasm, experience. Choreosonicity registers difference with each movement and vibratory enactment on the ground, even while being collective, social resistance to aversion. The politics of avoidance of black performance instantiates the choreosonic "stealing away" because one doesn't have long to stay any "here." The politics of avoidance is the perpetual and ongoing rupture against enclosure; it is the enactment of centrifugitivity as constant escape from being stolen and stilled.

The Great Awakening revivals—looked at as a series of interconnected spirited protocols regarding movement of the Spirit through "enthusiastic" corporeal motor response—was concerned with one's capacity for salvation. I briefly turn to these revivals because they share in a genealogical relation to Blackpentecostal aesthetics, particularly given the critique of the choreosonic "enthusiasm" such as shouting and spirited singing. The critique of enthusiasm was grounded in, and extended, a conception of economy. With the Awakening revivals there was a general concern about the ability to be saved, articulated as the expressed predestined will and desire of the sovereign, was bodied forth through a general problematic regarding the negro/African/black capacity for conversion. Predestination was equitably distributed—as resource, as an accumulation of capital—through including the negro in the category of the possible, while remaining radically committed to a theological-philosophical conviction of negro/African/black being-as-inferior.[105]

Cotton Mather's catechism for negro conversion, for example, did not allow for negroes to exist materially in equanimity; Mather never questioned negro inferiority but was merely concerned about negro capacity—as test, as "trial"—for conversion. Negro conversion was not even primarily for the negro's soul; it was to assure that the white capitalist was mindful of his property and his heavenly duties:

And such an Opportunity there is in your Hands, O all you that have any Negroes in your Houses; an Opportunity to try, Whether you may not be the Happy *Instruments*, of Converting, the *Blackest* Instances of *Blindness* and *Baseness*, into admirable *Candidates* of Eternal Blessedness. Let not this Opportunity be Lost; if you have any concern for *Souls*, your Own or Others; but, make a Trial, Whether by your Means, the most *Bruitish* of Creatures upon Earth may not come to be disposed, in some Degree, like the *Angels* of Heaven; and the *Vassals* of Satan, become the *Children* of God. Suppose these *Wretched* Negroes, to be the Offspring of *Cham* (which yet is not so very certain,) yet let us make a Trial, Whether the CHRIST who *dwelt in the Tents of Shem*, have not some of His Chosen among them; Let us make a Trial, Whether they that have been Scorched and Blacken'd by the Sun of *Africa*, may not come to have their Minds Healed by the more Benign *Beams* of the *Sun of Righteousness*.[106]

A candidate was not one that had obtained, but one that had been nominated for a possibility, for a chance. Such that even Mather's words are not fundamentally about conversion as much as it is about chance, opportunity, a generalizable concern over fortune, grounded in concerns about theophany, about the nature of a deity that would have such categorical distinction be enacted. The conversion of negro-servants in the houses of capitalists would allow owners to "try," to become "happy instruments," in the service of the king. The conversion of negro-servants was the would-be extension, and grounding principle, of the general conversion of Christianity to whiteness, and this conversion would happen by the fruits that were borne—by doing the work of the Lord, the work of the ministry, by paying obeisance to the Matthews 28:19 "great commission." The general conversion of Christianity to whiteness, of making whiteness and Christianity coeval, necessitated black servanthood, needed for blackness, blindness, and baseness to be a trinitarian theological-philosophical means for thinking the Other of salvation. Mather's is a theological self-determination rooted in the assumption of, on the one hand, white capacity for will, volition, and thought, and on the other hand, an ongoing concern about a general incapacity for will, volition and thought with the negro/negro-servant as the incarnation of such concern. As with Kant's general purposiveness, here in theology as well, the negro comes to stand in for a set of propositional worries about transcendence, the divine world, and salvation.

Following the tradition of Mather, Great Awakening revivalists George Whitefield and Jonathan Edwards aestheticized the general concern regarding capacity for salvation through injunctions against emotiveness and irrationality, utilizing the blackness of negro skin, utilizing those "that have been Scorched and Blacken'd by the Sun of *Africa*," as always already producing the appearance of the too "enthusiastic." Enthusiasm was a category that concerned the theological, philosophical, and juridical modes of cognition, at least since the formative moments of Enlightenment thought. Anne Taves makes such an argument:

> In the quest for an end to religious dispute, enthusiasm (along with superstition) held pride of place as the enemy of reason. All the moderate leaders of the early-eighteenth-century revival, therefore, took aggressive action to distance themselves from the threat of enthusiasm. Most of the moderates, including George Whitefield and Charles Wesley, actively discouraged bodily manifestations while they were preaching. Others, such as Jonathan Edwards in New England and James Robe in Scotland, not only discouraged these bodily manifestations, they joined with ministerial critics of the revivals, such as Charles Chauncy, and Enlightened skeptics, such as David Hume, in actively seeking to explain them.[107]

Enthusiasm, as a denounced category, shared with other concepts such as "delusions," "experience," "madness," or pathological "religious despair." And it becomes clear that these terms share in the rhetorics of dismissal for the choreosonicity of blacks above as "wild and barbarous," "uncouth," "a dismal howl," or "hideous noise."[108] Such concepts were aestheticized as manifestations of choreosonic force of Blackpentecostal aesthetics through the movements, spatial peregrinations, and attendant sonic productions of flesh in response to some divine call or encounter. At the same time that flesh becomes targeted as the site of regulation against religious enthusiasm, experience, and despair, is the same epistemological moment that flesh was being refashioned for the exploits of racial capitalism.

The foundational grounds for capital accumulation was based upon African bodies, African workers, African labor, according to Cedric Robinson. He discusses how "the significance of African labor for the development and formation of the commercial and industrial capitalist systems can be only partially measured by numbers," and that "first, African workers had been transmuted by the perverted canons of mercantile capitalism into property. Then, African labor power as slave labor was integrated into the organic composition of nineteenth-century manufacturing and industrial capitalism, thus sustaining the emergence of an extra-European world market within which the accumulation of capital was garnered for the further development of industrial production."[109] This transformation of worker into property into labor power as creating the condition of possibility of capital accumulation was aestheticized and critiqued as a question of enthusiasm. Jordana Rosenberg enters the discussion given her critical analysis of the historical uses, the historicity, of "enthusiasm." Looping Robinson through the opening Rosenberg lets us then reconsider the transformations from African worker to property to labor power. Of enthusiasm, Rosenberg states that "the contradictions of capital accumulation" can be "clarified by reference to enthusiasm's mediation of the antipodean relationship between the constitution of the sovereign state and ideals of subjective freedom and autonomy on the one hand, and the transformation of the legislative apparatus to execute and regulate the extraction of profit from a work force compelled to wage labor, on the other."[110] Enthusiasm, as a category of analysis and as a performance of transcendence and spirituality, enjoyed a transformation as part of this new temporality of western theological-philosophical epistemology. Enthusiasm indexed a secularist transformation, where secular here denotes the underside of the "work force compelled to wage labor," given the fact of the "invention of the Negro" that "was proceeding apace with the growth of slave labor," thus, "Black labor was pressed into service."[111] Simply, though enthusiasm on its surface is about feasibility of capital accumulation through wage labor, it hides the fact that there was a force of nonwage labor undergirding even the wage labor system of exploitation.

Rosenberg discusses capital accumulation—a concern for Robinson's analysis of the invention of the negro—as a "secret" process, one that "takes place in hidden or occulted ways," always "made up of a complex interweaving of financial, social, ideological, and structural transformations."[112] She further argues that accumulation, as secret, is "the complex manner in which profit is reinvested back into means of production" that necessitates "money's apparent vanishing."[113] The focus on wage labor would compel one to ponder the apparent vanishing of money as the apparent vanishing of black labor, the apparent vanishing of black flesh. Curiously, secrets have to either be held or given away, such that the withholding and dispersal of secret knowledge is always a performative, aesthetic praxis. Holding both Rosenberg's investigation of enthusiasm with Robinson's attention to the invention of the negro in tension produces an analytics for thinking the interrelation of invention to vanishing, or what

Peggy Phelan considers as the disappearance and nonontic nature of "performance."[114] For example, Phelan states, "Performance's only life is in the present. Performance cannot be saved, recorded, documented, or otherwise participate in the circulation of representations *of* representations: once it does so, it becomes something other than performance. To the degree that performance attempts to enter the economy of reproduction it betrays and lessens the promise of its own ontology. Performance's being, like the ontology of subjectivity proposed here, becomes itself through disappearance."[115] The relation of invention to vanishing applies necessary pressure on the assumption of performance's disappearance because enthusiasm as a contemptible, discardable religious concept for figures such as Jonathan Edwards and George Whitefield was scorned, at least in part, because of the temporal immediacy with which claims to divine encounter were posited. Rather than disappearance, what we have is the constant vanishing of the appearance of what is supposedly apparent, causing us to plumb the depths below any surface, to submerge ourselves in the underwater and underground of black social life. Enthusiasm shares with blackness in terms of extraction and abstraction as the transformation of capital accumulation. This transformation—as the invention of negroes, on the one hand, and the critique of spiritual, religious enthusiasm, on the other—forces an analysis of the ways in which enthusiasm was critiqued as an affect of the flesh. I am most interested in how flesh that produced such enthusiasm within the context of theology was thought. Who took up enthusiasm as a force and who dismissed it?

Rosenberg finds that the critique of enthusiasm was enabled by disagreements regarding "direct experience"—was it attainable, how to verify such claims and who would desire such an experience?—with God. David Hume said as much: "Enthusiasm arises from a presumptuous pride and confidence, it thinks itself sufficiently qualified to *approach* the Divinity, without any human mediator."[116] Additionally, "religions which partake of enthusiasm, are, on their first rise, more furious and violent than those which partake of superstition; but in a little time become more gentle and moderate."[117] And though "enthusiasm is destructive of all ecclesiastical power," it is necessary in order to produce Enlightened thought; it serves a teleological ideology of proper development of subjectivity.[118] Though Hume analyzed enthusiasm, not in order to support religion but to seek for its ultimate dissolution, and though he summarily deemed the force of enthusiasm as dangerous, because he thought the force of enthusiasm could not be sustained, it ultimately was not worrisome to him. He had to assume that enthusiasm was a personal thing, a private property that could belong to individuals rather than an ongoing ontological force of which people share and participate. His analytics of enthusiasm were refracted through the assumption of subjectivity. Hume critiqued the animatory force of Protestantism and for protesting itself. Hume could not conceive of enthusiasm as something other than "property" that self-possessed, self-determined individuals could repress rather than it being the vitality, the flight and escape, of perpetual rebelliousness. To have enthusiasm as proper to individuals, to the self-possessed transcendental subject would be to impose and restrict the radical potentiality of enthusiasm as transformational force. The enthusiasm Hume critiqued would also be the derangement (de-arrangement, otherwise choreosonic) of his philosophic thought. But he ingeniously elaborated upon what it looks like, what thought acts like, when it is inadequate to approach its object because of an imposition of regulatory, normativizing, arrangement. He placed within the enthusiastic tradition those organized, in process through refusing teleology, ecstatic socialities, commoners. However, the tools he brought, a regulative protocol, could both detect the potency but misread the potentiality.

There was, however, a critique of enthusiasm *within* decidedly theological discourse. When articulated thusly, enthusiasm was still the figuration of a problem for knowledge and capacity of the Other; enthusiasm carried the weight of racial/ist logic insofar as it indexed the essence of the purity, coherence, and stability of Islamic, Christian, and Jewish identities.[119] Anne Taves writes about the theological critique of enthusiasm as critiques of enthusiasm's "strange effects upon the body," the "raptures," "extasies, "visions," "trances" and "revelations." Enthusiasm also produced "swooning away and falling to the ground" as well as shrieks and convulsions.[120] These effects on the flesh had the capacity for transfer. When shrieking during a camp meeting, for example, it was noted that they "catch from one to another, till a great Part of the Congregation is affected."[121] Though as a Protestant and Calvinist, Jonathan Edwards argued that direct experience was both profound and possible, he repudiated the idea that those strange effects were resonances of such experience.[122] Rather, he placed direct experience in the realm of the spiritual as opposed to the corporeal. Even in this placing, he "viewed the new sense as obscured by sin," thus, "direct experience could not be trusted to provide assurance of one's salvation."[123] He was, in other words, profoundly cautious, profoundly worried, about the flesh, about its capacity to be moved. The critique of enfleshed manifestations of one's conversion experience challenged protoenthusiasts' claims that direct experience with God was the condition of possibility for corporeal motor and audible response. Edwards averted the very question of flesh by stating that the senses are inherently sinful and should be repressed and regulated. In order to critique the behaviors of converted flesh, he danced around the very possibility of bodily, sensual salvation.

The politics of avoidance of Blackpentecostal choreosonic performance was implied in each and every critical remark against the effects of the flesh as a response to a nonmediated encounter with divinity. Talal Asad argues that secularism is a product of modern Euro-American thought, that secularism "presupposes new concepts of 'religion,' 'ethics,' and 'politics.'"[124] There is a nonsecular resonance of the interarticulation of blackness, experience and imagination that echoes the volume of the noise before repression and regulation. The critique of enthusiasm is the aversion for—choreographic movement away from, sonic regulation of improvisation—the choreosonic force of blackness. As an immediacy of encounter, the critique of enthusiasm highlights a conception of blackness as capacious, sublime experience.

The circum-Atlantic trade that Joseph Roach writes about as the trading of coffee, sugar, and—most vulgarly—human flesh (all as cargo) was foundational to a global capitalist system that bore the necessity to reconceive choreographies by way of geographies, cartographies, and topographies, or simply, the "New World Project."[125] Both Denise Ferreira da Silva[126] and Willie James Jennings[127] discuss spatial logics as germane to the process of racialization, the ways the ground upon which imperialism was enacted had to necessarily be conceptually theologized and philosophized as chaste, as available for missionizing, exploring, and exploiting. This spatial logic is within the cleavage where there was likewise a necessity for a hearing logics that would similarly racialize-as-Other those would-be abductees. These lands, and their peoples, were available because of the purported lack of civility, lack of "true" religion and, thus, lack of the proper means toward Christian civilization (thus they would need to be compelled by violent force). They would not behave on the land as owners, and such refusal of behavior was the occasion for both their being displaced from it *and* their being thought categorically distinct theologically-philosophically *as* racialized.

The New World Project was always and everywhere the interarticulation of religious, economic, and racial/ist logics by means of a dissociative, self-alienating, violent force. The New World Project was enlivened by the concern for articulating this self-determination, this ability to be Enlightened, to think for oneself. And it is not the "determination" that is of import but the concept of "self" that is nothing other than a racial/ized category of coherence, stasis. On the one hand, the arrival of Europeans into the now New World, bringing along with them disease, foliage, and Christ, displacing indigenes and forcing them to work in mines (as only one such example), introduced a radically different relation to the land upon which one stood and, thus, a different, which is to say a theological-philosophical, worldview. On the other hand, uprooting millions from various nations and bringing them to climes and work conditions different from which they departed is part and parcel of this project of new theological-philosophical violence.[128] Flesh uprooted, transferred, displaced. Ways of life uprooted, transferred, displaced. Flesh and ways of life as the material configuration of theological-philosophical aversion. It is no wonder that enthusiasm—that concept which easily slipped, for the self-determined ones, into notions of experience, madness, and pathology—was targeted as the stumbling block to self-determination, to universality. It is no wonder, then, that enthusiasm had to have its material resonance as a manifestation on the exteriority of the flesh and that manifestation—so easily thought to belong only to those who lacked self-determination (thought, will, volition)—was radically critiqued as in need of regulation. The choreosonics of Blackpentecostalism was the constant and radical contestation of such displacement.

BY OCTOBER 18, 1821, at "nearly 70 years old," an enslaved woman named Jenny was mother of "several" children, though the one news report that tells her story does not tell readers how many she indeed had.[129] At nearly seventy years old, Jenny was accused of both thefts from, then the murder of, one Sidney/Sydney with her daughter Ritter as a possible accomplice. Though she never admitted to either of the charges, blood was found on her hat and tracks leading from Sydney's dwelling to Jenny's were found. "If the shoe fits," so the news report intimated, she had to "wear" the guilt of such crime. What intrigues many about this particular news item is not the crime, nor the fact of her children's melancholy at the event of their mother's murder, but the choreosonic environment that other "colored people" produced in response to the hanging of Jenny at the gallows:

> Few remained unmoved by the wild grief of Jenny's children, several of whom were present, and whose feelings on this trying occasion it is easier to imagine than to describe. Their sorrow seemed contagious. When the awful moment arrived in which the sheriff proceeded to the execution of his duty, numbers fled from the spot, and several hundreds of the colored people, squatted on the ground with their backs turned to the gallows, covered their faces with their hands, and uttered a simultaneous groan, which while it expressed their feelings, added not a little to the horror of the scene.[130]

The simultaneity of the groan is what resonates; it leaves the story of this particular Jenny perpetually open-ended, left at the moment of transition, unfinished. The simultaneous groans, the performance of Blackpentecostal choreosonicity—the crowd squatted and groaned—opens questions regarding the effects and affects of such choreosonicity. What did such vibration produce in the hearers as well as what was generative about such choreosonic sociality for the squatters? Adding to the horror was an intensification of the feelings of displacement that was witnessed by the "several" children who watched the murder of a mother. What this simultaneous groan enacts, it appears, is but another example of centrifugitivity—coterminous centripetal and centrifugal force—but beyond that, it is the choreosonic action of a collectivity, refusal of individuation. This collectivized response to horror is in *potential*; it is never engulfed, never exhausted, never fully representable or repressible, but is excessive in its force. This excess is constitutive of the resistance to such degradation. It is collectivized, an otherwise form and forum of life, a politics of and as avoidance of "sense" and enclosure.

Jenny von Westphalen was seven years old and, quite literally, thousands of miles away when the enslaved Jenny above was murdered by the state of Maryland. Four years his senior, Jenny would quickly become a childhood playmate, teenage friend, and early twenties lover before a marriage to Karl Marx would take place. Though their lives could be no more different, it seems—as von Westphalen was born to Prussian aristocracy—the connection between von Westphalen and the enslaved woman in Maryland is not reducible to, nor as tenuous as, their first names. What the news story in 1821 recounts is that Jenny refused to admit to any wrongdoing and that there was no confession before her being hanged. That is, she held conviction even beyond the point of death, even in the theater that would be her public demise. She was unrelenting. Not because she did not care for her children, it seems, but because "a good name" was her choice; she could not "give the consent that, nevertheless, she [could] withhold" to the conditions under which she was held and, ultimately, in which she died.[131] That ongoing refusal would be their point of connection, the lived experience and fact of her life that gave rise to and purpose for the choreosonic modality, the choreosonic sociality, and response of the gathered crowd, that refused to sever intellectual practice from fleshly ways of being in the world.

Jenny von Westphalen was similarly convicted, in her case, about the cause of communism, the redistribution of wealth, the rise and revolution of the working class, and, not unimportantly, the love she had for the man who would start a movement. Her father—Baron Ludwig von Westphalen—so impressed with the teenaged Karl, would talk to him often about politics, religion, philosophy, and the cause of socialism on walks in parks and through neighborhoods.[132] However, Ludwig was not merely impressed with Karl's acuity for knowledge; he also invited his daughter Jenny along for many of these conversations, and she, without a doubt, registered her thoughts, feelings, and personal resistances within the conversations as well. That to say, she was treated as an intellectual of equal standing, not only to her father, but to Karl as well. Jenny von Westphalen quickly grew accustomed to such conversations with Karl, and it was then that the seeds were planted for a lifelong love relationship full of itinerant living, communing, and commotion.

Married in 1843, Karl Marx itinerated because of his "radical" writings that were being censored in various nations. Because of such censorship— most undoubtedly, however, not only of Marx—he and Jenny moved around Europe several times and even considered a move to the Americas. What remained consistent throughout their movements, with their forced itineration, was the refiguration of the domestic sphere. The Marx household was a gathering space for fugitives and revolutionaries. Babies bounced on the knees of Friedrich Engels, cigar smoke from Karl wafted in the noses of friends and refugees. Karl and Jenny enacted a sociality of the commons by the refusal of the home to be a domestic, private space. Karl's and Jenny's lives were characterized by nomadism and exile, a type of mar-ronage, of being on the outside in order to build otherwise worlds based in, and as the critique of, the world from which one escapes. The Marxes were enacting communism and that performance was a necessarily social engagement with others.

But to return to Jenny. I want to point to a passage from one letter, writ-ten before their marriage, which elucidates another aspect of the Blackpen-tecostal politics of avoidance to which I am interested:

> Often when I thus suddenly think of you I am dumbstricken and over-powered with emotion so that not for anything in the world could I utter a word. Oh, I don't know how it happens, but I get such a queer feeling when I think of you, and I don't think of you on isolated and special occasions; no, my whole life and being are but one thought of you. Often things occur to me that you have said to me or asked me about, and then I am carried away by indescribably marvellous sensa-tions. . . . Oh, my darling, how you looked at me the first time like that and then quickly looked away, and then looked at me again, and I did the same, until at last we looked at each other for quite a long time and very deeply, and could no longer look away.[133]

What von Westphalen illustrates is the resistance to the averted gaze, and that resistance has within it the kernel, the seed, of erotic, libidinal desire. Each tried to instantiate a looking away from the other, each tried to allow the quickened image to linger in heart, in mind, without perpetual contact from the eyes, without sustained attention. According to Jenny von West-phalen, this was not a one-directional look askance; they both participated in such a sustained look, a choreographic look and look away until both, gripped by the view of the other, could no longer stand to look any else-where again. But each look away exceeded. A sound, a vibration, broke the frame of aversion. They were engaged, it seems, in reciprocal sound and sentiment, quickened by butterflies and nervous, youthful flights of fan-tastic fancy. Such that, at the time of her writing, all of von Westphalen's flesh would feel "marvellous sensation" at the very thought of Karl Marx.

Jenny von Westphalen's pondering Karl mentally caused within her an enthusiastic response, a complete union of mind and body, engulfed, as it were, in the desire for love, for fulfillment of such longing. No self-determination but, rather, a sought-after sociality. Such that she would be without words, where words bespeak the limit of emotion. Joy that was, indeed, unspeakable. What von Westphalen's letter contains is an instance of the politics of avoidance, and this politics, this way of life, this new form, new forum, is a declarative "yes." The sustained, enduring look—the refusal to look away—is an affirmation of life, the choreosonic force resisting the theology-philosophy of aversion. That is, the politics of avoidance is all about love, such love that emerges through sustained engagements and refusals to look askance.

The "fire fell," finally after waiting, after tarrying, after praying fervently and consistently in the home of Ruth and Richard Asberry, 214 North Bonnie Brae Street, April 9, 1906. The various seekers in the house that day— the Asberrys, Edward S. Lee, Jenny Evans Moore, William Seymour, for example—could not have known that their prayer and supplication would lead to a worldwide movement. All they knew is that they were seeking experience. And it is the enthusiasm, the experience of one Jenny Evans Moore that very night who closes this exploration of the choreosonics of Blackpentecostalism and its ongoing tradition. Moore, who would eventually marry the leader of the movement, William Seymour, had this to say in *The Apostolic Faith* newspaper in their May 1907 edition:

> On April 9, 1906, I was praising the Lord from the depths of my heart at home, and when the evening came and we attended the meeting the power of God fell and I was baptized in the Holy Ghost and fire, with the evidence of speaking in tongues. During the day I had told the Father that although I wanted to sing under the power I was willing to do what ever He willed. . . . [I]t seemed as if a vessel broke within me and water surged up through my being, which when it reached my mouth came out in a torrent of speech in the languages which God had given me. . . . I sang under the power of the Spirit in many languages, the interpretation both words and music which I had never before heard, and in the home where the meeting was being held, the Spirit led me to the piano, where I played and sang under inspiration, although I had not learned to play. In these ways God is continuing to use me to His glory ever since that wonderful day, and I praise Him for the privilege of being a witness for Him under the Holy Ghost's power.[134]

Like von Westphalen, Moore felt similarly "dumbstricken and overpowered with emotion"; however, this moved Moore not to speechlessness, but to broken speech, broken sound, broken voice through improvisational choreosonics. Though I will analyze "speaking in tongues" in the next chapter, here I want to think about what it means to have a vessel that dwells within that is broken, and that brokenness yields pleasure and joy, through choreosonic performance. What Moore bespeaks is that the fact of a something being in her previous to encounter with Pentecost; this something broke as a result of her desire, and this brokenness was a rupture toward fulfillment of immediacy of encounter with the Lord.

This Pentecost also allowed for Moore to sing "under power . . . words and music which" she had never heard before, which she had never, thus, rehearsed or prepared for the congregation. What she illustrates about the politics of avoidance that is foundational to Blackpentecostal choreosonics is what it means to become an affirmation, what it means to become, to enter and descend like an affirmation. Moore's singing not only made of her an instrument but gave her a new way to become an analog-organic machine against the brutal conditions of enslavement, its afterlife, the brutal conditions of capital exploitation. She was led to the piano by the Spirit and played thereupon, though never having done such previous to that situation. Her ability to contribute to the choreosonic environment rose to the occasion of its occurrence and did not precede its necessary utilization. That is, attention to Moore's movement in voice and across piano keys is a quantum theoretical movement that gives otherwise ways to think the sound and song of ancestors that worked plantations, that had labor stolen for the wealth accumulation of civil society. That something could be broken within, that which exists previous to encounter, is what Moore announces. Such that the singing and sounding on plantations were likewise breakings of some otherwise modality of being and existence in the service of sustaining and maintaining otherwise social form.

The choreosonics of Blackpentecostalism document—through movement, through sound—an ongoing class struggle; the aestheticization of class struggle happens with the yodel and the melismatic break, with the movement to the piano and singing in tongues. In order for this to happen, in order for the critique of the systems of marginalization and oppression to be generative, one must be open, one must be able to say, to sing, to seize upon a "yes," an ongoing affirmation of life against desired physical, emotional, psychic death. This "yes" emerges through a sociality and testifies to the limits and violence of normativity, of subjecthood grounded in western theological-philosophical constructions of the self-determined, affectable thing.

Georg Wilhelm Friedrich Hegel concluded that Africa did not have, nor belong to, History. According to him, "Africa proper, as far as History goes back, has remained—for all purposes of connection with the rest of the World—shut up."[135] Hegel conflated land with people, and he could not think Africa apart from negroes. Yet this inability to decouple a land from its people becomes the occasion to think categorical distinction of Africa from History, the former being defined by its total incapacity to be brought into, to be thought under the rubric of, the historical. As such, for Hegel, for theology-philosophy itself it seems, History, historical being, the historical moment all emerge from the capacity to produce exclusion, to produce categorical distinction in *some* ways (for example, Africa and History) while being unable to produce that very modality of thought otherwise (for example, Africa and the negro). This to say that—like Kant's Enlightenment thought that could not cognize the negro of Africa without a fundamental sociality of thought, without thinking with others as the very emergence of thought about blackness—Hegel likewise rubs up against his own delimitation, produces for us what delimitation of thought looks like, what it sounds like. Because for Hegel, the negro is a difficulty of thought, one that—because of such difficulty—causes him to want to give up thought, to refuse to think further, to repress imaginative capacity in the service of producing normative thought. We might call such normative thought the theology-philosophy-history of western civilization.

Hegel submitted his radical imaginative excess to theological-philosophical-historical constraint. It was the choreosonic vibrational sounded materiality of blackness, of Blackpentecostal aesthetics, against which the constraint of theology-philosophy-history served as refuge. The same modality of thought that refused a people a right to property—though they were transformed into property granting the capacity to produce normative citizenship and mental capacities to do philosophy and theology—also denied them History, denied them entry *into* the historical, denied their capacity to be historical being. All these capacities were granted and produced through excluding the *potentia* and *kinesthesia* of blackness, of Blackpentecostal aesthetic practice. Such that we might say, finally and again, that History is a categorically distinct mode of cognition that is fundamentally about denial, about aversion. And we might say, finally and again and only because of Sylvia Wynter's elaboration, that History is created through the coloniality of being/power/truth/freedom. Harriet Jacobs, the enslaved Jenny, Jenny von Westphalen and Jenny Moore were not attempting to be historical being; it was their performance through Blackpentecostal aesthetics that produced a critique of History. Theirs was the noise—joyful noise—of the excluded, the joyful noise breaking down the coloniality of History, of historical being.

The historical moment, and the mode of existence for its production, exists because of the episteme of its emergence. What we desire—and what Jacobs, Jenny, von Westphalen, and Moore show us is possible—are otherwise worlds without the necessity for such a distinction in terms of spatiotemporality. Such songs and sound—Blackpentecostal noise that is always grounded in joy—is a critique of such a normative world. What each gives are worlds of emergence, are modes of existence that are yet to come, choreosonic itineraries and protocols for the undoing of categorical distinction such that only after such undoing can we begin to be the old thing otherwise. The enactment of this world yet to come will not be grounded in teleology and linear time, such that through accepting and performing such incoherence, we can be formless here, now. Then, there. Blackpentecostal performance is *whenwherehow* to articulate want, and in such articulation, performs want in an otherwise manner altogether. Our figures elaborated performed want that was not grounded in the transcendental subject of History, performed want that was for love, performed want as the choreosonic call and plea, centrifugitivity. Want in this *whenwherehow* performs the interplay of surplus and lack, of excess and suppression, that is an ongoing condition of blackness. This performance is a mode of existence together, a critique of the existential crisis of a transcendental subject of History. Blackpentecostal performance is not a thing that can be owned, held, captured, though it can be carried—as breath—through, in and as exchange. It's all in the noise.

4

TONGUES

Having been said to be nothing, this is a love letter written to we who have been, and are today still, said to have nothing. This is a love letter written to a tradition of such nothingness. In having nothing, we putatively speak nothing. Such speaking echoes, such speaking reverberates, but such speaking is considered—in normative theological-philosophical thought—nothing. Nothing of consequence. Nothing of weight. Nothing of materiality. This is a love letter to a love tradition, a tradition that emerges from within, carries and promises nothingness as the centrifugal, centripetal, centrifugitive force released against, and thus is a critical intervention into, the known world, the perniciously fictive worlds of our making. Some might call this fictive world "real." Some might call this fictive world reality. Some might call this fictive world the project of western civilization, complete with its brutally violent capacity for rapacious captivity. This is a love letter to a tradition of the ever overflowing, excessive nothingness that protects itself, that—with the breaking of families, of flesh—makes known and felt, the refusal of being destroyed. There is something in such nothingness that is not, but still ever excessively was, is and is yet to come. This is a love letter written against notions of ascendancy, written in favor of the social rather than modern liberal subject's development. What emerges from the zone of nothingness, from the calculus of the discarded? If something makes itself felt, known, from the zone of those of us said to be and have nothing, then the interrogation of what nothingness means is our urgent task. The nothingness of possibilities otherwise, of living the alternative.

In Chapter 2, I began a discussion of Sapelo Island dweller, Bilali, talking about what came to be called *Ben Ali's Diary*. In that chapter, I discussed the directionality of the writing as an instance of a choreosonic performance of Blackpentecostal aesthetics. I return to the writing in *Ben Ali's Diary* here because it underscores something about blackness and nothingness in all its manifold capaciousness, in all its irreducible beauty. Bilali's writing is meditative speech and script, a mode of enfleshment on the page in both easily accessible and incoherent markings. A thirteen-page manuscript—five of which cannot be translated to any linguistic rhetoric or grammar, and thus remains opaque and impenetrable for any reader—written in the nineteenth century, it was given to Francis Goulding in 1859. Though discussed under the rubric of "autobiography," the document contains no formal identifying information about its author(s), is not a collection of dates and life occurrences, does not have in it information about ancestry or progeny. The writing begins with the opening benediction: "In the name of Allah, The Most Merciful The Most beneficent. Allah's blessings upon our lord Muhammad, and upon his family and companions, blessings and salutations."[1] It includes, "Using both the right and left hands, one puts water into the mouth at least three times, and puts water into one's nose three times [cleaning it]. One washes one's face three times [7:1–11], then wipes the right hand up to the [elbow] joint [*k`abain*], and the left hand up to the [elbow] joint [*k`abain*]."[2] And it includes the Adhan, the call to prayer, "Allah is Great, Allah is Great. I bear witness that [*a'an*] there is no god but Allah, I bear witness that [*a'an*] there is no god but Allah [9:1–14] . . . Come to prayer [*hi 'al salah*], come to prayer [*salah*]."[3]

What has befuddled translators is the near five pages that do not translate into any linguistic content coherent for readers at all that is at the heart—in the middle—of the document. Indeterminacy is at the heart of the textual matter for thought, forcing scholars to ask: Is the incoherent script the rehearsal of one who had not fully learned Arabic; is the script attempting to sound like what it looks like? More fundamentally, an ever-unasked series of connected questions: What is this incoherent text? What, with incoherence at its core, is the text as a whole? What is this nothingness at the core, at the heart, of the writing event's performance? What is the mode of existence, the beingness, of one—of ones—who would write such incoherence, such indeterminacies? Having been translatable text, why a breakdown in the middle? Why such nothingness at the interior of worship's itinerary and protocol? Nothingness has, at its core, meditation and celebration, often misunderstood because of its refusal to give itself over to rationalist projects of cognition and thought. The five pages of non-empty, nonreadable script speaks back against and is resistance prior to the articulation and enunciation of power. The script speaks against, in other words, the general conception of nothingness as pure emptiness and purely simple.

"Bilali's"—and the quote marks are important to index the indeterminacy of authorship, an indeterminacy that leaves open the question of authorial voice—graphemic markings serve to break down the distinction between script and speech, talk and text, and is a preface, a prelude, a prolegomenon to the music, the choreosonics, of nothingness. In a word, the nothingness of such script is anything but empty; it is, rather, full. Overflowing. Script otherwise, minoritarian speech. "Bilali's" writing is mystical in what is rendered but cannot be—refuses to be—said. Something is both given and withheld with incomprehensible script.

> What does the interior of the chalk look like? Let us see. We break it into two pieces. Are we now at the interior? Exactly as before we are again outside. *Nothing* has changed. The pieces of chalk are smaller, but bigger or smaller does not matter now. . . . The moment we wanted to open the chalk by breaking it, to grasp the interior, it had enclosed itself again. . . . In any case, such breaking up never yields anything but what was already here, from which it started.[4] (Emphasis mine.)

Like Martin Heidegger's chalk, "Bilali's" script breaks grammar, the word itself, but holds within each broken fragment, each severed piece of flesh through brutal violence, something of the sociality that made the script possible, the conditions and zones of emergence and horizon. Broken and laid bare is the concept of the bourgeois individual of enlightenment, the one who writes oneself into being through autobiographesis, through scripting histories in diaries, one that writes oneself into history, desiring historical being. Heidegger says *nothing* has changed. But what does this mean when broken apart, when broken down? That change has been applied to nothing, to the thing called nothing, to the set of capacities to be nothing. That nothing can change, that nothing can have change applied to it, that nothing can be broken and broken into, means that *nothing* is irreducibly full, irreducibly potential in its force. Nothing has *changed*, that which is considered nothing has been made to be, has become difference. Nothing has *changed*, that which is considered nothing has taken into its grasp, into its cupped hand like a ritual washing, objects as dispossessive force. The breaking of the chalk, the breaking of nothing and its capacity for change, makes intensely and intentionally evident the withholding of the centrifugitive force of black sociality. Having been, am, having been, will be.

SOLOMON NORTHUP BEGAN his narrative, first published in 1854, with the words "Having been . . .":

> Having been born a freeman, and for more than thirty years enjoyed the blessings of liberty in a free State—and having at the end of that time been kidnapped and sold into Slavery, where I remained, until happily rescued in the month of January, 1853, after a bondage of twelve years—it has been suggested that an account of my life and fortunes would not be uninteresting to the public.[5]

How can we understand something about Northup's *having* and, further, *having been*? What is presupposed with such a formulation? What is presupposed about being, about existence, about existence in black, about presupposition itself? *Having been* has within it the idea that there is something there, that something was there before the inaugural moment of its declaration. We can consider *having been* the perfect gerund and the subject of the sentence. Having is the present participle; been is the past participle. So though we can think of it as the perfect gerund, I want to consider the declaration that sets loose the narrative as the convergence of present and past, as a convergence that undoes notions of linear, progressive space and time. *Having been* announces— through unsaying, through the nothingness of such nonspeech—the otherwise, that which takes the form of the interrogative: What of the now? What of the soon to come? In the *having been* is the capacity for manifold temporality, an arhythmic modality of temporal measure against the line of Newtonian's smooth transition from past to present to future, from here to there. The *having been* produces, perhaps W.E.B. Du Bois might say, the unasked question of being, of the being of blackness as manifold and, as always, interrogative, anticipatory, antagonistic. Anticipatory insofar as the *having been* has horizonal thrust, posits a set of questions that are unasked, unvoiced, backgrounded, questions that are nothing but still there, unasked and unvoiced in their fullness. *Having been*, what are you? *Having been*, what will you be?

"Bilali's" writing includes "a collection of divergent glossia in which none is ostensibly placed as authoritative."[6] Consider, then, that which exceeds the glossia: the noise, that which was discarded, as the sonic substance, the speechifying of nothingness, the nothingness of glossolalia (glossolalia, about which more soon). The radical force of Bilali's incoherent script that frustrates translators can be generalized. Consider, for a brief example, the difference between the film and written narrative of *12 Years a Slave*. John Ridley and Steve McQueen read Northup's narrative and discarded the various modalities of sociality, sociality that Northup recalled—however—with devastating precision. Where was the friendship between Eliza and Rose? Where was the friendship between Northup and the Chicopees people, wherein he returned to the woods often to eat, talk, and dance with them, not as a mere spectator but as participant? Where were the children for whom Northup played the violin as he traveled from plantation to plantation, given he had extra time? Where were the "amusements"? Why does McQueen describe Northup's narrative as a Brothers Grimm fairy tale that ends "happy ever after"; why does he describe Patsey, several times over and again, as "simple"?[7] If Patsey was indeed simple, her fashioning of dolls from corn husks in the film was not evidence of her thriving in the face of brutal horrors; it was evidence of her simply not knowing how bad things were, her not cognizing the gravity of the environment in which she existed. This, of course, is erroneous. These were intentional choices, choices of filmmakers to display the brutality and horror of enslavement. There was an intentional repression of anything that could be considered "positive" because such a system of racial capital interdicts the very notion of positivity. What was given is a film that merely glanced at the text, a glance that could not account for the fullness of experience. The discardability of sociality—the imaging of social life as frivolity—as nothing at all, as nothingness, is enacted by a politics, by a worldview, by a theological-philosophical conviction that one needs be exceptional, individual, one needs to assert one's subjectivity and citizenship as coherent and stable. After submitting to such a theological-philosophical convention, such a conviction, black sociality registers as nothing at all, as pure nothingness, abject in its horror. The film depicts joy and a dance as simply momentary interruptions of ongoing trauma and utilizes much effort to suppress anything of the complexity of living life as enslaved. The only figure with complexity was the one that was to serve the hero's tale.

If "Bilali's" script serves as a method for thinking the nothingness of blackness, perhaps we can understand the incomprehensible text as ecstatic, as enthusiastic, as intensely and intentionally a breakdown of—a break with—grammar, an intensely and intentionally celebratory mood or reflection. Perhaps "Bilali's" text reflects the joyful noise of choreosonic black performance, the joy unspeakable of blackness, wherein what it means to be unspeakable issues forth from the performance of, the inhabitation of, happiness that is against reason and rationality. Michael Sells, in Mystical Languages of Unsaying, says:

> Every act of unsaying demands or presupposes a previous saying. Apophasis can reach a point of intensity such that no single proposition concerning the transcendent can stand on its own. Any saying (even a negative saying) demands a correcting proposition, an unsaying. But that correcting proposition which unsays the previous position is in itself a "saying" that must be "unsaid" in turn.[8]

But what we discover through "Bilali's" script, in the incomprehensible blackness, the incomprehensible celebratory nothingness of the script, is the fact that one can say without saying, one can give while withholding as a matter, as the scripted, etched, written materiality, of praise. To write that which enfleshes—that incarnates—itself as incomprehensible is to write nonreadability into the text, to write the necessity to think a different relation to objects, objects that are supposed to be easily captured as flesh on mediums, bateaus and skiffs. To write the unasked question of being into the text by making markings that do not appear to readers as readable, *Ben Ali's Diary* writes onto the page the question of being: What is this? And what of the one(s) who scripted such irreducible incomprehension?

Such that what is written in the incomprehensible text, in the nothingness of the sign, is the confrontation with the problem of the idea that text writes experience, that experience is easily turned into filmic scene, that cinematography captures precisely because what is being captured is an experience of nothingness, of objects who have nothing, objects who—like so many Patseys—are merely simple. The celebratory, loving mode of sociality Northup recalls in his text, indeed and again, is nothing but no less there, nothing but not empty. His text is a love letter to those described as nothing, those existing within the zone of nothingness. It is a love letter that is celebratory of a mode of sociality that is given in its unspokenness. This is to say the love and celebration, against representations of violence as a totalizing force, is not given to rationalist representation when such

rationalism is grounded in individual exceptionalism. Having been subjected to the totalizing force of violence, yet joy unspeakable and full of glory.

"Bilali's" text, inclusive of the unreadable five pages, also importantly presupposes a deity that can understand incoherence. Perhaps not simply a deity
but—because the text is a set of itineraries and protocols for worship—a community gathered by such incoherence as a mode of worship itself. It presupposes audience that would not deem the writing as incoherent, troubling the
assumptive nature of declaring of objects what they do not themselves declare.
The text resonates, it vibrates, it is both centripetal and centrifugal. The text is
centrifugitive, moving in multiple directions at once, gathering and dispersing, through meditation, affirmation, negation. Unspeakable joy spoken in its
being unsaid. But what to make of speaking, of performance, of black flesh in
its unsayability? Performance artist Alvin Lucier in his 1969 performance piece
titled "I Am Sitting in a Room" shows the resonance of an empty room, the
resonance of nothingness, making audible how that which is deemed nothing
has material vibratory force.[9] Lucier records the following words:

> I am sitting in a room different from the one you are in now. I am record-
> ing the sound of my speaking voice and I am going to play it back into
> the room again and again until the resonant frequencies of the room
> reinforce themselves so that any semblance of my speech, with perhaps
> the exception of rhythm, is destroyed. What you will hear, then, are the
> natural resonant frequencies of the room articulated by speech. I regard
> this activity not so much as a demonstration of a physical fact, but more
> as a way to smooth out any irregularities my speech might have.

After recording those words while sitting in a room, he goes through a performance process, allowing the technology of a tape recorder in the empty
space to play and record over and over again his voice. Eventually, the very
sound of his voice—the speech, the stuttering, the pauses—smooths and
one hears only the resonance that remains, the space itself. Nothing has
been caused to change and such change is a choreosonic fact. The material
vibratory force is nothing's ethical injunction, its ethical demand on the
world that would have such richness, such complexity, discarded.

There is a structural, irreducible, inexhaustible incoherence at the heart of
Northup beginning his narrative with the words *having been*, generative for
disrupting logics of liberal subjectivity grounded in forward progression across
space and time. The narrative begins with this incoherence, an incoherence

not unlike the disruption into other epistemologies of time, space, the sacred and secular, the theological and philosophical that came to be the displacement of flesh from land in the service of new world state juridical projects. *Having been* is the vibratory force of the ethical injunction that is not ever only about what Northup's life was and could be but about everyone who was displaced through brutal violence into the system of enslavement. If there is a universalizing impulse, in other words, it is in that all can make a declaration of irreducible incoherence: *having been*, am; *having been*, will be.

Fisk University was in the thicket of dire financial straits in 1871 when George L. White thought it his mission to organize a group of singers from the university for a fundraising tour. Amid dilapidated buildings and potential bankruptcy, White gathered nine singers and a pianist to sing throughout major cities with the hopes of averting the looming closing of the school. White so very much believed in the mission of the school that he was willing to risk his reputation and personal finances to journey to various cities with this unusual motley crew. Unusual insofar as these were no mere minstrel singers, no blackface performers, but were the true, real, authentic thing: black folks on a stage singing music from plantations, some Stephen Foster's melodies, anthems, and concert standards, so various newspaper articles recorded. "During the early days, the company had yet to establish the Negro spiritual as the main staple of its programs, performing instead 'white man's music,' mostly popular tunes, sacred anthems, and patriotic songs. White interspersed a few spirituals at times throughout the evening, but they were hardly the featured items."[10]

Organized five years previous to the first tour in 1871, Fisk University was formed through the philanthropy and religious beliefs of the American Missionary Association, a group that worked tirelessly for the abolition of the enslaved in the United States. Fisk University was thus established to educate colored people, men and women who envisioned educational achievement as necessary for integration into civil society. "Fisk University was a higher education institution committed to the principles of a classical education; its instructors strived to create well-rounded scholars with an appreciation for and keen understanding of what constituted beauty. . . . Fisk University sought every means possible to convince white Americans that African Americans were their equal."[11] And it was the group that would eventually be called the Fisk Jubilee Singers that saved the school from possible bankruptcy, performing on national and international stages beginning with their first performance in Ohio, October 6, 1871.

After months of training and only little public praise in the media, White decided to take a chance with the company, utilizing "spirituals" as the anchor for their performances. Such a risk was successful. Imagine: genuine, authentic negroes singing genuine, authentic plantation music, a spectacle unheard of before the Jubilee Singers's tours. But such spectacle, of course, came at a price. The music the Jubilee Singers performed had to be radically changed for wide audiences, for economic benefit to the school. Historian Mary Spence noted, "The spirituals sung by the young Fisk students needed altering—refinement or polishing, if you will—before presentation for audiences if they were to meet prevailing standards of 'culture.'"[12] More, "It is clear that White and his contemporaries felt that the performance of spirituals needed to conform to a shared set of rules that governed Western European music making before they could be worthy of consideration as art. Therefore, he engaged Ella Sheppard to arrange choral versions of spirituals, and together the two rehearsed the ensemble, aiming for precision and flawless choral blend . . ."[13] And it was in the space of the university that such training took place, where such learning of performative acumen was garnered. What is evident is that for the spirituals to become acceptable on the world stage—for the music to be considered art, to be worthy of the refined, the cultured—there had to be a reduction of the so-thought vulgarity, of the so-considered wildness and rudeness of voices. For the spirituals to become acceptable on the world stage, there had to be a removal of the nothingness, the nothingness in all its capacious plentitude—the sonic graphemes of irreducible incoherence—in their performance. There had to be a reduction of the noise, the ceaseless pulse and tremor of deformation and disruption, a reduction—in other words—of the joyful noise of black sociality.

Such training was not merely about the voice; it was also about the aspiration and movement toward becoming a subject, becoming a proper citizen against declarations and ideologies about the incapacity for negroes to rise to the occasion and fill in the borders of the human. Such training, in other words, gathered up and discarded the seemingly disrespectable aspects of black singing, of singing in blackness, in the service of white acceptance, in the service of proving blacks were just as good and human as whites. For example, a review of the October 6, 1871, performance stated,

"The unaffected simple fervor breathing forth the soul were remarkable and touching qualities of the performance. What might be done with such voices, subjected to early, thorough, and skillful culture, the singing of last night afforded a faint intimation."[14] Breathing. *Breathing.* The word that, in April 1906, would begin a critique of the fleshly blackness and inter-raciality of Blackpentecostal aesthetics.[15] That the reviewer uses the word *breathing* illustrates that the skillful culture towards which the Jubilee Singers should aspire would be achieved by discarding Blackpentecostal aesthetics. Subjected. *Subjected.* That the reviewer utilized the word *sub-jected* anchors a consideration of how the training of voices so construed was the movement toward subjectivity. Their performances on stages were, in other words, scenes of subjection, and the sound of subjection would be obtained through training, through enculturation. What they sounded like previous to such training and culture were mere intimations of that which would come through learning. This is a becoming-subject through the sonic, utilizing breath and voice to cohere. The training of voices set the foundation for a general pedagogy of one version—which is an aversion for black social life—of university studies, of a teleological principle for becoming a proper black subject.

This movement in the direction of training, culture—which is to say, subjectivity—is a fundamental feature of the debate regarding the nature of speaking in tongues that was set loose in the twentieth-century Blackpen-tecostal group. I do not denigrate or dismiss training, learning, and peda-gogy, generally (I am, of course, a college professor); rather, I am interested in the way training, learning, and pedagogy occurs, and what the objects of such desired affection are. There is a radical difference, it seems to me, between learning spirituals on plantations during working hours or while stealing away in brush harbors and praise houses, on the one hand, and learning them in private classrooms with the goal of perfecting through rehearsal, away from the social world, with the goal of fundraising, on the other. This latter mode of training, learning, and pedagogy is the condition for the emergence of the Kantian enlightened scholar discussed in Chapter 2, the emergence of the learned individual. This distinction has everything to do with the question about the nature of tongues speech and is an oper-ating distinction in the university generally, and black studies particularly.

Tongues. "When early pentecostals wanted to explain themselves to the outside world—indeed when they wanted to explain themselves to each other—they usually started with the experience of Holy Ghost baptism signified by speaking in tongues."[16] Speaking in tongues, as a mode of contemplative, meditative practice, is foundational for the Blackpentecostal imagination, for Blackpentecostal performance. Speaking in tongues is but one example of the Blackpentecostal capacity to give away that which one has received—utterance—in order to receive, and thus give, more. The initial Azusa Street movement was founded upon the belief in the "third work" of grace in the life of believers—the first as salvation, the second as sanctification or being set apart, cleansing, the third as the manifestation of speaking in tongues—as foundational for empowerment in the world. Given that many of the varied peoples that congregated on Azusa Street were marginalized based on race, class, and gender, the ability to speak, with boldness, with measured volume, from such a station, from such a configuration of lot and life, was to have speech emerge from the zone of those assumed to have no thought, to speak from such a position was to speak—while also being—nothing. And in so speaking from such a position, what was announced was a "disruption rather than the condition of a given epistemological line or chord."[17] As a defining feature of Blackpentecostal aesthetic practice, I focus on speaking in tongues because such an experience allows a way to think epistemology, to think the world of knowledge production otherwise.

Speaking in tongues has been described variously as "a special language gift which is used in praise and prayer, which can approximate to prophecy when interpreted" and as "unlearned human languages (xenolalia), heavenly/angelic languages or some spiritual language which defies description."[18] Vern S. Poythress elaborates a linguistic and sociological definition of speaking in tongues:

> *Free vocalization* (glossolalia) occurs when (1) a human being produces a connected sequence of speech sounds, (2) he cannot identify the sound-sequence as belonging to any natural language that he already knows how to speak, (3) he cannot identify and give the meaning of words or morphemes (minimal lexical units), (4) in the case of utterances of more than a few syllables, he typically cannot repeat the same sound-sequence on demand, (5) a naive listener might suppose that it was an unknown language.[19]

Though Pentecostal historians and theologians know of the distinction between xenolalia and glossolalia, few make much of the distinction. But perhaps much more is at stake. Concerned with a difference that seems to be nothing at all, I contend that concepts of personhood vitalize strains of Blackpentecostal Christianities at the turn of the twentieth century. What I mean, simply, is this: the way one thought the concept of speaking in tongues had consequences for how one engaged the world. There were initiatory debates about, and often frustration regarding, speaking in tongues; to amplify those debates and frustrations will prove useful for considering otherwise modes of social political organization.

But before we get to such speaking, some markings on a page. Some early Blackpentecostals engaged in what is known as "spirit writing," a form of writing that was not words or phrases, but extralinguistic writing that communicated divine messages. One such example is from 1914:

> under the anointing of the Holy Ghost, Elder W.G. Johnson wrote in an unknown handwriting which was interpreted by Bishop C.H. Mason as "Brother Johnson's call to Michigan." After arriving in Detroit on March 26, 1914 from their home in Memphis, Tennessee, Elder W.G. (Ting-a-Ling) Johnson and his wife, Mother Mary Mangum-Johnson began having services at Erskine and St. Antoine St. Later they worshiped on Catherine and Gratiot, also at 643 Beaubien and finally 623 Livingstone. The church at that time was known as Livingstone Street Church of God in Christ. This Church is now known as Seth Temple Church of God in Christ.[20]

Elder W.G. Johnson performed spirit writing and had the writing "interpreted" by Charles Harrison Mason. The written note attached states, "THE 'UNKNOWN HANDWRITING' OF ELDER W.G. JOHNSON WHICH WAS INTERPRETED BY BISHOP C.H. MASON AS A 'CALL TO MICHIGAN'." What we have with this glossographesis are markings for an emancipatory, liberatory project that privileges choreosonic indeterminacy—of the spirit, by the spirit—toward the unknown, toward the abyss and expanse of seeming nothingness. This unknown I elevate to the level of a general critique of modernity. The journey toward the abyss and expanse of seeming nothingness, prompted by the unknown is an emancipatory project: "This emancipation is achieved in a manner incomprehensible for the framing of what is supposed to be modernity's privileged discursive mode: subjectively grounded narrative writing."[21] Glossographia, also known as grapholalia, are the markings of incoherence and the irreducibility of discovery, markings of a general agnosticism at the heart of the Blackpentecostal prompt toward inspirited experience. Blackpentecostalism and agnosticism both share in the negation of desired stasis and stillness, a rejection of objects as impenetrable, of knowledge as exhaustible, the potentiality for further discovery expired. These writings "in tongues" illustrate the performative force of black glossolalia—a speaking, talking project, a choreosonic mode of performance. Black glossolalia is a potential deformation of the concept of liberal subjectivity, emancipating those of us that will make a claim for such performative force, into the endarkened logics of otherwise sociality.

The caption states that Charles Harrison Mason "interpreted" such markings, that he articulated—through the interpretation of the unknown while never claiming to "know" what each mark in its individuated grapheme meant—a mode of Blackpentecostal reflection that has indeterminacy at the core. Mason stated in his auto/biography (1924) that prayer was "given" to his mother to speak against the "baneful" nature of enslavement. Mason recalled that he entreated God to "give him a religion like that he had heard the old folks talk about and manifest in their lives."[22] For Mason, tongues, as a result of spirit baptism, was but another manifestation of the spiritual resource necessary for resistant life, for black sociality, during enslavement. Spirit baptism, tongues as a performative enunciation of such immersion, rose to its moment's occasion. Mason never denigrated the omens, visions, and folk customs and practices. Rather, he celebrated them as likewise divine workings. But more, where omens claim "knowledge," Mason asserted that spirit baptism plumbed the depths of the unknown: "The spiritual omens seemed to have given place to the power and mysterious working of the Holy Ghost."[23] Mason was also known for reading and interpreting what he called "God's handiworks in nature," tree roots, chains and other materials found that he believed had a divine message to be interpreted.[24] Mystery—the abyss and expanse of seeming nothingness—is cause for celebration. The mystery of black performance, the mystery of glossographia rehearses the generativity of agnosticism. This mode of spiritual reflection privileges the unknown, the nonsensical and nonrational; this mode of spiritual performance privileges incoherence.

But what are tongues? In an exposition about the capacity for tongue-talking to be a philosophy, a hermeneutic, a way of life, James K. A. Smith in *Thinking in Tongues* spends very little time discussing a general distinction at the heart of the very idea of tongues-speech as spiritual experience.[25] What sets his work in motion is the very thing that is repressed in his reflections about Pentecostal experience generally: a question of meaning. Tongues serve as exemplar for a specific uniqueness, uniqueness given as experiential knowledge in, of and for the world. But we are left to wonder: what is this thing, how does one receive—or how can one be open to—this process, this process of tongues speech? And why is there a black method, called tarrying, for such divine encounter? Smith brackets what he thinks as a merely theological question regarding tongues-speech but, as I will discuss below, the bracketing is an important and productive space of thought about subjectivity and personhood, performance and politics. This bracketing opens for me a space to articulate some issues regarding the nature of personhood that grounds spiritual practice.

This issue, the question, the problematic of tongues lets us travel curiously to the conceptual domains of essentialism and authenticity. And these categories have been played out in the crucible of black studies: assertions that a certain set of behaviors do not constitute blackness because that would be essentializing blackness to those behaviors ostensibly gathers up certain behaviors, ways of life, and discards those as adjunct to the theory, the essence, of blackness. Rather than thinking the relation that emerges through the performance and production of sociality, such assertions use the individual example in order to be a disruptive force in the very possibility of constituting blackness. Or the constitution of blackness comes to cohere around the violence done to black people, the so-thought history of the Middle Passage, enslavement and the afterlife of slavery, and racial trauma. Such that the constitution of blackness is grounded in what has happened to black people, an ongoing event of violence. Following the tracks laid by Zora Neale Hurston, how the performances of Blackpentecostal aesthetics were a movement against bourgeoisie aspirations, class-based critiques of working-class black American social life, critiques of authenticity end up being a critique of what *some* black folks do, implicating while simultaneously veiling, the ways class comes to mark, though muted, such stances. But not just class. There ends up being an uninterrogated and uncritical relation to asserting oneself as a liberal subject of Enlightenment thought, as an individual over and—yes—against the social.

For example, often "the black church" is reduced to a static entity, black Methodists and Baptists claiming that Blackpentecostal aesthetics were performed everywhere, not just in the walls of storefronts. "Everyone sang loudly and spoke in tongues," is one form the argument against the essentialism of certain aesthetic practices being Blackpentecostal takes. Such a claim—about the plentitude of such aesthetic practices any and everywhere—is dismissive of the ways there were rhetorical injunctions against such behavior during the initial moments of the Blackpentecostal movement, where speaking in tongues was uncouth and unacceptable behavior. People were excommunicated from families, had church memberships revoked and were lampooned in news media for being tongue talkers. If such behavior occurred in non-Pentecostal spaces, what is elided is the theological-philosophical thought inhering and emanating from those non-Pentecostal spaces. Blackpentecostals made a claim for, while others merely *allowed* or dismissed, such irruptions, such surreptitious moves of the spirit.

Smith "suggest[ed] that, at least on a certain level or from a certain angle, tongues-speech could be seen as the language of the dispossessed—or the language of the 'multitude.'"[26] I am sympathetic to such an understanding of tongue-speech but want to think more about the questions bracketed, questions regarding the theology-philosophy of those that speak in tongues from his general discussion. In his footnotes Smith states that he is against any understanding of "initial evidence" but rather believes that tongues-speech is but one spiritual gift among others. This theological assertion has resonance for the meaning of the practice and also the meaning of philosophizing from such a practice. But there is an even more fundamental, but likewise bracketed question: Is tongue-speech xenolalia or glossolalia?[27]

My reading through many firsthand accounts of those early Pentecostals in the twentieth century reveals an interesting distinction, nuanced though it may be, and this distinction falls along the lines of a categorical distinction that produces, and is produced by, racialization. Xenolalia is the ability to speak a foreign language—Spanish, French, Hindi, for example—without any knowledge of the language; glossolalia, by contrast, is the eruption and enunciation of irreducible, nonlinguistic, nonrepresentational vocalizing, ecstatic language, the speechifying of nothingness. A. J. Tomlinson, according to narratives recounted, spoke in languages he had never heard nor experienced previous to such divine encounter.

The Holy Spirit then used [A. J. Tomlinson's] "lips and tongue" to speak the language of the Indian tribes of Central America. After a little rest, the Lord directed his eye to Brazil, where the sequence of extreme suffering and speaking the native tongue repeated itself. The cycle continued, fixing next on Chile, then Patagonia, Africa, Jerusalem, Japan, northern Canada, back to his present home town of Cleveland, Tennessee, on to Chattanooga, then over to his natal town of Westfield, Indiana, and finally to the Indiana villages of Hortonville and Sheridan.[28]

He was taken on a journey through the world where language enunciation, without experience, was privileged as a mode of reflection and proselytizing. Tomlinson's recounting is of xenolalia and is foundationally about spatial organization, a settler colonial logic of expansion and conquering. All in the service of the supposed only wise God, the Saviour, with glory and majesty, dominion and power, both now and ever, all in the service of sovereignty. Ecstatic language was used to produce what Frank Wilderson calls "spatial and temporal coherence—in other words, Human capacity."[29] The capacity of the Human is to produce a mode of cognition that has settler logic as its core stability and structure. Xenolalic utterances resemble settler colonialist theological-philosophical imperatives because with xenolalic utterances is the concept of language as pure, coherent, stable in its enunciation, such that each language maintains purity. Blackpentecostal aesthetic practice is a disruption of such easy notions of purity.

Historian Grant Wacker calls these xenolalic utterances "missionary tongues":

> Belief in missionary tongues dated from the 1830s in Scotland, and continued a minor though persistent element of radical evangelical missionary strategy on both sides of the Atlantic throughout the late nineteenth century. But the concept came to serve as a veritable cornerstone of Charles Parham's theological system, for he taught his followers that all authentic tongues involved extant foreign languages.[30]

Charles Parham believed tongue-speech was xenolalia, foreign language. Responsible partly for teaching William Seymour, the black pastor of the important Azusa Street Mission and the leader of the several-years-long revival that spread worldwide from Los Angeles, Parham held strictly to the belief that Africanisms were a general problem for Christian reflection; Blackpentecostal aesthetic practices were antagonistic to theological-philosophical contemplation, to theological-philosophical thought. After visiting the Azusa Street Mission, Parham recounted his finding "the disturbing sight of white people freely associating with blacks and Latinos in 'crude negroisms' [which] sickened him; and he left the revival insisting that most of those claiming Holy Spirit's baptism were subject to no more than 'animal spiritism.'"[31] His thoughts about primitivism and Africanisms were rooted in an ideological disposition that could not cognize black capacity for thought, and he never fully committed to even the idea that blacks could be saved, much less filled with the Spirit. That he relegated such ecstatic behavior to the realm of the animal underscores the ways, for him, the animal and the black are constitutive racialist categories, categories that should be renunciated, shunned.

And this was not only true for Parham. It appears that many of the early Pentecostal doctrinal disagreements were likewise grounded in categorical distinction and racialization. This to say that when Pentecostalism began to elaborate a theology-philosophy of its thought, a constraint on the radical imagination, such thought was marshaled in the service of the perpetuation of racial distinction and purity, the maintenance of whiteness. Theology-philosophy, through the rubric of doctrinal correctness, was utilized in order to maintain a sense of categorical distinction. Though there were several declarations that the color line was washed away in the blood of Jesus, in the practice of this third work of grace, the actual practices were against such readings of the group.

> The 'love and harmony' was soon to be replaced by acrimony, and the 'miracle' overthrown by the re-drawing of the colour line through the Oneness movement. . . . During the years 1920 and 1921 the number of black ministers joining the Pentecostal Assemblies of the World steadily increased. Many became officials and members of committees and of the twenty-four 'Executive elders' in 1921, one-third were black. The increased involvement of black people in the leadership of the PA of W resulted in many racially prejudiced whites leaving.[32]

Assemblies of God was created through racist removal; it was therein that the "new issue" of Oneness doctrine was set in relief regarding formula for baptism.[33] This was the second issue; the first being the Finished Work teaching in which "colour was a significant factor in the split."[34] This doctrine was crystalized in William H. Durham's teachings in 1911, coming to Los Angeles, rejecting the view of ongoing sanctification. He argued that once saved and baptized with the Holy Ghost—tongues as initial evidence—work was complete, that sanctification was not indeed a third, necessary work. What if we think about Finished Work as the pronouncement of white supremacist logic, the same logic of xenolalia that does not take seriously ongoing need for renewing the mind. Seymour was a proponent of the third work, the necessity of sanctification, not least because though people participated in the phenomenology of tongues-speech, they still held within racialist ideology, racial distinction, desire for racialist control of the nascent group.

Seymour was not a proponent of the Finished Work doctrine because he experienced the way aesthetics were split from theory, how the intellectual practice of the choreosonics of Blackpentecostalism produced an occasion for the ongoing manifestation of racism in the hearts and minds of white Pentecostals. All this to say that racial categorization was a primary concern for the development of, not a practice but a *theology-philosophy*, a doctrine, of Pentecostalism. Such development would be the abatement of noise, the removal of the blackness, the severance of black from Pentecostal. Categorical racial distinction and purity is what *produced* the theological-philosophical reflection, the theological mode of thought, that justified several segregations and separations. The worry over the color line and its reestablishment was a worry about the refusal of categorical distinction in general, a general disavowal of sacred on the one hand and profane on the other, since these would have material-political effects in the world. How, for example, would white adherents to Blackpentecostal practice still be members of the Ku Klux Klan, how would they maintain their racial privilege and power in whiteness, if the practice of Blackpentecostalism undid for them the color line and its categorical distinction? No longer would the distinction of race/gender/class be operative, no longer sacred and profane, and thus, how to sustain a material-political separation from the people called black, people that are actively renouncing the very capacity for such distinctions to take place? Thus, a theology-philosophy, as doctrinal integrity, of Pentecostalism was created, a way to think it as a delimitation, as a dividing line rather than an open expanse. Such elaborations of doctrine—whether Oneness or Trinitarian, whether Finished Work or the Third Work of ongoing sanctification—veiled the fact of categorical distinction as a racializing project that would produce the possibility for racial severance and removal. This was an epistemic problem, a problem about the knowability of the world and performance practices.

Yet Blackpentecostals were willing to allow unknowability at the heart of the practice, were much more willing to think about tongues-speech as glossolalic, as incoherent. Henry Fisher, for example, stated, "The saints are being baptized with the Spirit. I too have received Him and have spoken in some kind of language, I know not what."[35] It is important to note that Seymour initially believed tongue-speech as xenolalic, no doubt because of his learning about the practice under Parham. Yet the rejection Parham produced created the grounds for Seymour to more robustly think a relation to tongues-speech that was not beholden to the theological-philosophical thought of his once teacher. And Charles Mason, of his experience at Azusa, stated, "I saw and heard some things that did not seem scriptural to me, but at this I did not stumble I began to thank God in my heart for all things for when I heard some speak in tongues I knew it was right, though I did not understand it."[36]

At issue is the concern about the epistemological moorings that inform the concept of tongues-speech as xenolalic performance. "Though the evidence remains sketchy, there are good reasons to believe that between 1906 and 1909 more than a dozen zealots journeyed to remote outposts on the mission field armed only with the conviction that they would be empowered to speak the native language when they arrived."[37] This is an argument not about the quantity but about the quality of the debate that is exposed with the xeno-, glosso-distinction. A. G. Garr and his wife believed so much in missionary tongues and the possibility for xenolalic utterance that they traveled—as did others—to foreign lands with hopes of converting nonbelievers.

> [A. G.] Garr felt certain the Holy Spirit was calling him and [his wife] Lillian to India as missionaries. He also felt certain that the Holy Spirit had miraculously enabled him to speak Bengali and Hindustani and Lillian to speak Tibetan and Chinese. . . . A resident missionary [in Calcutta] who knew Hindi told him that his gift of Bengali (a cognate language) was unintelligible. Garr refused to believe him and proceeded to preach to the Bengalis anyway. Failing, presumably after several tries, the couple moved to Hong Kong in October 1907, where they buckled down to the arduous task of learning the language the hard way.[38]

At the heart of the matter—between xeno and glosso—is a question, a Du Boisian problematic, about the foundational claims of and for identity: Is there a stable entity that is the locus of identity or is identity irreducibly incoherent, refusing stasis and stillness, is being irreducibly becoming, processual, verbing? Attendant to those concerns, just how to articulate a mode of personhood from those two ideations is of radical importance, an *a*theological-*a*philosophical matter enlivening the humanities from anthropology to sociology, from ethnomusicology to literary theory. Parham's ongoing misrecognition of negro capacity for knowledge and his aspirations toward xenolalia both articulate a general desire to, even when led by the spirit, fully cognize, fully know, fully conquer. It was another articulation of settler colonial logic.

This coheres with another oppositional distinction, between that of theoria and aesthesis, xenolalia taking up and literally enunciating the position of the former and glossolalia assuming and exhaling the position of the latter. "With Aristotle, *theoria* became abstract and cognitive contemplation of invisible, indivisible Being. It was the order of a rational discourse built on the principle of noncontradiction, of identity; *aesthesis*, on the other hand, became the locus of deceptive perception. . . . The final occultation of the sociopolitical dimension of *theoria* was achieved by the ontological move that placed it into the field of the real as the ideal, and *aesthesis* into the field of the sensible as illusion."[39] The epistemological separation of theoria from aesthesis means that aesthetics befalls as the deformational force against theoria, such that aesthesis encapsulates and is the force of the double, the force of that which exists previous to a theological-philosophical mode of thought, a mode of thought that produced absolute categorical distinction. Such that the "aesthetics of possibility" is meant to name a critical practice, a critical performance, of black sociality. The aesthetics of possibility where to be *of* possibility means to announce both *for* and *from* possibility. I argue that, as aesthesis, glossolalia does the same performative rupture of the very possibility of xenolalia. Like aesthesis is the grounds from which theoria is an abstraction, all language exists previous to call and encounter in unabstracted material form, in unabstracted material form as glossolalia.

Xenolalia is theoria, the enunciation of desired pure being, enunciated through the mastery of the language of the Other. Nahum Chandler theorized the assumption of "the question concerning the humanity of the

Negro," as a general problem for philosophical thought, of whiteness, of Americanness.[40] Theoria of pure being finds its announcement through speeched choreographies of a spatial logic that conquers the language of the Other quickened by God. The frustration to the *achievement* of xenolalia aside, what the aspiration as the project for xenolalia as tongue-speech unveils is a mode of subjectivity that depends upon the ever-expansive capacity to speak, while denying the cognizing value of such grammar. With xenolalia one could speak in, without having to think in the language of the Other, without having to ever think about the value of the persons that think and speak in that language. One could maintain a grammar and logic of settler colonial theological-philosophical thought, produced in the very language of the one that would be conquered.

Tongues-speech, xeno or glosso, is ostensibly beyond normative linguistic thought but in its very articulation, organizes a settler colonial logic—let's here call it American thought—or its critique. In other words, tongues-speech is a meditation on what it might mean to be a colonizer, a settler through lingual form as poetics, is meditation given in the not readily apprehended. The desire for xenolalia with Parham's disdain of Negroisms in mind yields "an apparently small but ultimately decisive formulation": "The problem at [the] root [of the question of America and the negro] is one of 'understanding.'"[41] Aesthesis-glossolalia is irreducibly incoherent and generative for a Blackpentecostal radical imagination; not the recovery of nonsense but the refusal of sense having the final say. Glossolalia—registering as nothing at all—is the movement into incoherence as a choreosonic form toward praise, toward divine encounter. Impurity is the grounds for such *a*theological-*a*philosophical speechifying, incoherence allowed as praiseworthy. And to speak in favor—and on the side—of glossolalia is also to favor interpretation over and against translation, about which more soon.

The conceptual grounds running through James K. A. Smith's declarations about tongue-speech is structured similarly to the conceptual grounds about revolution of the "American" variety, rehearsed through the refusal to think the likewise xeno-glosso distinction of the documentation of declaration, an initially spoken thing. The question about the possibility for the discovery of speech that would have utterance be considered to be pure language of the Other mines the curious "American" mind. Though the Acts 2 narrative of the descent of the Holy Spirit inclusive of speaking in tongues records various people hearing these tongues in their "own" language, the question of drunkenness sets loose the necessity for interpretation. Why? Though I am informed and influenced by Andrew Benjamin's argument that translation is the nature of philosophy,[42] I want to go in another direction to think about the question of interpretation, interpretation in the place of translation. What does that mean? An example:

> When in the Course of human events, it becomes necessary for one people to dissolve the political bands which have connected them with another, and to assume among the powers of the earth, the separate and equal station to which the Laws of Nature and of Nature's God entitle them, a decent respect to the opinions of mankind requires that they should declare the causes which impel them to the separation. We hold these truths to be self-evident, that all men are created equal, that they are endowed by their Creator with certain unalienable Rights, that among these are Life, Liberty and the pursuit of Happiness.—That to secure these rights, Governments are instituted among Men, deriving their just powers from the consent of the governed,—That whenever any Form of Government becomes destructive of these ends, it is the Right of the People to alter or to abolish it, and to institute new Government, laying its foundation on such principles and organizing its powers in such form, as to them shall seem most likely to effect their Safety and Happiness.[43]

This set of assertions was "a script written to be spoken aloud as oratory."[44] Jay Fliegelman states that "in the eighteenth century [the] world was revolutionized by an intensified quest to discover (or theorize into existence) a natural spoken language that would be a corollary to natural law, a language that would permit universal recognition and understanding" and rhetorically, "that new language was composed not of words themselves, but of the tones, gestures, and expressive countenance with which a speaker delivered those words."[45] I mention the Declaration of Independence for the American project because in it the performance of utterance as surface is assumed; the coarticulation of language and law enunciated through the declaratives within the statement. That to say that the Declaration purports toward a xenolalic understanding of itself, that it is axiomatic and that one only need understand the words themselves—those units of sentence measure—in order to make sense. What the Declaration as the performance of utterance produces is a way to think America: by speaking into existence without need for interpretation but simply translation. But, of course, the breakdown.

When this set of declaratives is orated from the crucible of the circum-Atlantic performance of trading in coffee, tea, sugar, and flesh, not a few of the words in the declaration need more than a mere translation, more than a simple xeno-logic. Who, for example, is the "we," and what does "men" encompass? Just how might one pursue happiness, and what is a people? The conceit of xenolalia is not merely that one could speak the language of the Other without thinking in that lingual form; it is also, and even more fundamentally, a conceit—even *the* American conceit—insofar as it does not cognize the relationship between any utterance and generativity of interpretation as irreducible. It is almost a resistance to thinking any utterance as a likewise materiality, but rather proposes that meaning is only surface deep and such surface is translatable. Andrew Benjamin describes translation in the ways I here describe interpretation: as necessarily plural, as necessarily irreducible, as anoriginal. For example, he says, "Literality or literal meaning emerges therefore as secondary effect. However it is a secondary effect that is never semantically pure. The consequence of this is that it denies to the literal the possibility of being prior and of having priority."[46] He also says, "The point that was being made is that any attempt to affix a fixed and static meaning to [any text for/of translation] necessitate[s] denying or refusing its inherent potential to open a different semantic space. The consequence being that what was primary, or anoriginal, was precisely this potentially conflictual ambiguity; potential semantic differential plurality."[47] When attending to the ways aesthesis is the deformational force of theoria after its having been made to be categorically distinct through theology-philosophy, I here offer interpretation as doing the work—the aesthetic practice—of laying bare the problematics of literality, of translation as producing literality. Interpretation is that which, in this work, announces the anoriginal nature of any word, phrase, concept.

Of breath, Charles Olson says, "And the line [of the poem] comes (I swear it) from the breath, from the breathing of the man who writes, at the moment that he writes, and thus is, it is here that, the daily work, the WORK, gets in, for only he, the man who writes, can declare, at every moment, the line its metric and its ending—where its breathing, shall come to, termination."[48] Glossolalia and glossographia are aesthetic uses of breath—as speaking, as writing—and point us toward life—irrepressible and inexhaustible modes of being in the world with others that Charles Parham and his desire for xenolalia could not cognize. What Olson gives us is a poetics of breath as writing practice—glossographia and not xenographia—that does not purport to be coherent or pure but that has the impurity of dilation, of respiration, of animus. Glossographia is not the language of the Other but a prompting toward more utilization of breath, whether great or slight. To be between the glosso's—between lalia and graphia, between speech and script—is to aestheticize breath as a way of irreducible, irrepressible life, in and as Spirit. The blackness, the tongue-speech, the tongue-script, the agnosticism, is a mode of life, a way of movement that takes the most mundane of resources in and around us for inhabitation, for the making of art. Art, not that has to renunciate the pleasures of the flesh as the Fisk Jubilee Singers were trained to do for a political economic project, but that grounds its being in the flesh, in the pleasures of the process of breathing, in the choreosonic force of Blackpentecostal performance. Breath is the space between script and speech.

THE UNIVERSITY SPEAKS in tongues. From Schelling to Nietzsche, from Du Bois to Derrida, concerns about the pedagogical processes of the university are grounded in concerns over language, over translation—as acts of displacement—on the one hand and interpretation—as acts of expounding—on the other. This distinction parallels Hortense Spillers's distinction of body from flesh and, as elaborated above, xenolalia from glossolalia. Whether understood as xenolalia or glossolalia, the purported gibberish that is speaking in tongues, particularly for the early Blackpentecostals during the twentieth century, was an object of ridicule and scorn. The various media accounts made claims regarding the backwardness, the primitivism, the hullaballoo of these incoherent speakers. Tongues-speech was a major disruptive force, interrupting and interrogating through performance modes of communicative efficaciousness, of linguistic coherence and grammatical rule. I here claim that the university, as a material and imagined space of thought, has Blackpentecostal aesthetic force of glossolalia running through it. Running through it yet engaged through aversion, engaged through desired repression. I further claim that there are ways to approach an object of study, and the choice of approach is of social and political consequence. There are both, however, xenolalic and glossolalic means to thinking objects of study and the university is animated by the debate over the efficaciousness of xenolalic and glossolalic utterance.

The university is animated by the debate with the desired gathering and discarding of glossolalic form in the service of xenolalic—which is to say neoliberal—ends. Xenolalia and glossolalia are means to approach an object. In the biblical tradition, Apostle Paul wrote specifically that if one speaks in tongues publicly within a congregation, that he desired there to be someone to "interpret" such speech. But the falling of the Holy Spirit in the book Acts of the Apostles demonstrates that people heard "in their own languages" what people were bespeaking. So between xenolalia and glossolalia are concerns about translation and interpretation. Between these two concepts, in other words, is a critical stance, a critical inquiry, a critical analysis of objects. "The imposition of a State language implies an obvious purpose of conquest and administrative domination of the territory, exactly like the opening of a road . . ."[49] Xenolalia operates by a peculiar conception of self and Other, and the conceit of xenolalia is not by imposing State language—of the Americas, for example—on the Other. What it does is, perhaps, more insidious. It imposes the *logic* of a State language through the refusal of linguistic difference, through the nonacknowledgment of idiomatic expression internal to the languages of the Other; it assumes that all one needs is translation, rather than interpretation. So not only does it assume that translation is more consequential than interpretation, but the *logic* is grounded in the necessity of the ongoing difference, the ongoing nonconvergence of the self and Other. Derrida was correct: the imposition of State language also is the imposition of a path, of forced entry into borders by allowing for the declaration of statehood on the one hand and then dispersing that statehood on the grounds of the Other. That one could be, following Denise Ferreira da Silva and Nahum Chandler, the *Other* of Europe assumes that Europe and its other are translational concepts, surface ideas, axiomatic. It is an imposition of the logic that is of violence, violation through perpetual coloniality of being/power/truth/freedom.

Language is used in the service of settler colonial logic. This is, perhaps, why missionary tongues—xenolalic utterances—appear to me to be a distinctly western theological-philosophical construction. Though the Acts of the Apostles narrative discusses the possibility of xenolalia, a question remains: Were the speakers speaking in various languages or were the hearers hearing in their own idioms? It seems that such a distinction is of utmost importance. One is a question of translation, the latter of interpretation. With xenolalia, missionary tongues-speech were utilized as paths toward the proliferation of a religio-cultural nation-state.

Tongues, particularly emphatic when enunciated through the force and conception of glossolalia, are sonic acts that stop short of being speech and with this refusal of speech, while giving utterance, a gift emerges: "What happens when such a speech act draws from the treasury of the linguistic system and, perhaps, affects or transforms it?"[50] Glossolalia retreats from the linguistic system through enunciating and elaborating vocables, aspirating sounded out breath without the need for grammatical structure or rule. Tongue-speech is nothing at all, in all its wondrous manifestation, in glorious plentitude. Glossolalia produces affect and transformation. Through xenolalia, however, there is the disappearance—as displacement and dispossession—of the Other. Catherine Malabou assists: "Language begins by making things disappear since to speak is to reveal the possibility of naming things in their absence, while also naming the absence. To speak is to lose. But in this instance, to be able to lose is also to be able to see, to be able to see what one loses, and to be able to say that one sees it."[51] More:

> There is, therefore, an originary violence at work in language, causing an irremissible schism between discourse and figure, sense and sensible, and idea and flesh. Given then, when we ask what it means to 'see a thought,' we must examine the distortion between the sayable as a gaping tear, rent at the edge of language, and sound out the power of the eye, which is both language and look, without being one more than the other.[52]

To seek an experience of speaking that stops short, literally, of such violence is what the glossolalic, the glossographic attempts; it is to revive the flesh from having been rent into—having been forced into being—a body through the "brush of discourse" or the mutilation of the flesh. Glossolalia returns to the originary scene of the crime where flesh was forced to dwell together with other flesh—severed, however, from the possibility of linguistic communication (the separating, the dividing up, the making categorically distinct through partitioning languages on ships, for example)— and at that site of exorbitant violence—violence for the establishment of a political economy—glossolalia speaks, not words, but the very stuff, the materiality, from which words come, glossolalia speaks the experience of nothingness, secretes—lets out into—the interior of inhabitation and refuge, compels an analysis of what such nothingness is, could be. Glossolalia speaks, enunciates, announces: originary difference, anoriginal brokenness atop which words—as coherent little things—float.

Standing atop strange planks, in strange (otherwise-than-) land on the sea—floating, as it were, like a journey toward coherence-as-language—Olaudah Equiano put his ear to a book with hopes that it would talk to him:

> I had often seen my master and Dick employed in reading; and I had a great curiosity to talk to the books, as I thought they did; and so to learn how all things had a beginning: for that purposes I have often taken up a book, and have talked to it, and then put my ears to it, when alone, in hopes it would answer me; and I have been very much concerned when I found it remained silent.[53]

On a boat, a "nowhere" in suspended space and time, Equiano's listening practice would be the foundations for a conversion experience grounded in the necessity for confession. Equiano's conversion is important to consider both because of the way he thinks language but also because of his submission to *and* critique of Calvinist doctrine. Equiano's listening to the text illustrates the way he wanted to find the noise, to hear the noise, and in such hearing produce otherwise than Calvinist doctrine, Calvinist thought. His engagement with the text would be a black noise that would continually deform his relation to Christianity, to providence, to what he called predestinarianism. "My mind was therefore hourly replete with inventions and thoughts of being freed. . . . However, as I was from early years a predestinarian, I thought whatever fate had determined must ever come to pass . . ."[54] Equiano's "knowledge of freedom"[55] was a choreosonic breakdown of and break with his thinking predestination doctrine, his knowledge and desire and movement in the direction of such freedom would have him, therefore, produce an otherwise relation to doctrinal integrity.

His talking to books and learning otherwise was in the "nowhere" of ships. The "nowhere" was also a case for radical sociality. Therein he heard and participated in noise making, noise listening, the nothingness of Blackpentecostal practice. Peter Linebaugh analyzed how the history of the slave ship highlights important features for the performance of resistance through the creation of Pidgin English: "The ship was not only the means of communications between continents, it was the first place where working people from the continents communicated. All the contradictions of social antagonism were concentrated within its timbers" and, additionally, "European imperialism also created the conditions of the circulation of experience within the huge masses of labour that it had set in motion. People will talk."[56] But the transformation of flesh into bodies into ledger balances—into, that is, nothing at all—could not reduce the irrepressible life that the enslaved carried in them and dispersed. The breath, literally of life, was in them and emerged to counteract the occasion of brutality and violence. The creative impulse was not obliterated but targeted towards the object of abjection: the purported severing off from the capacity for communication. Linebaugh said this about Pidgin English fashioned on the moving "nowheres": "It was a language whose expressive power arose less from its lexical range than from the musical qualities of stress and pitch," that "Pidgin became an instrument, like the drum or the fiddle, of communication among the oppressed: scorned and not easily understood by 'polite' Society."[57] Language was instrumentalized, used for varied insurrectional practices and resistances aboard these many floating cargo transports.

This to argue that glossolalia not only enacts a disruption of grammar and lingual form but also enacts spatiotemporal incoherence, produces a "floating nowhere" for celebratory speaking, for ecstatic praise against the very violence and violation that animated, and animates today still, our political economy. Glossolalia is the surplus of language and a line of flight. "The surplus, then, is a place, the place, that at the same time is atopical (atopique), that is to say, without place, without possible localization. It is the pure possibility of the place that gives rise without itself occupying a space, without taking care of its own space."[58] Furthermore, Stevphen Shukaitis says:

> One can find ways to use the institutional space without being of the institution, without taking on the institution's goals as one's own. It is this dynamic of being within but not of an institutional space, to not institute itself as the hegemonic or representative form, that

characterizes the workings of the nomadic educational machine. It is an exodus that does not need to leave in order to find a line of flight.[59]

We brush up against the Blackpentecostal prepositional aesthetic that yields directionality for thinking, and inhabiting, otherwise worlds within the constraints and limits of the given world. In Chapter 2 of this work, I discussed how Charles Harrison Mason talked about shouting, how—for him—it is praise *of, for,* and *to, in,* and *about* God. Shukaitis emphasizes how one can inhabit space without being of it, how one can be within without succumbing to institutional practices or desires. Like Mason's rendering of Blackpentecostal dance, Shukaitis participates in the Blackpentecostal aesthetic force of producing a space—momentary and temporary in its enunciation, emerging as a gathering during specific occasion never to occupy land or thought in concrete and immovable ways—in and against the grain of constraint.

Shukaitis expounded upon "a politics of knowledge constantly elaborated within a terrain of struggle," in the service of "the space of minor knowledges and experiences that do not seek to become a major or representative form, instead forming tools from discarded refuse and remains."[60] This is nothing other than a desire for an otherwise epistemology from which to think, to breathe, to be. Though the aesthetics of Blackpentecostalism are often relegated to being cognized theologically-philosophically as the merely aesthetic, the merely ornamental and, as such, the necessarily discardable, the excess that has no material force or import, what Shukaitis produces is a way to interrogate the ways in which Blackpentecostalism gets taken up as an object of study, but not as a mode *of*—for, and from—study itself. It is here, in the minor mode, in the excess epistemology, that offers a critical intervention into the inequities of the university. What is untrue is this: that Blackpentecostal objects might be graspable, might be apprehended through theological-philosophical projects, but they certainly do not constitute a disruption to the modality by which study occurs. Rather, these objects, these aesthetic practices that are nothing other than intellectual traditions, produce a force of dispossession equal in magnitude whenever grasped. They deform when taken up in normative projects. That normative projects, normative modes of study, do not detect such deformation is because of the logics of aversion.

Glossolalia—as opposed to, and in contradistinction from xenolalia—refuses representation and form through its elaboration as "heavenly language," which is another way to perhaps say *nothing at all*. It is a form of life that does not necessitate its ease of representation. It is a mode of existence that does not aspire to "stay" any "here," it is but another iteration of stealing away. One arrives only insofar as one finds temporary inhabitation, where one is always on the move. This is, in other words, fugitive speaking, criminal knowledge. To speak of nothing, from nothing, as nothing, to celebrate against the imposition of a crisis moment as old as modernity itself, is the Blackpentecostal aesthetic grounded, as it were, in possibility, in constant, reiterative, improvisational opening, unfolding. That one cannot be trained for such a speaking of nothing, of nothingness, of fugitive speaking, of refused grammar, slips between and allows for an analysis of translation and interpretation.

> Beneath the seemingly literal and thus faithful *translation* there is concealed, rather, a translation of Greek experience into a different way of thinking. *Roman thought takes over the Greek words without a corresponding, equally authentic experience of what they say, without the Greek word.* The rootlessness of Western thought begins with this translation. . . . What could be more obvious than that man transposes his propositional way of understanding things into the structure of the thing itself?[61]

Heidegger gives us traction here by disrupting even the desires that inhere to xenolalic utterance. For though xenolalia aspires to be the language of the Other, necessitating a mere translation, Heidegger disrupts an easy conception of translation. With the act of translation, it is not simply that words are placed into their proper language but there is a displacement of meaning through the experience of the speaker.

The way one understands the world, the way one engages and is structured by the world, is part and parcel of a translational project. It is the difference between "you're welcome" and "*de rien*," where the latter translates as, in one-to-one word fashion, "of nothing." The space, the gap, between *you're welcome* and *of nothing* indexes radically different approaches to the concept of gratitude, rooted in varied conceptions of personhood and Other. That something can be *of nothing* confirms the fact that *nothing*, indeed, *changes*. What one translates, in other words, is experience itself in all of its manifold capaciousness, in all of its irreducible agnosticism.

Xenolalia has an allergic reaction to plurality, to irreducible agnosticism, through displacement of the figural in the service of the literal. Xenolalic utterance is a desire for pure being, for pure literality, that is the ground of meaning but this purity can only be a displacement of that which stands before, that which has ontological priority. Xenolalia is a settler colonial claim on language whereas glossolalia is a disruption of—because it is the grounds for, the flesh of—language.

The university speaks in xenolalic tongues because the university was created for the concept and development of the scholar, for one to become a learned individual. Johann Fichte had much to say about the vocation of the scholar. For example:

> The skill in question is in part the skill to suppress and eradicate those erroneous inclinations which originate in us prior to the awakening of our reason and the sense of our own spontaneity, and in part it is the skill to modify and alter external things in accordance with our concepts. The acquisition of this skill is called "culture," as is the particular degree of this skill which is acquired. Culture differs only in degree, but is susceptible of infinitely many gradations. It is man's ultimate and highest means toward his final end qua rational and sensuous creature: toward complete harmony with himself. When man is considered merely as a sensuous creature, then culture is itself his final end. Sensuousness should be cultivated: that is the highest and ultimate thing which one can propose to do with it.[62]

What does the concept of harmony—particularly given the discussion above about the training of voices of the Fisk Jubilee Singers, a concept that has much purchase in musicological thought—have to do with notions of skill? When refracted through the training of the Fisk Jubilee Singers' voices, skill connects with class mobility, with aspirational desires to leave behind the so-called denigrated zone of nothingness, a zone whereby speech is unintelligible and nonrepresentational. The Fisk Jubilee Singers demonstrated the ways through which sound, cultivated through skill, was the grounds for the evidence of the very capacity to be enculturated and for the cultivation of culture itself.

Through Fichte we learn, however, that culture is the residue of that which has been suppressed and eradicated, the "erroneous inclinations which originate in us prior to" any awakening, great or small. Culture, then, is the result of suppression, the suppression of anoriginal glossolalia, culture is the bringing together of sensuousness with rationality after-the-fact of the suppression of originary inclination. Culture is the translation of the object, culture is the desire for xenolalic possibility; culture is an enunciation of theoria after its having been made categorically distinct from—by emerging out of the denigrated sensuousness and materiality of—aesthesis. For Fichte, the profession of a scholar is to attain mastery through the reduction and removal of ornamentation, of excess, otherwise translated, irrationality: "Man's final end is to subordinate to himself all that is irrational, to master it freely and according to his own laws. This is a final end which is completely inachievable and must always remain so . . ."[63] From where does the concept of irrationality emerge and what are the results of such an emergence? What has to be considered about thinking itself, about the capacities for cognition and the quivering of flesh, for any such declaration to be made about the necessity to repress that which stands before, that which emerges prior to, any such thing called rationality? Fichte would have that individuals work on themselves, as so many planks of wood in shops, to produce laborious habits of mind to manipulate the external world. Such that, for Fichte, the ensemblic motives of the senses—in all their vitality and openness to experience—should be cultivated, which is likewise to assert, should be cut, removed through serrational edge.

Fichte said, "It is not man's vocation to reach his goal. But he can and he should draw nearer to it, and his true vocation qua man, i.e., insofar as he is rational but finite, a sensuous but free being, lies in *endless approximation toward this goal* . . . perfection is man's highest and unattainable goal. His vocation, however, is to *perfect himself without end*."[64] Fichte thought the vocation of the scholar is not to simply be engaged in perpetual pursuits, but to be in the pursuit of a specific object: that of perfection, of purity, of pure being. To perfect oneself without end toward this object is to continually suppress and repress the anoriginal "irrationality" of our creatureliness. Fichte recognized, however, that this pursuit is productive of failure, of something that will never be realized. Pursuit becomes the inexhaustible. Like the Kantian desire for escape as the condition for emergence of Enlightenment, I am not interested in dismissing the critical force of ongoingness, perhaps as open-endedness, which Fichte posits is the work of the scholar. Rather, I am intrigued by the directionality of his claim.

His is a pursuit of perfection. But what if one is not after perfection but openness itself? What if the goal of endless restive movement and vibration is not to reach any mode of stasis and enclosure, is not to stay any where, but to ongoingly approach, to move toward—through varied directions—endless horizonal (of and toward the horizon) thrust? The cool thing about horizons is that they move along with you; any way you turn, there the horizon finds you. He needs a counterclockwise, counterintuitive, centrifugitive undoing of directionality, a practice of Blackpentecostal aesthetic performance.

from: a
to: dtim
Monday December 7, 2009, 10:16PM
Subject: Re: something
It's not that I wanted to possess you, though I certainly did enjoy and envision a future of us where we seized each other. And I never could master you but felt that each new morning occasioned things about you unexplored. Could it be possible to relate without ownership, to capture hearts while banishing jealousy?

I am a bit surprised about how upset I got about all of this last night while speaking to someone about some new sorta technology that can "perfectly reproduce" Art Tatum's piano playing. This technology has the ability to "listen" to music and recreate it. It kindasorta *sees what our brains react to* in order to infuse that in music performance. And I suppose I don't have a real issue with reproducing something. There's a guy—George Lewis, a musician and a pretty cool dude—in New York who has been using computer algorithms for years to improvise, to think about improvisation and subjectivity. And I'm down with all that because it seems he thinks of computer technology, not as opposed to human subjectivity but as part and parcel of it. I mean, you were the one that told me that the first meaning of computer was *one who computes*, that Dells, Macs and Gateways are only the newest mode of a really old concept.

So the issue I had with last night's conversation [aside from the fact that I was real close to my limit] was the pressure applied to the word *perfectly*, that something could be possessed, mastered sonically by machines only in order to reproduce it *perfectly*. But I wonder: what if the musician—Art Tatum, for example—was not trying to produce perfectly? What if, following Baraka's listening to and writing about Lady Day, one tries to create failure? Or, not even failure, but what if *perfection* is not part of the sociocultural vocabulary of a world, or not a thing desired in the first place? Like, isn't there an assumption that musicians and painters and all sorts of artists want to produce perfection? But what if they're not? Do we even think this refusal of desire is possible? That the norm could be on bending bent notes until even the bends are bent? And what is assumed when it is thought that a new mode of some old thing now, *finally,* can create perfection? what does it say about ingenuity and emotion and drive?

Anyway. So I began arguing rather forcefully against what the guy at the bar was saying about perfection and Art Tatum and his rather ridiculous assumptions. The technology he described seems to be nothing other than an enactment of a desire to possess and master without accounting for the underside of such declaration. It hallucinates the idea that the "original" producers had particular intent that could be fully realizable. Rather than asking how does the technology become another occasion to produce failure beautifully, it gets taken up to say that it can reproduce without failure. *More perfectly than even Art Tatum could've done* I think the dude said. Of course, there is likewise an assumption of an *essence* of music performance that can be found, that there is some ground-zero, some foundational claim to production of emotion and thought and drive.

And there seems to be, of course, the implication of an articulation of a critique of *authenticity* because if sound technology can "hear" Art Tatum "play" without his vivid thereness, then and of course, Art Tatum becomes inconsequential to the performance of Art Tatum. His materiality, his once-there flesh, becomes discardable chaff which the wind can drive away, at best. And, if the computer can reproduce perfectly what it has captured and mastered? Well, then no one has the ability to be authentic. And I know anti-essentialism is all the rage with its being against claims for authenticity but I don't even think the right questions are being posed. Like, what is perfection and how is it determined? If I said that Tatum's breath was just as consequential to his performance as his fingered weight on keys?

And what about the social field that was produced when Art Tatum played? These technologies are all about reproducing and perfecting originary genius and individuality when folks like Tatum [and maybe us all?] are constantly engaging in creating ways to be with others.

Then it finally hit me why dude last night was so wrong. I listened to the sermon *Let's Get it On* by Bishop Iona Locke again [for the, *how-many-nth* time?] earlier this morning. You know how we produce something other than but close to the concept of failure? She was preaching and in the moment of her *whooping* when the congregation is just all the way in it, screaming and clapping and providing that necessary background that isn't so backgrounded, she said

God said I will pour out my spirit . . . upon some *flesh*

and the congregation screamed back

All!

and then she came right back in

You talkin right. All! He said all *flesh!*

How would a technology account for that? She literally in her preaching moment opened up a space to allow the congregation to engage with her disarticulation of the scripture. She ruptured its flow, *some* flesh, knowing that the audience was right there with her production of something other than that which was correct. There is, of course, a world of difference between "some" and "all." But she realized the congregation as part and parcel of her preaching performance. Could the technology of perfection—rather than improvisation—*know* that she was going to exclaim *some* for the audience to respond as such? There is incalculability that is part of the performance, some aspect that cannot occur before such sitting down at piano benches or standing in pulpits. And if the organ wasn't there? And if the congregation wasn't standing and jumping and screaming?

She isn't the only one, though. It's like when folks are up exhorting the congregation, or when the organ breaks during shouting music :: there are all sorts of gaps and elisions and ruptures of sound, thought, texture, openings and forestallments that go against any such notion of "perfection " and reproduction that could ever be so termed.

These are the calling forth, not just *call and response* but *call and call,* some sorta accretion and accrual, layer upon layer upon layer, each word and phrase and scream and breath engaging and revising that which came before it, affecting subsequence. In such performance is the recognition that the congregation has some such knowledge in them that is animated by and likewise animates any such praise leader, devotional singer or preacher.

It's sorta like how when you'd exhort the congregation right before the preacher, or when you'd be giving words of encouragement during the momentary space between the dance and the "Yes, Lord" praise where some folks would still be praising and running while others would be hunched over and yet others still bent over with their hands rubbing on their outer thighs and over there would be Patty throwing her head back *AHHH!* and over here would be Jesse clapping incessantly and you would talk saying something like, *Take your seat if ya can . . . hahaha!*

Or you'd say something like *I don't know what you came to do but I come to praise the . . .*

You wouldn't, of course, include the final word, the word *lord* but would leave the statement, if ever so faintly, open-ended.

Or how you'd say *After all the things I been through, I stiiiiillll have jeeyuh . . .* quick, crisp, staccato-like and the congregation knew what that meant.

Of course, you'd have to be part of this social world to know that *jeeyuh* meant *joy* and that opening was also a space for folks to keep it going. The words don't necessarily cohere with what is desired. *We've got to move on* was as much a call for *not* moving on—for the Saints to keep praising—as it was to say that it was time to *turn over the service.* These are accents on and off the beat, not just slurred speech and weighted keys, but a way to inhabit a social antiphonal world. This world isn't about perfection. It's about the *power of the lord coming down* and I don't think you can account for that with algorithms, though algorithms can help get you there.

[And I am not against technology. The B-3 for me is quintessentially Pentecostal and without it, I wonder what the church world would sound like for black folks. and I'm still waiting on someone to write about First Church of Deliverance in Chicago using the Hammond in a black church setting, and how, curiously enough, the pastor was—what would they have said then? queer? a homophile? homosexual? gay? The technological, non-human machine that serves as foundational for the sound of this social world was first recognized as important by a someone very queer. There's gotta be something about dispersal, spirit and sound there. And maybe that *purported* imperfection's relation to the sound of Pentecost.]

It just seems that any desire for such perfection really spins out from a different sorta epistemological center altogether. Assumptions of clarity and rigor and rightness seem hella limiting to me. And there is never an accounting of how perfection—when it is achieved—may be merely another form of improv. Sometimes, I just wanna say: *leave this alone, let it do its own thing, if you wanna join it, cool but if you wanna perfect it? Stay back.*[65]

The problem, it seems, is with how objects become—and are the foundation for—a set of problematics. It is a problem, it seems then, with how one sees, hears, tastes, touches, smells an object, how one senses and experiences objects. But this problematic of sensual experience is grounded in refusal to openness and availability, which, on the lower frequencies we might say, is grounded in shoring up against sensuality. Nahum Chandler, again: "On what basis can one decide a being, and its character of existence, as one kind or another? What emerges as decisive at the limit and in the conceptual and propositional sense is the problem of grounding, in some fashion that would be absolute, a socially observable hierarchy that one might wish to affirm."[66] Denise Ferreira da Silva analyzes the ways that the other of European man was necessarily deemed "irrational" and how the very notion of irrationality, as such, is a racialized concept.[67]

We know of the stories wherein European men would encounter Africans or how they would encounter indigenous people—in the Americas, for example—dressed climate-appropriately; we know, also, how the encounter with indigenes in the Americas was a problem for European man because of a different ecological relationship with the world, one that did not presume land could be individuated and owned as private property. In both instances, European man deemed these others—through theological-philosophical thought—barbaric and savage because of sartorial adornment, because of the aesthetics of cloth and cover, because an otherwise epistemological ordering of world. European man would come to have a relation to the land that was fundamentally about a theological-philosophical ordering, theology and philosophy both being defined by their capacity to deem a people barbaric, savage, unholy, sinful. And such a declaration—as the grounds for theologizing and philosophizing—would mean the capacity, the availability, for obliteration and displacement was the mode of cognizing value, the mode of deciding what could and could not be "man." And this obliteration in the pursuit of the perfection of European man and civilization, the establishment of the identity of European man and its civilization.

Looped through Heidegger's notion that *trans*lation is about the evacuation and liquidation of experience into different terms, we might answer Chandler by emphatically asserting that the basis of the decision of being is what one allows to count as experience, always sensual. To follow Fichte, in order to suppress and eradicate the erroneous is to translate certain sense knowledges and to call it—whatever the "it" here would come designate—erroneous. To suppress and eradicate the erroneous is to make a claim, previous to situation, that the object of reflection is available to xenolalia; it is to hear the sensualness of the object and to make a claim about what is and is not necessary in and of the object for its being understood, for its very existence. It is, then, to do violence to the object through the abstractions of theology-philosophy of the beholder, the behearer, of the object. The scholar is created through this calculus—as the university—through the critical force given to the place of translation, the making of objects into xenolalic utterances.

Ralph Waldo Emerson thought the role of the scholar, particularly on these American shores, was to lead others after long periods of private preparation, absconded and away from publics:

> The office of the scholar is to cheer, to raise, and to guide men by showing them facts amidst appearances. . . . In the long period of his preparation he must betray often an ignorance and shiftlessness in popular arts, incurring the disdain of the able who shoulder him aside. Long must he stammer in his speech; often forgo the living for the dead. Worse yet, he must accept—how often!—poverty and solitude.[68]

Emerson's scholar is founded upon the necessity of solitude, aloneness. In this way, the scholar in the university approaches its objects through a xenolalic desire, through a desire to leave the zone of nothingness behind for a more stable, coherent, set of speaking—and thus subject-forming—practices. It is a mode of inhabitation that desires legitimation and validation from a one that stands above, outside; beyond it is legitimation and validation from one that vests within oneself the power of adjudication.

This is the impenetrability of the object as the foundations from western thought Foucault elaborates.[69] In this way, the university was never meant to be a place of refuge for minor life, minor language, which is to say, it was never supposed to be a place of glossolalic exchange, for a deepening into and journey within the dark expanse of nothingness as celebratory. Glossolalia, indeed, could be an object *to* study but not a method *of*—for, from—studying. Glossolalia is speaking in blackness. There is no resistance to considering blackness and black as objects *to* study. Resistance is in considering blackness and black objects as a collection of sensuous experiences that are life altering, a collection of sensuous experiences that are modes and models of intellectual practice. But is there a way to study with others, to have an intellectual practice grounded in the social? And what would be the consequence of such intellectual sociality?

Perhaps a Blackpentecostal aesthetic is elaborated in Emerson, perhaps against even Emerson's own mode of delimited thought. And this because of the way he describes a scholar through plurality: "The scholar is that man who must take up into himself all the ability of the time, all the contributions of the past, all the hopes of the future. He must be an university of knowledges."[70] The scholar is one that takes into oneself spatial and temporal measure, remakes it and gifts it to worlds. In such a taking in, one has the capacity to obliterate space and time, spatial and temporal coherence. It is to become an otherwise university. The scholar becomes only when they crystalize the plentitude of possibility. To be this otherwise university is to be capacious, to exceed the very borders and limitations of abstraction, to be open as and to flesh. To take into oneself time past and future is to disrupt spatial and temporal coherence, it is to interrupt smooth, linear, progressive chronologies. To take into oneself and to give out this *a*temporality-*a*spatiality is to be foundationally and irreducibly open for such indwelling.

What if the otherwise university were constituted with minor language, with minor life, in mind? What if it were animated by an indwelling, an outpouring of spirit, to the world? It would be an enactment of movement, of breath, in the service of reconfiguring life. It would be an enactment of Blackpentecostal aesthetic vitality. "What would that mean? An artistic movement dedicated to the reshaping of art, life, and politics that did not announce this to as many who would listen, but rather went about affecting its method of transformation on a minor scale?"[71] For Stevphen

Shukaitis, what is necessary for a reconfiguration project and process is a social intellectual practice of world-making, of recognizing that there is the capacity to produce "new word(s), new world(s)."[72] This capacity to produce otherwise is rooted in ongoing openness, a spiritual-material, *a*theological-*a*philosophical vulnerability. This openness and capaciousness, however, does not need to rise to the level of visibility, does not need to declare itself for its affects to be made nor felt in worlds. Indeed, visibility can be a problem.[73] Shukaitis is attuned to the problems of visibility as the only mode and model of movement: "The problem is that by declaring openly intents and methods to reshape art, life, and the relations of production, the avant-garde has tended to give away too much, to let its hand be shown too early. In other words, to leave it open to processes of decomposition and recuperation, where radical ideas are put to service within forms of social control and domination."[74] Visibility, apparentness, desires for the xenolalic, translation, all are submissions to ocularcentrism, to a world constructed based on the capacity to see, and to see clearly, and to have modes of ocular attention normativized as the most profound and meaningful way to affect change in the world. What is needed is a method of speaking that does not, even through its enunciatory force and elaboration, make itself apparent, make itself available for translational projects. Glossolalia, indeed, is the hesitance of speech through speaking; it is the hesitance and resistance to meaning, through enunciation.

BLACK STUDY SPEAKS in tongues, in glossolalic nothingness as celebratory. Institutional black studies is not coterminous, though it shares intimate relation, with Black Study. The former indexes an historical process in the mid-twentieth century and the latter indexes a mode of approaching objects, a form of intellectual practice, that resists the stilling and stasis of abstraction through language, and through quantifying.[75] Thus, Black Study—when taken up in institutional form as black studies—has always been concerned with the world, with the destruction of inequity and the imagining and material realizing of otherwise worlds, otherwise possibilities. For example, Martha Biondi argues forcefully that the founding of black studies at university institutions was part of the black revolutionary impulse of the late 1960s, not separate from it.[76] And from its foundations, black studies was always concerned with questions of globality, of nation-states and citizenship, and, particularly, for the concept of diaspora through class alliance and solidarity.

So a set of questions: How does aversion encapsulate the grounds for critique in and of institutional studies? How does what Derrida call the "as if"—the unconditional university—function antiphonally "previous to situation" that is inherent in Black Study as a Blackpentecostal aesthetic?[77] I turn to reflections on the modern university to think specifically about how a Blackpentecostal force can quicken institutionalization in the service of life, a life that could be, to speak about the university as if life, black life, life in blackness, is there (because such life is, is there, in the undercommons). As an enactment of *a*theological-*a*philosophical force, Black Study is aninstitutional, proffered by (having) being together as the condition of emergence for otherwise possibilities. Blackpentecostalism is fundamentally about having being-together as an irreducible plurality, irreducible density, inexhaustible journeys into the deep recesses of dark nothingness as resource, as reserve.

When considered as an aninstitutional mode of study, mode of social practice, Black Study compels an ongoing search through making of us all ongoing students. It would be like Apostle Paul telling new Christian believers that though he has not attained or seized the object of his affection, he would "press" toward such knowledge.[78] This, of course, is consistent with what Fichte opined about the scholar: that the scholar is one in perpetual pursuit. However, disrupting the logics of the aspiration toward perfection, Fred Moten and Stephano Harney offer, instead of the role of the scholar, the role of the critical academic: "To be a critical academic in the university is to be against the university, and to be against the university is always to recognize it and be recognized by it, and to institute the negligence of that internal outside, that unassimilated underground, a negligence of it that is precisely, we must insist, the basis of the professions."[79] Still, I believe the capacity for the university to be a plurality, a space of irreducible search in ways that follow Emerson's theorizing. I believe the university to be a great gathering of resources that should, it should be said, be exploited and put in the service of the search into the dark, dense folks of nothingness, the dark, dense folds of plentitude. What this would mean is paying attention to minor knowledges, minoritarian persons, not simply as raw material for analytics but as a means to transform the world. It would mean turning critical attention to those whom the political economy exploits through the unavailability of jobs, healthcare, and education in the cause of liberation and for the joy of learning. It would mean producing knowledge from within the social worlds deemed inappropriate for university life.

As such, the critical academic can exist in any space, the university inclusive, while troubling its frame, resisting its enclosure, breaking down the distinction between the inside and outside of the institution. The critical academic of Blackpentecostal institutional form might be the one, the ones, that carry blackqueer aesthesia, that trouble the frame and conceptual domain of normativity by producing queerness as a way of life. Blackqueerness, Blackpentecostal aesthetic practice, would not then be an identity but a method for reading and being in the world. The critical academic is a Blackpentecostal nomad, in search of ongoing experience, rich depth, sensuous movement. The critical academic speaks in tongues, in the glossolalic utterance against the imposition of the neoliberal university's institutionalizing of xenolalia as professionalization. The critical academic can produce otherwise universities, one not beholden to neoliberal logics, one that produces the *as if*—the unconditional—through speaking, and celebrating such elaboration of, nothingness. Such that glossolalia, which is to say Black Study, is the marking of unruly speech, unproprietous utterance, as the foundational soundings for celebratory praise, for change in the world. If "professionalization—that which reproduces the professions—is a state strategy,"[80] we find Derrida again haunting our analysis: we can say, then, that State language is a professional aspiration, and the neoliberal, normative university seeking to professionalize is seeking to produce certain language.

Both James Baldwin and June Jordan begin conversations about black English, consistent with linguists and social historians. They both write about how black English is the mark of black community, how in the language itself is the speechifying of sociality, of being together as the evidence of the unseen worlds, the unseen vitality and force, of blackness. For example, Baldwin asserted:

> Now, if this passion, this skill, this (to quote Toni Morrison) "sheer intelligence," this incredible music, the mighty achievement of having brought a people utterly unknown to, or despised by "history"—to have brought this people to their present, troubled, troubling, and unassailable and unanswerable place—if this absolutely unprecedented journey does not indicate that black English is a language, I am curious to know what definition of languages is to be trusted.[81]

And June Jordan stated:

White standards of English persist, supreme and unquestioned, in these United States. Despite our multi-lingual population, and despite the deepening Black and White cleavage within that conglomerate, White standards control our official and popular judgments of verbal proficiency and correct, or incorrect, language skills, including speech.[82]

In such an environment that conflates standard with white, it becomes no surprise that black language, language that exists on the other and under side of whiteness, is a force that disforms and disarranges the propriety of grammatical rule. Perhaps Baldwin was onto something: black English sets to question the idea of language itself. Just what is language if the communicative styles of the undercommons, the speechifying of black folks, the glossolalic utterances of Blackpentecostals are not considered language? Is the concept of language just another abstraction of theological-philosophical thought? Jordan's detailing of how English is only standard when white sets up the question: Should we want language that purports to coherence and stasis, that is used in the service of building a radically marginalizing nation-state? Should we desire language, when the logic of language through the cognized valuations of western theology-philosophy are grounds for settler colonialist violence? Or should we desire to speak the antithesis of language, social glossolalia?

If we answer yes to the latter, we would acquire "language" skills that are not interested in the production of citizenship and statehood, but are enlivened by what Édouard Glissant describes as "rooted errantry," which is "the knowledge that identity is no longer completely within the root but also in Relation."[83] Glissant goes on to call this errantry a poetics. So we can begin to think about the poetics of speaking in tongues, the poetics of glossolalia, the poetics of the dark expanse of nothingness, over and against the antipoetic force of xenolalia. I consider xenolalia to be an antipoetic force because it is not grounded in a relation of errantry and rootlessness, but in the capacity for pure representation, pure displacement from one language into another. As black language, as Blackpentecostal enunciation, the glossolalic makes a demand for "the right to obscurity," as Glissant would have, the right—that is, to nothingness in all its capaciousness.[84]

Ronald Judy in "Untimely Intellectuals and the University" is interested in how black studies became institutionalized as part of a neoliberal project:

What was needed was more civilization than science. This brings us back to understanding Black studies as originating as an extension of the university's intellectual project beyond the university. The research universities that so concerned Chapman with their vital administrative science took an interest in the newly freed slaves as objects of scientific research. . . . These early "scientific" studies of slavery rationalized the emerging socioeconomic order in which commercial growth was consistent with Blacks being categorized as essentially surplus labor. The rationalization was articulated in the scientific study of the inherent lack of civilization among Blacks. The scientific universities were concerned with Blacks only as objects of analysis and not as thinking, cultured subjects. It was in opposition to this scientific study of the Negro, and the progressive professionalization of science in the universities, that Black studies was first launched in Black cultural organizations . . .[85]

Let's call this translational project "the study of black objects," and given the modes through which this scientizing of civilization occurred, this translational project was a xenolalic othering of black objects. This xenolalia was utilized in ways to justify the marginalizing and oppressing of black people through economic structures. Much like the Fisk Jubilee Singers's need to repress accent, repress the unruly speech of plantations, repress and remove the nothingness from which they emerged in order to produce an economically viable stage show, the normative university's scientizing was entangled with an Africanist presence of American, of western, society. Judy moves us further still: "The academy's program of establishing the Negro's contribution to civilization is idealist in that it presumes that scientific contemplation of the Negro will reveal Negro thought self-knowingly manifesting itself in the world as World History."[86] This study of black objects is grounded in xenolalic displacement rather than interpretation of experience. It attempts to bespeak the nature, the structure, the value of the black object without ever considering the capacity for the object to speak, without ever thinking in the cognizing glossolalia of the undercommons. The tools of study that ground the neoliberal, normative university are given over to black objects rather than being of—for, from—such objects. Such that the utterances from the underground only show up as chatter, as noisome nothingness in need of dispelling through the making and marking coherent of speech. Xenolalic speech is abstraction, it is the modal enunciation that makes blackness into the object of aversion for the beholder with such desires.

Black Study, grounded in glossolalic search, is a general agnosticism that does not dismiss the journey, is a structure of belief, belief in the necessity of otherwise possibilities, otherwise being: "The wholly other has to do not only with the future of waiting but also with the possibility of a wholly other beginning. Belief—for such is the transcendental horizon of faith—always contains faith in another source: that everything could have been otherwise, that history could have happened otherwise."[87] I replace "other beginning" with otherwise possibility because Blackpentecostal aesthetics disrupt temporality and spatiality such that "beginning" would need recalibration. To be a student in such a study, in such an intellectual practice, would have individuals in the posture of sankofa, enacting, performing what it means to "go back and get it," where "it" here indexes the always possible otherwise, an otherwise that exists alongside and in antagonistic form to modernity, to western theological-philosophical thought. In the originary grounding of experience, what one has is always the capacity for plurality. Otherwise possibilities, otherwise being, are always existent in the anoriginal. Otherwise simply waits for interpretation. The black student practicing glossolalia continually returns to the source of language, the source of speech, to find that any utterance has within it the capacity for difference, for originary displacement.

To speak in glossolalic tongues is to believe in the plurality of experience itself, to perform and live into the otherwise. Black Study, here then, is a belief in an *a*theological-*a*philosophical mode of being in but not of the world. And this Black Study, a minor black studies, an aninstitutional black studies can exist within the space of the university. "To utilize the space provided by the university, not as a goal in itself, nor to assert one's right to such a space, but to accomplish something within this space. . . . It is what one does with this space that is the core politics within the university more so necessarily than the specific content. . . . It is a politics based more on process and ethics of transformation than the claiming of territory."[88] This minor black studies, this aninstitutional black studies, speaks out from cramped space, stuttered time, like Harriet Jacobs's habitation in a garret. It makes of constraint capaciousness through imagination, through the material movement against the desires for propriety and private property. This black studies is glossolalic utterance, it is in flight, in exodus, in the performance of marronage: modes of preparation that are always aesthetic.

Glossolalia, in other words and as opposed to xenolalia, is the speech of the undercommons. Glossolalia is capacious and expansive, open and irreducible, returning to originary grounds to find other possibilities, another way. "Once the question of the university is posed in these terms it becomes clear that the position of the individual student or academic and thus their relation to the university cannot be thought other than in relation to the broader considerations of human being as such, a concern that would then come to be re-expressed today in terms of citizens and, in the end, citizenship."[89] So we are thinking about an intellectual practice, a mode of study, that is not reducible to concepts of citizenship. Black Study posits a particular interruption of the historical, of historical being, through the celebration of glossolalic speech, against the historicizing projects grounded in Newtonian physics of smooth, linear, progressive time. June Jordan analyzes western history:

> Black American history prepares black people to believe that true history is hidden and destroyed, or that history results from a logical bundling of lies that mutilate and kill. We have been prepared, by our American experience, to believe that civilization festers between opposite poles of plunder and pain. And still the university waits, unavoidable at the end of compulsory education, to assure the undisturbed perpetuity of this civilization.[90]

Black Study is a performance, is the performance of Blackpentecostal aesthetics. It is not merely an ethnic notion, but a way to critically analyze the social forms, the economic conditions, that produced something called western civilization. Black Study, to return and produce another possibility, is the study of worlds, of world-making. It is neither neutral nor objective; it is not dispassionate nor unconcerned; it is not historical nor concerned with historical being, as each of these is grounded in the very epistemology of western theological-philosophical thought. Nathan Hare warned, "To remain impartial in the educational arena is to allow the current partiality to whiteness to fester. Black education must be based on both ideological and pedagogical blackness."[91]

Indeed, Black Study was performed in Harriet Jacobs's crawlspace, wherein she heard the voice of her children and those voices, those noises, was generative for a mother's care and concern. Black Study was enacted by Blackpentecostal Mamie Till-Mobley, deciding that the world would see what was done to her son, Emmett, deciding that an open casket—perhaps like her openness to the Spirit—was what was needed to quicken a movement for civil rights in the mid-twentieth century. Till-Mobley did not seek to translate her experience for newspapers and magazines; rather, she sought to show it, to speak it, to utter it with exuberant force, to show, speak and utter her love through the horrible scene of Emmett's destruction. Hers was a glossolalic form.

SILENCE PREOCCUPIES JAMES Baldwin. And this preoccupation with the concept of nothingness, of silence ad emptiness, is spatial and temporal. When considering the silence in *Go Tell It On the Mountain* (hereafter, *GTIOM*)[92] and *Just Above My Head* (hereafter, *JAMH*),[93] we can begin to think about repression, regulation, and repair with and against notions of the subject where what emerges is not a simple "I" or heroic figure but a social, a song, a sound, the closest of which might be the concept of together, of ensemble of noise. What Baldwin's engagement and critique of the sound of silence produces is the thing—the gather space for thought—against what he says as a "vivid aspect" of some of the white people he encountered who were surprised that he liked his mother:

> All kinds of people came into our joint—I am now referring to white people—and one of their most vivid aspects, for me, was the cruelty of their alienation. They appeared to have no antecedents nor any real connections.
> "Do you really like your mother?" someone asked me, seeming to be astounded, totally disbelieving the possibility.
> I was astounded by the question.[94]

Given Orlando Patterson's notion that enslavement and its afterlife created the condition of "natal alienation,"[95] it is important to think about how Baldwin here suggested that even with the horrors of enslavement and its classed, raced, gendered aftermath, that there is no alienation as such in black life, but it is fundamentally social. To think otherwise, for Baldwin, was cause for astonishment. Emerging from nothing means to carry something, a resource, from which to draw. Silence is never absolute, and its "putative emptiness" is a social construction. If silence is never absolute, then that which is there is a standing forth, a set of capacities. By way of Baldwin's insights into silence and its impossibilities, we may come to understand more fully the relationship of the nothingness to blackness. In both *GTIOM* and *JAMH*, silence as a concept poses the question of desire itself, cathecting to sight and thought by "locating" it either as the tunnel to or sedimentation in the US South. Baldwin presents the US South, then, as a set of potentials that must rigorously be resisted. If silence is the southern substance of things hoped for, it is evidence of the presence of overwhelming blackness.

The US southern soundscape is normally considered peaceful, tranquil, at rest.[96] The sounds of blackness (and blackness, here, is not of [merely] black people but a certain deregulated, unregulated, reckless, unending, always anticipatory expansiveness, an excessive hum or buzz that resists repression; following Burke in Chapter 3, sublime sounds of blackness as always carrying within the sound the capacity for violence) disturb the frame. Baldwin's engagement of the silence in and of the South is what both Mark Smith and White and White describe as "the white ideal of the plantation soundscape" as "not one of silence, but of quietude."[97] Silence, of course, is not the lack of sound, it is noise directed in a certain way, with certain modes of socially acceptable behavior and comportment. The "noise" of negroes singing was evidence of their contentment in the fields, so the story goes. Thus, what is theorized as a desire for quietude otherwise is what Baldwin writes against as the terror of spatially, sonically organized terror.

Baldwin is attuned to this dichotomy: in *GTIOM* and *JAMH*, the Harlem soundscape is replete with noise from cars, radios, subways, and Pentecostal church tambourines. The southern soundscape is characterized by its antithesis, with a certain anticipatory mode of hearing. The Southern landscape is written as a fundamental refusal of any noise but this refusal is a ruse. There is an incapacity to produce that which is most desired. This incapacity to produce normative form, normative order by way of the refusal of sound is what we are thinking about here. But first. How does silence preoccupy Baldwin?

Silence is a certain mode of inattention to some objects while, no doubt, privileging others, as silence is never all encompassing. It might be said, following Kant, to be the desire of enlightenment: "Enlightenment is man's exit from his self-incurred minority."[98] Silence is the forestalling of the sound's ever-expansiveness, of the ceaseless chatter and noise of nothingness, a nothingness that needs be discarded in order to produce the scholar, the learner.

As such, silence is the antithesis of the ceaseless pulse of vibration, the good vibration of noise, noise the foundation of sound and song. As a project of Enlightenment thought—as a mode of escape, as the exit and movement out—silence can be said to have epistemic characteristic: conceptually, it the desire to get to the heart of the matter, the truth of the situation, the irreducible agreeableness, the fundamental antimix. Silence—as an epistemological concern—is the regulation of thought from vibrational otherwise possibilities. Silence is the end and limit of concern, of thought, of engagement; it is rest. Silence is a category of desired purity and absolutism, under which there is no underneath, beneath which there can be no underground.

Nahum Chandler puts forth the idea that in western philosophy, "the Negro is produced as an exorbitance for thought: an instance outside of all forms of being that truly matter,"[99] and Baldwin answers this concern with choreosonic substance, with choreosonic mixture, with choreosonic force. If the negro is a problem for thought, choreosonics is the response. The South—as a concept—is not limited to states below the Mason-Dixon line. Rather, it is concept that accrues to itself and sediments the refusal to hear in a certain sort of way, the negation of the soundscape, it is a transformation of noise into nothingness, and then a discarding of such nothingness from earshot, from view. Baldwin produces silence as an exorbitance for thought as a means to critique the ways nothingness, the ceaseless noise of blackness, is discarded in normative theological-philosophical thought.

When Florence cried, Gabriel was moving outward in fiery darkness, talking to the Lord. Her cry came to him from afar, as from unimaginable depths; and it was not his sister's cry he heard, but the cry of the sinner when he is taken in sin. This was the cry he had heard so many days and nights, before so many altars, and he cried tonight, as he had cried before: "Have your way, Lord! Have your way!"

Then there was only silence in the church. Even Praying Mother Washington had ceased to moan. Soon someone would cry again, and the voices would begin again; there would be music by and by, and shouting, and the sound of the tambourines. But now in this waiting, burdened silence it seemed that all flesh waited—paused, transfixed by something in the middle of the air—for the quickening power.

This silence, continuing like a corridor, carried Gabriel back to the silence that had preceded his birth in Christ. Like a birth indeed, all that had come before this moment was wrapped in darkness, lay at the bottom of the sea of forgetfulness, and was not counted against him, but was related only to that blind, and doomed, and stinking corruption he had been before he was redeemed.

The silence was the silence of the early morning, and he was returning from the harlot's house. Yet all around him were the sounds of the morning: of birds, invisible, praising God; of crickets in the vines, frogs in the swamp, or dogs miles away and close at hand, roosters on the porch.[100]

There are two sides to Baldwin's silence to which we must attend. It is a break in the narrative. The silence moves and is moving. It is a "corridor," a channel through and bridge to which memory is recalled and relived. The silence in the Pentecostal church in Harlem—though brief, though pregnant, though anticipatory of sound to come afterward—was a momentary rupture and Gabriel is transported back to the South.

Astonishment is the depravation of the sensual domain, an unhinging shock out of self-possession by way of bewilderment or terror. Attunement to this passage opens up this idea. There is first Blackpentecostal noise of Florence's cry and Blackpentecostal theology of darkness through which she sounds, through which she moves. Gabriel is the moment of encounter; it is he who most fully apprehends these audiovisual actions. Then there was only silence in the church. The wicked ceased from troubling; the weary put at rest. This was a moment of astonishment, wherein Gabriel's senses were at their most acute: he was most sensitive to the Pentecostal noise, Pentecostal darkness and was fully seized with, taken up into, grasped by this blackness. At the apex of this acutement, he was also deadened to his senses: there was only silence in the church. A moment seeing nothing, hearing nothing, tasting nothing, feeling nothing, smelling nothing. Stupefied, stumped, staggered. Then released, into a new place, new time, new thought. The South.

I am arguing that with Baldwin, here, we find that the moment of reckless abandon that the religious tradition calls forth, the moment of unregulated praise, noise and terror is the occasion for transport, it is a moment of/after the encounter that blackness enacts for Gabriel's atemporal, memorial inhabitation. Transport to the South is not empty; it is full of the capacity to have thought, to have life, to have sound. In this

South, readers receive a glimpse of Gabriel's past, how and why he became a preacher, why he got saved. In that momentary eclipse of sound in Harlem, in that interstitial space opened up by withdrawal of a certain unregulated, deregulated sound, is an entire world. "He stroked her coarse, bowed head. 'God bless you, little girl,' he said, helplessly. 'God bless you.'" And then the break. Again. "The silence in the church ended when Brother Elisha, kneeling near the piano, cried out and fell backward under the power of the Lord. Immediately, two or three others cried out also, and a wind, a foretaste of that great down-pouring they awaited, swept the church."[101] Not merely a break in the narrative from present to past and present again, there is a literal break on the page, a white space between the past "God bless you" and the recommencing of Pentecostal fire. In that break, in that space of nothingness, a journey made, a journey of discovery, of otherwise possibility, of plentitude and overflowing capacity. In that break, in that space of nothingness, glossolalic force.

Baldwin, in *JAMH*, gives us the characters and relationship of Arthur and Crunch on which to ruminate to think about solutions—substances—to problems. Rather than repression, Arthur and Crunch's relationship is fecund social/sexual/choreosonic ground to explore by way of the proliferation and multiplication of desire. Desire emerged from below. But this was not mere desire for purity that the South would so require, that Burke would want to go as the unheard of blackness, but the movement toward an irreducible sociality heard in and through song, heard in and through sex, in and through the nothingness of blackqueer possibility. Arthur and Crunch's relationship is the audiovisuality of desired silence's antithesis: moans, groans, otherwise songs.

Arthur, Crunch, Peanut, and Red were in Tennessee—below the Mason-Dixon Line—singing the Lord's song in a strange land. "They have never been South before. They do not really like Nashville, but, at least, it looks like a city. This is a town, about twenty miles from Nashville—not far, unless you have to walk it."[102] At the end of the church service, they descended the stairs arriving "in the church basement, wide and deep and—beautiful."[103] We may want to consider the basement, below ground level, the underground, the submerged as a doubling of the below the Mason-Dixon Line, which is to say in the South. The South is not only geographic and topological, it is the resistance to the capacity of expanse; it is the epistemic, pedagogic withdrawal from openness. Lingering, even there in that thoughtscape replete with sonic materiality, is a sociality of blackness.

And it was in this below, in this South that Arthur's desire was quickened:

[Arthur] has never seen so insistent a smile. He does not, consciously, think it—it does not come to the forefront of his mind—but the smile makes him aware of his virginity, and all the hair of his flesh begins to itch. A little sweat begins at his hairline. He looks for Crunch, who has disappeared. Sister Dorothy Green is leading him, relentlessly, to a table.[104]

[Arthur] looks around the church basement again, seeing something for the first time. All those sisters, and all that cheerful noise, a warmth, as dangerous as lightning, and as comforting as a stove, fills the place. Laughter rings, gossip abounds: obliterating, for a moment, the endless grief and danger. He sees, but does not see, the swollen ankles, the flat feet, the swift, gnarling fingers, serving the deacons, repudiating the helpless condition, refusing, with a laugh, despair.[105]

The emergence of libidinal excess, an averted sociosexual gaze is the instantiation of the choreosonic substance of blackness the Southern landscape—in Baldwin's theorizing—would seek to diminish, repress, obliterate. Sister Dorothy Green was leading Arthur to the path of unrighteousness, smiling incessantly, knowingly, lustily. He looked away. Arthur averted his gaze, tending toward an absent presence, a haunting of and from Crunch. Arthur looked away to see nothing at all and in that look away, that glance, that gesture, was the displacement of the one in front of him toward a thinking of Crunch who was not there. This look, this turn to nothingness to explore its deep resources made audible the choreosonic force of the absent object, the songs that Crunch sang as a sociality of tonality where tones are dynamic: "To hear a tone as dynamic quality, as a direction, a pointing, means hearing at the same time beyond it, beyond it in the direction of its will, and going toward the expected next tone."[106]

In the averted gaze of Arthur was the capacity of the irreducible sociality of absence, the irreducible possibility of nothing—the sound and chatter of glossolalic performance—as soon to come in a form that had not been determined but tended toward him. Arthur was astonished by the smile of Dorothy. But he was overwhelmed by the vacuity of Crunch to the point of flooding, sweat forming on his forehead. The averted gaze toward the presence of nothingness was the occasion to consider fullness and the overwhelming of sonic substance. The gaze refused the surface, seeking otherwise, hearing the song Crunch sang, hearing the crunch and/ of Crunch. Averting his gaze, he avoided Dorothy, and desire was instantiated and made audible by the same gesture of the glance. With the gesture, two sides of being taken up—assumed and subsumed in—as well as being released—thrown down, thrown away—from desire. With Arthur's gesture, the substance of things hoped for and the evidence of things not seen, of nothing, exceeded capacity.

Sweat was the first substance. It was the materiality of desire forming at Arthur's brow. Something, really *nothing*, Arthur had not pondered— something remaining submerged—elucidated by this substance. It was the evidence of the hoped for Crunch. In that putative emptiness of a deep mysterious beyond—both in him while forming on him—was the condition of possibility for an abiding sociality, evinced by the very fact and lack of Crunch's materiality. Sweat would then be belief in the flesh, belief quite literally secreting out and onto the flesh. Knowledge was produced as substance, sweat, between hair and skin, at the edge, the hinge, the border. Only after Arthur was quickened with libidinal desire toward the absence of Crunch's lingering presence—in that same basement—was that space reanimated with the noise that was always present. By journeying into the space of nothingness, Crunch's absence, Arthur heard more, he heard in excess. He looked around the basement a second time—no doubt for Crunch—only to hear by way of the visual "cheerful noise," "laughter rings." This sound pulsed throughout the entire underground, which he occupied. This to say that there is an intense relay and syncopation of the visual and the sonic. Crunch withdrew from visual view, desire for Crunch beaded on Arthur's brow; Crunch withdrew from sight, askance vision opened up to the fullness of social life given in and as sound that was abounding and in abundance. Looking towards nothing at all, life.

The nonfulfillment of desire by Crunch's lack, by Crunch's absence, was tentative and thus on the edge, was incomplete and thus a journey into the capacious openness, the capacious open-endedness of nothingness. This nothingness was the condition whereby libidinal thought, social aspiration, emerged. What was grasped and given—through the choreosonic glance—was form, as knowledge learned was about the lack of something, the desire for something, a search into nothing. Baldwin presented an epistemological shift, a way to consider otherwise possibilities for a social intellectual project that is aligned with nothingness as a space of exploration. Baldwin presented an *a*theological-*a*philosophical mode of transgressive love, mode of transgressive learning, found in the no-space of lack, of absence, of nothingness.

THE UNIVERSITY WAS always in ruins.[107] The aesthetic vitality of Blackpentecostalism, the sociality of the undercommons, the glossolalia of the underground, made the university a ruinous place because the university never understood its objects of study as objects that study, objects that have and produce a mode of intellectual practice. Having been said to be, and to come from, nothing, Blackpentecostal aesthetic practice "ruins" the normative, neoliberal university, "ruins" such a zone of inhabitation in the service of producing otherwise possibilities. As carriers of such an aesthetic practice, black objects are ruinous. We must look to, travel to, journey below surfaces, dig deep in the expanse of capacious blackness, go beyond and look askance. It is there, in the otherwise zones of possibility, where a critical practice of pedagogy is enacted.

CODA

Otherwise, Nothing

Winds of 53 mph crashed against the lakeshore of Chicago for five days when October 29, 1929, arrived. It was fateful and fatal, indeed, but not simply for Chicago residents. Wall Street also felt its own tumult that day, the day marking Black Tuesday, the beginning of the Great Depression. Violent wind was blowing over and economically destabilizing the country, and Chicago was hit hard. Imagine, then, the resolve necessary to organize a choir during that fateful period in the face of such economic and ecological tumult. The First Church of Deliverance's choir, which would go on to international fame, held its first meeting that very day. Five years later, at 6:00 am in 1934, First Church of Deliverance aired their first radio broadcast, becoming the second radio broadcast of a "colored" congregation in Chicago. A few miles up the road in Evanston, Laurens Hammond was busily putting together the plans for a cheap organ that churches and novices could purchase. January 19, 1934, Hammond and his lawyers walked the patent to the office themselves, him promising that—during the economically disastrous period—he was ready to put hundreds of people to work, manufacturing the instrument that would come to bear his name. The patent was approved that very day and they went to work.

In 1939, music director for First Church of Deliverance, Kenneth Morris, conferred with Father Clarence Cobb in order to purchase one of those very new Hammond organs. "No church had had a Hammond organ prior to this, and people came from everywhere to hear First Church's revolutionary new instrument."[1] This idea, that First Church of Deliverance was the first church to purchase a Hammond organ would turn out to be a rumor, a narrative the church tells about itself. Because of the radio broadcast that already garnered popular appeal by 1939, with the sounds of the Hammond organ, people came from far and wide to see what they experienced sonically: Just what was this instrument with its, at times, "humanlike" voice?[2] "Cobb was able to attract to his congregation people from the ranks of the city's black middle and even elite classes because of his flashy personal style and promises of prosperity, but it was the emotionally demonstrative worship of his live radio broadcasts that made him a 'mass hero' among Chicago's poor and working class."[3]

Though the rumor of First Church of Deliverance's relation to the Hammond organ is important, there is a likewise rumor of blackqueer sociality that this particular church space served that interests me. "Former members of the First Church of Deliverance on Wabash Avenue remembered it as a major stop on the gay nightlife circuit in the 1930s and 1940s. The church welcomed gay people and Reverend Clarence Cobbs, along with many of his staff, was rumored to be gay," and "After attending the live broadcast at the church, which ran from 11:00 pm to midnight, club goers would simply walk from First Church of Deliverance to one of the area nightspots, usually the Kitty Kat Club, the Parkside, or the 430."[4] Eventually, the convergence of sound, subjectivity, and sexuality as a force of Blackpentecostalism would become a contentious, contestable debate. Blackqueerness was there, animating the social life of Blackpentecostal spiritual practice. As late as 1971, Anthony Heilbut wrote about how it was generally noted and accepted that "most immediately striking about many of the larger Holiness churches is the inordinate number of male and female homosexuals. As one singer bluntly put it, 'There's more sissies and bull daggers in the Sanctified churches, and they all think they're the only ones going to Heaven.'" Heilbut otherwise noted, "The Holiness church maintains a discrete and at times impenetrable mystique. It may be the blackest of institutions..."[5] That there was a moment in which there was an acceptance, not necessarily of the "lifestyle," but of the self-evidentiary nature of queerness inherent to Blackpentecostal aesthetic practice, that there was not a desire for violent removal and abatement, seems to me to illustrate the ways there was no theology-philosophy of queerness that could gather up and discard such aesthetics, such modes of life. It would not be until the theological-philosophical reduction of aesthetic force that such sociality would be figured as a problem for Blackpentecostal thought. Such that we might say the sound of the Hammond B-3 in Blackpentecostal spaces emerged from a queer sociality, from underground and otherworldly friendships and erotic relationships. Were musicians visiting the church before going to the Kitty Kat down the street, then telling their pastors about this object and the way it moved congregants?

The Hammond B-3 organ, and its ubiquity in the Blackpentecostal tradition can move us in such a direction. This instrument is used in store-front churches in impoverished inner cities and in new, modern mega-churches. The Hammond B-3 can be found in churches across the United States, in various countries in Africa, in England. It is a sound that has, in other words, spread. The Hammond B-3 organ has been taken up in Black-pentecostal spaces as the instrument, as the sound, of the movement. The Hammond B-3 organ's sound is an instance of blackqueer sonic presencing and enacts the politics of avoidance when the musician and instrument come together, sounding out in the space of congregations. The Hammond instrument is a "tonewheel organ," and tone wheels are "a system of spin-ning, steel, silver-dollar-sized" discs with "notched edges," resulting in "output [that] is more alive [and] organic . . . than what electronic organs can produce."[6] Though the Hammond instruments have sound presets that change the timbre and quality of the organ sound, there are also draw-bars that allow musicians to instantly change and control sound quality. Drawbar settings affect the loudness, the tones, the percussiveness of the instrument. "By pulling or pushing their drawbars, you could instantly sculpt your sound. If you want more high harmonics, just tug on the upper drawbars. To deemphasize the fundamental, shove in the white draw-bars."[7] The manufacturer warned against pulling out all the drawbars as a setting musicians should never use. However, in much Blackpentecostal performance with the B-3, particularly during moments of intense emo-tionality in church services, musicians often use that very setting, pulling out all the stops, so to speak, in order to be as voluminous as possible. Though Laurens Hammond had specific desires for the decorous use of the instrument, Blackpentecostal aesthetics not only obscured but popular-ized the unwanted. Drawbars "offer real-time control of the sound," and that real-time is generative for reconceptualizing temporality and spatial-ity, for thinking spacetime otherwise.[8]

To amplify the B-3 model, an external speaker cabinet has to be uti-lized. Though the Hammond Organ Company manufactured their own model, it was Don Leslie and the Leslie Company that had the best "fit" for the sound the Hammond attempted to produce. "The most popular Leslie speaker cabinet contains a high-frequency horn driver and a bass woofer, both of which are combined with rotating components. . . . The rotary components can rotate at high and low speeds, which adjustable ramp-up and -down times."[9] At the level of the machine itself, there is a necessarily sociality: for the machine to be heard, it necessitates some outside object to make the chord changes and progressions audible. Most fundamentally, the Hammond instrument differs from pipe organs because "the pipes themselves are spread out across a fairly wide range when constructed."[10] Pipe organs, in other words, are fashioned by the amount of room they require from any given space. For this reason, there are no pipe organs in domestic spaces; one would need cathedral-like space for such an instrument. In contradistinction, the Hammond organ was able to be compact and, in a way, portable (at 400 or so pounds), such that the achievement of the Hammond organ with the attendant Leslie speaker, we might say, is spatiotemporal compression, about which more soon. As a substitute for the pipe organ—because of the drawbars, the Leslie speaker cabinet and the touch-to-response ratio—the Hammond's "fast attack" made it a poor substitute,[11] but this failure, as its quick response to touch, would be its crowning achievement, making it perfect for the intense and quick "movement of the Spirit" in Blackpentecostal spaces.

The sound of the Hammond organ, particularly the B-3 model, would come to be the sound of Blackpentecostalism particularly and how the black church as an institution with historical force is imagined.[12] Described as sounding human, the Hammond organ offers a way to think about the breakdown between human and machines. Returning to Brother Steadfast's testimony given at Reverend F. W. McGee's Blackpentecostal church, January 28, 1930, him closing by asking for the Saints to pray "that I may be used as an instrument in his hand," this desire for instrumentality, I argue, structures the Blackpentecostal imagination such that any object can be sacrelized, made holy. People not only beat tambourines and stomp feet, but play washboards with spoons and blow whistles. The Hammond organ is in this tradition, the utilization of any object for sacred possibility. And in such making sacred of objects, the instrument is not the Hammond on the one hand or the musician on the other: the instrument is the sociality of the *spirit filled* musician with the musical object working together.

Being spirit filled breaks down the distinction, the categorical coherence of human and machine. This sociality of instrumentality is a respiratory performance. And fundamental to such an incoherence of human and machine is—like the aesthetic practices of whooping, shouting, noise-making and tongue-talking—the breath, black pneuma. The Hammond organ breathes on multiple levels: at the level of the musical object, the Leslie speaker gathers up and displaces the air within space in order for the object to be audible; it literally inhales and exhales air; it is, in other words, a breathing machine. The changes in speed of the Leslie speaker make such mechanical respiration audible; listen closely and you can hear the chop-chop-chop smooth out and speed up again. And on the level of the human and machine breathing together, what is it to be spirit filled? It is to be filled with breath, filled with air, filled with wind.

Given its prominence in the sound culture of America—heard not only in churches but in rock and roll, rhythm and blues, jazz, funk, soul—given its ubiquity, given the debates about authenticity and sound musicians have about the instrument, given the language used to describe its sounds, I want to consider the omission of the instrument from narrations and stories and analyses about black religiosity, music, and culture. Such omission seems to be audibly deafening, an aversive modality of thought, an aversion that is not unlike the racialized grounds for theology and philosophy. Is the aversion to discussing the instrument perhaps linked to its blackqueer origins within black sacred traditions? It remains to be explored if such is the case. But the proliferation of the sound of the Hammond B-3 in Black-pentecostal spaces emerged from a blackqueer sociality, from underground and otherworldly friendships and erotic relationships, so perhaps there is more there. Rumor and gossip about the queerness of musicians of these particular instruments within the space of the church abounds. There is, within this religiocultural space, a thinking together of the concepts of sound and sexuality.

Musician and critic Salim Washington offers that one way to think about sound in the Blackpentecostal tradition is as a technology: "Music in the Holiness churches can be used simply as a transformation of the mood and/or mind-set of the participants, but in the case of the 'shout,' music is used as a technology, through which a direct cause and effect takes place."[13] Technologies can be used as outlined in user manuals or can be used otherwise to create otherwise moods, otherwise meanings, with the same apparatus. The sound of the B-3 is ever present, and with the musician, complicates the generally accepted notion that Blackpentecostals are simply loud. The virtuosity of the musician allows us to overhear the dynamic nature of Blackpentecostal aesthetics. There are moments of quietude and others of cacophony, but always intense. The seeming omnipresence of the sound of the B-3 during church services, then, draws attention to what Avery Gordon calls the "seething presence" of all matters ghostly, the force of "the seemingly not there" that is perceptible, that is felt, that animates and is the foundation for movement, for behavior, for life and love.[14] The seemingly there and not there, faith as the substance of hope and as the evidence of things not seen—so the biblical book of Hebrews says—is on the edge. We wait and anticipate that something will happen, some mode of relationality enacted, some music played. I listen, I incline my ear towards the sounding and sounding out—from the first note to the last chord—of the B-3, "setting the atmosphere" for a particular kind of knowing, a certain modality for experiencing the world.

Attention to Blackpentecostal uses of the B-3 moves us further still by stopping short of Victor Zuckerkandl with his assertion that the dynamic quality of a tone is its will to completion.[15] What if tones weren't reaching for resolution or completion but were perpetually, ongoingly, open? Whereas Zuckerkandl believes that notes resolve to completion, I argue that Blackpentecostal engagements with the Hammond B-3 make evident the centrifugitivity of black social life. What we have, in other words, are tones that are not simply moving toward resolution but are on the way to varied directionality—not simply in a linear, forward progression but also vertically, down and up, askance and askew. What if, as open to openness, the sounds of the B-3 prompt in its hearers an intellectual practice of a reaching toward the beyond? Would not this reaching, this movement toward without ever seizing the beyond, instantiate ongoing anticipatory posture, an affective mode of celebratory waiting?

Black being is first a question of anticipation, and I mean anticipation precisely as an observation prior to proper time, an occurrence in advance of expected time. Anticipation, black being, is a disruption of and a break with the standard, the proper, the expectation of time as linear, progressive, forward propulsive. As a concern about being, about existence, the B-3's sonic thrownness—through the cen-tripetal and centrifugal spins of tone wheels and drum speakers—whether reaching toward the high ceilings and spacious layout of for-merly Jewish synagogues in neighborhoods like Newark, Detroit and Brooklyn or in the tight quarters and suffocating walls of storefront churches like those in which Helga Crane in *Quicksand* hearing con-gregants sing "Showers of Blessings," or John, Elizabeth, and Gabriel in *Go Tell It on the Mountain* find themselves, allow us to reconsider the concept of origin.

In James Weldon Johnson's *The Books of Negro Spirituals*, Johnson outlines the ways in which the authorship of Spirituals was constantly queried: Just who came up with such musical genius; who authored such songs?[16] Implicit in such a question about authorship is the con-cern about ownership that is grounded in the textual, in a worldview wherein reading is coeval to literacy, and textual-grammatical literacy is the privileged mode of thought and communication. This question of authorship, in other words, emerged in the same world that touted reading as the privileged practice toward freedom. Thus, when Spiritu-als could be transcribed and written are the moments when concerns of authorship emerged as a concern with urgent force. But what at times is called "soft chording," "padding," "talk music" or—most intrigu-ingly for me here—"nothing music" dislodges notions of authorship and genius as individuating and productive of enlightened, bourgeois, liberal subject from the capacity to create, to carry, to converge, to conceal.

"Nothing music"[17] is the connective tissue, the backgrounded sound, of Blackpentecostal church services heard before and after songs, while peo-ple are giving weekly announcements, before the preacher "tunes up" to whoop and after the service ends. Ask a musician, "what are you playing," and—with a coy, shy smile—they'll say, "nothing." Such musicked noth-ings are examples of what Samuel Delany says about the word: "The word generates no significant information until it is put in *formal relation* with something else."[18] Delany argues that with the introduction of each new word in a sentence, it acts as a modifier of everything that came before; such that meaning is emergent, meaning is of and toward the horizon. Meaning is made through relationality such that what Delany says about words in a sentence is consistent with what Zuckerkandl contends about tones in a sonic statement: to make meaning is to be in-between, in the interstice. But more, meaning is made through the inclined ear, through the anticipation of the *more to come* that *has not yet arrived*; this *more to come* is ever in relation to that which *is now* and that which has passed "*into the ago,*" as perhaps Heidegger would say. And we hear this in the musician's virtuosity: they uphold, they carry, they anticipate, through the performance of "nothing." "Nothing music" is not a song, nor predetermined melody. Perhaps *playing* is close to what I mean. The difference—musically—between playing "nothing" and improvisation, jamming or noodling is that perhaps with the playing of "nothing music," there is a certain lack of attention, a sort of insouiance with which one plays, a holy nonchalance: being both fully engaged in the moment while concentration is otherwise than the music, a nonchalance that is part of, while setting, the mood of the church service. Playing as a performance of conviction that is not reduced to the serious, decorous or pursuit of perfection. Playing is to anticipate change.

In this playing of "nothing," it is not that nothing is played, that nothing is heard; it is that what appears is the sound of the gift of unconcealment. Heidegger's understanding of Being and Time, perhaps through the theorizing of a gift, is animated by a Blackpentecostal anticipation of a sonic sociality. Anticipation is a sort of Heideggerian gifting that always retains—in its enactment—its force of foresight, foreboding. Heidegger says, "the gift of unconcealing . . . is retained in the giving."[19] Musicians unconceal—and uncompress—the play and the playing of nothing but retain, in the very playing out, the nothing from which the sounding out emanates. And when the drawbars are fully extended, perhaps we have a moment of "uncompression," of decompression. What one hears, what one anticipates, with each new chord and arpeggio is the movement toward the next chord and arpeggio; one hears the meaning of "I ain't got long to stay here," what it means, in other words, to "steal away." This is centrifugitive performance, criminal displacement of the concepts of genius and scholar because what these musicians play—and what we hear—they, and we, do not *know* though we certainly feel it, feel it pulling and tugging on us, at us, feel it attempting to move us toward some other mode of relationality.

from: a
to: a
Sunday November 29, 2009, 1:46am

Subject: . . .

mp,

I've gotta admit, I love the tendency in black gospel music to make any rhythmic song arrhythmic, to slow down standards so that the singer can play around and toy, tinker and trouble the structure. A mundane song gains new life by way of evacuating it of any such architectonics, yielding the song to a critique of normative modes of organization itself. 4/4 time and 3/4 time and 2/4 time become 0/4 time . . . or would it be 4/0 time, marking the possibility of infinite capacity for diffusion, difference, what Derrida might call that which structures differing and deferring, *différance*? Don't mind the faux-philosophical, opaque speak. Some shit I learned—rather, "learned" [yes, the scare quotes are necessary]—yesterday [or even still, more like, some shit I *read* that didn't make much sense to me at first read, so I copied and have been trying to think about it with the things that I know]. And I know I love how my own Aunt Janice would come to my church and how her "friend" Delores would play the organ for her. My Aunt Janice was queen of the arrhythmia that I'd hear in black pentecostal music. She'd take a song—something simple, a congregation song—like "This Is the Day"

This is the day, this is the day / that the lord has made, that the Lord has made

I will rejoice, I will rejoice / and be glad in it, and be glad in it

This is the day that the Lord has made / I will rejoice and be glad in it

This is the day, this is the day / that the lord has made

and whereas, during testimony service, we'd sing the song with the regular 4/4 structure, clapping on the two and four, my auntie would come sing during an afternoon service just before the preacher got up and she'd subject the entire song's structure to a melismatic critique. So you know how with melisma, instead of each note getting a syllable, one can sing multiple notes for one syllable of the song. So instead of saying *do-re-me-fa-so-la-ti-do* one would take the *do* and make it *do-oh-oh-oh-ooooh!* going up and down the scale. People like Kim Burrell or Darryl Coley, I suppose, are good examples.

My Aunt Janice would take that little testimony service, congregational song and sing it as a solo with Delores playing behind her. No rhythm. No structure. Rather, she built into the song ecstasy and surprise by way of the tension and release. She'd get up and say something like

> *ya'll pray for me, I'm hoarse, got a cold but god gets the glory on today.*
> *I'm gonna sing . . . well . . . I'm gonna sing . . .*

and she'd pause while Delores would play "nothing music" behind her, filling in the gaps and pauses and breaths with sweet organ music that would allow Aunt Janice a moment to think because she literally would never know what she'd want to sing but would allow the flow of the service to determine her song choice and how she'd deliver it. Since this one time was right before the preacher and the service was sorta dry and she wanted to give the preacher something on which to hold that would allow his sermon to escalate more easily, I'm guessing at least, she went for something familiar only to hold up its familiarity to scrutiny, only to show us that that which we thought we knew was that which we didn't know at all. Removing the rhythm while using words that we all knew very, very well meant that the substance of the song had to be found otherwise, that we had to *get into it* by her delivery, by the style she used that was, at the same time, its essence. Singing that which we all knew in a way that we did not and could know meant that we were all on a journey—with my auntie—of discovery.

So after her pondering, she came upon—which is to say, she discovered already there—the possibility for the arrhythmic version of the song, which is really when you think about it, just another kind of rhythmic offering, rhythmic critique. Kinda like how all squares are rectangles but not all rectangles are squares. Some concepts have folded in them other concepts. Rhythm as regularity is just another way to be arrhythmic. Right? So my auntie would close her eyes right before the first word, after having looked over and nodded to Delores, Delores still playing the "nothing music" waiting for the first words, not knowing what auntie was going to sing. Of course, auntie chose a different key than the one in which Delores was playing her "nothing music," so she immediately ran her fingers up and down the white and black notes to catch up to auntie, but so skilled she was that it took her but a quick second and she was there, right behind auntie, filling in while also anticipating.

Thi-ih-is . . . ih-ih-is oh oh oh oooh . . . the! day!

Well, to try and recount the entire rendition through typed words would only be to falsify what actually occurred. The written word can't really approach what happened live. Not at all. You would have had to have heard it. But you can at least imagine her singing this Lord's song in a familiar land but differently. It's as if my auntie would reduce the song to its component parts, examining the truth of each word and breath and note and break. The hesitant approach, I learned when I was much older, made the weary sad eyes she had whenever she sang make much more sense.

I've since learned that her best friend and organist—indeed, that Delores—was her on again, off again partner who was convinced as hell that hell was her destination and so life became a living purgatory for them both. Their intimate connection we'd hear as auntie sang while Delores played was nothing other than a melancholy—but also the momentary irruptions of joy, peace, hope, love—they both endured on a daily basis. The possibility for their intimate music making is that very thing that broke down all sorts of ideas about what rhythm, tune and time could be for any song. Auntie would sing down the heavens and Delores would play the hell out of that organ until we all shouted a bit, even those who'd never danced and those who didn't want to; she might've been what she preached against but she also had something in her that she wanted to give us whenever she sat on that organ.

Delores, we'd say, was a good organist. She did not lead the song but followed politely behind. She did not dominate the song but, rather, influenced it. She did this by having all of the drawbars for the B-3 pushed in except the 8' and 4', which were pulled all the way out to 8 (loudest volume). She, of course, would have the 32' bass drawbar pulled all the way out. There is nothing more soothing than the combination of the soft of the keyboard with the low bottom of the heavy bass. Carrying. Carrying as caring. The bottom and bottoming out of the testimony and song. She'd keep her setting like this while auntie sang the first two lines of the song, following, as I said before, a bit behind. Like a kind friend being led by the hand into uncharted territory. But after the dance and choreography of voice and pedal, organ and song, Delores would feel more confident and auntie would be more herself, eyes open now, having taken the microphone off the stand and holding it in her hand, prepared to walk a bit as she sang.

Delores would then pull out the 13/5', 11/3' drawbars to about 4 and the 1' drawbar to about 2 in order to add vibrancy and bounce and color to the sound. Still following, but not as far behind now. Still polite but more knowing still. After auntie'd sing "has made" in her long, drawn-out, arrhythmic manner, Delores would play the most delightful *turn around* which is like the end and beginning converging, an intro and conclusion at the same encounter. She, of course, pushed all the draw-bars back in again because auntie wanted to sing the same lines again from the beginning, leaving the *8'* and *4'* drawbars out but now exposing the *16'* as well, moving her hands up an octave because the *16'* necessitates this move.

I'm sure none of this makes sense to you and, even if it did, you don't care about drawbar settings but at least know that by the end of auntie's singing and Delores's playing, Delores would have exposed all of the drawbars pulled out to their fullest volume and the folks in the church would be up and loud and screaming in response *YEAH! YES! YESSAH! MMMMHMMMM!!!* and *MY MY MY* and other such things because of this song and dance auntie and Delores publicly engaged.

But you, of course and no doubt, are preoccupied with the curt but anything but simple question: Why? Why does any of this matter? And why linger in such a mundane conversation as drawbar settings and lesbians who cry and curse and feign coughs when called upon to sing? This is, at least in my mind, the very question that you allowed to pre-occupy you so much so that you never gave way to, or a way for, experience. You never could or would and never felt you should believe me when I'd exclaim your beauty, your brilliance. Of course, this is why you improvisationally asked me over and over again if I really actually thought that, if I believed it. You were beguiling, cunning, creative with the same query asked over and over again repetitiously until I too questioned if I meant it.

So why is it you like me
What is it you see in me
Do you really like me
Once someone comes around who really interests you, you'll leave me
You don't know anything about me
So what do you like about me
What things do you find attractive in me

I am not beautiful

None of these were questions, even if some appear at first blush to be. The problem, of course, is that you considered beauty to be kinesthetic, the project of movement that has been enacted and since you had the annoying tendency to deem your actions impotent, you thought the only beauty in you that others could possibly see a farce.

To me, beauty is not kinesthetic but rather potential. It is about the set of capacities to move *toward* movement that others, quite literally, sense. And I mean *sense* in its most profound and quotidian resonance, I mean taste and touch and smell and sound and sight. Your beauty, at least in the ways I detected it, was not wrapped up in what you've done [or, really, not done] but in the possibilities of discovering worlds together. This was the beauty of Delores's playing behind and with my auntie: the possibility for discovering, for happening upon something, for invention and improvisation. But my auntie's breaking the song into components also sounded out a similar concern that you'd announce each time you'd ask me the same question differently. She did not believe the words she was singing, so she exposed them to newness and revisement to see—maybe hear?—something *in* them that would betray some truth. She wanted the kinesthesia of the words rather than live in their potential. The funny thing is, the congregation *got* it, they felt the potential and praised accordingly. But for auntie and Delores, the potential was simply not enough, they needed some action, some movement.

But, of course when I think about it now, kinesthesia and *potentia* are not that different. Or, rather, they are both constructed from our social worlds and just like silence does not ever exist outside of a desire for it, and just like emptiness [of jugs, for example] is a ruse [a jug that is empty, Heidegger would say, is full with all the mixed properties that make air; to proclaim it empty is really to say that air is "nothing" but we know that this is not the case], so too is *potentia* a kind of movement [and likely that kinesthesia is also *potentia* with *différance*]. I mean, everything is always moving, in a state of flux. So even the notion of potential does not fully encapsulate the ways in which *potentia* is a form of movement. It is the motion of possibility, it is the stirring up [the gift? was I Paul to your Timothy?] of occasion, it is the flow of withholding.

What I mean is that *potentia* for me makes visible and audible the anticipatory nature of hearing. What we'd hear in auntie's announcement of a cold? The possibility for failure and not just of the song, even if not primarily the song, but the possibility for failure to produce the holy, sanctified and set apart subject deemed necessary for singing the Lord's song. What we'd hear in the first, hesitant, melismatic word *this* that she'd sing? The stirring up of a world of holy trouble. We knew, with that word, that the power of the Lord was sure to come down. The surprise would be in how we got there, not in the fact of us getting there because there was determined as achievable and achieved before she began. My auntie doesn't sing much these days and isn't invited out much either. Delores still plays, thankfully but they are rarely seen together from what I understand. Both of them got "delivered." Too bad they're no longer saved.

in potentia,

a.

HELGA CRANE WAS on the search for something. She spent the majority of Nella Larsen's *Quicksand*[20] trying to understand something about life, about love, something about a material-spiritual way to be in the world. Her being Other that was also, only and always her blackness, sent her on various migrations, both in the United States and internationally. Tennessee, Chicago, Harlem. She also traveled to Denmark where at first she felt relief. But soon after such relief, she felt she had become, to use Frantz Fanon, an object in the eyes of the Danes. Crane returned to the States, to Harlem specifically, because she missed the faces of, and comfort from, black folks who did not make her feel like an objection, like a question, like a problem.

One might say that she was on a journey, that Crane was committed to a general, *nonsecular* agnosticism that was at the same time the refusal of the *secular* western philosophical construction of atheistic stance that purports, in the most robust sense, the impossibility of further discovery for an object. What moves me about Crane is her continual dissatisfaction with the world as she knew it; her peregrinations were seeking for a fullness that she did not, and most certainly *could not* know existed previous to its discovery. But this lack of knowledge was not the occasion for a refusal to journey, nor a declaration of the nonexistence of such fulfillment. And that journey, from the US South to Chicago to Harlem to Denmark back to Harlem paused, if only momentarily, as she fell into the warmth and acoustic embrace of a storefront church:

> [Helga Crane] had opened the door and entered before she was aware that, inside, people were singing a song which she was conscious of having heard years ago—hundreds of years it seemed. Repeated over and over, she made out the words:
>
> . . . Showers of blessings,
> Showers of blessings . . .
>
> She was conscious too of a hundred pairs of eyes upon her as she stood there, drenched, disheveled, at the door of this improvised meeting-house . . . The appropriateness of the song, with its constant reference to showers, the ridiculousness of herself in such surroundings, was too much for Helga Crane's frayed nerves. She sat down on the floor, a dripping heap, and laughed and laughed and laughed. It was into a shocked silence that she laughed.[21] . . .
>
> There were, it appeared, endless moaning verses. Behind Helga a woman had begun to cry audibly, and soon, somewhere else, another. . . .
>
> Helga too began to weep, at first silently, softly; then with great racking sobs. Her nerves were so torn, so aching, her body so wet, so cold! It was a relief to cry unrestrainedly, and she gave herself freely to soothing tears, not noticing that the groaning and sobbing of those about her had increased, unaware that the grotesque ebony figure at her side had begun gently to pat her arm to the rhythm of the singing and to croon softly: 'Yes, chile, yes, chile.' Nor did she notice the furtive glances that the man on her other side cast at her between his fervent shouts of 'Amen!' and 'Praise God for a sinner!'
>
> She did notice, though, that the tempo, that atmosphere of the place, had changed, and gradually she ceased to weep and gave her attention to what was happening about her. . . . And as Helga watched and listened, gradually a curious influence penetrated her; she felt an echo of the weird orgy resound in her own heart; she felt herself possessed by the same madness; she too felt a brutal desire to shout and to sling herself about.[22]

She stumbled into a storefront church and into radical possibility that was opened to her by way of sound, intensity, fervor. Crane was always on the move, she continually found herself in spaces, seeking fulfillment, constantly moving but never settling, always willing to begin to search anew. She is the enfleshment of the material condition that "no finite or conditioned reality can claim to have reached its destiny" and her movements were always in the direction of a sociality.[23] Helga Crane's movements prompt the question: What is art? And, attendant, how is the storefront the production of art, the production of aesthetic practice?

Crane entered the church because, literally, it was serving as a refuge from the rainstorm occurring outdoors. It was there, in the community, open, serving its own purpose previous to her arrival: folks were there, praising there, singing there, joyous there, tarrying there, enacting radical sociality against the grain of sociological projects that would so have a constrained understanding of negro storefront Black-pentecostal churches as "Cults," as E. Franklin Frazier would describe them.[24] Crane entered the church because she didn't want to be wet any longer, wanted to dry off and calm her nerves. The materiality of the building was likewise a dwelling, open. There was no belief necessary for such material inhabitation. Belief is not what prompted her desire to be in the storefront, but a recognition of the conditions of the life she lived. Still, something happened.

Stumbling into the space, the sonic environment made a claim on her. The voices sang to her, the bodies came to her. The movement of sound, flesh, spirit. Falling on the ground, wet, she laughed. Somewhere between laughs, her engagement became serious. Her initial posture allowed her to listen, and listening opened to experience. The sounds of people singing, praying, praising—the sounds, generally, of the inspiring and expiring of breath, inhaling and exhaling, the aestheticizing of breathing in that tight, constrained space of the storefront—produced a bass, a bottom, a foundation upon which she could be carried. There was a resonance of the sounds, of the voices. She heard them. She inhabited them. She was, literally, covered—by sounds, by flesh—and we might say that this covering also was the refuge, at least at that temporal moment. And perhaps refuge is only ever temporal, only ever something that is carried and enacted rather than a place and a time. She sought and found it without having known it. She did not merely open up the church door but she allowed herself to be open to that which she heard, to what she felt. It was, for her, a terrifyingly joyful experience. The moment was of the dance and play of spirit, the choreosonic play of black sociality.

TONI MORRISON HAS written about *playing* in the dark, how there is an Africanist presence in American literature;[25] Judith Butler began her discussion of gender performativity in *Gender Trouble* by bespeaking how kids *play* and in such playing get in trouble:[26] So what is the relationship of play to presence, of play to performativity, that the organist, that the organ itself, furnishes forward for our consideration? To uphold, to carry, and to anticipate and move. These musicians organize sound in space in such a way as to produce three-dimensionality. Aden Evens would, I think, agree:

> Every sound interacts with all the vibrations already present in the surrounding space; the sound, the total timbre of an instrument is never just that instrument, but that instrument in concert with all the other vibrations in the room, other instruments, the creaking of chairs, even the constant, barely perceptible motion of the air.[27]

They are playing the air, gettin' down with the handclaps, getting' into trouble with the talking preacher, they gather the varied vibrations and channel them out through the sound of the B-3. But the thing they play, the thing with which they move congregants, is chord changes of nothing, the breaking of unconcealment to concealment. The musicians construct a narrative about and from nothing, through the available air compression and changes in the environment. No tone is excess, no harmony too egregious; each allows for discovery. If the presence that figures itself as "nothing" has the ability to move, to undergird, what does this mean about the status of the claim for being, for coming from, nothing? Perhaps lacking spatial and temporal coherence is a gift. It is to anticipate that there is, even in nothing, a multitude, a plenitude, a social world of exploration.

Nothing is *really* distinguishable between 1.1 and 1.2 unless we slip down between the crack of these two seemingly close numbers with the Density of Rational Numbers rule, that between any two rational numbers is a world of difference. Such that between any two rational distinct numbers, a and b, there is a rational number p such that

$a < p < b$

1.1—1.2

1.1, 1.11—1.2

1.1, 1.11, 1.111—1.2

1.1, 1.11, 1.111, 1.1111—1.2

1.1, 1.11, 1.111, 1.1111, 1.11111—1.2

1.1, 1.11, 1.111, 1.1111, 1.11111, 1.111111—1.2

1.1, 1.11, 1.111, 1.1111, 1.11111, 1.111111, 1.1111111—1.2

1.1, 1.11, 1.111, 1.1111, 1.11111, 1.111111, 1.1111111, 1.11111111—1.2

1.1, 1.11, 1.111, 1.1111, 1.11111, 1.111111, 1.1111111, 1.11111111, 1.111111111—1.2

Aden Evens says, "To hear a chord instead of isolated notes, to hear a pro-gression instead of a bunch of chords is to hear the implicated."[28] What is implicated at the outer limits of 1.1 and 1.2 is the anticipation for a get-tin down and diggin' deep, a movement away from the surface of things wherein one discovers a world ready for exploration. Even on a page, we detect a space made. Like Helga Crane, one only discovers movement by a momentary pause and rupture, by opening oneself up to the possibility of an otherwise. "To hear a pitch that does not change is to hear as constant something that is nothing but change, up-and-down motion. To hear is to hear difference."[29] If what one hears is difference itself, then what one anticipates is the means through which difference shows itself, the routes through which difference announces itself, not as a moment for denigra-tion but as a showing, as an appearance, worthy of celebration, praise. And this difference that is felt, that is heard, through anticipation, calls forth a sociality.

The sound of the B-3 participates in a relationship with the other sounds in the space, that the musician enacts—along with the architectonics, the noise and murmuring, the conversations and glossolalia, the foot stomps and vocable expirations—and this participation is the horizonal emer-gence for, and the grounds of, blackqueer relationality, Foucault's friend-ship as a way of life, an inventional A thru Z mode of coming together in otherwise, uncapturable, anti-institutional configurations with each sounded out chord.[30] What is desired from the playing of chords, I think, is to have the congregants scream in ecstasy, to yelp in pleasure, because of the anticipated but unexpected, anticipation as surprise and astonishment. What the sound of the B-3 lets us hear, then, is that Blackpentecostal aesthetics, black pneuma, the politics of avoidance, are all illustrative of the anoriginal density, uncompressed compression, that is fundamental to any creative practice, any form of life.

ACKNOWLEDGMENTS

How does one thank everyone with whom they have been in contact, every vibration and each instance of assistance, help, even resistance? How does one acknowledge and show gratitude for love and engagement shown, both big and small, that has allowed this manuscript to emerge in the form it has? This acknowledgement section, like all acknowledgments I presume, is an exercise in failure. But I will attempt to thank a few people that have helped me, that have allowed my thought to flourish in community with others. The thoughts throughout this book are not only mine, they are constituted by the various conversations and sittings, various meditations and listenings, to which I have been a part. I will, no doubt, forget to acknowledge very important people because everyone with whom I have interacted has affected my life – some in big, deep and others in smaller but still noticeable ways.

Without my parents, Ronald, Sr. and Roxann, this would be a very curious endeavor, a very curious writing exercise. Everything I sought to investigate was because of my upbringing and it was my parents' commitments to being Pentecostal, to loving neighbor and self as a practice of life, that first prompted my worldview such that this line of thinking, this modality of thought, could emerge. To Ronald, Jr., my brother, my friend. The various ways you have been a support to me is priceless and I am glad that, by accident of birth, you are my brother. This project is about you too, it's about us playing church as kids, about us trying to live in, while creating, new worlds. And to Earnest, my new brother, I love that you love my brother and care for him. I sit and write these acknowledgments in your house, Ronald, at the edge of Spring 2016. You and Earnest have allowed me space here to breathe, to listen, to write. I appreciate you both.

This project emerges from my studies at Duke as a doctoral student, is a huge revision and correction of the work I was able to do there under strong guidance and care. Without Fred Moten and Maurice Wallace, this writing would be very different. Each of you were intellectual giants but also kind, always pushed my own thinking but also great friends. Encountering the two of you at Duke was a godsend (and I still am agnostic!). To Ian Baucom, Willie James Jennings and Louise Meintjes, thank you all for the critical feedback that helped this project take on a life of its own; I am forever indebted to you. Amey Victoria Adkins, a model of what friendship is and can be. Though you are far, far away from me geographically, you're always in my heart. To Allison Curseen—the other AC—I'm glad that we ended up together as students and friends. Your continual support is so important to me. Damien Marassa, Jonathan Howard: I am glad to be part of a collective project with you. Thanks to Lindsey Andrews for listening to me complain, asking questions and giving me so much feedback; your friendship is invaluable to me. Thanks to Cathy Davidson for the continual support. Erica Fretwell, thank you for your constant encouragement and seeing things in my work that I did not know was there. To Alexis Gumbs: I would not have attended—even applied to—Duke, likely, had I not encountered you in 2007. I am so thankful for that meeting and your subsequent generosity and kindness. Karla Holloway, I am thankful to have gotten to know you and learned so very much.

I did not know that I would finish graduate studies and walk right into a great job with great colleagues but I have been thankful for the wonderful people at University of California, Riverside. Some people I'd like to thank there: Maile Arvin, Crystal Baik, Jayna Brown, Amalia Cabezas, Jennifer Doyle, Erica Edwards (thanks for supporting me for such a long time!), Laura Harris, Jennifer Hughes, Jodi Kim, Mariam Lam, David Lloyd, Dylan Rodriguez (you've been a great chair!), Sarita See, Setsu Shigematsu, Andrea Smith, Deb Vargas.

I have several best friends. Akira, we're getting old. Who knew 16 years ago that we would become so close? I'm thankful for every phone call, for your unwavering support and care. Kendal Brown, what can be said about our friendship and brotherhood? That ours is an enduring friendship, with ups and downs, good times and bad, has taught me so much about myself, about how to be a better person, about how to be present with others. Khalilah Liptrot for always being there when I call on long drives, for offering your home for me to rest and for always telling me that I can accomplish my goals, for offering me beds to sleep whether in Jacksonville or Harlem, for offering laughter and love, I am grateful. Jonathan Adams, you are one of the most gifted thinkers and kind people I know . . . I look forward to you continuing the generous and thoughtful work you're just beginning. And I am glad we can sing gospel and go to a bar together. Shydel James, we've known each other since junior high days and I am blessed to call you a close friend. Desiree and Imri Thompson for literally changing my life. Terrion Williamson, my sister, you mean such a great deal to me. And to Naomi Leapheart, your dedication and commitment to an otherwise world, to spirituality as a way of life, is beautiful and I am happy we journey together as friends.

A special thanks to Roderick Ferguson, Ronald Judy and Ann Pellegrini for the superb feedback. I was moved to know that you each read with care the writing and provided critical analysis, asked great questions and offered suggestions that I could use for the revision process. I hope the work lives up to the critiques gifted. And thanks to Imani Perry for your mentorship and compassion, for how you model for me a way to be a scholar that is concerned with living in the world in just and ethical and moral ways.

Paul Amar, Moya Bailey, Joshua Bennett, Sarah Blackwood, Felice Blake, Rizvana Bradley, Jennifer Morris Brockington, Rosa Echols Brown, Teresa Fry Brown, Simone Browne, Leslie Callahan, Nahum Chandler, Michelle Commander, Cornerstone Community Church, Brandon Thomas Crowley and the Myrtle Baptist Church family, Jessica Davenport, Tyler Denmead, Carol Duncan, Yvette Flunder, James Ford, Kwanda Ford, Mona Ford, Travis Foster, Max Foxx, Eddie Glaude, Stefano Harney, Randa Jarrar, E. Patrick Johnson, Imani Johnson, Javon Johnson, Elleza Kelley, Robin Kelley, Tom Lay, Eric Lott, Nathaniel Mackey, Jarrett Martineau, Summer McDonald, Sarah Mesle, Katherine McKittrick, Nick Mitchell, Peter Moore, Fari Nzinga, Yumi Pak, Courtney Patterson, Greg Person, Yolanda Pierce, Jemima Pierre, Lynice Pinkard, Alton Pollard, Shana Redmond, Matt Sakakeeny, Denise Ferreira Da Silva, Joel Smith, Damien Sojoyner, C. Riley Snorton, Emma Stapley, David Stein, Pamela Sutton-Wallace, Jasmine Syedullah, Elizabeth Todd-Breland, Kyla Wazana Tompkins, Anjulet Tucker, Rinaldo Walcott, Shakera Walker, Alex Weheliye, Bryant Woodford, Rochelle Wright-Jones: each one of you has contributed to my life in unalterable ways. Thank you.

Amaryah Armstrong, Kyle Brooks and Jamall Calloway, for our daily conversations that push the limits of my own imagination, to Donna Auston and Kameelah Mu'Min Rashad for being sisters when I've needed it, thank you all. Sarah Haley, I'm so glad we stumbled upon each other and share so many meals together. Sofia Samatar, through a chance encounter, I count you as one very dear to me. Your words, how you think and imagine, effects the way I go about my own work. And to Richard Morrison, thank you for your guidance during this journey.

Of course, this project was social and made possible by my engagement with other people. I am thankful for Ricardo Morgan, always sending me good things to hear, to see, to experience. Much analyzed in this project was sent to me from you. And to Timothy Fair, Angel Farley and Tracy Wright, thanks for the daily laughter. I am equally grateful for Nikki Young, Jeremy Posadas, Letitia Campbell and Susannah Laramee-Kidd for—to use a good churchy phrase—"bearing me up" and laboring with me ever since my days in theological training at Candler. Your dedication to shared, communal friendship and love with me has affected my life in ways I am still yet discovering. To Jamila Garrett-Bell and Ayanna Abi-Kyles, Cora Ingrum and Donna Hampton: you have each affected my life in ways that I still cannot describe. I am so humbled to know great women like you.

FOR THE INITIAL contact with Fordham University Press, for the flourishing conversation, for the joy of meeting and pushing the work to be published, I dedicate *Blackpentecostal Breath: The Aesthetics of Possibility* to the memory of Helen Tartar.

NOTES

INTRODUCTION

1. I use the term *Black Study* as opposed to black studies to intimate a relation between what gets institutionalized in the university as black studies, African American studies, Africana studies, ethnic studies, and multicultural studies beginning with the student protests on college campuses in 1968 with an intellectual practice that is always collective and resists institutionalization. This claim about the resistance to institutionalization will be argued throughout *Blackpentecostal Breath*; it is a claim that is the grounds for the project's genesis. Black Study is a term I first encountered in Stefano Harney and Fred Moten, *The Undercommons: Fugitive Planning & Black Study*, 2013. Several books and articles have been written about the history, emergence, sociology, and future of institutional black studies, and this work is both in conversation with and moving in another direction from that work. See, for example, Martha Biondi, *The Black Revolution on Campus* (Berkeley: University of California Press, 2012); John W. Blassingame, *New Perspectives on Black Studies* (Urbana: University of Illinois Press, 1971); Carole Boyce Davies et al., *Decolonizing the Academy: African Diaspora Studies* (Trenton, NJ: Africa World Press, 2003); C. L. R. (Cyril Lionel Robert) James and Anna Grimshaw, "Black Studies and the Contemporary Student," in *The C.L.R. James Reader* (Oxford; Cambridge, MA: Blackwell, 1992); Ronald A. T. Judy, "Untimely Intellectuals and the University," *Boundary 2* 27, no. 1 (March 20, 2000): 121–33; Ronald A. T. Judy, *(Dis)forming the American Canon: African-Arabic Slave Narratives and the Vernacular* (Minneapolis: University of Minnesota Press, 1993); Shirley Moody-Turner and James Benjamin Stewart, "Gendering Africana Studies: Insights from Anna Julia Cooper," *African American Review* 43, no. 1 (spring 2009): 35+; Hortense J. Spillers, "Peters's Pans: Eating in the Diaspora," in *Black, White, and in Color: Essays on American Literature and Culture* (Chicago: University of Chicago Press, 2003); Robyn Wiegman, *Object Lessons* (Durham, NC: Duke University Press, 2012).

2. Denise Ferreira da Silva, "To Be Announced Radical Praxis or Knowing (at) the Limits of Justice," *Social Text* 31, no. 1 114 (March 20, 2013): 44.

3. Saidiya V. Hartman and Frank B. Wilderson, "THE POSITION OF THE UNTHOUGHT," *Qui Parle* 13, no. 2 (April 1, 2003): 183–201.

4. Adam Fitzgerald, "An Interview with Fred Moten, Part 1," *Literary Hub*, accessed September 22, 2015, http://lithub.com/an-interview-with-fred-moten-pt-i/.

5. Cheryl I. Harris, "Whiteness as Property," *Harvard Law Review* 106, no. 8 (1993): 1707–91.

6. M. Shawn Copeland, *Enfleshing Freedom: Body, Race, and Being* (Minneapolis: Fortress Press, 2009).

7. Fred Moten, *In the Break: The Aesthetics of the Black Radical Tradition* (Minneapolis: University of Minnesota Press, 2003).

8. See, for example, Brady Thomas Heiner, "Foucault and the Black Panthers 1," *City* 11, no. 3 (2007): 313–56.

9. Nathaniel Mackey, *Bedouin Hornbook* (Los Angeles: Sun & Moon Press, 1997), 42.

10. Numerous histories and studies of Pentecostalism have been written. For a small sampling, see, for example, Estrelda Alexander, *Black Fire: One Hundred Years of African American Pentecostalism* (Downers Grove, IL: IVP Academic, 2011); Frank Bartleman, *Azusa Street* (Plainfield, NJ: Logos International, 1980); Ithiel C Clemmons, *Bishop C.H. Mason and the Roots of the Church of God in Christ*, Centennial ed. (Bakersfield, CA: Pneuma Life Pub., 1996); Paul Keith Conkin, *Cane Ridge: America's Pentecost* (Madison: University of Wisconsin Press, 1990); David Douglas Daniels, "The Cultural Renewal of Slave Religion Charles Price Jones and the Emergence of the Holiness Movement in Mississippi" (Union Theological Seminary, 1992).; Douglas G. (Douglas Gordon) Jacobsen, *Thinking in the Spirit: Theologies of the Early Pentecostal Movement* (Bloomington: Indiana University Press, 2003); Cecil M. Robeck, *The Azusa Street Mission and Revival: The Birth of the Global Pentecostal Movement* (Nashville, TN: Nelson Reference & Electronic, 2006); Nimi Wariboko, *The Pentecostal Principle: Ethical Methodology in New Spirit* (Grand Rapids, MI: William B. Eerdmans, 2012); Anthea D. Butler, *Women in the Church of God in Christ: Making a Sanctified World* (Chapel Hill: University of North Carolina Press, 2007); Cheryl Gilkes, *"If It Wasn't for the Women—": Black Women's Experience and Womanist Culture in Church and Community* (Maryknoll, NY: Orbis Books, n.d.); Cheryl Jeanne Sanders, *Saints in Exile: The Holiness-Pentecostal Experience in African American Religion and Culture* (New York: Oxford University Press, 1996); Grant Wacker, *Heaven Below: Early Pentecostals and American Culture* (Cambridge, MA: Harvard University Press, 2001).

11. Silva, "To Be Announced Radical Praxis," 44.

12. Hortense J. Spillers, "The Crisis of the Negro Intellectual: A Post-Date," *Boundary 2* 21, no. 3 (October 1, 1994): 66.

13. Gastón Espinosa, *William J. Seymour and the Origins of Global Pentecostalism: A Biography and Documentary History* (Durham, NC; London: Duke University Press Books, 2014), 48–49.

14. Ibid., 49.

15. Ibid.

16. Alexander, *Black Fire*, 115.

17. "WEIRD BABEL OF TONGUES: New Sect of Fanatics Is Breaking Loose; Wild Scene Last Night on Azusa Street; Gurgle of Wordless Talk by a Sister," *Los Angeles Times (1886–1922)*, April 18, 1906, sec. Editorial.

18. Kelly Brown Douglas, *Black Bodies and the Black Church: A Blues Slant* (New York: Palgrave Macmillan, 2012).

19. Ibid., 33.

20. Ibid., 168–69.

21. Tom Beaudoin, "Postmodern Practical Theology," in *Opening the Field of Practical Theology: An Introduction*, ed. Kathleen A. Cahalan and Gordon S. Mikoski (Lanham, MD: Rowman & Littlefield, 2014), 194.

22. Andrew E. Benjamin, *The Plural Event: Descartes, Hegel, Heidegger* (London; New York: Routledge, 1993), 5.

23. EL Kornegay, *A Queering of Black Theology—EL Kornegay Jr.*, n.d., 9, accessed December 13, 2015.

24. Marcella Althaus-Reid, *Indecent Theology: Theological Perversions in Sex, Gender and Politics* (New York: Routledge, 2002), 1–2.

25. James Baldwin, Fred L. Standley, and Louis H. Pratt, *Conversations with James Baldwin* (Jackson: University Press of Mississippi, 1989), 4–5.

26. RagtimeDorianHenry, *Deep Moaning Blues (Ma Rainey, 1928) Jazz Legend*, accessed December 21, 2015, https://www.youtube.com/watch?v=A-mRHNAeJXE.

27. Andrew R. Mossin, "'The Song Sung in a Strange Land': An Interview with Nathaniel Mackey," *The Iowa Review* 44, no. 3 (winter 2014), http://www.iowareview.org/from-the-issue/volume-44-issue-3-%E2%80%94winter-201415/song-sung-strange-land-interview-nathaniel-mackey.

28. Ibid.

29. Ibid.

30. Brian Priestley, *Mingus: A Critical Biography* (New York: Da Capo Press, 1984), 4.

31. Arthur Jafa, *Dreams Are Colder Than Death* (documentary, 2014).

32. For a discussion of anti-Muslim sentiment within the New Atheist movement, see, for example, Glenn Greenwald, "Sam Harris, the New Atheists, and Anti-Muslim Animus," *The Guardian*, April 3, 2013, sec. Comment, http://www.guardian.co.uk/commentisfree/2013/apr/03/sam-harris-muslim-animus.

33. See, for example, Talal Asad, *Formations of the Secular : Christianity, Islam, Modernity* (Stanford, CA: Stanford University Press, 2003).

34. Karl Marx, "On The Jewish Question by Karl Marx," 1843, http://www.marxists.org/archive/marx/works/1844/jewish-question/.

35. Fred Moten, *In the Break: The Aesthetics of the Black Radical Tradition* (Minneapolis: University of Minnesota Press, 2003).

36. Nimi Wariboko, *The Pentecostal Principle: Ethical Methodology in New Spirit* (Grand Rapids, MI: William B. Eerdmans, 2012).

37. Jean-Christophe Bailly, "The Slightest Breath (On Living)," *CR: The New Centennial Review* 10, no. 3 (winter 2010): 1–11, 269.

1. BREATH

1. Saidiya V. Hartman, *Scenes of Subjection: Terror, Slavery, and Self-Making in Nineteenth-Century America* (New York: Oxford University Press, 1997).

2. See Peter Linebaugh, "KARL MARX, THE THEFT OF WOOD, AND WORKING CLASS COMPOSITION: A CONTRIBUTION TO THE CURRENT DEBATE," *Crime and Social Justice*, no. 6 (October 1, 1976): 5–16; Peter Linebaugh, *The Magna Carta Manifesto: Liberties and Commons for All* (Berkeley: University of California Press, 2009); Peter Linebaugh, *Ned Ludd & Queen Mab: Machine-Breaking, Romanticism, and the Several Commons of 1811–12*, Pmplt (Oakland, CA: PM Press, 2012).

3. Peter Linebaugh, *The London Hanged: Crime And Civil Society in the Eighteenth Century*, 2d ed. (London; New York: Verso, 2006).

4. Nimi Wariboko, *The Pentecostal Principle: Ethical Methodology in New Spirit* (Grand Rapids, MI: William B. Eerdmans, 2012).

5. Ibid., 1.

6. Ibid., 155.

7. Geoff Kennedy, *Diggers, Levellers, and Agrarian Capitalism: Radical Political Thought in 17th Century England* (Lanham, MD: Lexington Books, 2008).

8. Harriet A. (Harriet Ann) Jacobs, *Incidents in the Life of a Slave Girl: Written by Herself* (Boston: Bedford/St. Martins, 2010).

9. Milton C. Sernett, *Harriet Tubman: Myth, Memory, and History* (Durham, NC: Duke University Press, 2007).

10. Sarah H. (Sarah Hopkins) Bradford, *Harriet Tubman, the Moses of Her People*, American Experience Series. (Gloucester, MA: P. Smith, 1981).

11. Olaudah Equiano, *The Interesting Narrative and Other Writings: Revised Edition*, rev. ed. (New York: Penguin Classics, 2003).

12. Laura Harris, "What Happened to the Motley Crew? C. L. R. James, Hélio Oiticica, and the Aesthetic Sociality of Blackness," *Social Text* 30, no. 3 112 (September 21, 2012): 53.

13. Frank B. Wilderson III, *Red, White & Black: Cinema and the Structure of U.S. Antagonisms* (Durham, NC: Duke University Press, 2010), 251.

14. Peter. Linebaugh, *The Many-Headed Hydra : Sailors, Slaves, Commoners, and the Hidden History of the Revolutionary Atlantic* (Boston: Beacon Press, 2000).

15. Jürgen Moltmann, *The Spirit of Life: A Universal Affirmation*, 1st Fortress Press ed. (Minneapolis, MN: Fortress Press, 1992), 1.

16. Veli-Matti Kärkkäinen, *Pneumatology: The Holy Spirit in Ecumenical, International, and Contextual Perspective* (Grand Rapids, MI: Baker Academic, 2002), 11.

17. Ibid., 17.

18. Moltmann, *Spirit of Life*, 4.

19. Estrelda Alexander, *Black Fire: One Hundred Years of African American Pentecostalism* (Downers Grove, IL: IVP Academic, 2011), 113.

20. I opine that prejudicial reasoning, which emerges out of racialist discourse of continental philosophy and western theology, is but one reason why William Seymour's Azusa Street revival became a nodal point from which Global Pentecostalism emerged. A student of Charles Parham—a white man living in Texas who also believed in the "third work of grace," the movement of the Spirit with tongues-speech as evidentiary— Seymour, under Parham's tutelage, was not allowed to pray with his classmates at church altars or to sit in the classroom because of the submission to discriminatory logics.

21. Kärkkäinen, *Pneumatology*, 25.

22. David Hadley Jensen, *The Lord and Giver of Life: Perspectives on Constructive Pneumatology* (Louisville, KY: Westminster John Knox Press, 2008), xv.

23. Moltmann, *Spirit of Life*, 4.

24. "WEIRD BABEL OF TONGUES," *Los Angeles Daily Times*, April 18, 1906.

25. Moltmann, *Spirit of Life*, 83.

26. Sylvia Wynter, "Unsettling the Coloniality of Being/Power/Truth/Freedom: Towards the Human, After Man, Its Overrepresentation—An Argument," *CR: The New Centennial Review* 3, no. 3 (2003): 257–337.

27. Chandler, *X—the Problem of the Negro*, 2014.

28. Evans E. Crawford and Thomas H. Troeger, *The Hum: Call and Response in African American Preaching* (Nashville, TN: Abingdon Press, 1995), 71.

29. Ibid., 17.

30. Ibid., 20.

31. Ibid., 26.

32. Glorayyy, *Dorinda Clark Cole (Why Do I Come Back For More) *Must See**, accessed December 1, 2015, https://www.youtube.com/watch?v=-HlCo2jMHcw&feature=youtu.be&t=3m26s.

33. Elvis Lewis, *Pastor Juandolyn Stokes "This Closed Door Will Be Your Best Opportunity" Part 1*, accessed December 1, 2015, https://www.youtube.com/watch?v=mtTLXipHwvE&feature=youtu.be&t=4m15s.

34. Paul Grossman and Cees J. Wientjes, "How Breathing Adjusts to Mental and Physical Demands," in *Respiration and Emotion*, ed. Yutaka Haruki et al. (Tokyo; New York: Springer, n.d.), 43.

35. Ronald Ley, "Respiration and the Emotion of Dyspnea/Suffocation Fear," in *Respiration and Emotion*, ed. Yutaka Haruki et al. (Tokyo; New York: Springer, n.d.), 66.

36. Yuri Masaoka, Arata Kanamaru, and Ikuo Homma, "Anxiety and Respiration," in *Respiration and Emotion*, ed. Yutaka Haruki et al. (Tokyo; New York: Springer, n.d.), 55.

37. Jean-Christophe Bailly, "The Slightest Breath (On Living)," *CR: The New Centennial Review* 10, no. 3 (winter 2010): 4–5.

38. Fred Moten, "The Case of Blackness," *Criticism* 50, no. 2 (2008): 177–218.

39. W.E.B. (William Edward Burghardt) Du Bois, "Last Message to the World," in *W.E.B. Du Bois Speaks: Speeches and Addresses, 1890–1919* (New York; London: Pathfinder, 1970), 355.

40. Toni Morrison, *Beloved: A Novel* (New York: Vintage International, 2004), 60, accessed November 29, 2010.

41. Gilles Deleuze, *Pure Immanence: Essays on a Life* (New York: Zone Books; Cambridge, MA: MIT Press, 2001), 27, 29.

42. Jared Sexton, "The Social Life of Social Death: On Afro-Pessimism and Black Optimism," *InTensions* 5.0, no. (fall/winter 2011): 28.

43. For an analysis regarding gender and homiletics, see L. Susan Bond, *Trouble with Jesus: Women, Christology, and Preaching* (St. Louis, MO: Chalice Press, 1999); Teresa L. Fry Brown, *Weary Throats and New Songs: Black Women Proclaiming God's Word* (Nashville, TN: Abingdon Press, 2003). For discussions of performance style, particularly of men, see Crawford and Troeger, *The Hum*; Frank A. (Frank Anthony) Thomas, *They Like to Never Quit Praisin' God: The Role of Celebration in Preaching* (Cleveland, OH: United Church Press, n.d.); L. Susan Bond, *Contemporary African American Preaching: Diversity in Theory and Style* (St. Louis, MO: Chalice Press, 2003); Henry H. Mitchell, *Black Preaching: The Recovery of a Powerful Art* (Nashville, TN: Abingdon Press, 1990); Kenyatta R. Gilbert, *The Journey and Promise of African American Preaching* (Minneapolis, MN: Fortress Press, 2011). And for an analysis of how gender is a spatial logic in the pulpit, see Roxanne Mountford, *The Gendered Pulpit: Preaching in American Protestant Spaces*, Studies in Rhetorics and Feminisms. (Carbondale: Southern Illinois University Press, 2003).

44. Jerma A. Jackson, *Singing in My Soul: Black Gospel Music in a Secular Age* (Chapel Hill: University of North Carolina Press, 2004), 4.

45. Julio Bermudez, "On the Architectural Design Parti," *University of Utah—College of Architecture + Planning (Website)*, n.d., 1, http://faculty.arch.utah.edu/courses/arch6971/parti.pdf.

46. Ibid., 2.

47. Nathaniel Mackey, *From a Broken Bottle Traces of Perfume Still Emanate: Bedouin Hornbook, Djbot Baghostus's Run, Atet A.D.* (New York: New Directions, 2010).

48. Susan Buck-Morss, "Aesthetics and Anaesthetics: Walter Benjamin's Artwork Essay Reconsidered," *October* 62 (October 1, 1992): 12–3, doi:10.2307/778700.

49. Brian. Massumi, *Parables for the Virtual: Movement, Affect, Sensation*, Post-Contemporary Interventions. (Durham, NC: Duke University Press, 2002), 5.

50. Italo Calvino, *Invisible Cities* (San Diego, CA: Harcourt Brace Jovanovich, 1974), 12.

51. Ibid., 27.

52. Ashon Crawley, *Moth's Powder* (Unpublished manuscript, 2012).

53. Hortense J. Spillers, "Mama's Baby, Papa's Maybe: An American Grammar Book," in *Black, White, and in Color: Essays on American Literature and Culture* (Chicago: University of Chicago Press, 2003), 206.

54. Judith Butler, *Bodies That Matter: On the Discursive Limits of Sex* (New York: Routledge, 1993), 2.

55. Michael Inwood, "Thrownness and Facticity," in *A Heidegger Dictionary*, Blackwell Reference Online (Blackwell Publishing, 1999), http://www.blackwell-reference.com/public/book?id=g9780631190950_9780631190950.

56. Michael Wheeler, "Martin Heidegger," in *The Stanford Encyclopedia of Philosophy*, ed. Edward N. Zalta (winter 2011), http://plato.stanford.edu/archives/win2011/entries/heidegger/.

57. Massumi, *Parables for the Virtual*, 6.

58. Ibid.

59. Hortense J. Spillers, "Interstices: A Small Drama of Words," in *Black, White, and in Color : Essays on American Literature and Culture* (Chicago: University of Chicago Press, 2003), 165.

60. Michel De Certeau, *The Practice of Everyday Life* (Berkeley: University of California Press, 1984).

61. Barcroft TV, *The Boy Who Can See Without Eyes*, accessed December 1, 2015, https://www.youtube.com/watch?v=Wby1CIhnYWI.

62. Massumi, *Parables for the Virtual*, 14.

63. Ibid., 9.

64. Michel Foucault, Robert Hurley, and Paul Rabinow, "Friendship as a Way of Life," in *Ethics: Subjectivity and Truth* (New York: New Press, 1997).

65. Ibid., 136.

66. MonsieurBaudelaire, *Billie Holiday—Strange Fruit*, accessed December 1, 2015, https://www.youtube.com/watch?v=h4ZyuULy9zs.

67. maya h., *Nina Simone—Strange Fruit*, accessed December 1, 2015, https://www.youtube.com/watch?v=tqbXOO3OiOs.

68. "Strange Fruit," *Wikipedia, the Free Encyclopedia*, December 3, 2012, http://en.wikipedia.org/w/index.php?title=Strange_Fruit&oldid=526086426.

69. Jean-Christophe Bailly, "The Slightest Breath (On Living)," *CR: the New Centennial Review* 10 (2010): 1–11, 269.

70. Manthia Diawara, "One World in Relation Édouard Glissant in Conversation with Manthia Diawara," *Nka Journal of Contemporary African Art* 2011, no. 28 (March 20, 2011): 5.

71. Trudier Harris, *Exorcising Blackness: Historical and Literary Lynching and Burning Rituals* (Bloomington: Indiana University Press, 1984), 2.

72. Joseph R. Roach, *It* (Ann Arbor: University of Michigan Press, 2007), 3, accessed November 30, 2010.

73. Ibid., 2–3.

74. Ida B. Wells-Barnett and Ida B. Wells-Barnett, *On Lynchings* [electronic resource] (Amherst, NY: Humanity Books, 2002), 25.

75. Ibid.

76. Ibid., 31.

77. Ibid., 30.

78. Susan Olzak, "The Political Context of Competition: Lynching and Urban Racial Violence, 1882–1914," *Social Forces* 69, no. 2 (December 1, 1990): 395.

79. Ibid., 396.

80. Khalil Gibran Muhammad, *The Condemnation of Blackness: Race, Crime, and the Making of Modern Urban America* (Cambridge, MA: Harvard University Press, 2010), 59.

81. For a robust discussion of homoeroticism at the site of lynching violence, see Robyn Wiegman, "The Anatomy of Lynching," *Journal of the History of Sexuality* 3, no. 3 (January 1, 1993): 445–67.

82. "Emphysema Definition—Diseases and Conditions—Mayo Clinic," accessed December 13, 2014, http://www.mayoclinic.org/diseases-conditions/emphysema/basics/definition/con-20014218.

83. Masaoka, Kanamaru, and Homma, "Anxiety and Respiration," 55.

84. Nahum Chandler, "Originary Displacement," *Boundary 2* 27, no. 3 (2000): 250.

85. Olzak, "The Political Context of Competition," 401.

86. Jonathan Markovitz, *Legacies of Lynching: Racial Violence and Memory* (Minneapolis: University of Minnesota Press, 2004), 10.

87. Wells-Barnett and Wells-Barnett, *On Lynchings*, 64.

88. Zora Neale. Hurston, *The Sanctified Church* (Berkeley, CA: Turtle Island, 1983), 79.

89. J. L. (John Langshaw) Austin, *How to Do Things with Words*, William James Lectures , 1955 (Cambridge, MA: Harvard University Press, c1975).

90. Orlando Patterson, *Slavery and Social Death: A Comparative Study* (Cambridge, MA: Harvard University Press, 1982), 5.

91. James Allen, *Without Sanctuary: Lynching Photography in America*, 7th ed. (Santa Fe, NM: Twin Palms, 2005), panel 25.

92. See, for example, Natasha Barnes, "On Without Sanctuary," *Nka Journal of Contemporary African Art* 2006, no. 20 (September 21, 2006): 86–91; James H. Cone,

The Cross and the Lynching Tree (Maryknoll, NY: Orbis Books, 2011); Raphael Hörmann and Gesa Mackenthun, Human Bondage in the Cultural Contact Zone: Transdisciplinary Perspectives on Slavery and Its Discourses (Münster: Waxmann Verlag, 2010); Anne Rice, "How We Remember Lynching," Nka Journal of Contemporary African Art no. 20 (September 21, 2006): 32–43.

93. Cone, Cross and the Lynching Tree, 31.

94. Denise Ferreira da. Silva, Toward a Global Idea of Race, in Borderlines (Minneapolis, MN) v. 27. (Minneapolis: University of Minnesota Press, c2007).

95. Immanuel Kant, Critique of Pure Reason (London; New York: Penguin, 2007).

96. Leigh Raiford, "Lynching, Visuality, and the Un/Making of Blackness," Nka Journal of Contemporary African Art no. 20 (September 21, 2006): 22.

97. Jacques Derrida, Archive Fever: A Freudian Impression (Chicago: University of Chicago Press, 1998).

98. Wariboko, Pentecostal Principle, 23; Victor Zuckerkandl, Sound and Symbol, Bollingen Series 44 (New York: Pantheon Books, [1956–73]).

99. Wariboko, Pentecostal Principle, 25.

100. Michel Foucault, The History of Sexuality, Vol. 1: An Introduction (New York: Vintage, 1990), 143.

101. James Baldwin, Giovanni's Room (New York: Delta, 2000), 25.

102. Gwendolyn Brooks, Maud Martha, a Novel (New York: Harper, 1953).

103. Kathy Bennett, "Lynching," The Tennessee Encyclopedia of History and Culture, December 25, 2009, http://tennesseeencyclopedia.net/entry.php?rec=816.

104. Craig Scandrett-Leatherman, "Rites of Lynching and Rights of Dance: Historic, Anthropological, and Afro-Pentecostal Perspectives on Black Manhood after 1865," in Afro-Pentecostalism: Black Pentecostal and Charismatic Christianity in History and Culture (New York: New York University Press, 2011), 104.

105. C. H. Mason, The History and Life Work of Elder C. H. Mason, Chief Apostle, and His Co-Laborers (N.p.: n.p., 1987).

106. Scandrett-Leatherman, "Rites of Lynching and Rights of Dance: Historic, Anthropological, and Afro-Pentecostal Perspectives on Black Manhood after 1865," 105.

107. Ibid., 95, 96.

108. Cheryl Gilkes, "If It Wasn't for the Women—": Black Women's Experience and Womanist Culture in Church and Community (Maryknoll, NY: Orbis Books, n.d.), 43.

109. Toni Morrison, Beloved (New York: Longman, 1998), 88–89.

110. Nahum Chandler, "Of Exorbitance: The Problem of the Negro as a Problem for Thought," Criticism 50, no. 3 (2008): 347.

111. Ibid., 348.

112. Achille Mbembe, "Necropolitics," Public Culture 15, no. 1 (January 1, 2003): 21.

113. Morrison, Beloved, 60.

114. Mbembe, "Necropolitics," 21.

115. Fred Moten, "Preface for a Solo by Miles Davis," *Women & Performance: A Journal of Feminist Theory* 17, no. 2 (2007): 218.

116. Sylvia Wynter, "Unsettling the Coloniality of Being/Power/Truth/Freedom: Towards the Human, After Man, Its Overrepresentation—An Argument," *CR: The New Centennial Review* 3, no. 3 (2003): 257–337.

117. Mbembe, "Necropolitics," 25.

118. Ibid., 28.

119. Michael Hardt, *Commonwealth* (Cambridge, MA: Belknap Press of Harvard University Press, 2009), 79.

120. For a discussion of "nevertheless" and "in spite of" that prompts this discussion here but that though goes in another direction, see Jared Sexton, "People-of-Color-Blindness Notes on the Afterlife of Slavery," *Social Text* 28, no. 2 ,103 (June 20, 2010): 35.

121. Elizabeth Grosz, *Space, Time and Perversion: Essays on the Politics of Bodies* (New York: Routledge, 1995), 96, 97.

122. Chandler, "Originary Displacement," 281.

123. Michelle Koerner, "Line of Escape: Gilles Deleuze's Encounter with George Jackson," *Genre* 44, no. 2 (summer 2011): 174.

124. Ibid., 173.

125. Gwendolyn Brooks, "Speech to the Young / Speech to the Progress-Toward," in *I Can Make a Difference: A Treasury to Inspire Our Children*, ed. Marian Wright Edelman (New York: HarperCollins, 2005), 23.

2. SHOUTING

1. Nahum Chandler, "Originary Displacement," *Boundary 2* 27, no. 3 (2000): 249–50.

2. Cheryl Jeanne Sanders, *Saints in Exile: The Holiness-Pentecostal Experience in African American Religion and Culture* (New York: Oxford University Press,, 1996).

3. Bryan Wagner, *Disturbing the Peace: Black Culture and the Police Power after Slavery* (Cambridge, MA: Harvard University Press, 2009), 62.

4. M. Allewaert, "Swamp Sublime: Ecologies of Resistance in the American Plantation Zone," *PMLA* 123, no. 2 (March 2008): 341–42.

5. Samuel R. Delany, *Neveróna, or: The Tale of Signs and Cities-—Some Informal Remarks Towards the Modular Calculus, Part Four* (Middletown, CT: Wesleyan Press, 1993), 52.

6. Timothy James Lockley, *Maroon Communities in South Carolina : A Documentary Record* (Columbia: University of South Carolina Press, 2009), iii.

7. Michelle Koerner, "Line of Escape: Gilles Deleuze's Encounter with George Jackson," *Genre* 44, no. 2 (summer 2011): 174.

8. Sally Price, *Maroon Arts: Cultural Vitality in the African Diaspora* (Boston: Beacon Press, 1999), 1.

9. Ibid., 16.

10. The "politics of avoidance" will be fully explicated in Chapter 3. However, briefly, the *politics of avoidance* is ontological, and we find a strain of its historicity in the performances of the always (mis)read as excess and excessive moves and programmatics of black social dance. The politics of avoidance is an "insistent previousness evading each and every natal occasion" (Nathaniel Mackey, *From a Broken Bottle Traces of Perfume Still Emanate: Bedouin Hornbook, Djbot Baghostus's Run, Atet A.D.* (New York: New Directions, 2010), 42.

11. See Frank Lambert, *Pedlar in Divinity: George Whitefield and the Transatlantic Revivals, 1737–1770* (Princeton, NJ: Princeton University Press, 1994). Of Whitefield's Calvinist leanings, he states that Whitefield "asserted that only God's actions were efficacious in redemption, effecting salvation through nothing less than a 'union of the soul with God' resulting in the 'one thing needful,' the new birth. God's grace alone saved men and women; human merit played no role whatever. As early as 1740, Whitefield split with his mentor, John Wesley, over the doctrine of 'universal redemption,' the idea that salvation was available to all who would accept it. Whitefield clung to a strict predestination whereby the sovereign God elected whom he wished to save" (15). It will be important to note, in the chapter about *glossolalia*, that salvation depended upon the written text. "The central role of reading in Whitefield's conversion is noteworthy because of the scant attention historians have given to print in the evangelical revivals. The focus has been on the orality of the evangelist's ministry, suggesting that the religious awakening represented a face-to-face world in retreat before the oncoming tide of rationalism in print. From the outset, the printed word had a profound influence on Whitefield both in informing his own understanding of experimental faith and in conveying the gospel to a transatlantic audience" (17). It seems that predestination might seem to dovetail conveniently with the ability to read; the capacity for salvation is regulated by the ability to read.

12. Denise Ferreira da Silva, *Toward a Global Idea of Race*, in *Borderlines*, v. 27 (Minneapolis: University of Minnesota Press, 2007).

13. Toni. Morrison, *Playing in the Dark: Whiteness and the Literary Imagination*, William E. Massey, Sr. Lectures in the History of American Civilization, 1990 (Cambridge, MA: Harvard University Press, 1992), 6.

14. Ronald A. T. Judy, *(Dis)forming the American Canon: African-Arabic Slave Narratives and the Vernacular* (Minneapolis: University of Minnesota Press, 1993), 46.

15. Ibid., 34.

16. J. L. (John Langshaw) Austin, *How to Do Things with Words*, William James Lectures, 1955 (Cambridge, MA: Harvard University Press, 1975).

17. Judy, *(Dis)forming the American Canon*, 35.

18. Higginson, *Army Life in a Black Regiment*, 28.

19. Diana Taylor, *The Archive and the Repertoire: Performing Cultural Memory in the Americas* (Durham, NC: Duke University Press, 2003).

20. Sterling Stuckey, *Slave Culture: Nationalist Theory and the Foundations of Black America* (New York: Oxford University Press, 1987), 16.

21. Michael A. Gomez, "Muslims in Early America," *The Journal of Southern History* 60, no. 4 (November 1, 1994): 682.

22. Art Rosenbaum and Johann S. Buis, *Shout Because You're Free: The African American Ring Shout Tradition in Coastal Georgia* (Athens: University of Georgia Press, n.d.), 169.

23. Nathaniel Mackey, *Atet A.D.* (San Francisco, CA: City Lights Books, 2001), 123–24.

24. John Fanning Watson, *Methodist Error, Or, Friendly, Christian Advice, to Those Methodists, Who Indulge in Extravagant Emotions and Bodily Exercises* (Trenton, NJ: D. and E. Fenton, 1819).

25. Ibid., 22, 27.

26. Judith. Butler, *Undoing Gender* (New York: Routledge, 2004), 19.

27. Cornelia Bailey and Christena Bledsoe, *God, Dr. Buzzard, and the Bolito Man: A Saltwater Geechee Talks about Life on Sapelo Island* (New York: Doubleday, 2000), 1.

28. There is contention as to the attribution of authorship of this collection of writings, though. Ronald Judy argues that authorship may be multiple and that, perhaps, only sections of the text may have been authored by Bilali himself, though this is difficult to determine. See Judy, *(Dis)forming the American Canon*, 271.

29. Bailey and Bledsoe, *God, Dr. Buzzard, and the Bolito Man*, 157–58.

30. L. A. Michael, *The Principles of Existence & Beyond* (Lulu.com, 2007), 175.

31. Mackey, *From a Broken Bottle*, 34.

32. All quotations are taken from Rosenbaum and Buis, *Shout Because You're Free*.

33. Orlando Patterson, *Slavery and Social Death: A Comparative Study* (Cambridge, MA: Harvard University Press, 1982).

34. Lorenzo Dow Turner, Katherine Wyly Mille, and Michael B. Montgomery, *Africanisms in the Gullah Dialect* (Columbia: University of South Carolina Press, 2002), 202.

35. Gilles Deleuze says, " The tired no longer prepares for any possibility (subjective): he therefore cannot realize the smallest possibility (objective). But possibility remains, because you never realize all of the possible, you even bring it into being as you realize some of it. The tired has only exhausted realization, while the exhausted exhausts all of the possible." See Gilles Deleuze, "The Exhausted," *SubStance* 24, no. 3 and 78 (1995): 1.

36. Michel Foucault and Duccio Trombadori, *Remarks on Marx: Conversations with Duccio Trombadori* (New York: Semiotext(e), 1991), 27.

37. John Wesley, *John Wesley* (New York: Oxford University Press, 1980), 90.

38. Zora Neale. Hurston, *The Sanctified Church* (Berkeley, CA: Turtle Island, 1983).

39. Ibid., 103.

40. Ibid., 106.

41. Grant Wacker, *Heaven Below: Early Pentecostals and American Culture* (Cambridge, MA: Harvard University Press, 2001), 99.

42. For another of Hurston's quotes, see page 28 above. Hurston, *Sanctified Church*, 91.

43. We might even, because of Fanon, consider the shout traditions as guerilla warfare, a particularly violent intervention into emergence into the normative subject position. See Frantz Fanon, *The Wretched of the Earth* (New York : Grove, 1968), 85.

44. Mackey, *From a Broken Bottle*, 11.

45. C. H. Mason, *The History and Life Work of Elder C. H. Mason, Chief Apostle, and His Co-Laborers* (N.P.: n.p., 1987), 53.

46. Ibid.

47. Mason, of course, was involved in postemancipatory, reconstruction battles about the meaning of the divine, of the spirit, of the prayers of his ancestors. The black holiness movement of which Mason was a part spanning roughly 1896–1906 contended with the black Baptist movement, making claims that the theology of the very rhetoric of being a "Baptist Church" was not a biblical precept and, thus, should be done away with. For a robust treatment of this history, see David Douglas Daniels, "The Cultural Renewal of Slave Religion Charles Price Jones and the Emergence of the Holiness Movement in Mississippi" (Union Theological Seminary, 1992).. For example, Daniels describes the various schisms that took place at the now historic Mt. Helm (Baptist) Church, its various renamings such as the Church of God and the Christ's Tabernacle that they desired in order to be more consistent with what they believed to be biblical mandates. The church specifically wanted to separate from "Baptist" churches and "from all creeds, denominations, associations and conventions . . . because of the evils in them" (32). This was the theological ground in which Mason found himself making a space.

48. "A Minnesota Preacher's Testimony," *The Apostolic Faith*, March 5, 1907, February–March edition.

49. "WEIRD BABEL OF TONGUES: New Sect of Fanatics Is Breaking Loose; Wild Scene Last Night on Azusa Street; Gurgle of Wordless Talk by a Sister," *Los Angeles Times (1886–1922)*, April 18, 1906, sec. Editorial.

50. Immanuel Kant and Thomas Kingsmill Abbott, *Kant's Critique of Practical Reason and Other Works on the Theory of Ethics*, 6th ed., new impression, with memoir and portrait (London: Longmans, Green, 1927), xliv.

51. Immanuel Kant and Allen W. Wood, *Basic Writings of Kant* (New York: Modern Library, 2001), 281.

52. Ibid., 294.

53. For a discussion about "impenetrability" as the basis for Enlightenment thought, see Michel Foucault, *The Birth of the Clinic*, 3rd ed. (New York: Routledge, 2003).

54. See what Menninghaus says regarding "disgust" as causing aversion for Kantian philosophy in Winfried Menninghaus, "'Disgusting Impotence' and Romanticism," *European Romantic Review* 10, no. 1 (1999): 203.

55. Kant and Wood, *Basic Writings of Kant*, 133.

56. Sarah H. (Sarah Hopkins) Bradford, *Harriet Tubman, the Moses of Her People*, American Experience Series. (Gloucester, MA: P. Smith, 1981).

57. Silva, *Toward a Global Idea of Race*, 59.

58. Kant and Wood, *Basic Writings of Kant*, 275, 276.

59. Ibid., 306.

60. Ibid., 307.

61. Foucault, *Birth of the Clinic*, xiv.

62. Kant and Wood, *Basic Writings of Kant*, 312.

63. Ibid., 42–43.

64. Andrew E Benjamin, *The Plural Event: Descartes, Hegel, Heidegger* (London; New York: Routledge, 1993), 3.

65. See specifically Kant's writing about the transcendental aesthetic of space in Kant and Wood, *Basic Writings of Kant*, 44, 45, 47.

66. Ibid., 49.

67. Ibid., 50.

68. Sylvia Wynter, "Unsettling the Coloniality of Being/Power/Truth/Freedom: Towards the Human, After Man, Its Overrepresentation—An Argument," *CR: The New Centennial Review* 3, no. 3 (2003): 257–337.

69. Immanuel Kant, Robert B. Louden, and Günter Zöller, *Anthropology, History, and Education* (Cambridge; New York: Cambridge University Press, 2007), 32.

70. See, for example, "Black Mo'nin' in the Sound of the Photogragh" for a discussion of the "glance" in Fred Moten, *In The Break: The Aesthetics of the Black Radical Tradition* (Minneapolis, MN: University of Minnesota Press, 2003).

71. Kant, Louden, and Zöller, *Anthropology, History, and Education*, 59, 61.

72. Ibid., 156–57.

73. Ann Taves, *Fits, Trances, & Visions: Experiencing Religion and Explaining Experience from Wesley to James* (Princeton, NJ: Princeton University Press, 1999) notes how many conversions, particularly that occurred as a result of Methodistism, were due likely to the "small group" nature of their meetings. Methodists had a different ecclesial structure that gave "exhorters"—those who were not trained as clergy—much latitude in leading services. These services often were

not about preaching but unified experience. The Separate Baptist tradition was similar.

74. Jonathan Edwards, "Sinners in the Hands of an Angry God," *The Jonathan Edwards Center at Yale University,* 1739, http://bit.ly/whKWvX.

75. See "New York City Plot" for a full treatment of this episode Junius P. Rodriguez, *Encyclopedia of Slave Resistance and Rebellion* (Westport, CT: Greenwood Press, 2007), 347–49.

76. Edwards, "Sinners in the Hands of an Angry God."

77. Toni Morrison, *Playing in the Dark: Whiteness and the Literary Imagination,* William E. Massey, Sr. Lectures in the History of American Civilization; 1990 (Cambridge, MA: Harvard University Press, 1992).

78. Silva, *Toward a Global Idea of Race,* 97.

79. Chandler, "Of Exorbitance: The Problem of the Negro as a Problem for Thought," *Criticism* 50, no. 3 (2008): 354.

80. The idea of "enthusiasm" will be explicated in Chapter 3, based on Rosenberg's historical analysis of the concept. See Jordana Rosenberg, *Critical Enthusiasm: Capital Accumulation and the Transformation of Religious Passion* (New York: Oxford University Press, 2011).

81. Hortense J. Spillers, "Mama's Baby, Papa's Maybe: An American Grammar Book," in *Black, White, and in Color: Essays on American Literature and Culture* (Chicago: University of Chicago Press, 2003), 203.

82. For example, "Viewed locally, the prayer meetings of the classes appear to have been the engine of the revivals. Conversions apparently proceeded apace even in the absence of preachers, and preachers seemed to have particular difficulty silencing congregations when their sermons had been preceded by a successful prayer meeting." See Taves, *Fits, Trances, & Visions,* 90.

83. Ashon Crawley, *Moth's Powder* (Unpublished manuscript, 2012).

84. See specifically chapter 2, "The Strange Career of Bras-Coupé," in Wagner, *Disturbing the Peace.*

85. Margaret Washington Creel, *A Peculiar People: Slave Religion and Community-Culture Among the Gullahs* (New York: New York University Press, 1988), 299.

86. See Anthea D. Butler, *Women in the Church of God in Christ: Making a Sanctified World* (Chapel Hill: University of North Carolina Press, 2007).

87. Saba Mahmood, *Politics of Piety: The Islamic Revival and the Feminist Subject* (Princeton, NJ: Princeton University Press, 2005), 56.

88. Daniel Alexander Payne and John Hope Franklin Research Center for African and African-American Documentation, *Recollections of Seventy Years.* (New York, Arno Press, 1968).

89. Winfried Menninghaus, *In Praise of Nonsense: Kant and Bluebeard* (Stanford, CA: Stanford University Press, 1999).

3. NOISE

1. Philipp. Schweighauser, *The Noises of American Literature, 1890–1985: Toward a History of Literary Acoustics* (Gainesville: University Press of Florida, 2006), 4.

2. Edmund Burke, *A Philosophical Enquiry into the Origin of Our Ideas of the Sublime and Beautiful, and Other Pre-Revolutionary Writings*, Penguin Classics. (London; New York: Penguin Books, 1998), 149.

3. Ibid., 150–51.

4. Ibid.

5. Mark M. Smith, *Listening to Nineteenth-Century America*, illus. ed. (Chapel Hill, NC: University of North Carolina Press, 2001), 10.

6. Meg Armstrong, "'The Effects of Blackness': Gender, Race, and the Sublime in Aesthetic Theories of Burke and Kant," *The Journal of Aesthetics and Art Criticism* 54, no. 3 (July 1, 1996): 275, doi:10.2307/431624.

7. Burke, *A Philosophical Enquiry into the Origin of Our Ideas*, 275–77.

8. Ibid., 279, 280.

9. Ibid., 218, 282.

10. Ibid., 285.

11. Shane White and Graham White, *The Sounds of Slavery: Discovering African American History through Songs, Sermons, and Speech* (Boston: Beacon Press, 2006), xi–xii.

12. Leigh Eric Schmidt, *Hearing Things: Religion, Illusion, and the American Enlightenment* (Cambridge, MA: Harvard University Press, 2002), 4–5.

13. Jordana Rosenberg, *Critical Enthusiasm: Capital Accumulation and the Transformation of Religious Passion* (New York: Oxford University Press, 2011).

14. Schmidt, *Hearing Things*, 103.

15. Ibid., 3.

16. David D Daniels, "'Gotta Moan Sometime': A Sonic Exploration of Earwitnesses to Early Pentecostal Sound in North America," *Pneuma* 30, no. 1 (2008): 5–32.

17. Gastón Espinosa, *William J. Seymour and the Origins of Global Pentecostalism: A Biography and Documentary History* (Durham, NC; London: Duke University Press Books, 2014), 66.

18. Willie James Jennings, *The Christian Imagination : Theology and the Origins of Race* (New Haven, CT: Yale University Press, 2010).

19. Johannes Fabian, *Time and the Other: How Anthropology Makes Its Object* (New York: Columbia University Press, 2002).

20. A full discussion about the concept of possessive individualism is beyond the bounds of the analysis here. For a robust explication of the concept, see C. B. Macpherson, *The Political Theory of Possessive Individualism: Hobbes to Locke*, reprint ed. (Don Mills, Ontario: Oxford University Press, 2011).

21. Georg W. F. Hegel, *The Philosophy of History* (PLACE: Cosimo, Inc., 2007), 99.

22. Frank B. Wilderson III, *Red, White & Black: Cinema and the Structure of U.S. Antagonisms* (Durham, NC: Duke University Press, 2010).

23. Sylvia Wynter, "Unsettling the Coloniality of Being/Power/Truth/Freedom: Towards the Human, After Man, Its Overrepresentation—An Argument," *CR: The New Centennial Review* 3, no. 3 (2003): 257–337.

24. Denise Ferreira da Silva, *Toward a Global Idea of Race*, in *Borderlines*, v. 27 (Minneapolis: University of Minnesota Press, 2007), 80.

25. Steven Salaita, "Inter/nationalism from the New World to the Holy Land: Encountering Palestine in American Indian Studies" (Undisciplined Encounters, University of California, Riverside, 2014).

26. John S. Mbiti, *African Religions & Philosophy* (Portsmouth, NH: Heinemann, 1990), 16–17.

27. Cedric J. Robinson, *The Terms of Order: Political Science and the Myth of Leadership* (Albany: State University of New York Press, 1980).

28. Cedric J. Robinson, *Black Marxism: The Making of the Black Radical Tradition*, Third World Studies (London: Zed Press, 1983), 170.

29. Hortense J. Spillers, "Interstices: A Small Drama of Words," in *Black, White, and in Color: Essays on American Literature and Culture* (Chicago: University of Chicago Press, 2003), 155.

30. David S. Ferris, *Walter Benjamin: Theoretical Questions* (Stanford, CA: Stanford University Press, 1996), 24.

31. For a discussion and interrogation of 1492 as the inaugural moment of a new world order, see Sylvia Wynter, "1492: A New World View," in *Race, Discourse, and the Origin of the Americas: A New World View*, ed. Vera Lawrence Hyatt and Rex Nettleford (Washington, DC: Smithsonian Institution Press, 1995).

32. Christine M. Korsgaard, *Kant: Groundwork of the Metaphysics of Morals*, trans. Mary Gregor and Jens Timmermann, 2d ed. (Cambridge: Cambridge University Press, 2012).

33. V. Y. Mudimbe, *The Invention of Africa: Gnosis, Philosophy, and the Order of Knowledge* (Bloomington: Indiana University Press, 1988).

34. Ibid., 17.

35. Nahum Dimitri Chandler, *Toward an African Future—of the Limit of World* (Newport Beach, CA: Living Commons Collective, 2013), 10.

36. Nathaniel Mackey, *From a Broken Bottle Traces of Perfume Still Emanate: Bedouin Hornbook, Djbot Baghostus's Run, Atet A.D.* (New York: New Directions, 2010), 34.

37. Harriet A. (Harriet Ann) Jacobs, *Incidents in the Life of a Slave Girl: Written by Herself* (Boston: Bedford/St. Martins, 2010).

38. Ibid., 69.

39. Ibid., 65.

40. Ibid., 10.

41. Diana Taylor, *The Archive and the Repertoire: Performing Cultural Memory in the Americas* (Durham, NC: Duke University Press, 2003), 2.

42. Jacobs, *Incidents in the Life of a Slave Girl*, 59.

43. Ibid., 40.

44. Saidiya V. Hartman, *Scenes of Subjection: Terror, Slavery, and Self-Making in Nineteenth-Century America* (New York: Oxford University Press, 1997), 20.

45. Mackey, *From a Broken Bottle*, 29–30.

46. Martin Heidegger, *On Time and Being.* (New York: Harper & Row, 1972).

47. Ibid., 6.

48. Ibid., 16.

49. Daphne Brooks, *Bodies in Dissent: Spectacular Performances of Race and Freedom, 1850–1910* (Durham, NC: Duke University Press, 2006), 67, accessed November 29, 2010.

50. Personal correspondence.

51. Jacobs, *Incidents in the Life of a Slave Girl*, 69.

52. Ibid., 93.

53. Karl Marx, "On The Jewish Question by Karl Marx," 1843, 13, http://www.marxists.org/archive/marx/works/1844/jewish-question/.

54. Ibid., 21.

55. Ronald A. T. Judy, *(Dis)forming the American Canon: African-Arabic Slave Narratives and the Vernacular* (Minneapolis: University of Minnesota Press, 1993), 33.

56. Rev F. W. McGee, *Rev. F.W. McGee Vol. 2* (Portland, OR: Document Records, 1992).

57. Jon Michael Spencer, *Black Hymnody: A Hymnological History of the African-American Church* (Knoxville: University of Tennessee Press, 1992), 156.

58. Tomas Harris, *"Yes Lord" Praise at Pentecostal Temple COGIC- Memphis, TN,* accessed December 1, 2015, https://www.youtube.com/watch?v=vuisScVJphg.

59. See particularly chapter 8, "The Church of God in Christ," in Jon Michael Spencer, *Black Hymnody : A Hymnological History of the African-American Church* (Knoxville: University of Tennessee Press, 1992).

60. Quoted in *Down Behind the Sun: the Story of Arenia Cornelia Mallory*, in ibid., 159.

61. Cotton Mather and Paul Royster, "The Negro Christianized: An Essay to Excite and Assist That Good Work, the Instruction of Negro-Servants in Christianity (1706)," *Electronic Texts in American Studies*, January 1, 1706, http://digitalcommons.unl.edu/etas/28.

62. Robert Ryland, *The Scripture Catechism for Coloured People* (1848; reprint, Richmond, VA: Harrold & Murray, 1971).

63. Janet Duitsman Cornelius, *"When I Can Read My Title Clear": Literacy, Slavery, and Religion in the Antebellum South* (Columbia: University of South Carolina Press, 1991), 46–47.

64. Peter Linebaugh, *Ned Ludd & Queen Mab: Machine-Breaking, Romanticism, and the Several Commons of 1811–12*, pamphlet (Oakland, CA: PM Press, 2012), 10.

65. Ibid., 11.

66. Ryland, *Scripture Catechism for Coloured People*, 93.

67. For an example of tarrying, see *Butts Miracle Temple "Old Fashion Tarring Service" Part 1*, 2009, https://www.youtube.com/watch?v=USS5WuaFDws.

68. Lindon Barrett, *Blackness and Value: Seeing Double* (Cambridge: Cambridge University Press, 2009), 66.

69. Cornelius, *When I Can Read My Title Clear*.

70. Ibid., 16.

71. This is what my colleague Rochelle Wright-Jones stated about Blackpentecostal noise in a personal communication (July, 2012).

72. David D. Daniels, "'Gotta Moan Sometime': A Sonic Exploration of Earwitnesses to Early Pentecostal Sound in North America," *Pneuma* 30, no. 1 (2008): 12.

73. Ibid., 17.

74. "WEIRD BABEL OF TONGUES," *Los Angeles Daily Times*, April 18, 1906.

75. David D. Daniels, "'Until the Power of the Lord Comes Down': African American Pentecostal Spirituality and Tarrying," in *Contemporary Spiritualities: Social and Religious Contexts*, ed. Clive Erricker and Jane Erricker (London; New York: Continuum, 2001), 178.

76. Samuel A. Floyd, *The Power of Black Music: Interpreting Its History from Africa to the United States* (New York: Oxford University Press, 1995), 50.

77. Anthony Heilbut, *The Gospel Sound: Good News and Bad Times - 25th Anniversary Edition* (N.P.: Limelight Editions, 1997), xxiii.

78. Shane White and Graham White, *The Sounds of Slavery: Discovering African American History through Songs, Sermons, and Speech* (Boston: Beacon Press, 2006), 21.

79. Ibid., 22.

80. Ibid., 24.

81. Ibid., 31.

82. I get the idea of "pious disposition" from Saba Mahmood's *Politics of Piety: The Islamic Revival and the Feminist Subject* (Princeton, NJ: Princeton University Press, 2005). For example, she says, "The process of cultivating and honing a pious disposition among the mosque participants centered not only on the practical tasks of daily living . . . but also on the *creation* and *orientation* of the emotions such a disposition entailed" (140, emphasis mine). What I think happens with the various sonic resources utilized during the production of work songs is the creation and orientation of emotions antithetical to the work that is being produced.

83. Art Rosenbaum and Johann S. Buis, *Shout Because You're Free: The African American Ring Shout Tradition in Coastal Georgia* (Athens: University of Georgia Press, n.d.), 66.

84. Karl Marx, *Grundrisse: Foundations of the Critique of Political Economy (rough draft)* (Harmondsworth, England: Penguin Books, 1973), 46.

85. Cedric J. Robinson, *Black Marxism: The Making of the Black Radical Tradition*, Third World Studies (London: Zed Press, 1983), 4.

86. Ibid., 82.

87. Ibid., 113.

88. Denise Ferreira da Silva, *Toward a Global Idea of Race*, in *Borderlines*, v. 27 (Minneapolis: University of Minnesota Press, 2007), 53.

89. Karl Marx, "On The Jewish Question by Karl Marx," 1843, http://www.marxists.org/archive/marx/works/1844/jewish-question/.

90. Linebaugh, *Ned Ludd & Queen Mab*, 8.

91. Ibid., 23. Steven Hahn's work comprehensively illustrates the various ways in which enslaved people resisted their condition by the destruction of tools, by "community building" (41), stealing education, etc. See Steven Hahn, *A Nation Under Our Feet: Black Political Struggles in the Rural South, from Slavery to the Great Migration* (Cambridge, MA: Belknap Press of Harvard University Press, 2003); Steven Hahn, *The Political Worlds of Slavery and Freedom*, Nathan I. Huggins Lectures. (Cambridge, MA: Harvard University Press, 2009). For other accounts, see Eugene D. Genovese, *Roll, Jordan, Roll: The World the Slaves Made* (New York: Vintage Books, 1976).

92. Linebaugh, *Ned Ludd & Queen Mab*, 32.

93. Floyd, *The Power of Black Music*, 6.

94. Ibid.

95. White and White, *Sounds of Slavery*, 30.

96. Marx, *Grundrisse*, 50.

97. From Rev F. W. McGee, *Rev. F.W. McGee Vol. 2* (Document Records, 1992); for the specific testimony, link here http://www.youtube.com/watch?v=drsXBOkA3BM&t=2m20s.

98. Daniel Patrick Moynihan, "U.S. Department of Labor—History—The Negro Family—The Case for National Action," accessed April 6, 2011, http://www.dol.gov/oasam/programs/history/webid-meynihan.htm.

99. Daniel Alexander Payne and John Hope Franklin Research Center for African and African-American Documentation, *Recollections of Seventy Years* (New York: Arno Press, 1968), 254.

100. Ibid., 255–56.

101. Rosenbaum and Buis, *Shout Because You're Free*, 41.

102. Adrian Piper, *Out of Order, Out of Sight* (Cambridge, MA: MIT Press, 1996), V2, 130.

103. Moten, *In the Break*, 1.

104. Édouard Glissant, *Caribbean Discourse: Selected Essays*, CARAF Books (Charlottesville: University Press of Virginia, 1989), 133.

105. See particularly the introduction, in Jordana Rosenberg, *Critical Enthusiasm: Capital Accumulation and the Transformation of Religious Passion* (New York: Oxford University Press, 2011).

106. Mather and Royster, "The Negro Christianized: An Essay to Excite and Assist That Good Work, the Instruction of Negro-Servants in Christianity (1706)," 1.

107. Ann Taves, *Fits, Trances, & Visions: Experiencing Religion and Explaining Experience from Wesley to James* (Princeton, NJ: Princeton University Press, 1999), 19.

108. White and White, *Sounds of Slavery*, 30.

109. Robinson, *Black Marxism*, 112, 113.

110. Rosenberg, *Critical Enthusiasm*, 4.

111. Robinson, *Black Marxism*, 119, 120.

112. Rosenberg, *Critical Enthusiasm*, 15.

113. Ibid., 16.

114. Peggy Phelan, *Unmarked: The Politics of Performance* (New York: Routledge, 1993).

115. Ibid., 146.

116. David Hume, Stephen Copley, and Andrew Edgar, *Selected Essays* (Oxford; New York: Oxford University Press, 1993), 40.

117. Ibid.

118. Ibid., 41.

119. In *Critical Enthusiasm*, Jordana Rosenberg argues that the resistance to enthusiasm was at least partially Islamophobic: "Eighteenth-century discourses about religion . . . often turned to Islam as an exemplification of the dangers of enthusiasm." As early as the seventeenth century, "conversion to Islam was represented . . . as an act that involved the combination of seductive deception with some degree of force" (49). And the focus on Islam's relation to Christianity as a question of enthusiasm as a monotheistic religion "meant that enthusiasm had become both a hermeneutical . . . as well as a historical" question (51). What I am thinking here is along the lines and in the same direction as the critique of nonessentialist discourse in Nahum Chandler, "Of Exorbitance: The Problem of the Negro as a Problem for Thought," *Criticism* 50, no. 3 (2008): 345–410. He argues that African enslavement practices were a philosophical set of concerns that were always material. As a philosophical concern, "The question is an ontological one (even if it is not radical or rigorously fundamental): on what basis and in what manner can one decide a being, and its character of existence, as one kind or another? What emerges as decisive at the limit and in the conceptual and propositional sense is the problem of grounding, in some fashion that would be absolute, a socially observable hierarchy that one might wish to affirm. At this juncture, I can begin to name

the philosophical appurtenance of the distinction in question, for the only manner in which such a claim could be made was to assume, in the ontological sense, that a distinction was absolute, oppositional, or pure, that in an analytical sense it could be understood as categorical. On that basis then, one could insist upon the categorical difference of the 'Negro' (or African) and the European (or 'White')" (355). I argue that the category of enthusiasm as marking the difference between the proper forms of religio-cultural constitutions of citizens is a symptom of the already emerging discourses of and philosophical considerations about blackness.

120. See all of chapter 1, "Explaining Enthusiasm" for the full conversation, in Taves, *Fits, Trances, & Visions*, 22.

121. Ibid., 31.

122. Ibid., 38.

123. Ibid., 39.

124. Talal Asad, *Formations of the Secular: Christianity, Islam, Modernity* (Stanford, CA: Stanford University Press, 2003), 2.

125. Joseph Roach, *Cities of the Dead* (New York: Columbia University Press, 1996).

126. Silva, *Toward a Global Idea of Race*.

127. Willie James Jennings, *The Christian Imagination: Theology and the Origins of Race* (New Haven, CT: Yale University Press, 2010).

128. See all of "Part 1: Displacement," in Jennings, for a detailed discussion of ground and uprooting as necessary for the theological project of imperialism.

129. "Public Execution," *National Advocate*, November 3, 1821, vol. IX, issue 2537 edition.

130. Ibid.

131. Fred Moten, "Preface for a Solo by Miles Davis," *Women & Performance: A Journal of Feminist Theory* 17, no. 2 (2007): 218.

132. Mary Gabriel, *Love and Capital : Karl and Jenny Marx and the Birth of a Revolution* (New York: Little, Brown and Co., 2011).

133. Jenny Marx, "Letter from Jenny Von Westphalen to Karl," in *Marx Engels Collected Works*, vol. 1 (International Publishers, 1975), 695–98, http://marxists.org/archive/marx/letters/jenny/1839-jl1.htm.]

134. Jenny Moore, "MUSIC FROM HEAVEN," *The Apostolic Faith*, May 1907, vol. 1, no. 8 edition.

135. Georg W. F. Hegel, *The Philosophy of History* (New York: Cosimo, Inc., 2007), 109.

4. TONGUES

1. Ronald A. T. Judy, *(Dis)forming the American Canon : African-Arabic Slave Narratives and the Vernacular* (Minneapolis: University of Minnesota Press, 1993), 240.

2. Ibid., 240–41.

3. Ibid., 242.

4. Martin Heidegger, *What Is a Thing?* (Chicago: H. Regnery Co., [1969, c1967]), 19–20.

5. Solomon Northup et al., *Twelve Years a Slave* (New York: Penguin Books, 2013), 5.

6. Judy, *(Dis)forming the American Canon*, 226.

7. *12 YEARS A SLAVE | Steve McQueen Q&A*, 2013, http://www.youtube.com/watch?v=KrLEXgUncKw&feature=youtube_gdata_player.

8. Michael Anthony Sells, *Mystical Languages of Unsaying* (Chicago: University of Chicago Press, 1994), 3.

9. *Alvin Lucier—I Am Sitting In A Room*, 2011, http://www.youtube.com/watch?v=2jU9mJbJsQ8&feature=youtube_gdata_player.

10. Toni P. Anderson, *"Tell Them We Are Singing for Jesus": The Original Fisk Jubilee Singers and Christian Reconstruction, 1871–1878* (Macon, GA: Mercer University Press, 2010), 39.

11. Ibid., 98.

12. Ibid., 101–2.

13. Ibid., 102.

14. Louis D. Silveri, "The Singing Tours of the Fisk Jubilee Singers: 1871–1874," in *Feel the Spirit: Studies in Nineteenth-Century Afro-American Music*, ed. George Russell Keck and Sherrill V. Martin (New York: Greenwood Press, 1988), 107.

15. "WEIRD BABEL OF TONGUES: New Sect of Fanatics Is Breaking Loose; Wild Scene Last Night on Azusa Street; Gurgle of Wordless Talk by a Sister," *Los Angeles Times* (1886–1922), April 18, 1906, sec. Editorial.

16. Grant Wacker, *Heaven Below: Early Pentecostals and American Culture* (Cambridge, MA: Harvard University Press, 2001), 35.

17. Fred Moten, "Preface for a Solo by Miles Davis," *Women & Performance: A Journal of Feminist Theory* 17, no. 2 (2007): 217, 218.

18. Mark J. Cartledge, "The Symbolism of Charismatic Glossolalia," *Journal of Empirical Theology* 12, no. 1 (January 1, 1999): 37.

19. Vern S. Poythress, "Linguistic and Sociological Analyses of Modern Tongues-Speaking: Their Contributions and Limitations," *Westminster Theological Journal* 42, no. 2 (spring 1980): 369.

20. For the image, see "Michigan/Ontario Council of Bishops, Church of God in Christ, Inc.," accessed April 25, 2016, http://www.cogicmica.org/mi-history.htm.

21. Judy, *(Dis)forming the American Canon*, 24.

22. C. H. Mason, *The History and Life Work of Elder C. H. Mason, Chief Apostle, and His Co-Laborers* (N.p.: n.p., 1987), 14.

23. Ibid., 24.

24. For an extended discussion of Mason and "signs," see Yvonne P. Chireau, *Black Magic: Religion and the African American Conjuring Tradition* (Berkeley; London: University of California Press, 2006).

25. James K. A. Smith, *Thinking in Tongues: Pentecostal Contributions to Christian Philosophy* (Grand Rapids, MI: William B. Eerdmans Pub. Co., 2010).

26. Ibid., 148–49.

27. See, for example, footnote 2 on page 124, footnote 56 on page 146 James K. A. Smith, *Thinking in Tongues : Pentecostal Contributions to Christian Philosophy* (Grand Rapids, MI: William B. Eerdmans Pub. Co., 2010).

28. Wacker, *Heaven Below: Early Pentecostals and American Culture*, 36.

29. Frank B. Wilderson III, *Red, White & Black: Cinema and the Structure of U.S. Antagonisms* (Durham, NC: Duke University Press, 2010), 251.

30. Wacker, *Heaven Below*, 45.

31. Estrelda Alexander, *Black Fire: One Hundred Years of African American Pentecostalism* (Downers Grove, IL: IVP Academic, 2011), 28–29.

32. Iain MacRobert, *The Black Roots and White Racism of Early Pentecostalism in the USA* (New York: Palgrave Macmillan, 1988), 73.

33. Ibid., 69.

34. Ibid., 66.

35. Ibid., 163.

36. Mason, *History and Life Work of Elder C. H. Mason*, 17.

37. Wacker, *Heaven Below*, 45.

38. Ibid., 49.

39. Judy, *(Dis)forming the American Canon*, 46.

40. Nahum Chandler, "Of Exorbitance: The Problem of the Negro as a Problem for Thought," *Criticism* 50, no. 3 (2008): 354.

41. Nahum D. Chandler, "Of Horizon: An Introduction to 'The Afro-American' by W.E.B. Du Bois—circa 1894," *Journal of Transnational American Studies* 2, no. 1: 6, accessed March 10, 2012, http://escholarship.org/uc/item/8q64g6kw?view=search.

42. Andrew E. Benjamin, *Translation and the Nature of Philosophy : A New Theory of Words* (London; New York: Routledge, 1989).

43. "Declaration of Independence—Transcript," accessed September 27, 2010, http://www.archives.gov/exhibits/charters/declaration_transcript.html.

44. Joseph Roach, *Cities of the Dead* (New York: Columbia University Press, 1996), 12.

45. Jay Fliegelman, *Declaring Independence : Jefferson, Natural Language & the Culture of Performance* (Stanford, CA: Stanford University Press, 1993), 1–2.

46. Andrew E. Benjamin, *Translation and the Nature of Philosophy: A New Theory of Words* (London; New York: Routledge, 1989), 38.

298 *Notes*

47. Ibid., 58.

48. Charles Olson and Robert Creeley, *Selected Writings of Charles Olson* (New York: New Directions, 1966), 18–19.

49. Jacques Derrida, *Eyes of the University: Right to Philosophy 2* (Stanford, CA: Stanford University Press, 2004), 8.

50. Ibid., 3.

51. Catherine Malabou, "An Eye at the Edge of Discourse*," *Communication Theory* 17, no. 1 (2007): 18.

52. Ibid.

53. Olaudah Equiano, *The Interesting Narrative and Other Writings: Revised Edition* (New York: Penguin Classics, 2003), 68.

54. Ibid., 339–40.

55. Fred Moten, "Knowledge of Freedom," *CR: The New Centennial Review* 4, no. 2 (2004): 269–310.

56. Peter Linebaugh, "All the Atlantic Mountains Shook," *Labour / Le Travail* 10 (October 1, 1982): 109.

57. Ibid., 111.

58. Catherine Malabou, "Another Possibility," *Research in Phenomenology* 36 (2006): 123.

59. Stevphen Shukaitis, "Infrapolitics and the Nomadic Educational Machine," in *Contemporary Anarchist Studies: An Introductory Anthology of Anarchy in the Academy*, ed. Randall Amster (London; New York: Routledge, 2009), 167.

60. Ibid.

61. Martin Heidegger and Albert Hofstadter, *Poetry, Language, Thought* (New York: Harper Perennial Library, 1975), 23.

62. Johann Fichte, "Some Lectures Concerning the Scholar's Vocation," in *Philosophy of German Idealism: Fichte, Jacobi, and Schelling*, ed. Ernst Behler (New York: Continuum International Publishing Group, 1987), 8–9.

63. Ibid., 9.

64. Ibid.

65. Ashon Crawley, *Moth's Powder* (Unpublished manuscript, 2012).

66. Chandler, "Of Exorbitance," 355.

67. Denise Ferreira da Silva, *Toward a Global Idea of Race*, in *Borderlines*, v. 27 (Minneapolis: University of Minnesota Press, 2007).

68. Ralph Waldo Emerson, "The American Scholar," in *Selections from Ralph Waldo Emerson*, ed. Stephen W. Whicher (New York: Houghton Mifflin Company, 1960), 73.

69. Michel Foucault, *The Birth of the Clinic*, 3rd ed. (New York: Routledge, 2003).

70. Emerson, "American Scholar," 79.

71. Stevphen Shukaitis, "The Wisdom to Make Worlds: Strategic Reality & the Art of the Undercommons," 2, accessed December 24, 2012, http://eipcp.net/transversal/0311/shukaitis/en.

72. Nathaniel Mackey, *From a Broken Bottle Traces of Perfume Still Emanate: Bedouin Hornbook, Djbot Baghostus's Run, Atet A.D.* (New York: New Directions, 2010), 63.

73. Peggy Phelan, *Unmarked: The Politics of Performance* (New York: Routledge, 1993).

74. Shukaitis, "The Wisdom to Make Worlds: Strategic Reality & the Art of the Undercommons," 2.

75. For a treatment of the ways blackness and statistics came to bear on one another historically, see Khalil Gibran Muhammad, *The Condemnation of Blackness: Race, Crime, and the Making of Modern Urban America* (Cambridge, MA: Harvard University Press, 2010).

76. See, for example, Martha Biondi, *The Black Revolution on Campus* (Berkeley: University of California Press, 2012). In this work, Biondi argues forcefully that the founding of black studies at university institutions was *part* of the black revolutionary impulse of the late 1960s, and not separate from it. And from its foundation, black studies was always concerned with questions of globality, of nation-states and citizenship, and, particularly, for the concept of diaspora through class alliance and solidarity.

77. Jacques Derrida, "The Future of the Profession or the Unconditional University (Thanks to the 'Humanities,' What Could Take Place Tomorrow)," in *Deconstructing Derrida : Tasks for the New Humanities*, ed. Michael (Michael A.) Peters and Peter Pericles Trifonas (New York: Palgrave Macmillan, 2005).

78. Philippians 3:14.

79. Fred Moten and Stefano Harney, "The University and the Undercommons SEVEN THESES," *Social Text* 22, no. 2 79 (June 20, 2004): 105.

80. Ibid., 106.

81. James Baldwin, "If Black English Isn't a Language, Then Tell Me, What Is?" in *The Price of the Ticket: Collected Nonfiction, 1948–1985* (New York: St. Martin's/Marek, 1985), 651.

82. June Jordan, "Nobody Mean More to Me than You and the Future Life of Willie Jordan," *Harvard Educational Review* 58, no. 3 (August 1988): 364.

83. Édouard Glissant, *Poetics of Relation* (Ann Arbor: University of Michigan Press, 1997), 18.

84. Édouard Glissant, *Caribbean Discourse : Selected Essays*, CARAF Books (Charlottesville: University Press of Virginia, 1989), 2.

85. Ronald A. T. Judy, "Untimely Intellectuals and the University," *Boundary 2* 27, no. 1 (March 20, 2000): 127.

86. Ibid., 131.

87. Malabou, "Another Possibility," 117.

88. Shukaitis, "Infrapolitics and the Nomadic Educational Machine," 168.

89. Andrew Benjamin, *Democracy and the University: Notes on Fichte's "Some Lectures Concerning the Scholar's Vocation,"* 2–3, accessed February 21, 2013, http://www.thelondongraduateschool.co.uk/blog/andrew-benjamin-on-democracy-and-the-university/.

90. John W. Blassingame, *New Perspectives on Black Studies* (Urbana: University of Illinois Press, 1971), 30.

91. Ibid., 3.

92. James Baldwin, *Go Tell It on the Mountain* (1953: reprint, New York: Dial Press, 1963).

93. James Baldwin, *Just Above My Head* (New York: Dial Press, 1979).

94. James Baldwin, *The Price of the Ticket: Collected Nonfiction, 1948–1985* (New York: St. Martin's/Marek, 1985), 687.

95. Orlando Patterson, *Slavery and Social Death: A Comparative Study* (Cambridge, MA: Harvard University Press, 1982).

96. Mark M. Smith, *Sensing the Past: Seeing, Hearing, Smelling, Tasting, and Touching in History* (Berkeley: University of California Press, 2008); Mark M. Smith, *How Race Is Made: Slavery, Segregation, and the Senses* (Durham: University of North Carolina Press, 2008); Mark M. Smith, *Listening to Nineteenth-Century America*, illustrated edition (Durham: University of North Carolina Press, 2001); Shane White and Graham White, *The Sounds of Slavery: Discovering African American History through Songs, Sermons, and Speech* (Boston, MA: Beacon Press, 2006).

97. White and White, *Sounds of Slavery*, xiii.

98. Immanuel Kant and Allen W. Wood, "Answer to the Question: What Is Enlightenment?" in *Basic Writings of Kant* (New York: Modern Library, 2001).

99. Chandler, "Of Exorbitance," 355.

100. Baldwin, *Go Tell It on the Mountain.*, 102–3.

101. Ibid., 128.

102. Baldwin, *Just Above My Head*, 175.

103. Ibid., 177.

104. Ibid., 177–78.

105. Ibid., 180.

106. Victor. Zuckerkandl, *Sound and Symbol*, Bollingen Series 44 (New York: Pantheon Books, 1956–73), 137.

107. Bill Readings, *The University in Ruins* (Cambridge, MA: Harvard University Press, 1996).

CODA: OTHERWISE, NOTHING

1. W. K. McNeil, *Encyclopedia of American Gospel Music* (New York: Routledge, 2005), 264.

2. http://www.chicagofestivals.net/music/gospel-music/chicago-gospel-music-timeline

3. Wallace D. (Wallace Denino) Best, *Passionately Human, No Less Divine : Religion and Culture in Black Chicago, 1915–1952* (Princeton, NJ: Princeton University Press, n.d.), 115.

4. Ibid., 188.

5. Anthony Heilbut, *The Gospel Sound: Good News and Bad Times—25th Anniversary Edition* (New York: Limelight Editions, 1997), 183, 173.

6. Mark Vail, *The Hammond Organ : Beauty in the B*, 2d ed. (San Francisco: Backbeat Books, 2002), 10.

7. Ibid., 35.

8. Ibid., 42.

9. Ibid., 12.

10. Ibid., 13.

11. Ibid., 14.

12. For an example, see, *Greater Harvest Reunion Choir Musical: Scripture, Prayer & Praise*, 2012, https://www.youtube.com/watch?v=OpaVcZ1Megw.

13. Salim Washinton, "The Avenging Angel of Creation/Destruction: Black Music and the Afro-Technological in the Science Fiction of Henry Dumas and Samuel R. Delany," *Journal of the Society for American Music* 2, no. 2 (2008): 239.

14. Avery Gordon, *Ghostly Matters: Haunting and the Sociological Imagination* (Minneapolis: University of Minnesota Press, 1997), 195.

15. Victor Zuckerkandl, *Sound and Symbol*, Bollingen Series 44 (New York: Pantheon Books, 1956–73).

16. James Weldon Johnson et al., *The Books of American Negro Spirituals [Printed Music]: Including The Book of American Negro Spirituals and The Second Book of Negro Spirituals* (New York: Da Capo Press, 1969).

17. Listen, for example, to the music backgrounded in Bishop Iona Locke's prayer here: http://theregen.net/music/bilprayer.mp3

18. Samuel R. Delany, "About 5,750 Words," in *The Jewel-Hinged Jaw: Notes on the Language of Science Fiction*, rev. ed. (Middletown, CT: Wesleyan University Press, 2009), 2.

19. Martin Heidegger, *On Time and Being* (New York: Harper & Row, 1972), 6, 7.

20. Nella Larsen, *Quicksand*, Dover Books on Literature and Drama. (Mineola, NY: Dover, 2006).

21. Ibid., 102–3.

22. Ibid., 103–4, 105.

23. Nimi Wariboko, *The Pentecostal Principle: Ethical Methodology in New Spirit* (Grand Rapids, MI: William B. Eerdmans, 2012), 1.

24. Edward Franklin Frazier, *The Negro Church in America*, Sourcebooks in Negro History (New York: Schocken Books, 1974).

25. Toni Morrison, *Playing in the Dark: Whiteness and the Literary Imagination*, William E. Massey, Sr. Lectures in the History of American Civilization, 1990 (Cambridge, MA: Harvard University Press, 1992).

26. Judith. Butler, *Gender Trouble: Feminism and the Subversion of Identity* (New York: Routledge, 1999).

27. Aden Evens, *Sound Ideas: Music, Machines, and Experience*, in *Theory Out of Bounds*, v. 27 (Minneapolis: University of Minnesota Press, 2005), 6.

28. Ibid., 19.

29. Ibid., 1.

30. Michel Foucault, Robert Hurley, and Paul Rabinow, "Friendship as a Way of Life," in *Ethics: Subjectivity and Truth* (New York: New Press, 1997).

INDEX

9–11, 37, 39, 40–41, 88, 101–2, 104, 207; "nevertheless" and "in spite of" responses, 74, 80, 81–82; Spirit (Holy Ghost) in, 159–62, 193, 207–9; tradition of, 5, 7, 9, 21–22, 24, 135

Blackpentecostal practices: dancing, 7, 28, 92, 107, 136; excessiveness of, 23–24, 159, 166; noisemaking, 4–7, 28–29, 98, 139, 142–47, 149, 151, 159, 161, 166–68, 174, 196, 205, 214, 268; "nothing music," 257–58, 260; shouting, 4, 28, 38, 91–92, 93–111, 119, 130, 132–38, 146, 169, 182, 225, 287n43; singing, 7, 29, 60, 159–61, 182; speaking in tongues, 4, 5, 7, 10, 29, 39, 88, 162, 168, 193–94, 206–17, 220–21, 239, 268; spirit baptism, 10–11, 209, 215; spirit writing, 208; tarrying (Tarry Service), 4, 10, 28–29, 91, 144, 159, 166–69, 210; testifying (Testimony Service), 28–29, 39, 43, 81, 91, 144, 159–63, 168–69, 259; whooping, 4, 5, 7, 27, 38, 42–43, 46–50, 55, 59, 65–66, 75, 83–84, 231

black pneuma, 30, 38, 40–41, 44, 48, 59, 67–68, 77–80, 83, 86, 175, 255, 269

Blackqueerness, 238, 247, 252–53, 255, 268

black social life, 6, 22–23, 29, 37–38, 69, 78, 105, 146, 205–6, 209–10; black English and, 238; Islamic influence on, 97. See also sociality

Black Study, 3, 8, 24–25, 27, 210, 236–38, 241–43; vs. black studies, 236, 239–41, 275n1, 300n76

black womanist theology, 12, 14, 16, 20

Blassingame, John, 94

blues, the, 12–16, 18–21, 255

breathing, 27, 30, 32–50, 55, 59–75, 78–86, 103, 115, 136–37, 206, 255; during childbirth, 156–57; in poetry, 219–20; sociality of, 40, 62

Brooks, Daphne, 156

Brooks, Gwendolyn, 76, 84

Brown, Kendal, 31

Brown, Michael, 79

Buck-Morss, Susan, 52–53, 54

Burke, Edmund, 139–42, 244

Burrell, Kim, 259

Butler, Judith, 59, 267

Butts Miracle Temple COGIC, 166

Calvinism, 28, 86, 92–94, 126–28, 134–35, 143, 223

Calvino, Italo, *Invisible Cities*, 55, 61, 62, 79

catechism, 163–65, 182–83

categorical distinctions, 3–5, 11, 13–15, 20, 30, 42, 73, 82, 84, 86–87, 93, 213; in Kant, 111–24; noise and, 139, 140, 142, 145

centrifugitivity, 95, 103–4, 106, 107–8, 145, 169, 180, 182, 190

Certeau, Michel de, 61

Chandler, Nahum, 24, 31, 41, 79, 87, 127–28, 150–51, 216–17, 221, 233–34, 245, 295n119

Chauncy, Charles, 184

choreographic protocol and itinerary, 28, 92–94, 135; philosophy as, 114

choreosonic performance, 23, 28–29, 63, 91, 93–96, 99, 102, 104, 108–9, 112, 137–38, 146, 159, 160, 167, 182, 190; Baldwin and, 245; Jacobs and, 152–55; repetition in, 163

church ceilings, 129–31

Church of God in Christ (COGIC), 24, 44, 76–79, 104, 160, 162, 208

ciprieré communities, 88–91. See also marronage

Clark, Twinkie, 132

207, 211–12, 214–17, 220–22, 226–27,
239–42. *See also* Blackpentecostal
practices: speaking in tongues
Gordon, Avery, 256
Great Awakening revivals, 28, 92, 98,
114, 123–24, 134, 137, 182–84

Hahn, Steven, 294n91
Hammond, Laurens, 251, 253
Hammond B-3 organ, 45, 232, 251–57,
261–62, 267–69; Leslie speakers,
254–55
Hare, Nathan, 242
Harney, Stephano, 237, 275n1
Harris, Cheryl, 6
Harris, Laura, 37
Harris, Sam, 25
Harris, Trudier, 64
Hartman, Saidiya, 24, 33, 154
Hegel, Georg Wilhelm Friedrich, 15; on
Africa, 146–47, 195
Heidegger, Martin, 60, 83, 89, 155, 199,
258, 263; on translation, 226, 234
Heilbut, Anthony, 169, 252
Higginson, Thomas Wentworth, 95
historical being, 28–29, 147–48, 149–51, 169
historicity (and the historical), 8, 147–
48, 151, 195–96
Holiday, Billie, 63–64, 65, 230
Holiness Pentecostal Church, 21-22
Hooke, Robert, 143
Hume, David, 120–21, 184, 186–87
Hurston, Zora Neale, 105–6, 107, 159, 210

impenetrability, 112, 116, 121, 137, 198,
209, 235
Islam, 25, 96–101, 171, 295n119
"I've Been Down in Jesus' Name"
(song), 163

Jackson, Jerma, 49

Jacobs, Harriet, 35, 48, 151–55, 157–58,
196, 241, 242–43
Jennings, Willie James, 188
Jenny (slave), 28–29, 189–91, 196
"John Brown's Body" (song), 95
Johnson, James P., 18
Johnson, James Weldon, 179, 257
Johnson, W. G., 208
Jordan, June, 238–39, 242
Judy, Ronald, 94, 159, 239–40, 286n28

Kant, Immanuel, 11, 28, 73, 92, 109–24,
141–42, 150, 175, 244; aversion in, 111–
13, 115, 121–23, 179, 288n54; on race,
120–23, 129, 141, 195; on time, 118–19;
transcendental aesthetic in, 116–18,
120, 126, 147, 150, 165
Kärkkäinen, Veli-Matti, 39
kinship, 70–71
Koerner, Michelle, 83, 90
Kornegay, EL, Jr., 15–16, 17, 20
Ku Klux Klan, 214

Labat, Jean-Baptiste, 121
LaBelle, Patti, 111
Lambert, Frank, 285n11
Larsen, Nella, *Quicksand*, 257, 264–67,
268
Latrobe, Benjamin, 142
Lee, Edward S., 10, 193
Lewis, George E., 229
"Lift Him Up" (song), 160
Linebaugh, Peter, 164, 174, 223–24
Locke, Iona, 231
Locke, John, 53, 70
Lockley, Timothy James, 90
Los Angeles Ministerial Association,
145
Lucier, Alvin, 203
Luddites, 173–74
lynching, 27, 63, 64–80, 82, 115;

pneumatology, 27, 38–42, 83. *See also* black pneuma
Pound, Ezra, 19
Poythress, Vern S., 207
preaching, 42–46, 231–32; female approach to, 44–46, 49–50, 60–61, 83–85
predestination, 28, 86, 127, 147, 182, 223; literacy and, 285n11
primitivism and superstition, 25, 143, 150, 158, 178–79, 184, 186, 209, 213, 220
purposiveness: Kant on, 122–24, 183; in theology, 129

queer theology, 17; church attendance and, 31, 252-53

racialization, 11–12, 25, 30, 172, 188, 211, 213–15
racism, 1–2, 3, 5, 182, 214
Raiford, Leigh, 73
Rainey, Ma, 19
Ridley, John, 201
Ring Shout, 28, 93, 95–97, 101–4, 106–8, 119, 130, 135–36; Payne on, 178–79
Roach, Joseph, 64–65, 188
Robe, James, 184
Robinson, Cedric, 149, 171, 184–85
Roof, Dylan, 22–23
Rosenberg, Jordana, 185, 295n119
Ryland, Robert, 163, 165

Salaita, Steven, 148
Sanders, Cheryl, 87–88
Sapelo Island, 99–102
Saul, Scott, 21
saut. See Afro-Arabic traditions
Scandrett-Leatherman, Craig, 77–78
Schmidt, Leigh Eric, 143–44
scholars: Emerson on, 234–35; Fichte on, 227–28, 237
screaming, 69, 73, 75, 102, 105, 156–57

secularism, 14, 28, 158, 185, 188
self-determination, 171, 172–73, 176, 183, 189, 195
Sells, Michael, 202
Seymour, William, 9–11, 41, 104–5, 108, 145, 193, 212, 214–15, 279n20
Sheppard, Ella, 205
Shukaitis, Stevphen, 224–25, 235–36, 241
silence, 74–76, 168; in Baldwin, 243–46
Silva, Denise Ferreira da, 8, 24, 27, 31, 114, 127, 147–48, 188, 221; on irrationality, 233; on self-determination, 172–73
Simone, Nina, 63–64, 65
slave narratives, 32–33, 34–36, 94, 152–54, 156, 200
slavery, 5, 37, 70, 80, 82, 83, 94–95, 102, 125–26, 128, 166–67, 169–72, 184–85, 188–89, 209, 210, 243; catechism and, 163–66, 182–83; Islamic presence in, 97; Luddism and, 174; in New Orleans, 89; "scientific" studies of, 240; slave ship communication, 153, 223–24; social death under, 70, 78, 80 102; sound of, 153–54, 169–71, 244
Smith, Bessie, 18
Smith, James K. A., 209–10, 211, 217
Smith, Mark, 244
sociality, 61–62, 74, 136, 141, 176; in Islam, 96, 99; Jacobs and, 158; Northup and, 201–2; Tubman and, 113
Spence, Mary, 205
Spencer, Jon Michael, 161
Spillers, Hortense, 23–24, 31, 59, 60–61, 64, 128, 149, 167, 220
spirituals and gospel music, 102, 155, 204–6, 257, 259
Stanley, William, 71, 73

Stokes, Juandolyn, 44, 45–46, 49–50, 60–61, 66, 83–85
"Strange Fruit" (song), 63, 65
subjectivity, 4, 24–25, 28, 179, 181, 206; blackness and, 122
sublime, the, 115, 118, 139–42, 244
Sufism, 101

Tatum, Art, 229–31
Taves, Anne, 98, 129, 184, 187, 288n73
"Testifyin' Meetin'" (song), 160, 163
Thelwall, John, 164
theological tradition, 11–18, 20, 44; delimitation of thought in, 143, 145, 165, 181, 214; direct experience in, 186–88; performative practices in, 25–26, 158
theology-philosophy dyad, 4, 5–6, 26, 30, 38, 86, 139; aversion in, 178–81, 195, 212–13, 233–34. See also Kant, Immanuel
theory vs. aesthetics, 94, 106, 159, 214, 216–17, 228
"This Is the Day" (song), 259–60
Till-Mobley, Mamie, 243
time: linear (western), 33–34, 75, 82, 87, 119–20, 146, 148, 150, 200, 242; Kant on 118–19; Heidegger on, 155; potential, 148–49, 160; work and, 172, 175
Tomlinson, A. J., 211–12
translation vs. interpretation, 217–22, 226, 234
Tubman, Harriet, 35, 113
Turner, Lorenzo Dow, 96, 97, 103

Underwood, Ben, 61–62

universities. See glossolalia: the university and

vestibularity, 31, 149, 167, 172

Wacker, Grant, 105, 212
Wagner, Bryan, 89
Wariboko, Nimi, 33–34, 74
Washington, Salim, 255
Watson, John Fanning, 98
Wells-Barnett, Isa B., 27, 65–69, 72, 74, 76
Wesley, Charles, 184
Wesley, John, 105–6
Westphalen, Jenny von, 29, 190–93, 196
White, George L., 204–5
White, Shane and Graham, 169, 174–75, 244
Whitefield, George, 92, 127–29, 135, 183–84, 186, 285n11
whiteness, 6, 13, 25, 66–67, 69, 71, 80, 146, 175, 213; Christianity and, 183, 214; language of, 239; silence and, 74–76
white supremacism, 22–23, 72, 148, 214
Wilderson, Frank, 212
Woodman, Britt, 21
Wright-Jones, Rochelle, 293n71
Wynter, Sylvia, 41, 81, 147, 151, 195–96

xenolalia. See glossolalia
xenophobia, 180–81

"Yes, Lord" (song/chant), 161–63, 165–66, 167, 232

Zarruq, Ahmad, 101
Zuckerkandl, Victor, 19, 74, 256, 257–58

COMMONALITIES
Timothy C. Campbell, series editor

Roberto Esposito, *Terms of the Political: Community, Immunity, Biopolitics*. Translated by Rhiannon Noel Welch. Introduction by Vanessa Lemm.

Maurizio Ferraris, *Documentality: Why It Is Necessary to Leave Traces*. Translated by Richard Davies.

Dimitris Vardoulakis, *Sovereignty and Its Other: Toward the Dejustification of Violence*.

Anne Emmanuelle Berger, *The Queer Turn in Feminism: Identities, Sexualities, and the Theater of Gender*. Translated by Catherine Porter.

James D. Lilley, *Common Things: Romance and the Aesthetics of Belonging in Atlantic Modernity*.

Jean-Luc Nancy, *Identity: Fragments, Frankness*. Translated by François Raffoul.

Miguel Vatter, *Between Form and Event: Machiavelli's Theory of Political Freedom*.

Miguel Vatter, *The Republic of the Living: Biopolitics and the Critique of Civil Society*.

Maurizio Ferraris, *Where Are You? An Ontology of the Cell Phone*. Translated by Sarah De Sanctis.

Irving Goh, *The Reject: Community, Politics, and Religion After the Subject*.

Kevin Attell, *Giorgio Agamben: Beyond the Threshold of Deconstruction*.

J. Hillis Miller, *Communities in Fiction*.

Remo Bodei, *The Life of Things, the Love of Things.* Translated by Murtha Baca.

Gabriela Basterra, *The Subject of Freedom: Kant, Levinas.*

Roberto Esposito, *Categories of the Impolitical.* Translated by Connal Parsley.

Roberto Esposito, *Two: The Machine of Political Theology and the Place of Thought.* Translated by Zakiya Hanafi.

Akiba Lerner, *Redemptive Hope: From the Age of Enlightenment to the Age of Obama.*

Adriana Cavarero and Angelo Scola, *Thou Shalt Not Kill: A Political and Theological Dialogue.* Translated by Margaret Adams Groesbeck and Adam Sitze.

Massimo Cacciari, *Europe and Empire: On the Political Forms of Globalization.* Edited by Alessandro Carrera. Translated by Massimo Verdicchio.

Emanuele Coccia, *Sensible Life: A Micro-ontology of the Image.* Translated by Scott Stuart. Introduction by Kevin Attell.

Timothy C. Campbell, *The Techne of Giving: Cinema and the Generous Forms of Life.*

Étienne Balibar, *Citizen Subject: Foundations for Philosophical Anthropology.* Translated by Steven Miller. Foreword by Emily Apter.

Ashon T. Crawley, *Blackpentecostal Breath: The Aesthetics of Possibility.*

Terrion L. Williamson, *Scandalize My Name: Black Feminist Practice and the Making of Black Social Life.*

Jean-Luc Nancy, *The Disavowed Community.* Translated by Philip Armstrong.